BLOOD OUT OF STONE

WHAT HAPPENED TO THE NORWEGIAN 'LEBENSBORN' CHILDREN MUST BE TOLD. THE RELENTLESS STORYTELLER OF THIS TRUE STORY OF THESE CHILDREN OF SHAME REVEALS THE TRUTH BY GRIMLY SQUEEZING STONES OF DIFFERENT KINDS

BRAM VERHOEFF
WITH ROB VANSPRONSEN

authorHOUSE®

AuthorHouse™ UK
1663 Liberty Drive
Bloomington, IN 47403 USA
www.authorhouse.co.uk
Phone: UK TFN: 0800 0148641 (Toll Free inside the UK)
UK Local: (02) 0369 56322 (+44 20 3695 6322 from outside the UK)

Published by AuthorHouse 09/12/2022

ISBN: 978-1-7283-7440-6 (sc)
ISBN: 978-1-7283-7441-3 (hc)
ISBN: 978-1-7283-7439-0 (e)

Print information available on the last page.

This book is printed on acid-free paper.

CONTENTS

PROLOGUE

FRIDAY JUNE 25, 2010, HURDAL, NORWAY

Odd Gripar

The land that is now called Norway was His quintessence of creation: rain worn rocks, resilient bush and fertile misty greyness in all directions. For ever reborn after Ragnarök, like the sprouting of purple fireweed after forest fires, it was His universe and His dwelling place. The man in the truck observed it all with his green eyes, sensing the branches of the world-tree Yggdrasil, the tree of life, encircling all his surroundings. He rolled open a window and inhaled the fresh breath of God, like he was drinking mead. Yes, the world was moving on.

The sun had barely set during the night. Just south of him, the sun would be high above the sky and his world should be bathed in the bright sunlight. However, he had just driven into a dense fog that was rolling off Lake Hurdalsjøen. It created a heavy blanket that made driving a challenge. There was just enough visibility to see about thirty meters ahead. Up to this point, he was making good time and was expecting to arrive at his destination early. He glanced at the gauges. His clock told him he had been on the road for nearly ninety minutes and his speedometer told him he was going at a snail's pace. Well, actually, it was registering just north of 75 km/h.

Good thing he wasn't driving an ordinary Scandinavian pickup truck; Gripar was sitting high in his crimson-coloured Ford F650. Decked out with a chrome roll-bar, fog lights, and a winch, it was a formidable beast. Sure, he had to endure the harassment of his colleagues who teased him about having 'small-penis syndrome'. The truth be told, Gripar was entirely comfortable with his masculinity. He knew it was possible to both own a big truck and have a big... Suddenly something darted onto the road. Cursing, he swung the steering wheel, nearly clipping a Red Deer that was intent on getting to the other side. He almost missed the sign declaring he had now entered the municipality of Hurdal.

Gripar wasn't sure what to expect when he got there and he wasn't sure why he was even involved. Was it because he was a police inspector in the Kripos, the Norwegian National Criminal Investigation Service? Without a doubt, a crime had been committed. But, strangely, for some reason yet unknown, he was specifically selected to be an integral part of the investigation. He glanced over at the passenger seat where several pictures lay. Earlier today, he had spent a considerable amount of time poring over these pictures. They were various shots of the same scene: three men sitting on a crudely constructed wooden bench. They were sitting upright; each one arranged in a different posture than the others. It didn't take years of police training to figure out these men weren't alive anymore. Gripar found an envelope with the pictures and letter in his postal box this morning. It had been delivered sometime during the night. When he checked the surveillance camera at his home, the camera caught a man with a short grey beard wearing a hoodie sweater and sporting a pair of aviator-style sunglasses. That this package was delivered to his home address rather than to his office suggested this was something personal.

The pictures were disturbing, for sure. Even more so because they didn't depict a typical crime scene. There was no blood. The bodies looked pretty much unmolested. Somebody had taken great care to arrange the bodies of three dead men into a kind of montage. All three were sitting on what looked like a crudely constructed wooden bench - each uniquely arranged into a particular pose. Gripar noted their lifeless eyes were staring straight ahead. He couldn't help but wonder what their dead eyes were fixated on. Who nailed their wooden seat together, and why? The photographer took various shots from different angles and different lighting. It occurred to Gripar, more than once, that these photographic scenes presented themselves like pieces of morbid art. Gripar wondered if the three men were randomly killed for this or if they were purposely selected. Was there a reason for three bodies? Lots of questions begging for answers, Gripar thought grimly to himself.

Then there was the letter that accompanied the photos. It comprised a single sheet of white paper. It had an artistic touch to it. The person who did this was concerned with presentation and style. About a quarter of the way down, centred, was typewritten in a bold and large font: "*Judge the living and the dead*". A couple of line spaces under that was also bolded and centred: "*The Three Witnesses*". The font size was larger than the first sentence. Then, underneath these two lines was a little rhyme: "Go find the three, their confessions are free, but you'll have to kick in for the price of fame: the press will also be informed about this game." At the bottom of the paper was a strange icon:

The letter was signed: *The Wolfsangel.*

On the back of the paper was a set of directions on how to locate the actual subjects of the photograph.

Gripar rubbed the back of his head in a vain attempt to get rid of a smouldering pain. The pain had been building up throughout the drive, likely because of the intense concentration required to navigate through the dense fog patches. He figured he should be making eyes on the first landmark described in the letter. Just as he was beginning to think he had missed it, Gripar breathed out a sigh of relief as he caught the faint sightlines of the elementary school.

The fog obfuscated the actual distance and he ended up driving past the turn-off. He stifled a curse, swerved onto the shoulder and hit the brakes. Throwing the transmission into reverse, he drove backwards until he reached the gravel road. He was relieved to find it was marked Odemarksvegen. Taking a deep breath, he swung the wheel and gunned forwards. The tires eventually gripped the road but not before spreading some gravel across the pavement.

After passing the elementary school on his left, Gripar began scanning upward, looking for the tell-tale of the power lines, which he soon spotted. He continued for a few minutes until he spied the trail, roughly the width of a small truck. Making another right, he navigated the narrow trail another three hundred meters or so, as per the instructions on the paper. He stopped and killed the engine. Gripar took a deep breath and exhaled slowly. His body was still tense from the drive, and now the anticipation of seeing in real what was foreshadowed by the photos.

He swung open his door and jumped out. He scanned the landscape to assess any potential hazards. The fog had pretty much lifted by now, but tiny vapour particles were still suspended in the air. This made the wooded hillside feel even more desolate. Suddenly, Gripar's body shuddered. This startled him because he wasn't usually prone to hypnic jerks. Gripar recalled his mother telling him as a boy that this feeling suddenly grabs you when you walk over somebody's grave. I guess that's a good sign that I am close, Gripar thought to himself. Nevertheless, he felt a general uneasiness at being directed out here by some stranger for some unknown reason. He concentrated on the surrounding area. The landscape was rather dull and unappealing; the power lines and trees seemed incongruent and the tracks below the lines were filled with rocks, stumps, and bits of concrete rubble. He looked up at the hills and spotted, not too far away, a stately white building. That must be the Hurdal Verk. During the War, it served as an orphanage for the Lebensborn children. Now, it was a collegiate.

Since that was the key landmark, he knew for certain he was in the right place. He made a slow but methodical search for the building structure that was described in the letter as a bunker, partly underground and partly above ground. After about fifteen minutes of rummaging through the low-lying shrubbery, Gripar was beginning to doubt that this structure even existed. Sweat was running down his back, gluing his shirt to his skin. He felt an insect climbing up one of his legs under his pant legs. When he stooped down to take care of the annoyance, he saw it. About ten meters ahead there was an unnatural elevation in the land. As he walked towards it, he could feel a slight adrenaline rush.

He estimated this structure to be roughly three by three meters and between ten and twenty years old. So, this is the place where the "Three Witnesses" are supposed to be on display. After a brief search, thankfully, Gripar discovered the opening, hidden by grass sod and rocks. He thought about the shovel he carried in the back of his truck and wished he had the foresight to have taken it with him. He glanced back at his truck, parked some distance away, heaved a sigh and went to fetch it. The clouds were drifting apart, and the sun was peeking through the cracks. After a brisk run, Gripar arrived at his truck, stepped inside and drove a little closer to the bunker. Gripar then grabbed his shovel and equipment bag and headed back to the opening.

He quickly cleared the sod and rocks and found a wooden door. He grabbed the attached copper ring and gave it a strong tug. Gripar suddenly found himself flat on his ass. The door had opened surprisingly easily and had caught him off guard. Gripar was chagrined to discover the hinges were actually well greased. A black plastic sheet separated the open door and the inside. When Gripar shoved the black plastic aside, an overwhelming smell of must and decay washed over, forcing him to step back. He filled his lungs with fresh air, held it, and opened the plastic once again. After some fumbling, he managed to pin it down and stepped back to let the stench pass by.

After waiting a couple of minutes to allow fresh air from the outside to waft in, he grabbed his flashlight and tool bag and stepped inside. He stayed at the threshold and was careful not to disturb anything before the crime scene investigation team arrived.

It was cold and bare inside. Gripar flicked on his light and the beams immediately caught three bodies sitting straight up beside each other on a rough wooden bench. It was an eerie sight - the light beams cast dark, grotesque shadows on the ceiling and walls. Yet, there was no doubt this was the subject of the photograph. The eyes of the corpses sunk deep into the hollows of their sockets, staring out at the wall, their flesh still covering their skeletal frames. Gripar shone his light on the wall that faced the three. The mystery of what the dead men were staring out was solved. They were staring at words scribbled with red paint: "*judge the living and the dead*". A single line with a sharp hook at both ends and a transversal stroke at the centre, underlined these words. Gripar recognized the symbol of the Wolfsangel. In some twisted way, this bunker evoked memories of a chapel where a very young Gripar attended a memorial service with his parents for a war veteran.

He knew he had to act fast; the rhyme on the back of the paper suggested that the press had also been warned and they could be here any minute. He took out his newly acquired iPhone 4 and snapped about a dozen pictures of the site. He stepped back outside to retrieve a roll of red and white Police tape from his equipment bag. After securing the crime scene before anybody else arrived, he dialled his boss, Chief Inspector Walter Svendsen, to let him know he found and secured the crime scene. Svendsen promised to notify the local police district as well as assign somebody from the crime scene investigation team to take over. Gripar hoped it wouldn't take long for their crews to arrive.

Gripar shivered again as he stared out at the countryside, his eyes searching for movement. In the brief moment between scanning the hills and catching the sound of vehicles approaching, he couldn't shake the feeling that he was being watched.

Wolfsangel

From a distance, concealed behind a grove of bushes, Wolfsangel continued to watch the drama unfold. He reached into his backpack and took out a can of Coke, pushed the tab in, and took a deep draught. He remembered the many nights he had lain in bed, listless, plagued with a sense of inadequacy and uncertainty. Now, for the first time in a long while, he felt content. The time had finally arrived. The Brobdingnagian stage has been set, the curtain has been drawn open, and now the three supporting characters can began their roles in the epic drama of Eirik.

Wolfsangel allowed a brief smile to play on his face. The woman's advice was spot-on. This prologue had played out as he had hoped. It did its job as a teaser—a hook, if you will–to get them wondering about what happened and why. They will eventually find out his purpose. Not now, though.

He took out his binoculars and trained them on Gripar, the tall police officer who had taken charge of the scene. "Well, Gripar," he whispered. "I wonder whether you still remember me? It was so long ago when we first met. You don't realise it yet, but you have an eminent part to play in this epic. Don't worry, though, I will nourish your role carefully. You will wonder, along with me, why things happened the way they did. At the end of our journey, you'll discover, albeit unwillingly, that I did not do wrong. Like you told me, the dead need to be judged."

Wolfsangel sensed Eirik's anticipation. Of course Eirik was coming along. After all, he is main character of this epic journey.

There was no other way.

Nothing happens without a reason.

PART 1

NOTHING JUST HAPPENS

Summer 1993, Hurdal, Akershus, Norway

Wolfsangel

A light-green Passat sat parked by a clump of trees. Inside, the lone occupant had tilted his seat all the way back to catch a few winks of sleep. A thunderstorm had rolled on through the area during the night, and now, early in the morning, the cloud cover was breaking up and the sun's rays were forcing their way through the cracks. Some of those rays managed to ply their way over the face of the sleeping person.

Through the haze of sleep, Wolfsangel realised Eirik had pushed through. It had been quite a while since that happened. Some people might think he was schizophrenic or just plain nuts. It wasn't true, of course. He was always in full control of his mental faculties. Sure, he could hear and see someone who no one else could hear or see. But when Eirik spoke or when he looked him straight in the eyes, Wolfsangel always maintained a grip on reality. It did take some getting used to. In the past, Eirik would randomly scream at him or scold him. Over time, Wolfsangel had discovered ways he could get Eirik to quiet down, even to the point of being able to shield his thoughts and feelings from Eirik. It took concentration, but he could do it almost every time—when he was awake. He wasn't quite fully awake now.

Dazed and confused, he said, "Eirik? What are you doing here? You're … You're still alive?"

There was no response. The man stared disconsolately at the distance.

Wolfsangel became urgent. "Look at me! You still know me, don't you?"

Eirik ignored him. His face was awash in a haze of sadness. After what seemed an eternity, he slowly turned his head towards Wolfsangel. He still did not respond.

Wolfsangel was losing his patience. He raised the volume of voice until he felt he was shouting at Eirik. "Come on, man. Say something! What are you doing here? What do you want?"

Suddenly, without warning, Eirik jolted up, his back ramrod straight, his shoulders back, his eyes locked ahead. *My father was head of the Gestapo in Norway from 1942 to '45 and responsible for the deportation of at least 532 Norwegian Jews.*

After a moment, when it seemed that Eirik wasn't going to say more, Wolfsangel asked him, "How well did you know your father?"

I am not a Nazi. Eirik slumped back into the seat and slowly turned to him. *Like you seem to be. That tattoo. That of the Wolfsangel?*

Wolfsangel smiled sardonically. "I'm no Nazi. I'm the Wolfsangel! That is my new identity. I don't hunt and kill wolves, though. I hunt the truth!" Wolfsangel caught and held Eirik's eyes as he said this. He couldn't decipher Eirik's look. Was it sadness? Depression? Hurt?

Eirik smiled hesitantly and nodded. *It's a good thing that old Mikkel died in your arms before you had the chance to interrogate him.*

Wolfsangel scoffed. "A good thing for him, maybe. If I had known then what I know now, I would have literally torn him apart." He could feel anger welling up inside. He glanced at Eirik and said softly, "Mikkel used to have you in control, right?"

A moan escaped Eirik's lips. *Norway gave him free reign to do whatever he wanted. We, children of SS soldiers, had no choice but to suffer. Nowhere else in the world were German war children treated so horribly.*

Wolfsangel could see on Eirik's face the memories were flooding in, almost overwhelming him. Eirik paused. *Thousands killed themselves or became insane from being confined in mental institutions or were raped and humiliated in, oh, so many ways.*

"But you were lucky—you survived."

Eirik shuddered. *Luck? Survived?* Taking a deep breath, he spoke monotonically, *I should never have been born. My people are nothing but a pox on Norway.* He beckoned, inviting Wolfsangel to look at him. When he did, Eirik's eyes bore deeply into the soul of the Wolfsangel. His voice became impassionate. *You are a survivor. It is now time. It is now time for the sacrifice. You know what you have to do.*

At those words, Wolfsangel bolted up in his seat. The haze and fog of sleep suddenly dissipated. His heart pounded in his chest. He regarded the black portfolio on the seat beside him. It contained the journal papers he had been reading before falling asleep. When he looked out through the fogged-up windows, he could feel the isolation. He wasn't, however, alone on this hill. On the other side of the car was a small mound some twenty metres away. The mother and her son were chained in that secluded, underground space.

He became aware that his temples were throbbing. He tried easing the pain by rubbing them with his thumb and forefinger. He never discussed Eirik with anyone, never told anybody about him. They would not understand anyway. Depressed and angry as hell at everything in his life, he had walked away from home years ago. He was unable to find rest anywhere. Ultimately, he found some form of peace, yes, with this man, Eirik. Who would understand that?

The distant rumble of thunder brought Wolfsangel out of his reverie. He glanced down at the portfolio. Neatly printed on the front cover:

Psychiatric Hospital Fylke, Oslo

Client: Eirik Tijsker, born July 26, 1943, in Hurdal

Dr. Robert Thomassen

The last entry in the notebook was made in 1978. Wolfsangel made a quick mental calculation. That's fifteen years ago. Fifteen. No more entries after that. Where could Eirik be now? I must find him.

He stepped out of his car; his joints stiff after sleeping in that tight space. Like a cat, he stretched all his limbs starting with his arms and ending with his legs. He punctuated the exercise by breaking wind. The fresh air and cool temperature had triggered his bladder. After a deep yawn, he turned his back to the car and aimed at a green mossy stone. He noticed an insect making its way over a large stone and decided to deluge it with a tsunami of urine. A smug smile drifted over his face as he watched the insect fight to find its footing and then, after a brief struggle, get swept away. That'll teach him not to mess with the Wolfsangel.

He stepped into the bunker and immediately shivered. It wasn't because of the cold interior. It was an involuntary reflex as he savoured what Eirik had told him: the time is now. Wolfsangel could feel the tension in his gut rising—an excitement was building. The journey had begun. He covered his face with a balaclava, reached out, and switched on the small LED lamp he placed there earlier.

There was a startled reaction at the far end of the bunker. It reminded him of a time in his childhood when he and his friend would sneak into a barn at night. Clutching a baseball bat, they would suddenly turn on their torches, and in the brief moment when the mice were frozen as the light startled them, they would swing their bats, hammering away at as many mice as they could. This time, it was a middle-aged man and an old woman, sitting in front of a table on a crudely built wooden bench. They suddenly lifted their hands to shield their eyes from the light. He could see the terrified look on their faces.

Wolfsangel nodded in satisfaction. They were still here. Not that he expected otherwise. He had cuffed their legs and chained them to the anchor in the ground. The two of them had spent the night in cold and darkness at the mercy of a stranger. Rubbing his hands together, he addressed the two of them. "Well, it's morning. Now you two can get to work."

Walking towards them, he said, "You don't have to be so scared. Yes, I'm Wolfsangel, but I am not hunting wolves; I am hunting the truth." Wolfsangel reached the table and leaned towards them, hands gripping the edge of the table. He alternated his attention between the son and the mother. The mother just stared helplessly at her lap. The son, on the other hand, made a feeble attempt to stare back defiantly. "All I want from the two of you is an honest report and a confession." The son couldn't maintain eye contact. Wolfsangel smiled to himself. He got those two exactly where he wanted them. Stepping away, he continued to focus on the son. "Those transcripts of Eirik's sessions in Fylke—very interesting. I'm glad you found them and were able to pass them along to me."

"I don't know why I kept them. They're useless to me. I don't understand Eirik, and I don't understand my father," he stammered.

The Wolfsangel slammed his fist on the table, making both the man and his mother jump. His eyes bore into the old lady's. "You know how Norway destroyed her own Lebensborn children like troublesome weeds?"

The woman whimpered while her son put his arm around her protectively. "What do you want from us?"

"Get started with your assignment. Write everything you know about Mikkel's involvement with Eirik. Don't leave anything out!"

The terrified old woman and her son looked at each other and nodded. Wolfsangel leaned in closer and hissed, "If I am not satisfied, I will torture one of you while the other watches." He pushed a Toshiba laptop that had been sitting on the table towards them. He had already set it up last night, but his guests had obviously not noticed it in the darkness.

They had also not noticed something else that finally caught their attention. Someone else was in the room. He was sitting opposite the two, surrounded by dark shadows. He was immobile, and because of the lighting, it was impossible to distinguish the shape properly. He sat there as if he were attending a family reunion.

The son noticed first. "Who is that?"

Wolfsangel saw them taking a good look at the figure. It sat like the image of Rodin's Thinker, and his ghostly eyes stared at them from the other side of the room. It seemed like a big doll, but their intuition told them it had been a real person. "He will not disturb you. Now get to work. There is some food and water at the end of the table. Help yourself. But do not for a minute think that I will be satisfied with anything less than the truth. Do you understand?"

Not waiting for a response, Wolfsangel walked out again and locked the thick door behind him.

Back at his car, he found some food and water he had packed for breakfast. He glanced at his watch. Five past eight. A perfect time to call. He took out his cell phone and dialled a number. Far away in Germany, in the town of Bochum, a phone rang in the flat of an old man. He hoped the old man would pick up.

After several rings, a wheezy voice came on the line. "Guten Morgen, Hellmuth Patzschke ..."

"Ich bin es, ..." There was an audible gasp and then silence on the other end. Wolfsangel waited for a reply. "Wirst du nicht etwas sagen?"

Finally, the old man spoke. "What! You are still alive?"

"Yes, of course I'm still alive. What did you think?"

"Aber ... Wait a minute. I don't understand." Wolfsangel heard the man swallow and cough. A few seconds later he spoke again. "I was told that you were dead! I received an official letter in the mail."

"You sound so disappointed that I am actually alive," Wolfsangel chuckled.

"No. No, of course not. I am very relieved. But I'm a bit shaken. You know, I've never talked to a dead person before. What happened? Where are you now?"

The Wolfsangel couldn't contain the grin in his voice. "I am now in Hurdal and I did it. I carried out a successful mission. Mikkel. He is officially dead. He looks good, though. I wonder how long it will take before those two recognize him..."

The old man interrupted him. "What happened to you? How come they thought you were dead?"

Wolfsangel decided to have some sport with him. "I'll tell you later. I'll come visit you in about a week or so."

"Nein nein, bitte!"

Wolfsangel heard a catch in the old man's throat and sighed. He stepped out of his car and started pacing as the memories flooded back. "Where shall I begin? When I visited you the last time, remember I told you that I was committed to staying in the Legion for two more years? Well, this spring was exactly five years since I signed that first contract in 1988. I tell you, it was a hell of an end to those five years. I was in Sudan and there were four of us on a reconnaissance mission when we got ambushed. A sudden fury of bullets rained down on us. I was driving and for whatever reason-it makes no sense to me-I somehow managed to avoid being hit. I was focussed on getting us out of harm's way. I raced like the devil. There were bodies of my comrades everywhere. Of course, a front tire blew and I lost control, crashing into a tree. I didn't want the vehicle to fall into the hands of the rebels, so I tossed a grenade in it. I got the hell out of there before the noise and flames alerted the rebels to my position."

"Hmmm ... your lifeless comrades were totally cremated," Hellmuth mused. "But you. You survived. Was für eine Geschichte! So, I guess that's why the organization figured you were also dead." There was silence on the other end. "I'm glad you survived, so relieved. Then you just fled to Norway?"

"What do you mean 'just fled'? Hell, first I had to go through a few extremely difficult weeks of survival. I'll tell you about that later, but I was in France three and a half weeks ago."

"Were you in Aubagne at the head office?"

"Yep. I totally caught them off guard. You should have seen their faces when I walked through the door. After I told them what happened, they wanted to know if I would sign an extension."

"Did you?"

"No. I thought about it, but I had enough of the Foreign Legion. They don't really give a damn about their people. I figured this was a sign that I needed to find somewhere else to go."

There was a pause and then the old man said gruffy, "But you could have reached out to me and told me you were alive. I really did mourn for you! I even started drinking again. I was drowning my grief in alcohol."

Wolfsangel didn't know whether to believe him. The old man was given to histrionics on occasion. "I'm really sorry. I didn't know they sent you that Death Notification letter. That must have been a shock to your system."

The old man grunted, seemingly placated by the sincerity in Wolfsangel's voice. "Do you need money?"

"No, I've got plenty. They gave me a good bonus, probably hoping that I will change my mind sometime in the future."

"So, now what?"

"I've put Eirik's plan in motion. I left France and took the express train to Hirtshals and then the ferry to Larvik. You know something. When I arrived in Norway, I felt like I was coming home."

"Yes, yes", Hellmuth said impatiently. "I'm sure it was. Now, did I understand you right? You have the old one, the old Thomassen, in that bunker of yours? Isn't he dead?"

"Yes, that old bastard is dead. I've got his corpse as well as his wife and son in the bunker."

"His corpse? You were able to find the old one back?"

"It wasn't a problem." Wolfsangel recalled his trip up north to the mountainous area of the Dovre National Park. There, about five years ago when he was just eighteen years old, he buried the old psychologist's body high in the mountains among the alpine plants and grass into the cold of the permafrost in the ground. At those temperatures, corpses will remain in good condition. Even the body of old Mikkel which was already rotten to the core.

"Well, I hope he won't turn into maggot food too quickly now."

"Don't worry," Wolfsangel reassured him. "I've taken care of that."

There was a pause as the old man waited for Wolfsangel to explain. Wolfsangel was comfortable with the silence. He had learned years ago the less others knew about his plans, the less likely things would go wrong.

The old man seemed to understand. He didn't press. "And this bunker? Nothing is going to happen to the body? It's hidden well?"

"Oh, yes. It's just outside of Hurdal. I hid it well. You can't tell where it is until you are just about on top of it. I used a lot of treated wood for bracing. After all, right now I do not know when I will meet the others. Could take years."

He took a sip of water as the old man seemed to be processing what he had just said.

"Let me help you. Please. I am old, but I am very capable, you know that. Besides, I could use some adventure in my life right now." The excitement was obvious in his voice.

Wolfsangel rolled his eyes. He figured the old man would eventually get to this request. There was no way he wanted Hellmuth tagging along. He grunted noncommittally. "I need to find Eirik. I need to know if he is still alive."

"Ah, yes. Eirik." A silence fell, until Hellmuth spoke up again. "If you won't let me help you, can you at least keep me up to date?"

Wolfsangel nodded. "Of course. Robert Thomassen has transcripts of various sessions Eirik had with Mikkel. I'll make sure you get a copy of them and any other reports that Robert comes up with. That's the best I can do for you."

The old man sighed. "Of course. I'd rather be working with you, though. But I understand." Wolfsangel knew that he didn't but respected the old man for not pushing.

Wolfsangel promised to stay in touch and ended the call. He shivered, but this time it was because a cold breeze was nipping his bare arms. He glanced up at the sky and noticed that dark clouds had crept in, blocking the sunlight. He returned to his car and decided to re-read the transcripts stored in his portfolio. The first entry was written nearly sixteen years ago.

Wednesday, December 28, 1977 / Psychiatric Hospital Fylke, Oslo / Client: Eirik Tijsker, Born July 26, 1943 in Hurdal / Dr. Robert Thomassen / Conversation # 1: Research into cause problems

"I am a rat with mud fever, I never knew that."

"Why?"

The patient in front of me cleared his throat, swallowed, yanked at his knitted sweater, and snapped his neck with a movement. "Yes, rat. Your fellow Doctor Else Vogt Thingstad understood. She stated - shortly after the war - that we were retarded, infected rats. I still do not understand why I had not noticed that. Rats from the sewers make people sick."

He sniffed two or three times: "I can even smell it, that nauseating sewer air. Rats rotting there." He shrugged and looked at me questioningly with his clear blue eyes.

"I only smell Fylke. Tell me about your parents, are they still alive?"

"Mother is dead. I think that Father still lives, somewhere in Germany, of course. I do not know him. Dare not to. I learned that all German soldiers were bad people."

"Do you think so now?"

He was silent for a moment, then said, "That is not possible … all bad, isn't it? But there are bad people. Olaf, he was from here, a real Norwegian. He …"

Silence filled the air, the man sighed deeply, then straightened his back. "I have long tried not to linger in my past, I became hard and strong. Your father took care of that, I think. It went well, until I … saw myself again, as a piece of vermin."

"When they found you ten days ago, you were almost frozen to death. Fortunately, those children found you, otherwise you would have been dead now."

"Happy …? Who will miss a stinking rat?"

"Your wife, your children …?" I saw the man cringe. "There are people who care about you. But there are also very annoying traumas that have a lot of power over you. I suspect you have often decided to ignore these, haven't you?" He nodded in agreement. I continued, "Many of the German war children, the Tyskerbarn, have gone mad and have stepped out of life. But it is almost 1978 and the war ended 33 years ago. You … let me read here, yes, you have even emigrated, married, children, work. What happened to you, what made you end up in this psychiatric hospital?"

"Surviving is not easy, doctor, I have fought, hoped, loved and almost got free, almost … forgetting that I really am only a German war child."

I did not say anything. The thirty-five-year-old man in front of me had recovered from freezing, thanks to his strong body, and a gentle warm-up process. Still, Eirik was psychologically far from healthy, and easily lost his mind. He saw him rubbing his knees hard, groaning weirdly, swallowing, and looking at his pale hands.

He fascinated me, I had heard from my father of the Lebensborn children.

Robert Thomassen, Fylke, Oslo

Wolfsangel looked up from the transcripts. He again felt a sudden loneliness and isolation. He knew it was more than a physical feeling. Reading this transcript hit a nerve deep inside of him. Many years ago, he happened to overhear Eirik in a deep discussion with his wife about identity and shame. Eirik felt so much shame that he was a 'Lebensborn' child. Wolfsangel wasn't exactly sure what a Lebensborn was, so he did some reading. He was stunned to learn that the Lebensborn was a Nazi project created by Heinrich Himmler in 1935. His idea was to procreate racially superior children. The Norwegian women were especially considered prime breeding vessels because they tended to produce blonde and blue-eyed children - hallmarks of Aryan racial purity the Nazi's were looking for. Wolfsangel had no idea that between ten and twelve thousand Lebensborn children were born in Norway. That was a significant number of war children for a population of just under four million people. At that time, Wolfsangel really couldn't understand, though, why a person would feel shame because they are Lebensborn. Who cares what other people think? Shame is nothing more than allowing other people to impose their definitions of identity on you. You alone can either receive that identity or choose to reject it. Wolfsangel had come to realise that it wasn't quite that simple.

Hellmuth and Eirik, in their own unique circumstances, were pawns in the Third Reich's dialectic of identity and racial purity. Hellmuth, the German Gestapo officer, committed to doing his part in carrying out Hitler's master plan. Eirik, the Norwegian Tyskerbarn, a product of that commitment. So, how did he, the Wolfsangel - three generations removed from the Great War – become part of the synthesis?

It was a good question. Was it fate? Was it destiny? Amid a chaotic and unsettled youth, he had stumbled across Hellmuth, a man who knew exactly what he wanted to get out of life. He brooked no nonsense when he found out that Wolfsangel's life was like a pinball, bouncing from situation to situation and every time it looked like he would escape, he got catapulted back into the chaos. Without consulting Wolfsangel, Hellmuth arranged to have the Foreign Legion interview him. While he didn't initially see it that way, this turned out to be the best thing that ever happened to Wolfsangel. He was now in his late twenties, still young and deeply infused with experiences and skills that he would need to make a grand life for himself. The Foreign Legion had certainly turned his life around.

He had to pause his life, though, for the time being. He had been commissioned to undertake a unique quest. There was no opportunity to refuse and no chance to back out. At the center of all this stood Eirik.

Wolfsangel caught himself staring into the distance, the transcript still in his hand. He continued reading:

Monday January 9, 1978 / Psychiatric Hospital 'Fylke, Oslo / Client: Eirik Tijsker (1943) / Dr. R. Thomassen / Conversation # 2: 26 June 1943 - summer 1950

I asked Eirik if he wanted to tell me about his life. He nodded but remained silent. After insisting on my part, he moved to the edge of his chair, looked at the floor and started talking.

I do not know what happened to my life. I am the son of a German military officer and a Norwegian girl. That makes me a war-love-baby. Since my father was a pure German, I have a certificate of descent somewhere that proves that I and my sister are also purebred. I found that out from my mother. She received the ceremonial SS dagger and candle standard, made in Dachau, used in my christening ceremony. I also found out from my mother that I was actually christened Erich and my sister was christened Evelina. We had to have pure German names. After all, we were the future of Hitler's master plan. My mom renamed us Eirik and Esther so that our names wouldn't stand out like sore thumbs. Not that it really helped us.

I remember nothing from the Lebensborn home in Holmestrand, except the sweet face of my nurse, Mirre; but that's maybe because we lived with her for a few years after the war. I still know her, by the way. Hurdal was very peaceful until the evil Olaf Andersen came into our lives. I was four and a half or five years old when I saw him for the first time. Olaf was husky and tall. I had never seen anyone who was so strong. I was afraid of him and hoped he would leave, but he and Mirre got married. Often, he was gone, which I approved of. In his presence, I felt an impending doom. Then Olaf bellowed that he did not like having two German children in the house, and a slut on the couch.

I had to pee one night. I walked quietly to the bathroom, closed the door and sat down on the toilet. It was very quiet in the house, but it seemed like something was going on in the hallway. It stood still in front of the bedroom, our room. I felt a presence, slipped from the toilet, pulled my pants up and crept to the door. Quietly I opened it and investigated the hallway. Nothing. Suddenly a colossal hand grabbed my neck and I petrified instantly. Another hand grabbed my …

He said, 'Listen carefully, stinky swine, I can do what I want with you. Your species has no rights. If you do not do what I want, I pinch your throat shut and do the same with your sister. When you two will be buried, I have a party. Do you understand? Everyone hates you, Tyskerbarn. You are just vermin, dirty rats, war weeds.' Olaf spoke very softly, but his words penetrated deep into my marrow. I did not dare to protest. I could not say anything, my voice stopped working. That was the first moment in my life that I realized that I was only a German war child, a Tyskerbarn. Olaf pulled me back to the bathroom, closed the door, and the Norwegian scoundrel abused me for half an hour. Demons screamed in silence in my head. From that day on, Olaf could do all he wanted.'

Eirik shrugged his shoulders and continued: My own fault. I should have never been born. One evening, when Mirre had a night shift in the hospital where she worked, he picked me up again. No one knew that Mama was at home. But she was, asleep in a chair. She later said that she woke up because she had heard something. I was in the bathroom and just held Olaf's penis in my hand when she opened the door. I felt deeply ashamed. Not Olaf. He had a big grin on his face. Mother saw and understood everything. She ran to the big man and pushed him backwards. Nothing happened. Olaf stood there, naked and ruthless like a wild beast. Then Olaf gave her a push. 'Why do you worry about that piece of vermin?'

She jumped forward, slapped him in the face, then put her nails from both hands in his face. With a big stroke, shrieking like a madman, she ripped the face of Olaf open. Olaf screamed and turned to the mirror and looked at the damage. It hurt him, he was in a lot of pain, he shrieked, raged! He turned back to mama and his eyes shone like those of a wild animal.

'You whore, you ungrateful bitch. I will teach you.' He took her, and I saw how he grabbed her everywhere. He picked up mama and bore her - roaring like a monster - to his bedroom. She tried to get away, but he did not give her a chance. He hit her with clenched fists and laughed. She fell on the bed, tried to protect herself with her hands, but Olaf could not be stopped anymore. He dived on her.

From the threshold of the bedroom I and my sister were forced to watch.

The sadist roared like a bull!

My mother did not move anymore, yet he still screamed at her. 'Stupid German bitch, this is your own fault. Daring to tempt me? Well, I'll bring it on.'

He walked past us, we drew back, terrified, but he did not pay any attention to us. Moments later I heard a car start and drive away. It was the service car of Hurdal Verk, which Olaf often used to drive home. He was gone.

Crying all the time, we washed mother. We dressed her with her nightdress as good as we could. Mama was totally apathetic. I think she felt nothing and could not think. That night we were in bed together, but we shuddered and trembled, even when there was such a thing as sleep.

The next morning, I saw Mamma get up, she grabbed a pair of scissors, and cut her hair. Then she walked away. I followed her, she walked to the neighbours. The police arrived just when Mirre came home again.

I think Olaf stayed away for a week, when he was there, he smelled of spirits and smoke. His cheeks still showed the nail scratches. I saw his drooping shoulders as he told the agents, 'She seduced me, and then I could no longer hold myself. Sorry, Mirre, but you should have never allowed that woman to live in your house. Once a whore, always a whore.'

I think he had to apologize. I still do not understand that Mirre did not send him away. Then finally the house on the Vestside road became available. It is still there, by the way, I was there recently. It is opposite the local campsite and a pizzeria with red painted wooden panelling. There, on the other side of the road, is an old and derelict hovel, nobody lives there anymore. In the year 1949 it was not exactly a hovel then, but that did not matter much. Mama was only eight and twenty years old at the time.

My school time in Hurdal was not bad. At that time, I was not aware of the fact that I was exceptionally lucky. My fate was actually unusual for the Tyskerbarn. Everywhere in Norway the so-called German war children were bullied and harassed by students and teachers. Their mothers continued to be called sluts and their children were often removed from their homes. I heard later that many Tyskerbarn were locked up in mental institutions, without anyone ever doing research. A war girl was tied with a dog leash by her foster father for a long time, a swastika scratched on her forehead.

But I was safe with mom and my sister Esther. In 1950 we moved to Jessheim, 50 kilometres to Oslo.

Robert Thomassen, Fylke, Oslo

Wolfsangel felt the rage boiling up inside as he finished reading. He imagined turning that cowardly Andersen into a fleshy blood-stew. "Olaf. Olaf Andersen. You will pay for this," he growled. He suddenly felt caged and constrained inside his car. He jumped outside. Taking some deep breaths, he eventually calmed down and got his breathing under control. Thanks to his Foreign Legion training he was getting better at regulating his emotions. After another bout of arm and leg stretches, he decided to visit his guests. People might not believe it, but he wasn't particularly titillated holding these two innocent people hostages. It was something that had to be done for a higher purpose.

"How's your assignment coming along?" He asked the two. They both assured him with many bobs of their heads that they were almost finished.

Wolfsangel nodded and made it look like he was going to leave again. However, he turned back to them and said, "By the way, that guy over there across the room. Isn't he an old acquaintance of yours?"

He saw them shrug and exchange puzzled glances. "Maybe you don't recognise him without his hat." From a dark corner he took a cane hat and put it on the head. "I'm fairly certain he never went anywhere without this on, right?"

With that, he exited the bunker, leaving the door open so that not only would the heat and light get in, he could also listen to their reaction.

It was the mom that figured it out first. “Oh. I know that hat.” Her breath stopped suddenly. Then she screamed. “That’s Mikkel. That’s father. Robert, that man stole Mikkel right out of his grave! Mikkel! Mikkel, is that you? Oh dear God, that’s Mikkel!” She screamed for what seemed a solid minute until eventually the bunker became silent, punctuated by a few sobs.

Wolfsangel imagined the son was holding on to his mother, calming her down. He heard Robert’s voice. “He obviously has excavated father’s body and placed it here. This is the work of a sick and dangerous man. Come on, mother, drink something here. We are still here, and my real father is not there. He is in heaven. This is just his body. Do not look at him and let’s get this assignment finished as quickly as possible.”

Wolfsangel stepped away from the bunker and briefly wondered why he just did that to them. He could have left Mikkel completely alone and they would not have been the wiser. His father once told him that some people deal with their pain and hurt by transferring it to other people.

Whatever. Maybe he did get his jollies from other people’s pain.

He got back into his car and read the next entry in the transcripts:

Monday January 23, 1978 / Psychiatric Hospital ‘Fylke’, Oslo / Client: Eirik Tijsker (1943) / Dr. R. Thomassen / Conversation # 3: 1950 - 1953

R.T.: During this conversation client Eirik Tijsker tells about his youth in Jessheim, Ullensaker

Mama got a job and suddenly a lot changed in my life. The newly built Gardermoen Hotel was looking for a capable person who could manage the cleaning of this hotel. Mama who had done administrative and business management work for the Germans during the war, got the job. We lived at an unpaved road near the Trondheimsvegen. On the right is a school with a lake in front. I liked that school; there were probably more war love children that were not aware of it. I later heard that the German-war-children of Kinderheim Godthaab, half an hour's drive west of Oslo, in the Haslum district, were put in homes with insane people, often until they were adults. No, despite the sadistic atrocities of Olaf Andersen, I had it better than many of my kind. Besides, Olaf wouldn't come back in my life. So I thought at that time.

At the elementary school, I was sometimes bullied, but I knew how to strike back. It is a pity that he is no longer alive, but otherwise you should ask a boy named Lasse about that one time. Lasse was someone who liked to hurt other children. Three years older than me, five centimeters taller and at least 20 kilos heavier. Lasse challenged me to fight him, scolded me, really badly wanted to teach me a lesson, but things went very differently. Ha, I can still see him lying beneath me, pleading for mercy. The big bully of the Romerike School. It was as if someone had pressed the red button, the 'off' button. Lasse disappeared into the shadows. I later heard that he became extremely fat.

Time and death, they know each other well. I, mother Anna and sister Esther seemed to be able to escape the sharp edges of Norwegian revenge on war children. We were free. Mama received a lot of appreciation for her work, I am sure she was very reliable and effective. She earned better and better. The Romerike School was safe and the farmer and his wife, on whose yard we lived, were good for us. We got the milk for nothing as well as the firewood, because I liked working hard to help the farmer. They had no children at home anymore, and we became dear to them.

I have never seen my father. Lebensborn children grew up without fathers. At school I learned that all Germans were bad people. Mama said that father also had good sides, but I heard at school that my father had arranged a transport of Jews.

It was summer; we had been living in Jessheim for a whole year, when Finn Undredal came into our lives.

One day a police car drove into the yard and an officer got out. He took the time to look around. I was nine or ten years old and came out with a wheelbarrow full of manure. I asked him, 'What can I do for you?' I remember how he turned his eyes before he answered me. Later I knew him, Finn Undredal was his name and he originally came from Flåm. He was not as tall as Olaf Andersen, not so strong, but bulkier, fatter.

My mother was regularly harassed by Finn Undredal, anywhere, sometimes in plain sight on the street. He must have been convinced that everyone thought he was strong and handsome, a hero like Marshall Johnny Mack Brown in the Western Blazing Bullets. I later heard that he once offered himself generously for sexual services, but mama refused. That made him angry: here was a German whore who refused a true Norwegian!

I remember it was autumn: rainstorms, hail and biting cold. Nature first takes on warm autumn colours, but then the autumn storms come and a colourless time commences. I remember how we longed for beautiful white snow.

On a dark, cool evening in October, Finn Undredal appeared. We did not hear him coming into the yard. Someone knocked on the door, I opened, and there he was. Suddenly he grabbed my head and hit it hard against the cupboard that stood in the hallway.

'Damn imbecile, vanish!' The big man shouted as he stepped inside.

I felt nothing for a moment, everything became black before my eyes, and I collapsed like a bag of potatoes. This lasted only briefly, and I became aware of everything again. I heard Finn Undredal laugh sadistically and I immediately remembered Olaf. At first, I was very scared, but then it became freezing cold inside me. I stood up and walked into the living room. Finn Undredal had thrown mama on the couch and hit her hard. I saw him loosen his belt and saw the fear in mama's eyes.

'I do my duty, bitch. You gave yourself to a German and produced two bastards; now I'm going to punish you for ignoring us, real Norwegian men.'

If he had not been so stuck in his own story, he would have noticed me. I took two large glass bottles that were used for milk. They were waiting to be rinsed out later - two sturdy glass bottles.

I snuck up to Finn Undredal and allowed no other thoughts, no fear and no pain, to come into my brain. Finn Undredal lowered his pants, bending for a moment.

When Undredal's head lowered, I struck, confident and hard. The bottle burst into shards. He grabbed his head, staggered and sagged on his knees. He shook his head; a trickle of blood ran across his forehead to his eyes as he looked around. I threw the neck of the milk bottle aside and took the second one in my right hand. Undredal shook his head a few times. He tried to get up, but just as he regained his sense of balance and staggered upwards, I brought the other bottle into action. He tried to miss the blow and stooped, but I counted on it and hit him hard on the right side of his head. The cop fell, the left side of his head catching the edge of the table. He collapsed, face upwards, groaning, staring blankly.

Now he was completely helpless. My mother, yes, I still see it in my mind. She stood up and looked down at him with utter contempt. Powerless and baffling was he, a small stream of spit ran from his left mouth over his cheek to his ear.

I collected the pieces of glass but kept an eye on him constantly. He wanted to get up, but he could not. I think he'd never been so scared; he pissed in his half-sagged pants. He cried and implored: 'Please, let me go. I will never do it again, please.' He whimpered like a scared dog.

Anna bent her head close and spoke in a penetrating way. 'You retarded fool! My German lover was a real man, not a coward like you. Now…' She pointed, 'Go to the door like a dog, and do not dare to lift your wretched head.'

With great difficulty, Finn turned and crawled to the door with his pants down on his knees. For a moment he looked at me, totally humiliated. I opened the door for him, and with his pants still half off, he continued to crawl. Just as he was outside with his hands, I kicked him hard and he fell forwards, landing on his face. I slammed the door behind him.

But later came his chance to regain some of his self-confidence, to take revenge for all his pain. It happened on a dark and cold night, that of January 22nd, 1952. I had gone with my sister that afternoon to Nordbytjernet Lake. A group of young people drove an old car without an exhaust pipe across the ice on the lake. The ice had not been strong enough everywhere and the car had cracked the ice in a few places and made a few holes. The car eventually even fell right through. The young people had come out quite quickly, even laughing, but the front of the car stuck out of one ice hole, the back on the bottom of the lake. My sister and I had really enjoyed the spectacle!

Shortly after supper we missed Esther. We called her and searched everywhere on the farm, until I discovered some of her footsteps going in the direction of school.

'Mama, she has been here. I think she went back to the lake', I said and together we ran, following the tracks. She had crossed the Trondsheimvegen and walked to the parking lot of the school. We walked past a parked car, but our attention was on the lake. It was awaiting us, white and dark at the same time, a big dark hole threatened thirty meters away. It was quiet, deadly silent. Nowhere a sign from Esther. Then I saw a few footsteps in some snow on the ice.

Suddenly Finn Undredal was behind us. He looked hypocritically curious and asked what we were doing there. We ignored him, and I ran to the hole and jumped into the water without hesitation; it was up to my chin, and within a few seconds I found my sister. She was weak and did not breathe anymore. With the help of mama, we brought her ashore. I had no feeling in my body anymore, but I did not bother to think about that.

Officer Undredal did not help, he smoked a cigarette. After taking a few more drags, he walked slowly to the car and picked up the police radio. After a deep sigh, he called the hospital for an ambulance.

Mom and I had to make up a report of all relevant events that evening. We concluded that Finn Undredal must have seen Esther. She walked past his car, onto the ice. He must have seen her, must!

It was full moon, clear sky. She probably slipped and got into the hole. Of course, she has tried to get out, and all that time he must have been watching. Oh, it still makes me so angry. In my mind's eyes I see her white-cold hands slipping from the edges of the ice.

Why did he not do anything? He must have seen her walk past; why? Such a sweet little girl.

Robert Thomassen, Fylke, Oslo

It took a lot to surprise the Wolfsangel, but in this case, he had to read the report through twice. All this information about Undredal was new to him. He had no idea this happened. Eirik obviously withheld this information for some reason. Wolfsangel had to admit the conclusion reached by Eirik and his mother about Undredal using this situation as an opportunity for revenge was most likely accurate.

He felt the familiar feeling of a rage boiling up inside of him again. If you are still alive, Finn Undredal. He didn't finish the thought.

Wolfangel had read enough for the time being. Between Olaf and Finn, he had enough rage inside of him to single-handedly take on Saddam Hussein. Of course, he noted ruefully, his physical body might disagree with his mind. His muscles still ached from building the bunker. It took him many long days to hand dig the hole, construct the bunker, and then cover the 3 by 3-meter structure with grass sod, stones, and assorted items of construction waste.

He was feeling restless and out of sorts. He needed to do something. Securing the transcripts in the portfolio, he pulled on his balaclava and checked up on his guests. He found Robert talking quietly with his mother, but all conversation ceased when they noticed him coming through the door. Wolfsangel didn't care. It was a good thing that they were silent, otherwise there was a distinct possibility that one of them would say something that would trigger his rage. Without acknowledging either of them, Wolfsangel grabbed the laptop and went back outside to read what they had written.

Obviously, he wouldn't accept their first draft. There was no doubt in his mind that they would hold back important details because they didn't want to embarrass the family name. Wolfsangel stepped inside and shook his head. Robert and his mother stiffened. He threw a package on the table. "Here's a new external battery for the laptop. I am going to take a hike. It will take a while before I am back. Use that time to double check what you have written and ensure that you have told me everything there is to know about Mikkel and Eirik Tijsker. I mean, everything. Even if it is embarrasses you." Then, shaking his finger at them, he warned them, "It had better be the truth and nothing but the truth."

Robert nodded and glanced at his mother. She was looking at Wolfsangel with venomous eyes, refusing to nod her head. Wolfsangel was pleased to see large drops of sweat beading on both their foreheads. They were taking him seriously. That said, Wolfsangel knew he needed to end this sooner than later before something went awry.

Wolfsangel got into his car, not entirely sure where he should go or what he should do next. When he was with the Foreign Legion, he didn't have to make decisions and plans about what to do next. He simply followed orders and did what he was told. In the absence of the order and structure of the Legion, he felt melancholic. The rage he felt earlier was now replaced with angst and apprehension. There was a throbbing pain coming from the back of his head. He tried to massage the pain out while at the same time taking in the landscape, hoping to ground his emotions.

He had a strong urge to confront Finn Undredal so he made that his starting point. Based on what Eirik wrote in his journal, he should look for the fat man in Jessheim. Wolfsangel took a deep breath and exhaled slowly. He repeated that procedure a couple more times to achieve a more emotional balance. Jessheim was about a thirty-minute drive south of here.

About half of that would be driving along the Hurdalssjoen Lake. There was something about bodies of water that relaxed him.

Less than six minutes later, Wolfsangel drove through the village of Hurdal. As he approached the roundabout, he spotted a huge man wearing a checkered shirt. The man was waiting for traffic to clear so he could cross the street. Wolfsangel leaned across his steering wheel, seeking a closer look. His face broke into a wide grin. "Well, today is my lucky day". He knew the man had to be close to seventy-five years old, but his muscular and rough build belied his age. The man clearly had the look of a mean fighting dog.

The Wolfsangel pulled up right beside the man and rolled down his window. He sized up the man contemptuously.

"What the fuck do you want?" The man glared at Wolfsangel. Wolfsangel met his glare, slowly gathering up some liquid. Suddenly, he hocked a loogie that splattered on the man's shoe. "Your time will come, asshole". He calmly rolled up his window and drove off to Jessheim.

Settling in for the thirty-minute drive, Wolfsangel turned on the radio to listen to some good tunes. He was pleasantly surprised when one of his favourite songs, *Call of the Wintermoon*, came on. It was sung by the heavy metal group, Immortal, and it so touched the heart of what Wolfsangel was trying to accomplish these past few years.

Buried beneath the mountains of frost
Years of silent sorrow grim and dark
My winterwings of evil sleeps in eternal nights
In death cold crypts of snow
The moon chimed my return
With the blackstorms I came
And not with the winds

He thought about Mikkel, the bunker, and Eirik. He relished how those years of silent sorrow, grim and dark, were going to be smashed wide open by the blackstorms of the Wolfsangel. Who knew that heavy metal music could be so profound?

Just before he entered Jessheim, he exited the E6 and refuelled at a large Esso service station, not far from the International Gardermoen airport. As he filled his tank, he thought about how to go about locating the man. The problem was, he only had a name - Finn Undredal - and a general area - Ullensaker.

Wolfsangel went inside to pay for his petrol, a plan forming in his mind. After throwing down enough cash to cover the petrol, he added in a few more Kroners. Casually, he asked the attendant, “Say, I’m looking for a guy named Finn Undredal. Do you know him?” He looked carefully at the woman’s eyes and immediately noticed a reaction. Wolfsangel couldn’t believe his luck today. It’s almost like the gods were smiling on him. She definitely knows him.

“Why, who wants to know?” She replied, averting her eyes.

Ah, he thought, she hates him. That’s good to know. Out loud, somewhat angrily, “The bastard owes me money and I want to collect.”

“He’s a bastard, all right,” she agreed, finally looking at Wolfsangel. “He was married to my friend’s sister, but the guy couldn’t keep his hands off the girls. Especially the young girls.” He noticed her whole body shudder at the thought.

“So, does he still live here?”

She nodded. “Ten minutes away in Algarheim.”

“He used to be with the police, right? Is he still with them?”

“Used to be,” she said. “But not anymore. He once tried to rape a teenage girl after he put her in the drunk tank. I guess she wasn’t as drunk as he thought or hoped. She screamed and got the attention of another police officer. Well, he got caught with his pants down. Literally. That was the end of his career."

Wolfsangel smirked as he recalled a similar story in Robert's transcripts. Clearly, Undredal thinks with his dick rather than his brain. "Do you happen to have an address? I would like to pay him a visit."

"No, I don't have his address, but I know that he works as a labourer at a manufacturing plant in Algarheim. You could probably catch him there."

He turned to leave. Offhandedly, he threw out, "Thank you; there will come a day when you will be glad that you have helped me so well."

She grabbed his arm. Fixing her gaze on him, asked, "Are you going to hurt him?" Wolfsangel noted that her neck became flush and surmised she would be quite happy to hear he would do just that.

He smiled at her as he turned again to leave. "There most definitely will be pain. How much will depend entirely on him."

As he walked toward the door, his eye fell on The Jessheim Herald sitting in a newsstand. He stopped when he saw a familiar name. On the front page was a photo of a lake with the headline: 'Mysterious fish mortality in our Nordbytjernet Lake.' He recognised the name of the lake in front of the Romerike School.

After grabbing a bite to eat at a local restaurant, Wolfsangel drove back to the bunker, feeling rather pleased with himself. This was certainly a worthwhile trip. He felt good about the next step, although he had to wrap up this step very soon because the Thomassens were getting close to falling off the edge. His plan would be in serious jeopardy if that should happen. As he pulled up to the tree grove near the bunker, he made sure that the two of them could hear his return.

He decided to give the two in the bunker another minute and picked up Thomassen's transcripts and started reading where he left off.

13 February 1978 / Psychiatric Hospital 'Fylke, Oslo / Client: Eirik Tijsker (1943) / Dr. R. Thomassen / Conversation # 4: 1953-1958

After the death of my dear sister, I slowly, but surely, slid down to the world of psychiatry, to the white sheets, to treatments, to pain and anesthesia.

After my sister's funeral I was broken, mentally broken, and plunged into the dark world of depression. I could no longer deal with life. One day I was found somewhere, I could not talk and was completely confused. They took me to Fylke; I was ten years old.

I've been here before, Doctor Thomassen.

Years later I heard someone say that the domain of psychiatry at that time was in the hands of scary atheists. Yes, you hear it right; they watched their world through Darwinian glasses. Their heroes experimented with people before, during and after the war.

Me and many other Tyskerbarn were strong genetic material, as such very welcome in the hands of experimental psychiatry. One of the most ambitious scientists in psychiatry at that time was your father, Mr. Mikkel Thomassen. Great was his name, all over the world.

I've been here until I was fifteen, but I have no idea what happened to me here. My thoughts do not get it together yet painful electroshocks, drugs, hypnosis, and numbness, I got totally loco. I forgot everything, even the memories of my sister's death. I felt nothing when I thought of her, nothing! How is that possible? What happened to me?

On August 26, 1958, I was discharged from the hospital, declared healed by your father, Dr. Thomassen, Senior and reunited with my mother Anna.

I was physically strong, but there was something wrong in my head, the blueprint had changed. I was no longer the same son as before.'

Personal notes R.T.: I went deeper into the fate of the Lebensborn children and read that they were even supposed to be infected with a fascist bacillus.

Whatever that may be. Hard to believe what was done to these children: leashed like beasts, locked up with false dogs, survived among feral pigs, tortured with boiling water, hot fire pokers and burning cigarette butts. Yes, it was exactly the same as what Joseph Mengele did in Auschwitz. Children and their mothers were abused by the Norwegian and American Secret Service CIA for LSD experiments, medical trials and open brain surgery, in which pieces of brains were removed from living persons.

Robert Thomassen, Fylke, Oslo

Wolfsangel sighed deeply and pondered how even the gentle Norwegians succumbed to inflicting such atrocities on their fellow citizens. He really should thank Robert profusely for these reports. They provided so much more information than he expected or hoped for. For the first time in his life, he really began to understand Eirik and the mission he was on.

Wolfsangel carefully put the transcripts and the other papers in his portfolio and went back to the bunker. He stood in the open doorway, his whole body framed by it. He heard the old woman sobbing while Robert beckoned him. "Come in. We're done. We have nothing more to add. You can torture us as much as you want, there is nothing left for us to tell."

Just as Robert finished speaking, his mother howled. "What did you do, you monster?"

Wolfsangel must have had a look on his face because Robert quickly stepped in. "She's not talking to you but to the corpse."

Wolfsangel understood – sort of – and looked at the computer. He made a show of carefully checking over what they had written. He wasn't worried. He knew they were sufficiently scared to do what he asked and believed Robert when he said they had nothing else to say.

He gave them both a hard look. "I am satisfied." Their relief was palpable. Both started to laugh and cry at the same time.

He allowed them a moment or two to celebrate and then continued "I am willing to let you go. But, there's one condition. You do not tell anyone about this until I give you specific instructions to do so. There will come a time when you can share everything with others, but that may take years. When that time has come, I'll call you, Robert Thomassen." He paused to stare at each of them. "If this gets out before its time, I will hunt you both down. Are we clear?"

Both nodded vigorously. Even the old lady. He grabbed a plastic bag from his pocket and noticed their scared looks. "Now, do not be afraid, this just contains an anaesthetic. It's the only way I will take you back to safety. This won't hurt, I promise you." The two were hesitant but Wolfsangel was confident their desire to escape this hell hole would overcame their distrust. They gave each other a hug and walked with Wolfsangel to his car. When they were both sitting in the back seat, Wolfsangel administered each a dose of Sevoflurane via an inhaler. It didn't take them long to become too weak to sit up and eventually slip into unconsciousness. After locking up the bunker and removing any traces of him being in the area, he got into the car.

For one meditative moment he looked around the deserted parking terrain. There was definitely relief that he had finally got started. There was a sense of elation as well as some trepidation. He had made a dead person speak; but who can judge what he has done? God? The survivors of the German war children perhaps? Do they have an inherent right to condemn their executioners even though they are dead?

He made his way to the Jessheim where, half an hour later he transferred the two of them, still unconscious, to Robert's car, parked close to the Gardermoen hotel.

As he drove out of the abandoned parking lot, Wolfsangel wondered if it would be possible to learn to forget what happened in the past. People sometimes say that the feeling of loss disappears by itself. He shook his head. Learning to forget was impossible. Does loss, pain and suffering make us wise? No, because then the whole world would be wise. Would he come back to Hurdal and finish this? He wasn't sure. That question did not have a straightforward answer. After all, he was now driving in the opposite direction. He supposed that was a metaphor of his life right now. He seemed to be always the reluctant driver, trying to put this whole thing behind him and move on. He would do this by throwing himself into his work, taking on the most dangerous missions possible. Unfortunately, Eirik never seemed to forget him. He would suddenly appear, usually when he was on an adrenaline rush, brutally smashing someone or something or rattling his machine gun and tasting blood. Yes, then Eirik would nod at him. But there were also times Eirik would suddenly appear when he was relaxed or celebrating victories. There were even the very exceptional times when Eirik would appear when he was laughing at something. Each time, he would hear Eirik's voice from a hidden place somewhere in his head. Wolfsangel knew as certainly as the sun would rise in the morning there was more. There was going to be no escape. It was crystal clear to him: he carried Eirik and his sacrificial stone with him for the entire duration.

He sighed and slumped down in his seat. Jessheim disappeared behind him in the night. His next stop was Germany to deliver a special parcel.

August 1993, Bochum, Germany

A gray-blue high-speed passenger train raced into the city of Bochum, Germany, and made a stop at platform three in the Hauptbahnhof station. Almost immediately after it came to a halt, another train on the other side of the platform started gathering speed in the opposite direction. Wolfsangel sat by the window right next to the door. It was a habit of his when travelling by train to sit near an exit. He noticed a gaggle of students hanging around on the platform waiting for the train to make its final stop and open its doors. They were laughing at each other, girls with short shirts and boys with black leather coats. They were jostling each other, trying to predict where the door would finally stop and who would get on first. Meanwhile, the occupants on the train were leaving their seats and scrambling for the same exit door. To Wolfsangel's amusement, a rather obese woman had managed to be the first in this car to get in front of the doors. As the doors finally swung open, she tried to step out, her fleshy legs struggling to find secure footing. She was fighting a losing battle against the crowd of incoming students. Suddenly, the first of the students stopped short while the others behind bumped into each other, surprised that they weren't moving. They eventually found out why. The figure of Wolfsangel had filled the doorway, and the students froze.

He really wasn't that much older than them, but he suspected his world was vastly different from theirs. He watched the young folks in silence. Maybe it was his piercing eyes or maybe it was because they intuitively felt an aura of danger, but invisible hands seemed to disperse them off to the side rather quickly. The lady nodded her thanks to him as they both stepped onto the platform.

Wolfsangel walked out of the station, orientated himself and then strode onto the Kortumstrasse. He wore an ineffable smile on his face. Why not? Wolfsangel was on his way to the flat of Hellmuth, a former SS Nazi who wore that title like a badge of honour.

The air here was cold and dank and it chilled Wolfsangel to the bones. He was glad he had the foresight to grab a warm coat before leaving for Germany. He shivered again. A heavy blanket of clouds draped the sky, signalling an impending rain shower. It was three o'clock in the afternoon, although it felt later in the day. He turned right on the wide Bruckstrasse. A moment later he stood in a small square, which was partially used as a terrace for a Turkish restaurant. He found the number of the flat. It was number 15.

Just as he was about to push the buzzer to be let in, an elderly lady with a pug nose, large dangling hoop earrings, and sporting a flamboyant pink, blue and green jacket, opened the door. She wasn't about to let him through. She stopped directly in front of Wolfsangel. He couldn't quite stifle a cough. Clearly the lady had anointed herself with a copious amount of perfume, not the pleasant-smelling stuff, either. Wolfsangel wasn't quite sure what to do. He was trapped by a wall of flesh and odour. He made like he lived there; he gave her a nod, stepped aside, and then was ready to pop past and bound up the stairs. She had other plans. She grabbed his arm, giving it a tight squeeze, and asked him in a raspy voice where he was going. When he told her who he was going to visit, she smiled, held the door open for him, and said, "Salute him on my behalf." He thanked her, walked to the stairwell, while the automatic exterior doors closed behind him.

Moments later Wolfsangel was at the door of the war criminal Hellmuth Reinhard. He had already been here twice; the first time, five years ago, had not been very successful at first. The old man had wanted to hit him, even to shoot him. Wolfsangel grinned at the memory. He didn't start the encounter on a positive note when he rudely called up at the entrance and asked to be let in: "In the name of Erich, the son of your whore, Anna."

At the time, the old man's belt missed a few loops. And now? Well, over the phone, he seemed like he's got it together a bit more. Wolfsangel shrugged. At least something good had come from that encounter. Hellmuth did get him into the Foreign Legion. If that had not happened, he would be dead now or locked up in a prison because of his unrestrained anger.

So, here he was, for the third time, standing at the door of the former SS man. He knew it wasn't unusual that many former SS men were still alive in the 1990s. He had heard from Hellmuth many alumni still supported each other through thick and thin. They would hold regular reunions where veterans could share memories and laugh at the same old jokes.

Wolfsangel knocked on the door and yelled, "Let me in, in the name of Erich, the son of your whore Anna." He waited.

The door opened a crack and the old Hellmuth peered out. "Huh. I see they let you out of the mental hospital. Are you on a day pass?"

Wolfsangel let out a guffaw as the door swung open. Helmuth looked like a young puppy, so happy he was there again. He laughed and gave Wolfsangel a friendly tap on his shoulders.

"How nice to see you again. Come in. Did you arrive here after stopping past your girlfriend for a conjugal visit?"

"No. Why do you ask?"

"My eyes are watering from the perfume that's clinging onto your clothes. Oh wait. That smells like old lady Schubert."

Wolfsangel raised his eyebrows. "Speaking of conjugal visits, she asked me to salute you. Is that a euphemism for something? Are you making forays into enemy territory, by chance?"

Hellmuth deftly evaded that question. "I'll bet you want a good German ale. Sit down and I'll get you one. Then you can tell me everything that's happened since your last visit."

The two of them sat in the living room drinking a Hefeweissbier. The usually silent Wolfsangel did most of the talking. "I went to Henrik Ibsensweg in Oslo and stood there, Hellmuth, on the spot where you met that young Norwegian woman, Anna Pederson."

The former SS man, rubbing his unshaven chin, said softly, "Oslo, September 25, 1942. I can still see and hear the bombs scraping across the road."

"Scraping bombs, eh. You already talked about that last time. I took a look, and yes, the building where the Gestapo had its administrative headquarters is still there. The roof is still very steep. No wonder those bombs did not go off on the roof but slid onto the street."

The old man had told the story before, but he clearly wanted to relive those glory days. "Ah, young man, it was such good weather, the sky was blue. Suddenly I saw those three English Mosquitos. They were coming at us at more than 450 kilometers per hour. Far behind them, I could make out at least two of our German Focke 190 aircrafts. They tried to intercept the English, but the Mosquitos came out of the blue and had too much of a head-start."

Wolfsangel leaned forward. “And you knew what they came for. But tell me again. Why did those bombs not immediately explode on the roof of the headquarters?”

The old man chuckled, clearly enjoying this story. “You should know that Mosquitoes carried heavy bombs that weren’t supposed to detonate immediately. Imagine they did, what would happen to those low flying planes? Why, they would be in grave danger.” He laughed at his own pun. “So, they designed a way to delay detonation by using chemical retarders. In this case, when the bombs were dropped on the Gestapo headquarters that day, they did not go off right away. In fact, one bomb shot over top of the roof, another did not explode. Some went straight through the roof and came out the back side, and a few slid along the steep roof onto the street.”

“Chemical retarders? That’s how they did it?” Wolfsangel missed that detail the first time he heard the story.

The old man nodded and continued, wrapped up in his memories like a fuzzy blanket. “There were more than a hundred civilians on the street and a waiting tram stuffed full of passengers. The quiet reverie was shattered by the sudden approach of the English planes. Time seemed to go in slow motion.”

At this, Hellmuth’s voice started cracking. “By the time the shadows of the planes had peeled away from the ground, they had dropped about half a dozen bombs. I distinctly remember hearing a child calling for her mamma. Then, my instinct kicked in. I dove behind a tree and rolled into the foetal position. First came the light. Then the hellish ear-splitting noise, followed by the shock waves. People were thrown off their feet, bodies splattered around. The tram turned over while glass sprayed around like hail. I felt a scorching blast of air over me which was quickly replaced by the cooling of the breeze. Friend, enemy and everything in between were united in death, pain and total desperation. Dust and blood covered the bodies.”

It was a compelling story and Wolfsangel was caught up in it again, just like last time.

Hellmuth paused, got another two bottles of beer and returned, deep in thought. Wolfsangel nodded. He was able to imagine it all; his Foreign Legion experience had taken care of that.

Hellmuth paused to open the two bottles and then went on.

"Again that … ghostly silence, as if time, horrified, took a breath. I stood up, stunned. I found a tree to lean against as I tried to orientate myself."

Hellmuth glanced at him for a moment, probably hoping that Wolfsangel was suitably enthralled by his story-telling. He cleared his throat for effect and continued. "The tram had been caught in the explosion and was thrown on one side. I saw a gaping hole in the roof of the Gestapo headquarters; a bomb had gone in, but it hadn't exploded. I walked to the tram and did my best to help people climb out. A number remained inside, screaming … screaming. I pushed in and helped some. I did what I could."

"You met her then?" Wolfsangel asked.

"When I looked up, I saw her…" He swallowed and continued. "She was helping some elderly people who were clearly in a state of shock. I called to her through the broken windows. She nodded; she had already seen and recognized me. We worked together until we were exhausted, then we went to my flat."

"I guess you didn't tell her you were married?"

"No, that's not true. Believe it or not, but I did tell her I was married and was planning to stay married. But when we looked into each other's eyes, we realized only one thing was relevant at that time." He took a deep breath, sighed, and looked out the window for a moment.

"That you were destined for each other?" Wolfsangel coughed inaudibly; he had to make an effort to hide his distaste.

Hellmuth either did not notice it or chose to ignore it. He got up and started pacing around the room. "Yes. Yes, we could honestly tell our children later that we loved each other very much."

"And, that justifies everything?"

"Well, I am alive." There was a slight pause. "But it does not always feel right." Hellmuth's gaze slid over Wolfsangel who was wearing a short sleeved black T-shirt. His eyes lingered on the black tattoo, a vertical wolf's hook, on the left upper arm. His eyes went from the tattoo to the face. "Did you bring Erich's papers?"

"Yes, copies. You may still be able to find a clue about why he went missing. You never know. The reports by Robert Thomassen, from 1978, are very interesting! I think you will be able to find everything about your son that you have missed." Wolfsangel got up and looked outside to the square in front of Hellmuth's flat on Grosse Beckstrasse. He craned his neck to get out the kinks, stretched his arms, and then said, "He might be dead, but – like you - cannot believe it. I really need to know for certain."

The old man shook his head. "No murder without a corpse. Can there still be a conviction?"

"I don't need a body to convict the guilty but imagine …" He wandered off in thought as a photograph on the wall caught his attention. It was a black-and-white photo showing two men in official SS clothing. One was holding a baby while the other was holding a dagger to the breast of the baby. In the background was a picture of Hitler. He turned to Hellmuth. "Is that you? What's going on here? Looks like a ritual involving human sacrifice?"

"What the heck? No. That baby is Erich! I am the one who holds him. This is a photograph of his christening ceremony. The dagger was used as a symbol of unwavering loyalty and enduring obligations to the cause. The candle stand, made in Dachau, is a gift to the parents."

"That's interesting." Wolfsangel had never heard of an SS christening. "Why the gift?"

"Well, he is…was a pure Aryan child. Our hope at that time was that the Lebensborn children would eventually rule the world."

"Well, that plan didn't work out as intended." Wolfsangel said this more to himself as he shook his head. He tore his eyes from the photo and turned to Hellmuth. "I'm actually hungry. Shall we go out to eat something?"

"It's early, but there is a good restaurant across the street, the Rietkotter. Come, we'll eat there. I'll even pay."

"Good idea, especially if you're paying. I have the confession of Mikkel Thomassen here. I'll share it while we eat."

They walked out of the flat together, took the elevator down. Wolfsangel could swear that the scent of old lady Schubert still lingered in the entrance.

As they crossed the square, Hellmuth paused and pointed to the older white three-story building with the red roof. "See, that's why I chose that restaurant. It was, I believe, built more than two hundred years ago. During the war, Bochum was mercilessly bombed by the Allies and thousands of people died. The city was a ruin after the war, but this restaurant proved indestructible."

Pointing to the more modern building next to it, walled-in mostly with glass, "Look beyond the past, the new Germany. Modern, strong and resurrected to a new life. Our race will prevail, just as the Führer prophesied."

Wolfsangel didn't say anything. He was partly amazed and partly amused after all these years at how entrenched Helmuth was in the Nazi ideology. These guys were certainly committed to the cause.

His thoughts were interrupted by a large group of middle-aged troublemakers. They nearly took up most of the sidewalk as they passed by them. They were clearly possessed by a Peter Pan syndrome: talking loudly to themselves, pushing and shoving each other while laughing insanely at each other's antics. Wolfsangel found himself being elbowed in the ribs a couple of times. He swore at them and was rewarded by a cigarette butt flicked his way. It took some effort, but Wolfsangel decided to ignore this - for now.

The two of them eventually made their way into the restaurant and found a table. After they had settled in and the waitress had taken their drink order, Hellmuth asked, "What are you going to do now? You're still young. Did you get started on something a bit more long term?"

"I'll be fine." Wolfsangel shrugged off the concern but was well aware that the former SS man was not fooled at all by Wolfsangel's cavalier attitude. The old man, of all people, would understand the danger of suddenly being without a war.

"Oh, really? You only feel the fear of war when it becomes silent around you. You remind me of one of my brother's sons. His name is Hellmuth, too. They named him after me." There was a look of pride on Hellmuth's face. He leaned in closer to Wolfsangel. "You know. You should talk to him if you ever want a well-paying job. He is only three or four years older than you. He looks like you, or rather you look like him."

Wolfsangel nodded and deliberately changed the subject. "Anna. Did you ever feel like going back to see her, especially when she was still alive?"

Hellmuth's face clouded. Leaning back, he took his time answering the question. "Yes, I've attempted several times, but in the end, it never worked out. It really didn't."

"I don't understand. How come you were never arrested after the war? No Nuremberg for you?"

Just then, the waitress appeared with their food order. They both ordered a traditional German dish since that is what this restaurant was known for. As Hellmuth cut into his schnitzel, he answered the question. "You're correct. No Nuremberg for me. During the war, I didn't use my real birth name. I used the surname, Reinhard. It wasn't until much later, around 1964, somebody figured out that I was Hellmuth Patzschke. I guess when my real name eventually appeared on a health form, someone noticed it and reported it to the authorities. The timing was impeccable. I was actually on my way to Norway to see Anna. As I was waiting for the ferry, I was arrested. I was tried and sentenced to four years in prison. It was in prison when I received a letter from Mirre Andersen from Norway letting me know that Anna had died."

Now Hellmuth looked away from his guest, his eyes were momentarily soft and moist. Then, hardening his face, he turned and looked Wolfsangel. "At that moment, I felt that I had failed as a man. I wanted then and still want now to go back, and utterly destroy all those people who caused her misery and death."

The young man nodded slowly. Revenge, he understood. Anger against injustice too.

Hellmuth mistook that look. He threw his hands in the air and started shaking. "I mean it, man, the Norwegians have been as bad as we Nazis were. No much worse!" He leaned forward and stuck his index finger in Wolfsangel's face. "We Nazis still believed in something, but those cowards could only rise from their stinking graves by teasing our wives and children and giving them no choice but to take their own lives. Oh! How I would like to drown those cowards by holding their heads in a pail of their own shit."

He took a few deep breaths and got control again.

Wolfsangel looked at Hellmuth. The two of them were quite different. The old man wore his emotions on his sleeve whereas he felt a deep, quiet, smouldering rage.

They finished their meal in silence. When the plates and cutlery were cleared, they ordered coffee.

Wolfsangel took out the large envelope he had carried with him. "So, Hellmuth, are you ready for Mikkel's testimony?"

Hellmuth's hands were shaking slightly as he grabbed it out of Wolfsangel's hands. "Unbelievable how you managed to make a dead person speak."

While Wolfsangel drank his coffee and thought about that group of rude assholes that passed them on the sidewalk, Hellmuth read the report written by Robert Thomassen and his mother in the freezing cold of the Hurdal hills.

It really was an impressive stack of papers. Page after page filled with the facts Mikkel's son and wife were able to recall in their anxious hours in the bunker. Wolfsangel watched as Hellmuth paged through them thoughtfully.

Hellmuth put the stack down on the table. Looking at the young man in front of him with admiration, "You really have made the dead speak."

Wolfsangel nodded. "Read the last one and let me know what you think."

As the old man read through the report, Wolfsangel continued to watch his face. It was an open book. Grief etched the lines in his face deeper and his eyes became moist.

20 February 1978 / Psychiatric Hospital 'Fylke, Oslo / Client: Eirik Tijsker (1943) / Dr. R. Thomassen / Conversation # 5: 1959 - 1966

Eirik Tijsker

Dr. Thomassen wanted me to talk about my formative relationships outside of my immediate family. I guess he wants to know how a guy like me could find a girl and eventually get married.

Well, even heavily traumatized young people grow physically. I managed to move through puberty fairly well during my years in Oslo. I remember as a kid I couldn't wait to grow up. I wanted to be tall and strong. For the longest time, I was one of the shortest kids in my class.

Looking back, I know that I wasn't good at dealing with people. Being constantly bullied at school, losing my sister, and having no father around was harder on me than I realised. I had trust issues and, like the typical nerd, I immersed myself in solitary activities that required brain skills and not people skills. I loved working with complex technical designs and I eventually found work with a company that deals with fishing equipment. One of the highlights for me was learning about beam trawling. Beam trawling started in the Netherlands and proved to be a leading edge for fishing on the North Sea at that time.

January, 1961, stands out for me. I remember it was very cold and the yard was busy getting ships ready to go when the spring thaw hit. Once the ports were free of ice, all these ships had to be ready.

At that time, a steel cutter from the Netherlands was parked there, not there for repairs, but for study purposes. The owner, who was also a shareholder in the Geir shipyard, had rented the boat out to the shipyard for two months so that we could study the latest fishing techniques. Albert Romkes, a fisherman from Urk, came by at the end of February to check on the progress of our study of his boat. We seemed to hit it off because we were both excited about boats and equipment. One day, he asked me to join him for lunch at a local restaurant. He bought me lunch. During our lunch, he wanted to know if I had any ideas about improving fishing equipment. He seemed genuinely interested in what I thought so I told him about my idea of improving the fuel efficiency of his cutter. At the moment, the cost of diesel fuel is relatively cheap, but the way things are going in the world, fuel prices are going to rise. This rising cost will eat into the profit margin.

Albert was intrigued and wanted to know what my solution to that was. I told him that there are at least two things that could be done. First, construct the various parts of the boat with lighter material and second, design it so that it is more wind resistant. He right away saw the implications of that - less diesel, same revenue, more profit. He asked me to flesh out my ideas on paper.

It was that lunch that started me on my journey to the Netherlands and eventually to a relationship with the most wonderful girl a guy could ever dream of. For the next four weeks, the two of us worked out my ideas and made modifications to his cutter. We worked well together and through this relationship, I discovered that Urk, the place where he came from, really interested me. Urk is a fishing village whose people fished on the entire North Sea, the English Channel, the Dogger Bank and even on the Atlantic Ocean. What a freedom! According to Albert, the beam trawl was instrumental in bringing great prosperity to Urk. Nobody expected that - not Urkers nor the rest of Holland.

When I remarked that Urk was lucky, Albert grew quite serious and said that there is no such thing as luck. It is all a blessing from God.

I was intrigued with Urk. Albert told several stories how the village had to fight hard to overcome difficult challenges. That's apparently the miracle of Urk: Together with God confidently moving forward. Clearly, Urk is a close-knit Christian community. According to Albert, the fishermen are home every Sunday to go to church.

At one point, Albert said that I should come out to Urk once and see for myself. He did warn me that their women are not easy to handle. After all, when the men are at sea, family life circles around the mothers. I didn't know if he was serious or not about me coming out to visit Urk. But, a couple days later, he repeated his invitation. He offered to not only give me a job but also assist me in getting the immigration paperwork done.

The more I thought about it, the more I realised that I wanted to go. I talked to my mother about it and her advice was, 'My dear son, you are now 19. Go away from this God forsaken country and build a new life somewhere else.'

So, I left Norway and settled on Urk (yes, apparently 'on Urk' is the correct way to phrase that. Urkers are quirky people and like to remind everybody that they live on an island). Here I am, a nineteen year-old pimply-faced kid leaving his mother and striking out on his own. It really was a beautiful thing. The first half a year was like a dream. It felt like a warm bath, a rebirth, a new life. The only problem was that my daily food always included fish, but I eventually grew to love it.

I chose to attend the Petra church, initially because of one particular lovely lady. Her name was Marianne. Sixteen years old, but very mature for her age. She had a real zest for life. I still remember how she drove recklessly on a high-powered Puch-moped through the narrow alleys and streets. Above her bed, she had a James Dean poster. Her friends were a group of older boys who also drove around on mopeds like Royal Nord, Kreidler and Zundapp. Ah, it doesn't mean anything to you? To me it did.

We started to hang out occasionally, and eventually our friendship grew. She once told me I looked like Paul Newman. I think that was a compliment. On Sunday evenings a group of us from church would often walk the Raadhuisstraat. The Urk giant 'de Gus' was there, always accompanied by his friend, who was known as 'captain.' Somehow, we were drawn towards each other, I mean Marianne and me. One time she asked me if I looked like my father, I honestly said I had never seen him. I told her that I was a child of a German soldier and a Norwegian woman, and that I had a hard time with that. I told her about my sister. But about my time here in Fylke? No.

In 1966, we got engaged to be married. We wanted to let my mother know so we made plans to go to Norway. We had to hurry because my mother was very sick. I was shocked when I saw her in the hospital. Even though she was only forty-five years old, she could have easily passed for a person twice her age. It is a good thing that we got there as quick as we could. She lived only seven days after our arrival. Fortunately for all of us, her mind was clear - she had no pain or fear of death.

She was very glad we were there and for the first time, she talked extensively about my German father. Just moments before she passed away, she grabbed my arm and said, 'Eirik! Do not forget Esther … remember her!' We stayed until the funeral was over. Family was invited, but nobody came, only Mirre and her friend Rannveigh. Mirre, how angry she was. I've never seen anyone so sad and so angry at the same time.'

Robert Thomasson

The former SS man slumped in his seat, embarrassed that tears were freely flowing down his face. "This is all my fault. I handed my son over to the wolves in Norway while I fled back to Germany. I didn't realise until now how much I have hurt him and Anna."

Wolfsangel sat silent, watching as the guilt, anger, and grief surged through the old man's veins like a poisonous cocktail.

When they eventually left the restaurant, the sun was beginning its descent behind the buildings. The town's nightlife was burgeoning. Up ahead, outside a Turkish restaurant, a group of swarthy men stood on the sidewalk, talking loudly in a foreign language and laughing at the passers-by. Wolfsangel noticed that Hellmuth behaved rather nervously as they approached this group. Even though he tried to give the men a wide berth, a couple of them stared at them and then each other, laughing in derision. Wolfsangel felt his rage starting to percolate but Hellmuth pressed on, ignoring what was going on around him.

The two of them walked back to Hellmuth's flat in silence. In the elevator, Wolfsangel turned to Hellmuth. "Have you had a run-in with those Turks?"

Hellmuth looked at his shoes and stayed silent.

"Hellmuth, you must be honest with me. What happened?"

Hellmuth nodded, but still said nothing. They entered the flat and when the door was locked, Hellmuth turned to Wolfsangel. He sighed deeply and started talking. "Well, you know what they say, a leopard never changes its spots. I hate those inferior people. What are they doing here in my Germany? Those foreigners pollute our land and race. They are nothing more than parasites. I even see German girls falling for them. Can you imagine: German blood with that cursed, inferior, stinking…?"

No wonder Hellmuth wanted to make sure he was in his private residence before spouting off that vitriol. Wolfsangel cut him off. "Tell me what happened."

Hellmuth stopped for a moment to control himself. "It started with that Turkish restaurant. Ever since it opened, they have been hanging around here. One day, a few months ago, they were standing in front of their restaurant, just like tonight. When I walked by, I discovered they were flirting with a couple of young German girls. Well, I quietly spoke to one of the girls and just reminded her of her superior race. I was very polite. I just told her that she should and could do better than that." Hellmuth shrugged his shoulders.

"Go on."

"That stupid girl turned around and told her Turkish friend what I had said."

"Did he whack you?"

"Worse. Three of them grabbed my arms and neck and dragged me inside that stinking restaurant. The owner tried to stop them, but they snapped at him. I don't know what they said, they were talking in their pig language. They forced me onto a chair and while I sat, they stood around me. One guy we saw tonight, the one with the large earring, said, "We are grey wolves. We are Turkish and Muslim. I guess you are probably an old Nazi.

"I said something like 'we were allies … 'and 'there were Muslims who helped us', but he slapped me across the face and told me to be quiet. Actually, he told me to shut my pig's head! Then, hitting himself on the chest like he was some hero, he proceeded to explain to me that they are the people to watch. They do everything better than us old Nazi losers."

Wolfsangel snorted.

Helmuth continued, trying to mimic the accent of those Turks, “For more than a hundred years, we - Turks - have been removing minorities; just ask the Armenians and Christians. We made them slaves, without rights, we took their homes and killed millions. We systematically exterminated these dhimmis, transported them in livestock trucks, made them perish in concentration camps and deserts. But we get away with it. We’ll always get away with it, no Nuremberg for us. Do you know why? Because we are better than you.”

Wolfsangel guffawed, mostly at the horrible imitation of their accent. Hellmuth didn’t crack a smile, he started pacing, becoming more agitated. “I tried to get up and leave, but somebody hit me from behind and told me to shut up and stay seated until they said I could go. Well, Earring Goon held his stinky garlic face just in front of me and told me that they are quite simply superior. After all, they have been systematically liquidating the weak by burning churches and killing piles of Armenians for more than a hundred years. Then one of the goons grabbed my head and held a burning cigarette near my right eye and told me to go to our German police, what are they going to do? It’s my single word against all of them.”

Wolfsangel felt that rage start to percolate again. This was more serious than he thought. Not that the SS didn’t deserve a taste of their own medicine. If there was any group of people who knew the power of terror, it was them. However, as he surveyed the old man, he saw Eirik being bullied. “Did they let you go after that?”

Hellmuth looked embarrassed. “The guy with the earring grabbed my nose and twisted it. Hard. It was so painful, it brought tears to my eyes. They all scoffed. ‘Cry as much as you want. Soon we will be in charge. It won’t take that much longer because we are Uber-Nazis. By the way, we know where you live.’ With that, they grabbed my arms, dragged me to the door and threw me out.”

“That was the same group of men that we passed outside?” Wolfsangel asked.

"Yes. I recognized most of them today from my previous encounter." Hellmuth sniffed his nose. Reliving this memory brought up the humiliation he had suffered earlier. "The owner of the restaurant was a nice man, though. He came to talk to me a couple of days later to see how I was doing. He didn't know how to stop them from attacking me."

The two of them were silent for a minute or so. This was interrupted by a sudden loud noise of laughter and glass breaking. Wolfsangel glanced out the window. Hellmuth's neighbourhood looked like it had been taken over by a group of street thugs.

Wolfsangel glanced at the tough old man and felt a rage coming into him. Too many Norwegians denied their actions shortly after the war, but the facts were there. They denied the fact that they'd forced prisoners of war to clear a minefield. They still deny their debt to Lebensborn children. They're so proud of their cowardice. A plan began to form in his mind. "Do not worry about those assholes," he growled.

The old man remained silent, lost in thought. Wolfsangel stood up, looked for and found a bottle of quality whiskey. Outside a discordant thunderstorm broke out, lighting the sky with firebolts, portending the rage building up inside of Wolfsangel. While the two men spoke upstairs, the group of men in the streets found shelter. Death itself kept watch over them that night, but they did not know it at that moment. The old clocks of the old Catholic St. Peter and Paul Church told Wolfsangel it was ten o'clock.

"I have to go away for a moment, back in half an hour. Give me your Walther."

Hellmuth looked at him quizzically but complied.

Wolfsangel left Hellmuth's flat with an old SS pistol and two rolls of grey duct tape in his coat pocket. He walked past the restaurant and looked inside. There were nine or ten people sitting in a booth. He recognized the man with the earring. He first cased out the surroundings, the plan solidifying in his mind. The rain had temporarily cleared the street of pedestrians. Pleased with how things were shaping up, Wolfsangel stepped into the restaurant, took off his coat and ordered a coffee. He watched the man behind the counter prepare the drink orders for the group.

Wolfsangel caught his eye. "What's your name?"

"My name is Mohamed, and you?" Mohamed passed on a tentative smile and rubbed his moustache.

Wolfsangel ignored the question. "You're not German. Are you Turkish?" Mohamed nodded furtively and continued to work in silence.

A fat, dark-skinned man with a big moustache said something in his language and the others laughed. Wolfsangel turned and saw that they were looking at him. It was about him. Good. The man with the earring laughed hard, in direct eye contact with Wolfsangel.

"Piece of shit, pisslik", drawled Earring Goon studying the sinister face of Wolfsangel. His eyes narrowed as he recognized him. "Hey, you were just that old guy, right? That Nazi loser with his purebred talk, that despicable kafir."

Wolfsangel kept a steady gaze on that fat face while taking another sip of his coffee. It's good to be sure of your target. That's him for sure. An ungrateful asshole in a hospitable country. He slammed his cup down on the table and said, "Germans do not deny what they have done in the past, that is their power. Tell me, what did you people do to Christian Armenians?"

Earring Goon looked at him and laughed. "Oh, I see. That old fart told you about our conversation. Why don't you two just hang yourselves already?" Then, slowly turning his back to Wolfsangel, Earring Goon said something in Turkish to the others. They grinned maliciously at Wolfsangel.

Well, that was enough pleasantries for Wolfsangel. He did a quick survey of the restaurant, then turning to the man behind the counter, "Mohamed, you are the owner of this outfit?"

"Yes, well, along with my married brother. He is vacationing with his family in Turkey at this moment."

"Ok. Lock the door."

"What. Why? We close at eleven o'clock, there's still a couple of hours left ..." Distracted, the man looked at his watch. When he looked up at Wolfsangel, he was staring into the face of a man who was deadly serious about getting that door locked.

Speaking calmly, but sharply, "It's time for a Wannsee meeting, right?" He looked around, they were grinning at him like a group of aggressive hyenas. Behind the desk Mohamed looked at him quizzically, but made no move to the door.

Wolfsangel wiped his mouth with a napkin then and stepped over to the nearest man. It was the fat man with the moustache. Without so much as a second glance, he reached back and grabbed the handle of his gun. Fat Moustache Goon had no idea what was coming. Wolfsangel stuck his face right into the fat man's face, the putrid smell of bad breath almost knocking him out. Fat Moustache Goon, with a wide smirk, took a puff from his cigarette and blew the smoke into Wolfsangel's face. Without blinking, Wolfsangel took out the pistol and shoved the barrel onto the chest of the fat man. Looking straight into his eyes, Wolfsangel pulled the trigger. The shot was muffled by the belly fat. Wolfsangel watched as the smirk turned to surprise and then shock as Fat Moustache Goon looked down and saw his blood spurting from his body.

The restaurant became still. The arrogant looks fled the faces of those sitting there and terror replaced it. Totally stunned, nobody spoke a word.

Wolfsangel caught the eye of Mohamed and shook his head in the direction of the door. The man quickly scrambled to the door and locked it.

"Now, lower those shades and close them completely." The shades came down very rapidly. The rest of the men simultaneously watched as the lifeless body of their fat friend slumped over, his face frozen with the look of shock.

"Okay. Get on the floor, all of you. On your stomach and hands on your back." The men did as they were told.

Wolfsangel called Mohamed and gave him the rolls of duct tape. "Wrap tape around their wrists and ankles. Make sure it is tight."

Earring Goon found his voice and whimpered. "Hey, man, what the hell is going on? What do you want?"

His mouth shut quickly when Wolfsangel turned to him and shoved his gun into that man's ear. "Keep your pie hole shut." The man immediately acquiesced, slumping back into his seat.

Giving the impression that he was on the verge of losing his self-control, Wolfsangel snarled at the group of men. "I want an Endlösung from you guys. Is that clear?" There were a lot of heads bobbing up and down.

He was, in fact, completely in control. Despite what it might look like, he did not hate foreigners. In general, they integrated slowly but surely. After three generations they were all like full-blooded natives. But Hellmuth's story had made him angry as hell. He pushed the barrel of his gun a little deeper into the ear of Earring Goon. Wolfsangel, pleased to see the man wince in pain, hissed, "One squeak and I will perforate your brain in the name of Eirik."

Mohamed was just finishing taping the legs of the last goon. Within a short time, nine men were lying on the floor, all tied up with duct tape. Wolfsangel then tied the owner himself and checked his work. Some were not tied enough, they got a few extra wraps of tightly bound tape.

Wolfsangel peered into a room behind the bar. There was a small storage room where Wolfsangel found a sharp knife on a shelf. He took it and further inspected the room. Walking back to the men on the floor, "We're going to continue this meeting in a back room. Since you can't get there on your own, I will drag you in one by one."

The heavy corpse of the fat guy was the first one out. Wolfsangel grabbed his legs and dragged the body, leaving behind a small trail of blood. Wolfsangel unceremoniously swung him into the back of the room and then kicked him in the groin. He made sure the other men heard him snarl. "Laugh at me, blow smoke in my face. Really, fatso?"

He walked back to where the rest of the men were on the floor. He immediately noticed an odour of urine and faeces. A smile landed on his face as he realised that some of them were facing the same shame and humiliation as Hellmuth. He growled at them. "Pigs are unclean, right?"

He waited a moment, not really expecting them to answer his rhetorical question. Well, the rhetoric was soon going to be reality. He grabbed the second man's legs and pulled him to the room.

Eirik sang in his head and the knife did what it had to do.

Wolfsangel dealt with them one at a time, leaving Earring Goon for last. He bent over the man's head and whispered in his ear. "You silly fool! You should never, ever threaten a Nazi!" He grabbed the man by the ears and dragged him to the room. He noticed a trail of wetness left behind the man being dragged. He grinned. "So, you pissed your pants, did you. You really are an Uber-Nazi."

Mohammed, he didn't kill.

Wolfsangel locked the storage room with the keys he had taken from Mohamed. He set out to clean up the place and remove all traces of his presence. The restaurant was, of course, empty so he put the chairs back on the tables, grabbed a mop and wiped the trail of blood left by Fat Moustache Goon. Then he gathered all the dirty dishes and put them in the kitchen sink. He switched off the lights and in the dark, he opened the shades a bit so when people wanted to look inside, that was possible. There was nothing special to see here.

When he stepped outside, he discovered it was still raining. He hurriedly locked the door and dropped the keys into the nearest storm drain. He walked around the block just to make sure nobody was following him and then, when he was sure nobody was, he dashed across the street and into the flat building.

It was a restless and nervous Hellmuth who opened the door and let him back in.

Wolfsangel placed the gun on the table. "Here is your Walther back. I fired a shot, one."

Helmuth looked distressed. "What? Who did you shoot?"

"Döner kebab, veal or chicken. I'm not sure. You will find out later."

Old Hellmuth looked at him and nodded in understanding. He took the gun and put it on the counter. "All right. I am curious, you left no trace, I assume?"

Wolfsangel gave him that look. "Of course not. Just think of this as a present from Eirik." Grabbing his backpack, he turned to Hellmuth. "Please give me the number of that namesake of yours. I'm leaving now."

Hellmuth took a block of papers, ripped one off and wrote a phone number he retrieved from a red book. Handing the paper to Wolfsangel, he gave instructions on where he could find Hellmuth Junior. "Let me hear how you made out with Little Hellmuth, okay? I want to know what your next steps will be. Erich never did that, which is too bad because I would have loved to help him."

"I will do that," Wolfsangel said in a conciliatory tone, although he was pretty sure he wouldn't.

"Maybe you can also send a postcard once in a while." The old man, eyes downcast, suddenly looked lonely. "It's so nice to get mail." He raised his eyes and added, "Send one to your home as well, even if you have forgotten them and think you do not need them. They probably think, like I did, that you are dead."

Wolfsangel thought about his family. What family? He didn't have a family. After a few seconds, the younger man responded. "I promise you that I will do that. Talking about forgetting, old man. Did you ever go to the graves of your own daughter and your lover?"

Hellmuth paused. "You're right. You're absolutely right. I have no excuse. The next time you come here, I will have put flowers on their graves." Wolfsangel gave him a skeptical look. Hellmuth stepped closer, looked up into the dark eyes. "You don't believe me? I will! I swear it to you."

Wolfsangel saw the man's sincere eyes and remembered that at one time he had been an SS Gestapo man. Their motto was 'Meine Ehre heißt Treue' – My Honour's name is Loyalty. That meant loyalty until death. The past led the way before them.

He stepped out of Hellmuth's flat, into the hall. Turning around, "A son looks up at his father. What do you think? If Eirik had known you better, would he have been proud of you?"

The old man was silent, and his face fell. Wolfsangel knew that Hellmuth's failure to help Anna and their children plagued his conscience. He scratched his chin but remained silent.

Wolfsangel understood. This had been a very difficult day for Hellmuth. "Goodbye, old friend. It might take a long time, but you will see me again." He nodded his goodbye, turned and took the stairs down.

Wolfsangel walked back to the Bochum Hauptbahnhof knowing that there would be no train leaving for Norway at this time of the day. He had glanced at his watch earlier and saw that it was much later than he thought. That's okay, he contemplated. I have no plan, no home, no work, but I have lots of money and time. He saw there was a train leaving soon for Amsterdam and decided it was as good time as any to visit his home country. He purchased a ticket at the kiosk and boarded the train a few minutes before it left.

He was still coming down from the high he felt as those asshole Turks got what was coming to them. It didn't bother him in the least that he just snuffed out the life of nine human beings. His time in the Foreign Legion instilled in him that Machiavelli principle: 'People should either be caressed or crushed. If you do them minor damage they will get their revenge; but if you cripple them there is nothing they can do. If you need to injure someone, do it in such a way that you do not have to fear their vengeance.' Wolfsangel saw no point in trying to teach those arrogant pricks a lesson. It would be lost on them and Hellmuth would end up suffering more. This way, Hellmuth could live in peace and the world got rid of useless people who contribute nothing positive to German society.

Eventually, though, as the night wore on, the high was slowly replaced with a touch of melancholy. As the train sped towards his childhood home, he saw his steady reflection in the foreground of the window while in the background the landscape, shrouded in darkness, sped past. His mind wandered to his childhood and how things seemed so certain back then. When the teen years hit him, he couldn't wait to get the hell out. He longed for freedom and adventure. And now? He caught himself thinking about finding a special someone and settling down to raise a family. Wolfsangel shook his head. Okay, that was so absolutely ridiculous; it actually brought a momentary smile to his face.

He got up and went to the concession to purchase a cola. By the time he reached Amsterdam, nearly four hours after leaving Bochum, he had resolved to get his life back on track - pun intended. The mission of Eirik would have to be put on hold. He found the paper in his pocket with Hellmuth, Junior's phone number and decided to give him a call as soon as practical. The years in the legion were not wasted time, but now it was time to start another career.

Hellmuth Junior was everything Wolfsangel expected him to be. A few days after calling him from Amsterdam, Wolfsangel met him in a Berlin restaurant on Friedrichstrasse. The man sitting across from him was tall, blond, with chiselled features. Three years older than him, Hellmuth looked very much like the typical Aryan. Wolfsangel suspected Hellmuth would have made Hitler proud.

"I bet the old man has already called to tell you about me," Wolfsangel said.

Hellmuth took a sip of his coffee and fixed his eyes on Wolfsangel. There was a rather lengthy pause while Hellmuth took a couple more sips, his eyes never leaving Wolfsangel's face. It was a bit unnerving, but Wolfsangel decided to wait out the silence. Finally, with a small smile playing on his face, Hellmuth nodded. "Yes, my uncle Hellmuth vouches for you. I do not know how you did it, but you impressed the hell out of him. And he doesn't impress easily. After all, when you have somebody like me, there is not a lot of room for improvement."

Wolfsangel grabbed a napkin and daubed his mouth, wiping away the imaginary crumbs. He returned the stare, not sure if he was serious or joking. His face didn't offer any clues.

Without missing a beat, Hellmuth continued. "So, I heard you were in the Foreign Legion?"

"Yes. The full five years, then an honourable discharge. And you?"

"KSK, Kommando Spezialkräfte, an elite military unit in the German army. One day, I just up and quit. I am now a private security guard. That's not really my thing either."

"Oh?"

"I need more action. Look at me. Can you see me just hanging around rich people making sure their money and their lives are safe? I've been doing some research and there are a few private mercenary companies that work worldwide. They are looking for people with military training and experience. I think they would even take you."

Wolfsangel kept eating and remained passive. Hellmuth dug something out of his pocket. It looked like a newspaper clipping. He carefully unfolded it and set it in front of Wolfsangel. "Isn't this your work?"

Wolfsangel scanned the article. It was from the Westdeutsche Allgemeine Zeitung:

Ten men brutally murdered in Bochum, survivor insane

The bodies of ten men were found by the Kriminalpolizei in a storage room of a Turkish restaurant in Grosse Beckstrass. One of the men had been shot to death while the remaining nine had their hands, feet, and throat cut. One of those nine had his intestines pulled out. All of them likely died a slow and painful death.

The owner of the restaurant is currently in the psychiatric ward in the St. Josef Hospital. Police speculate that he may have been present when the murders took place.

At this time, there are no leads as to either who murdered these ten men or what the motive might be. There has been a recent rise in anti-Turkish sentiment and there is some speculation that this might be the result of a turf war between the Turkish community and a neo-Nazi group.

An elderly couple who lives near the restaurant said, "'Of course, we think it's very bad about those dead, but those Turkish cocks always fight, don't they? Let them cut their throats in the backcountries of Turkey. This neighbourhood changed because of the arrival of these Turks. They bothered us a lot."

Comprising 3.4 percent of the population, Turks are the second largest group of immigrants in Germany. Seventy-four percent of these immigrants do not have professional qualifications. The majority of Turks insist on maintaining their Turkish identity and cultural heritage. Although none of them wants to be associated with these atrocities, a new Turkish café will soon be opened in this city, where Turks can feel at home in their own culture.

Wolfsangel shrugged, trying to play it cool, but he couldn't help it when the corners of his lips started to creep upward.

Suddenly, Hellmuth's face split into a wide grin. "Come on, man, you know it is. You've got what it takes. So, what do you think? Are you interested in money, adventure, danger, and women? Surely, that's got to appeal to you."

Wolfangel had already made up his mind earlier. "You know, I think we have the same interests," Wolfsangel smiled. "Let's do it. If you hang around with me long enough, I'll show you how you can improve."

Hellmuth burst out laughing. "I know a company that is looking for people just like us."

In the days that followed, they found work at Blackwater, a newly formed company that ran its operations out of the United States. Its training grounds comprised nearly three thousand hectares of wetlands constantly drenched by black, smelly, decaying peat water. The inaccessible private facilities of Blackwater were located on the border of the states of North Carolina and Virginia. Both Hellmuth and Wolfsangel were amazed at the versatility of this company. It was a one-stop shop for countries or organizations who had lots of money to hire a professional army. This army was well trained to eliminate terrorists through extremely dangerous but effective means. Its secretly train army units were able to extract deeply held information. Really, everything and anything was possible as long as somebody was willing to pay the price. What surprised Wolfsangel the most, though, was how the United States regularly hired these mercenaries surreptitiously to fix up the dirty work of the CIA.

It didn't take Blackwater long to realize these two young men were gifted with a natural and intuitive ability to quickly learn a wide range of defensive and attack methods. They were soon deployed in Africa where they protected both interests and lives. Mercenaries do not always kill; they also save lives. They protect food transport, disabled drug gangs and dare to stand literally between ordinary soldiers and dangerous radical terrorists. But, as the two of them soon found out, the Blackwater swamp held some deep and dark secrets that occasionally bubbled to the surface. Clinging to the two of them was an odour reeking of murder, torture, theft, looting, and bribery.

Time flew by. Life for Wolfsangel was both surreal and adventurous. It had been a long time since he had this degree of contentment and peace. He revelled in the primal feeling of being a warrior; of being a man. The two of them fought side by side, feeling like young gods. Their lives became separate from the rule of law and largely free of responsibility for others.

Yet, in spite of this freedom, there were those unexpected moments, usually at night, when Eirik would insert himself. Apparently, he wasn't going to let Wolfsangel forget the injustices that he had pledged to right. In the depths of his sleep, Wolfsangel occasionally heard desperate cries. It was the helpless cries of someone suffering deep agonies. It came from within Wolfsangel but it was not from him. He found he could usually assuage the cries when he would whisper, "I will not forget you, I promise."

This situation changed in the Spring of 1996. Much to his consternation, Wolfsangel found himself unable to mollify Eirik. Eirik became more and more insistent, refusing to be silenced.

The end of May 1996, Vanderhoof, British Columbia, Canada

It started when Hellmuth approached Wolfsangel with a new assignment. "We're heading out to Alaska. There's a remote place called Bokam Mountain on the south end of the panhandle."

Wolfsangel found a map and the two of them located the area.

"What's our mission?" asked Wolfsangel.

"The details are a bit sketchy right now. They are on a need-to-know basis. From what I've been told, our client is interested in that particular area because they believe there may be a pocket of rare earth minerals in the mountainside. They are hoping to sneak in and grab some geological samples for testing. If it turns out they are right, I suspect they will make some large investments in American mining companies."

"Okay. So, how does that involve us? We're not geologists or tour guides."

Hellmuth nodded. "True, but the stakes are high. China has all but cornered the market on mining these rare earth minerals. Which, by the way, are used in the production of high-tech military applications. Our client is expecting some trouble from both the Russians and the Chinese who are closely monitoring the area by satellite. This could turn out to be a dangerous mission, so our company was hired to protect the geologists and make sure they get in and out safely with some samples. We were specifically assigned because of our experience in accessing and working in remote areas. And, of course, my intelligence, charm, and good looks." While Wolfsangel did the eyeroll, Hellmuth clapped him on the shoulder. "So, pack your bags, buddy, we're heading out to Alaska."

With that, Hellmuth left the room, leaving Wolfsangel studying the map. His eyes were drawn to a small town almost directly east of Bokam Mountain. He could feel his temples throb and realised that it had been a while since he felt that. He looked up and saw Eirik staring at him, the pain etched all over his face.

Wolfsangel shook his head as if trying to clear the cobwebs from his brain. He wasn't expecting this, and it caught him off-guard.

Vanderhoof, Canada. Wolfsangel remembered the place and who lived there, even though it had been almost three years since he had read the journal and reports. He felt a deep shame swallow him. He had gotten his life back together and found some meaning and purpose, but he neglected his mission. "Yes, Eirik, I know what I need to do."

With that, Wolfsangel convinced Helmuth to make a slight change in their itinerary. They were going to make a brief stop-over in Vanderhoof so that Wolfsangel could visit a distant family member. Their plan called for flying into Vancouver International Airport, hopping on another flight from Vancouver to Prince George, then renting a truck and driving to the coast after a stop in Vanderhoof. When they arrived at the coast, they would be able surreptitiously to sneak into the Alaska panhandle without alerting any of the American authorities. It was a great plan.

Four days later, the two of them drove into Vanderhoof. This town of more than four thousand didn't seem very special to Wolfsangel. It consisted of a monotonous arrangement of one chain hotel after another. He did, however, get his first glimpse of the well-known Canadian icon called Tim Hortons.

Wolfsangel shook his head. "What the heck is so special about this place? Why would anyone want to leave Europe and choose this place to settle down? It seems so boring and nondescript."

Hellmuth grunted. "I know how we can liven this place up. I did a bit of research. This place has a decent airport which annually holds a fairly famous air show. Maybe we should tell Blackwater to hold our upcoming Entebbe Liberation action training here. They are looking for a suitable place and this town and airport definitely have the room for it. It's pretty private up here. And, look at that, there's a bar that we can hang out after training."

Wolfsangel tried to visualize holding an Entebbe Liberation training exercise here. He couldn't. The exercise was about freeing a commercial airline from armed terrorist hijackers. The original operation took place at the airport of Entebbe in Uganda in 1976. The Israeli army stormed a plane that had been hijacked by a terrorist group who demanded the liberation of some Palestinian militants captured by the Israelis. It was a highly successful mission, in part because of the intense training that took place. All the hijackers were killed while the Israelis lost one person - Jonathan Netanyahu - the brother of the future prime minister of Israel. The Ugandans, who supported the hijackers, also didn't fare very well. They lost forty-five soldiers and eleven of their fighter planes. The exercise was highly sophisticated. Wolfsangel couldn't see it happening here.

Hellmuth spied an A & W fast food restaurant. "A hamburger joint. Let's stop here and get some food and figure out how you are going to find your relative. You are absolutely sure he still lives here?"

Wolfsangel gave him his best disdainful look. "Of course. He's Dutch. He's here. They don't move around much." Truthfully, though, he wasn't totally sure.

They were just starting to down their hamburgers and root beer when they were interrupted by a teenage boy who seemed to be aimlessly wandering around the seating area clutching a fly swatter in his left hand. As he approached their table, he suddenly swatted the back of the booth where Hellmuth was sitting. To his credit, Hellmuth didn't flinch. He looked up into the wild eyes of the boy and growled at him to get lost.

The boy ignored Hellmuth and made a beeline to another table where he swatted the tabletop numerous times, each time he let out a giggle. Fortunately, there were no customers sitting there.

"Hey, mental Theo, there is a fly over here." A big-bushy bearded lumberjack hollered at him. At that, the boy headed straight for that table. Wolfsangel heard the thwack of the swatter as it hit the tabletop. It was accompanied by the raucous laughter of the table mates. Wolfsangel slid out of this booth and stood up. He caught the boy's attention. "Hey, come here. I'll buy you a hamburger."

The boy burst into a big smile as he skipped over to their table. "I'll have a teen burger. I'm a teen, so that is why I want a teen burger. Do you have an uncle burger? Is that what you have?" He peered at Wolfsangel's tray of food.

Hellmuth smirked and said to no one in particular. "Actually, he's having a momma burger."

Wolfsangel pointed to the booth across the aisle from them and told the boy to sit there while he fetched the boy's food.

Wolfsangel was glad he wasn't sitting with him. The boy both ate and talked to himself at the same time. Food and spittle flew out his mouth as he engaged himself in a highly animated conversation about god, broken necks, farming, and everything in between. When the boy had put the last morsel of food in his mouth, he stood up, spread his hands and blessed them as if he were a minister. "May the Lord bless you and keep you. Yes, there is salvation also for you." The boy intoned.

Wolfsangel winced slightly as he felt the wetness of a hamburger bun hit his cheek, cling for a moment, and then fall off. "Amen". Hellmuth and Wolfsangel replied solemnly.

"Theo Weerstand!" An intense and demanding voice rang out. Almost as if they had practiced this before, all three heads - Wolfsangel, Hellmuth, and Theo, turned around in unison to see where that voice was coming from. A very attractive young woman walked out from behind the counter and approached the boy. She stopped Theo's performance with a gentle hand and looked at the two mercenaries. Both just stared at her like two boys taking in their first dirty magazine. Hellmuth, of course, was enchanted by her beauty. Wolfsangel, on the other hand, was startled when he heard the boy's last name.

"Thanks for being kind and feeding him." She explained, "I know he is a bit weird, but he can't help it. He has autism and his parents don't look after him very well."

Wolfsangel was the first to speak. "Weerstand? Did you say his last name is Weerstand?"

The woman nodded.

He continued, "That's a Dutch name. It means resistance."

"Hmm. Is that what it means? Resistance?" The young woman put her arm around Theo who promptly pushed it off. "He occasionally lives with his parents but goes to a psychiatric hospital in Prince George regularly. So please ignore him, he only harms the flies." Then, turning to Theo,

"You are good at that, aren't you? So, our customers won't be bothered by those critters."

Hellmuth finally found his voice. "Did you just feel that?" He looked around the room and planted his feet firmly on the floor. "Either that was an earthquake or you just rocked my world."

The young woman looked at him blankly, processing what he just said. Then, bursting out laughing, she told him, "My name is Hannah." Within seconds, Hellmuth had steered the conversation away from Theo and the two of them began a conversation about things to see and do in this town.

Since Hannah had finished her shift and the conversation was heading in the direction Hellmuth was hoping it would, Wolfsangel figured he had a lot of time on his hands to get some information from the teenager. Meeting him here was a stroke of luck for Wolfsangel. Weerstand was the surname of Eirik's wife, Marianne. He was pretty certain he had found the brother-in-law.

"Your surname, Weerstand, that's a Dutch name. Are you from Holland?"

Theo looked at him with remarkably wide eyes. "My father is from the Netherlands, from a place called Urk. I have never been there myself."

"Well, fancy that. I actually know where Urk is. So, what does your father do here? Vanderhoof is far from the sea, a pretty desolate place for an Urker."

"Desolate. That's an interesting word." Wolfsangel watched Theo's face as he repeated that word several times to himself. "Desolate means lonely. Yes. That is a good word for this place." After repeating the word a couple more times, Theo continued, "My father is a farmer. Cows, milking, well..." With a gesture he showed that he had a low opinion of this profession.

Wolfsangel exaggerated a surprised expression on his face. "An Urker? Here as a farmer? My goodness, he is a long way from the sea. I can't believe I came across an Urker who is not a fisherman. I want to know more about him. What do you think? Can I talk to your father?"

"Maybe." Theo strained his neck muscles. "You never know with him. He's often in bed, sick. Yep, pretty sick. But he can talk. Even when he is in bed." Theo's eagle eyes spotted a fly that just landed on a table. Within a flash, the fly had met a swift death at the hand of Mental Theo. He raised his hands in victory and then turned back to Wolfsangel. "And mother is also at home. Mother is always at home. She has A.L.S. Do you know what that is? She talks very strangely, she can't move her lips very well. Well, all of her muscles can't move very well. I think she is desolate."

He stopped to look around for more flies, raising his swatter in a warning gesture. "You know, she's… she's not crazy. I'm not crazy either. I have a doctor's note that says so. Our farm is close to the highway, the third road left, number thirty-six towards Burns Lake. It has a lot of flies. Yes sir, a lot of them." He decided that he was finished speaking and went back on the prowl for any recalcitrant flies.

Wolfsangel scratched his head as he thought about Eirik's brother-in-law. Things, it would seem, aren't all a bed of roses for him. That's good. Justice is already being served. Maybe all he needed to do was give a gentle nudge.

He heard a tinkle of laughter and spotted Hellmuth with a solemn expression on his face and Hannah in a full blush. The mating ritual was in full swing. Wolfsangel felt sorry for the girl. She had no idea that she was caught in a master's web. Wolfsangel was somewhat envious of the free and easy way Hellmuth had with females - especially the good-looking ones. They seemed naturally attracted to him. "It's the eyes," Hellmuth once told him. "If you look like a wary cat, always expecting trouble, you'll never attract anyone. You're like the cat with his ears back flat, growling, ready to attack at the first sign of trouble. Come on, you need to trust that not everybody is out to get you. What's really hidden behind those eyes of yours? Is it only revenge and toughness? Get over it. Females get turned off by that."

Wolfsangel took those words to heart and since then did some self-reflection. There was a good deal of truth to what Hellmuth said. His thoughts were often consumed with revenge and violence. A shaft of loneliness hit his stomach and, for a fleeting moment, he felt some long suppressed emotions bubbling upward.

As Theo approached his direction, Wolfsangel asked him, “Well, what do you think, Theo? You think your father and mother would like a visit from me?”

Theo grinned and nodded happily. “We haven’t had a visitor for at least five years. Come on, I’ll make coffee for you.”

Wolfsangel shouted over to Hellmuth. “Hey, Romeo. Do you feel like going on a visit? Theo just invited us over to his place.” Hellmuth grunted something about he’d rather wait here at the restaurant, but Wolfsangel was free to take his time. Wolfsangel shrugged his shoulders, turned to Theo and said, “He is too busy. It’s just going to be the two of us. Come with me, I’ll drive us to your place.”

“Yes, that would be swell. What should I do with my bike?”

“Throw it in the back of the truck.”

Theo laughed and clapped his hands. The two of them walked out together. Theo thrust his chest forward and walked on his toes. After a couple of unsuccessful attempts – he refused Wolfsangel’s help, he finally managed to throw his old bike into the back of the truck. He triumphantly climbed into the box and sat down with his back against the cab. Wolfsangel shook his head. Clearly this young man had internalised his place in the social order. “Theo,” Wolfsangel barked. “Get in the cab. There is lots of room for you.”

Theo’s face was awash with pleasure as he scrambled out and took his place on the passenger side. You’d think he was sitting on a throne. The only thing missing was him waving to a crowd of adoring fans.

The farm was quite easy to locate as Theo had given him very precise directions. Less than fifteen minutes after leaving the restaurant, Theo pointed to a smattering of buildings and announced their destination was close. Even from the road, it was pretty evident that the farm was in a state of disaster. Wolfsangel guided the truck through the long access road. Every once in a while, he had to steer clear of a rusty farm implement that made its final resting place in the middle of the road. Just before he pulled up at the house, a couple of skinny dogs came out to bark their displeasure of being invaded. When they finally stopped at the house, Wolfsangel looked around. The place was in utter shambles. The house was missing most of its siding. There were old fence posts, wire racks, and empty cardboard boxes strewn all over the place. The yard had clearly not been kept up for many years - weeds and other obnoxious plant life had invaded. The outbuildings were all in a state of decay. The whole place looked and smelt like it was dying a slow death.

Theo had already tossed his bike out the side of the truck and tugged at Wolfsangel's coat. "They're probably in the living room. Come with me."

They entered the house through a door at the back. Theo explained that this was the mud room. Wolfsangel considered the room aptly named. Theo guided Wolfsangel through an obstacle course of boots, shoes, and tools strewn all over the floor before they entered the kitchen. Wolfsangel wrinkled his nose as he took in the disaster that deluged the kitchen. There were dirty dishes piled precariously all over the counter. The floor was littered with moulding food articles. Anaemic plants stood their ground in the solitary window sill. The nauseating smell compounded by the myriad of flies buzzing around made the mighty mercenary's stomach give a slight heave. He half expected Theo to start attacking the flies. However, Theo was on a mission. They were almost through the kitchen. As they passed the stove, caked with layers of grease, dirt, and fly shit, Wolfsangel glanced at a frying pan sitting on the stove. It contained three blackened sausages nestled in a gelled pool of whitish grease. Theo noticed his gaze and explained. "Nice, eh? Made of elk meat. You want to try one?" Wolfsangel decided to pass on the offer.

They escaped the kitchen by exiting through a set of double doors into the sitting room. Almost immediately, Wolfsangel's nose was further assaulted by an overpowering stench of urine and old sweat. The room was darkened by closed blinds; it took a moment for his eyes to adjust. Eventually, he made out a dumpy old man lounging on a decrepit lime-green recliner. Wolfsangel was distracted by a strange wheezing sound and he turned his gaze towards the sound, just making out a frail woman sitting in a wheelchair next to a couch. A few empty bottles of whiskey stood on an end-table next to the recliner. Neither of them seemed to notice the visitors. Their faces were glued to the television.

"Mom. Dad," Theo spoke up. "Do you know who I met? Someone who knows the Weerstand family of Urk. Dad, nice hey? From Urk. Weerstand." The woman looked up at Wolfsangel, but the man closed his eyes. Theo turned off the TV and immediately walked back to the kitchen. Wolfsangel first looked at the woman; her complexion was pasty and her eyes were sunken. She clearly had difficulty moving her head because she only moved her eyes to look at him. Her lips started to move, but at first no sound came out. Eventually, with great difficulty, she managed to ask in a halting voice, "Who are you, young man?"

He introduced himself and said that he had become curious when he heard from Theo that their surname was Weerstand. "That name is very common on Urk, I know a certain Eirik who married a Weerstand girl."

At the sound of that name, the old man seemed to come alive. He struggled to push the footrest in and leaned back. Fixing his eyes on Wolfsangel, a sneer formed on his face. He cleared his throat, swallowed, and croaked, "Did Marianne Weerstand send you?"

Wolfsangel smiled to himself. He had hit the jackpot. "No. It was actually Eirik who suggested that I might drop in. Do you know him?"

The man pounded his head on the back of the recliner a couple of times as if he wanted to shake it clear. He had to work through a coughing fit before he could speak again. "Hah! So it is Eirik who sends you? Hey, woman, what do you know? Finally Urk sends someone to check how I am doing here."

The man grabbed both armrests and leaned forward to stare directly at Wolfsangel. He tried to look intimidating, but was failing miserably. Just like everything else around here. Wolfsangel couldn't take the man seriously. His red face and discoloured nose suggested years of alcohol consumption. His hair was stringy and greasy, pathetically trying to hide the significant hair loss on the top of his head. His sweater was full of stains and his fly was wide open. Fortunately, the fruit did not appear to have escaped the loom. The man spoke in a raspy voice. "Yes, I am Allard. I am Allard Weerstand. I am the brother of Marianne. I am the brother-in-law of Eirik." He finished his statements with an expectant look.

Wolfsangel wasn't sure what Allard expected his reaction to that news would be. He kept his face neutral. The two of them continued to stare at each other for what seemed an eternity. Neither willing to break off the eye contact. Finally, Allard caved and shouted at Theo in the kitchen. "Theo, make yourself useful, pour us some coffee!" Pointing at Wolfsangel, he barked. "Sit down".

Wolfsangel sized up the mound of laundry heaped on the chair. He actually couldn't tell if it was clean or dirty. He used his elbow to bulldoze the mound off and sat down. He made a mental note about burning his clothes when he got to the hotel in Prince Rupert.

The woman in the wheelchair managed to turn her neck a bit further. Nobody spoke – each looking at the floor, waiting for the other to start. Wolfsangel heard Theo muttering in the kitchen as he filled the kettle with some water. Allard managed to find a bottle residing nearby with a swig or two left. He squeezed the bridge of his nose, swallowed hard, then cleared his throat. No words came out. After swallowing a second time, he finally spoke. "I emigrated to Canada in 1968. It was winter; I went by boat, as most emigrants did at that time. I landed in Halifax and then took a train out West. It wasn't my choice to leave Urk. It was something that I had to do. I eventually ended up in northern British Columbia. There was lots of work either in the sawmills or in the nickel mines. I eventually saved enough money to buy a cattle ranch near the town of Smithers - just up the road from here. The ranch didn't do well, so I sold it and bought this place in Vanderhoof."

Wolfsangel nodded. "You said it wasn't your choice to leave Urk. What made you leave, then?"

"Nobody wanted me there. I was banished, puked out!" He sneered. "If you want the truth, I can give it to you." He paused, waiting for Wolfsangel to respond. When he didn't, Allard continued. "I will tell you the truth. I did not trust that strange guy Eirik. I don't know what my sister saw in him, but I knew he was bad news. I figured I would take a trip to Norway and determine what this guy's story really was. Well, it didn't take me long to find out I was right about him. He was hiding something."

Allard paused, probably for dramatic effect. He reached for another empty bottle and attempted to drain the last few remaining drips into his mouth. Then, leaning forward as if he was going to reveal a state secret, he spoke in a hushed voice. "His last name was not Tijsker. No, I found out he was a tysker, a German war child. I also found out that Eirik's real father was a Nazi. He had been a real Jew hater and hunter. A Gestapo dog of the worst kind. So, when I came back, I did my duty as the elder brother and confronted Marianne with these facts. I told her that she must end this relationship. Immediately." He leaned back on his chair, a smug smile on his face.

Wolfsangel nodded an encouragement to continue.

Allard did. "Of course, the bitch defended her lover. She said that he had done nothing wrong. It wasn't his fault that his real father was a Nazi. It doesn't matter, I told her, he comes from the wrong breeding. She was a much better person, she didn't need to marry some Nazi-lover's bastard kid.

"Well, Eirik overheard me talking to my sister and that damned Norwegian got so angry, he took a broom handle and nearly beat me to death. He came up from behind. I had no chance at all to defend myself. I was in such bad shape that I ended up in the hospital for days. Fortunately, I missed their wedding. When I got out, I discovered that everyone was against me. Marianne and Eirik had obviously worked hard behind my back to drag my name through the mud. They were successful. No matter how hard I tried, nobody believed the truth of my side of the story. That's why I left and never returned." With that, he nodded, furrowed his brow, and hollered to Theo to hurry up with the damn coffee.

If you ask an Urker to tell a story, he will tell you the whole story, Wolfsangel thought to himself. Theo stepped in with two mugs of coffee. He handed one to his father. The second cup he handed to Wolfsangel. He grabbed it from Theo, not sure what to expect. He was slightly mollified when he didn't find anything floating on the top. Then, to Wolfsangel's surprise, the coffee not only smelled pretty good, but it also actually tasted good, too. As Theo turned to sneak away before his dad found something else for him to do, Wolfsangel called a thank-you after him and then turned back to Allard. "You're a true Urker. You sure know how to tell a story is such detail."

Allard took that remark as a compliment and grinned. "That's right. My only regret is that I didn't get a chance to marry an Urker woman." He cleared his throat again and jabbed a thumb at the wheelchair. "Now I'm stuck with this mutant and the child from hell. Nobody from Urk has ever dropped in for a visit. Not even my only sister."

He exhaled loudly through his nostrils and added sarcastically, "Marianne and her SS-bastard."

Wolfsangel decided it was time to poke the bear. He spoke quietly but pointedly. "I don't quite understand your story. Why did Eirik become so angry that he was willing to beat you to death? Surely, it wasn't simply because you told his fiancé that she shouldn't marry him?" Wolfsangel took a hard stare at Allard. Allard shifted uneasily in his seat, probably realising now that this visitor knew more than he let on.

Allard met the gaze head on. "Marianne probably told you some cock and bull story. You can't believe everything she says. She is trying to cover up her mistake in marrying that low-life Tyskerbarn."

Inwardly seething, Wolfsangel never flinched. He kept his eyes on Allard. "Marianne? No. She never mentioned you. I didn't realise that she even had a brother. That is until I heard Eirik's story about what happened just before the wedding." He reached into his pocket, eyes never waving from Allard's face, and took out a sheet of paper. "This is a report from one of Eirik's psychiatrists who talked with him about a certain traumatic event. Shall I read it to you?"

Allard trembled slightly and then grew defiant. "I don't give a damn. It's just lies anyway."

Wolfsangel started to read.

27 February 1978 / Psychiatric Hospital 'Fylke, Oslo / Client: Eirik Tijsker (1943) / Dr. R. Thomassen / Conversation # 6: Night before wedding day

Marianne and I were married in 1967, a beautiful day of course, but the night before was terrible. I will tell you everything, what does it matter? On the night before our wedding day, Marianne stood in front of a large mirror to enjoy her wedding dress. She enjoyed her youth, her life, her clothes, and the thought of tomorrow. Yes, she felt beautiful. She heard her brother Allard walking down the hall to his own room but got a weird feeling at one point and looked back, where she saw Allard standing in the door opening. He scratched his obvious erection and laughed at her. He walked in, but she said, 'Disappear, brother, get away from me.'

But he said, 'No, I will not. I need you now. Let me have you once, only once.'

She pushed him away. 'Get out of here! You should be ashamed!' But he kept insisting. Then she slapped him, hard in the face. He grabbed her and threw her to the floor. "Shall I be ashamed? Don't you know anything about that future man of yours, that Eirik? He's the son of a Nazi whore, and if you're not quiet now and give what I want, I'm going to spread the news that you're also a Nazi whore!'

Fortunately, she managed to get her hand around his testicles and squeezed as hard as she could. Allard screamed loudly.

At that moment I was walking across the street, my mind totally occupied with her. I heard the scream and ran inside, up the stairs and saw the open door. Marianne ... Allard ...? For a second, I stood in the doorway. He had her hands pinned above her head. I did not see Marianne's face; they did not notice me. I did not know what to do, petrified, until I heard Allard say, 'Nazi whore.' That one word brought back everything: all my memories, pain, traumas, humiliations, everything.

Again, I experienced the rape of my mother and my great impotence. I became insanely mad! Never in my entire life have I been so angry. He had to die. I put him upright, embraced him and squeezed all the air out of his lungs, looking straight into his eyes.

He would have been dead if Marianne had not stopped me. Allard emigrated shortly afterwards, I never saw him again. I slept badly that night, but fortunately still managed to celebrate the next day. It went well for years, until my daughter looked at me through the ice. Her name was Anna Esther, after my mother and sister. I still miss her.

/ Robert Thomassen, Fylke, Oslo, 1978

Through the narrative, Allard made it a point to express his disdain. Several times he had rolled his eyes, drummed his fingers on the armrest, and muttered "not true - pathetic" under his breath.

When Wolfsangel had finished reading, his eyes bored into Allard's. "So, you raped your sister. You're a real class act." Suddenly, Allard jumped out of the recliner. Wolfsangel was mildly surprised at how quick Allard could move. With spittle flying everywhere, Allard yelled, "You motherfucker. You've just been playing me. You've come here to kill me, haven't you?"

Wolfsangel's eyes remained steady on Allard's. Haven't you," he yelled he yelled again. "That Nazi-loving whore sent you here to get revenge."

Wolfsangel stood up and looked around. "Look around you. Look at your place. Look at your house. Look at yourselves. You are a complete and utter loser. Nothing more than pus from a popped pimple. No, I'm not going to kill you. I don't have to. You are already dying a slow, painful death. That is by far the sweetest revenge anybody could hope for."

At that, both of them became aware of a gurgling noise coming from the wheelchair. Wolfsangel's best guess was that the woman was laughing. Allard jumped over to her, probably intending to hit her. Unfortunately for him, his feet got tangled up in the mound of laundry on the floor, and with a cry of rage, he fell facedown on the floor.

Wolfsangel decided his mission was complete; it was time to leave. As he walked to the kitchen, he could hear Allard screaming obscenities at him. Theo was bent over the stove poking into the frying pan with a fork. Clearly, he had decided to heat the sausages because Wolfsangel could see the grease splattering all over the stove. Wolfsangel put his hand on his shoulder and thanked Theo for taking him here. He felt sorry for the lad. Theo ignored him, concentrating on the sausages while moaning, "Flies … there are so many flies." Wolfsangel briefly considered taking Theo back to town when a shot rang out. Instinct and training took over and Wolfsangel dove behind the kitchen table. When he looked up, he saw an engaged Allard pointing a shotgun at him, screaming, "You motherless asshole. You come here to judge me? I am Allard Weerstrand. My father fought in the war against those bastard Nazis. He gave up his life for his country. My sister is a traitor for whoring herself to them." Allard continued to rant while waving the shotgun wildly about. It was a single-barrelled shotgun, so Wolfsangel knew there was no immediate danger. He stood up, ready to grab the rifle out of the old man's hands but stopped when another sound and smell caught his attention. He turned his head and saw a trail of flames from the stove down to the floor and all over the body of Theo. With a shock, Wolfsangel realised that the shot intended for him struck Theo in the neck, bursting one of his carotid arteries. The frying pan had been dragged off the stove and hot grease had splashed all over the place. Theo was clutching his throat while blood was gurgling up around his hands. Wolfsangel knew from experience there was little he could do to save Theo. He assessed the situation and saw that the grease had caught fire on the stovetop and the flames were quickly spreading. Allard didn't seem to notice, he was still yelling and screaming at him, waving an empty shotgun. The flames were soon rapidly spreading across the kitchen, finding lots of fuel to feed its fury. It wouldn't be long before the whole house would be engulfed in flames. Wolfsangel made a quick decision. Taking one last look at Theo, the flames catching his clothes, he walked out the door to his pickup truck.

On their way to Prince Rupert, Hellmuth finally asked him, "So? Was your side trip successful?"

Wolfsangel didn't know how to answer that one. Over the course of his work, he experienced the utter misery of the world. The world was a crappy place. How do you define success in this world? He supposed that at least Theo and his mother found freedom in death. That was a success. Allard had died in abject misery. That was a success. As for him, he still had no idea if Eirik was alive or dead. He looked over at Hellmuth and shrugged his shoulders.

Hellmuth understood. "You should see if you can find trained people to investigate whether Eirik is alive. You need to find answers. I don't think you can do it on your own."

"I know. You're right. What about you, did you find success in Vanderhoof?"

Hellmuth grinned. "Most definitely, my friend. Most definitely."

Wolfsangel rolled his eyes and contemplated on how simple his life might be if success was measured by the number of female conquests.

The two of them carried out their mission in Alaska efficiently and effectively. They were able to return to the United States with their heads held high, having given their clients everything they asked for. As a result, the two of them had secured a favoured position in the company and essentially were given the pick of the jobs. Time flew like shadows; hours became days, days became months, and the months turned into a year. Nothing in Wolfsangel's life seemed to remain the same. The present was always past, except for Eirik, who did not languish. Wolfsangel's life raced on, without resting points. Even though he chased people into their graves, his nemesis always slumbered somewhere.

January 13, 1997, Berlin, Germany

Wolfsangel heard somewhere that nearly a quarter of all people surveyed identified themselves as procrastinators. That's one label he did not want attached to himself. He truly did not believe he was one to loiter, linger, or lollygag. In fact, he considered himself self-disciplined and focussed.

Okay. Who was he kidding? That was true in all areas of his life except for his mission regarding Eirik. With Eirik, he was definitely lollygagging. As he considered this, he had to ask himself why this was so: Was it his quest for perfectionism because his mission was still so vague in Norway, or was it to avoid Eirik, who existed deep inside him like an undiscovered cancer? For whatever reason, he just couldn't get himself to finish it. Why not? Was he afraid to meet Eirik face to face and discover that he is actually alive? A voice interrupted his reverie.

"Good grief, what the hell is bothering you?"

Wolfsangel came out of the clouds and back to Berlin. He was sitting in a pub with Hellmuth. They had just arrived yesterday from a stressful few months in Yemen. He looked up and found Hellmuth staring at him with a questioning look. "Nothing. Just contemplating on the complexities of life."

"You know what your problem is, don't you? You make life too complicated by over thinking everything. Well, not everything. When we are at work, in the middle of a crisis, your instinct kicks in. You know what to do and you do it. When it comes to Eirik, somehow you can't get your shit together."

Wolfsangel grunted and Hellmuth shrugged. "I'll tell you what. You spend the rest of the evening contemplating, and I'll spend the rest of the evening doing something a bit more, shall we say, fun." He pulled out his cell phone and within a few minutes not only had his evening, but his entire weekend planned with one of his many female friends strategically located in various cities around the world. Slipping his phone back into his pocket, he stood up. "Okay, I'm off like a Jewish foreskin. What are you going to be doing for the next little while? It looks like we have at least two weeks off until we get our next assignment."

"Don't know yet. Maybe I'll head back home to Chesapeake Bay to do some ice fishing or snow skiing. Don't let your foreskin worry about me, I'll figure something out."

Hellmuth laughed. "Go with your instincts, brother. We'll keep in touch." The friends said goodbye with a firm hug. Wolfsangel decided to take a stroll down Berlin's famous 'Unter den Linden' street on his way back to the hotel.

It was late afternoon and the temperature was hovering just south of zero degrees. Of course, after being in Yemen, the temperature felt darn near minus thirty, and Wolfsangel was looking forward to relaxing in his room, perhaps watching some TV.

As he walked in the lobby of the Grand Berlin, he decided to first grab a hot cup of coffee at the lounge to take up to his room. To his surprise, his ears caught the sound of someone speaking Norwegian, the language of Eirik. He scanned the room and located the source. A bespectacled man, with a shaven head and a bearded chin, was sitting at one of the tables across from a slender woman with hair dyed light-red.

As the server made his coffee, he decided to listen in and figure out who these people were. He was surprised at how much of the language he actually understood.

The man was gesticulating. "I will never forget it. November 9, 1989. What a party! It was so awesome."

She nodded. "But the Soviets?"

"Ha, they were flushed down the toilet together with their wall when Schabowski said every DDR citizen was free to cross the border." The man scratched his shaved skull and pushed his glasses higher up his nose.

Wolfsangel studied the man. He guessed the guy was a scholar visiting Germany to study the history of the Berlin Wall. The woman was probably his travelling companion. Definitely not a prostitute. She seemed too into this guy for that. The woman seemed genuinely interested in what the man was talking about. The man used his hands a lot while talking about the fall of the wall. Wolfsangel couldn't figure out that relationship. The man seemed as boring as an accountant at a beach party. The only interesting thing about him was his wild hand movements.

When the server had finished preparing his coffee, Wolfsangel continued to observe the Norwegians. They were oblivious to him. An idea popped into his head. He caught the eye of the server and requested three pints of German Ale and a side of sliced Berliner curry sausages. When it arrived, he grabbed the tray and headed out to their table.

He put the tray down on their table and spoke to them in Norwegian. "Hey, there. You guys are from Norway. Fancy a pint and curry sausage?"

The two were startled, taking a moment to register what was happening. Suddenly, the man stood up and nodded vigorously. "Yes! Please have a seat and join us."

The man introduced himself as Stein Bratt, student of History and Political Science at the University of Trondheim, Norway. He did most of the talking. Wolfsangel noted that Stein didn't even ask him what his name was. He also didn't bother introduce the girl.

The three of them drank beer and ate sausage while Stein continued his treatise on how the fall of the Berlin Wall was one of the most important events in the demise of the Soviet Union.

When Stein finally ran out of things to say, the red-haired girl started a completely unrelated thread about love for the earth and nature, about matriarchal society, goddesses and feminist occultism. Wolfsangel decided that she likely wasn't a fellow scholar with Stein. He wondered why Stein would even need a companion since he seemed to be full of himself anyway.

Eventually, Stein glanced at his watch and got up. "We're going to a cool Rammstein concert tonight. Starts in half an hour. Do you feel like joining us?"

"No, that's okay. Thanks for the offer." Wolfsangel would have liked to be at that concert, but the thought of spending more time with those two didn't appeal to him. He was really hoping he could have engaged them in some conversation about Norway and maybe tease out some information. Unfortunately, Stein was more about himself than anything else.

"If you change your mind, let me know. Here is my cell phone number. We can save you a spot." Stein handed him a paper. "We definitely don't want to miss it. We drove twelve hours from home just to be there."

"Are you guys staying here at the Grand Berlin?"

Stein shook his head while the girl looked a bit aggrieved. "Heck, no. We can't afford that. We're sleeping in my car and then heading back first thing tomorrow morning. We just came here to get out of the cold and grab a bite to eat."

Wolfsangel decided he had enough. He got up and headed towards his room. As he stood waiting for the elevator, he felt a yearning in his soul. He wanted to be alone tonight so he headed back to the lounge to purchase a bottle of whiskey. That night, as he drank the whiskey, he reflected on the reason for the yearning in his soul. He realised it was brought on by those two Norwegians as a flood of memories washed over him. At the centre, of course, was Eirik. He saw his face, his clear blue eyes. There was no human on this green earth that had had more influence on his life. Yet, he had no idea where he was and if he was still alive. He desperately wanted to believe that he was. As he downed one glass, he immediately refilled it with another whiskey. At the very least, he had to locate Eirik's body. He might find peace if he knew for sure he was dead.

The next morning, he woke up early with a slight hangover. He opened the drapes to his window and looked over the street. He had enough of Berlin. It was time for something else. He had two weeks before he had to report back to work. Not quite sure yet where he wanted to go, he decided to draw up a plan after breakfast.

As he walked into the lobby, he was met with a surprise. That same couple from Norway were sitting on a couch. As soon as they spied him, the girl jumped up and waited for him to approach. She looked like hell. Her face drooped, there were bags under her eyes, and she wore the same clothes as yesterday. The young man, Stein, didn't bother to get up. He looked like he was in some pain. There was a big bandage around his head, bruises around his bloodshot eyes and he was missing a front tooth. They both seemed very upset.

Wolfsangel approached them. "Hey, you guys look a mess. What happened?"

The girl explained. "We haven't been able to sleep all night. After the concert, we came back to our car and got mugged. They took pretty much everything including all our money."

"Bunch of monkeys, imbeciles, goat fuckers." The man tried to sound angry, but it was hard for Wolfsangel not to grin as his words were punctuated by whistling sounds.

"Stein tried to defend us, but there were four or five thugs. They beat him up pretty badly, as you can see. We talked to a police officer earlier this morning, but we're probably not going to get our money and belongings back."

"You'll see. They'll do nothing, those fucking fascist assholes." Stein grabbed his head and groaned.

"We decided to come back here and see if we could find you." She paused to take a deep drag on her cigarette. "We have nothing except for our car. The only problem is that we can't get in because the keys were also taken. Is there any way you could help us out?" She made a desperate but pathetic hand gesture.

Wolfsangel thought quickly. "I see. You know what? It looks simple to me. You have a car and want to go back to Norway. Right?"

"Absolutely. We both want to get the hell out of here," the girl said. "But Stein won't be able to drive in that condition - at least, not the full twelve-hour drive. And I don't have a driver's license." She sighed desperately and added, "Even if we could get into the car, we don't have any money for gas. We have nothing left!"

"Where is that car?" Wolfsangel asked. It turned out it was parked nearby. "Come with me. I have an idea."

With some difficulty the two stood up and stumbled to a side street where the car was parked. Thanks to his training in the Foreign Legion, Wolfsangel had become an expert in breaking in and start all kinds of vehicles. With little effort he opened and started the Volkswagen.

For the first time this morning, both Stein and the girl had a smile on their face. "What if I do the driving," Wolfsangel said. "It's not that far, only twelve hours."

They looked at him in amazement. "You'd do that for us," asked the girl?

"It just happens that I have some time and I don't have any definite plans. Norway's as good a place as any to spend the next week or so. If you trust me, we can leave immediately." The two did not take time to consult. Stein immediately dove into the backseat. He found a pillow to put under his head and within minutes was dead to the world. The girl got into the front passenger seat, also quickly drifting off. They were both dead tired.

Wolfsangel drove through Hamburg, Kiel, through Denmark and arrived at Hirtshals for the ferry to Oslo. He was getting tired. Glancing at his watch, he realised that he had been driving straight for more than twelve hours, stopping only to fill up with fuel. He was looking forward to the break on the ferry. He booked the crossing and thirty minutes later they drove up onto the ferry. When they sailed into the middle of the waters of the Skagerrak, he woke up his two guests. The two of them were very groggy and quite uncommunicative. When they eventually went to the restaurant on the ferry, it was Wolfsangel who paid for the food.

After eating, Stein stretched and looked frankly into Wolfsangel eyes. "Man, you saved us. I will never forget that. If you are ever in Trondheim, please stop by for a visit."

"Hmm. I'll definitely keep that in mind. I don't really have any business in Trondheim yet, but who knows. I'm sure we'll keep in touch." The rest of the crossing went well; the two of them finally woke up and the atmosphere became pleasant. Wolfsangel realised he wasn't used to being around students for social purposes. Despite each of their individual quirks, this was a refreshing change from the people he normally dealt with. The young people thought deeper, wanted to learn something new, and sought connections.

When they arrived in Oslo, Wolfsangel got the car started for Stein and was ready to part ways. Stein finally asked him the question that Wolfsangel was expecting. "I can't imagine that your real name is Wolfsangel. Why do you call yourself that? I know it's none of my business. I'm simply curious."

"No, not at all. That's my identity until … I've found what I'm looking for."

Stein nodded and decided not to pursue that any further "Fair enough. You are entitled to anonymity. I hope you find whatever you are looking for. If you get the chance, visit me in Trondheim. I would love to help you."

Wolfsangel nodded, ready to walk away.

"I mean it. What, exactly, are you looking for?"

Wolfsangel studied Stein, trying to decide how much to say. He figured he didn't have much to lose. "I'm looking for a man, he's probably dead, but I want to know for sure."

"Well, give me his name and I'll see what I can do."

"His name is Eirik, Eirik Tijsker."

"I know it sounds silly, but have you already asked the police?"

"When he disappeared, they searched, but..." He shrugged.

"I really want to help, man, really. I owe you. I'll do some digging."

They said goodbye. Wolfsangel caught a taxi to a hotel in Oslo. It was nearly four years after his conversation with Robert Thomassen and his mother since he was in Norway again. The next day he was going to rent a car and drive to Hurdal.

1997, Hurdal, Norway

"I am ready for the next step, Eirik." Wolfsangel was feeling good. For the first time in a long time, he felt grounded and in control of his mission. This must have something to do with coming home. He parked his rental car at the Spar supermarket in Hurdal. Three bottles of cheap whiskey lay in his trunk. As he stepped out of his car, his eyes narrowed and he took a deep breath. The air was fresh, the temperature was below zero, the sun was well on its journey.

Yesterday, Wolfsangel felt saturated with his past and unsure of his future. He figured that life was just testing him. He wasn't going to be weak anymore. In fact, nobody was going to stop him. Today, he was going to make quick work on his promise.

He flashbacked to nine years ago when he first embarked on his mission. He chuckled, shaking his head. No doubt about it. It was a complete disaster. Back then, he was young, aimless, and angry. Totally messed up with the promise he had made to Eirik. Even so, Wolfsangel savoured that moment now. It was a defining one for him.

It was in Oslo, also during the winter. He was following the old man as he went on a solitary walk through a small park. The sun was setting behind the hills and darkness was slowly creeping in. The old man shuffled on - deep in thought. Something must have caught his attention because he looked back and saw this stranger moving fast to catch up. A look of fear crossed his face, and he increased his gait. It didn't matter much. Within a few seconds, Wolfsangel caught up beside the old man. He hissed, "Hi Mikkel. It's me. Do you remember me?"

The old man stopped and took a good look at the Wolfsangel's face. "No, I don't know you", he retorted.

Wolfsangel hissed, "Let me see if I can jog your memory a bit. Do you remember 'Eirik', you know, the Tyskerbarn?"

Recognition slowly dawned on the old man's face. "Him?" He exclaimed. "Go away, I've got nothing to say to you."

"Oh, but you do." Wolfsangel grabbed his arm "You've got lots to say. I am dragging the weight of the past for somebody, and you are going to help me release that weight. I have made a promise and I am going to keep it."

"So," the old man croaked, "So what? … I don't care about your stupid promise. I am going home." Mikkel shrugged off Wolfsangel's hand and started moving again, trying to get the old bones and muscles in a higher gear.

"No, old man, your home is somewhere else." Wolfsangel whispered and grabbed him by the scruff of his jacket. "You're going to die and your new home will be in hell! So tell me about it. Tell me what happened to him, what did you do to Eirik? Why? Tell me now, tell me! I have a right to know!"

But the old man struggled, trying to pry the hands off him. "I have no idea what you are talking about … I have nothing to tell … I am not responsible … Please, just leave me alone." His left knee gave out and he stumbled to the ground.

The Wolfsangel did not let go but dragged Mikkel up to his knees. He could feel himself losing it. He couldn't restrain himself any longer. He put his face right up to the old man's, raised his voice and yelled, "Tell me, you fucker. I … have … a … right … to … know." Each word was punctuated with a violent shaking of the old man.

Suddenly Mikkel's eyes widened, seemingly popping out of his head. He tried to fist-pound his heart, but it was a feeble attempt. His eyes went out of focus and his eyelids slowly closed. It didn't register immediately with Wolfsangel that the old man was having a heart attack. He watched as Mikkel tried to focus his eyes. His lips moved, but no sound came out.

When he realised what was going on, "Wait, old man." He ranted, "You still have to tell me. Don't die on me now! I want to know the truth! The truth!"

Mikkel didn't listen. He had breathed his last and Wolfsangel found himself grasping the lifeless body by the collar of his coat. He had made a huge blunder. This man would never confess anymore, he had moved on.

Even now, Wolfsangel could feel his anger starting to build. He wasn't sure who to direct it more towards - himself or Mikkel. Revenge should have been his. Be that as it may, never again would he make this mistake. Never again would any of them be able to hang on to the precious truth. It rightfully belongs to him first and then the rest of the world. Wolfsangel got lucky this time by finding Eirik's journal and having Robert remember enough about his father.

He took some deep breaths and got his emotions back in control. He knew he was much better prepared now to finish what he had started. He pulled out a cigar as he scoped the lay of the land. The plan he had worked on last night was still a good one. His bunker, with its lifeless inhabitant Mikkel, was less than a kilometre West as the crow flies. He saw the row of power poles that snaked up the hill to Hurdal Verk. To the East of him was the street that would lead him directly to the farmhouse where his next confessor lived. Sometime this afternoon, east will meet west, Wolfsangel thought humorously.

After he had finished his cigar, he headed back to his car, which was still standing at the Spar supermarket. He drove west to the old farmhouse and found a place to park out of sight. He grabbed his supplies: a 250 ml clear plastic water bottle filled with chloroform and a small towel. It was 16:30 and Wolfsangel noted with satisfaction that the lighting was perfect. The long shadows and low lighting suited his purposes perfectly. He crept up to the house. With the frozen ground, his shoes made no noise. He peered through one of the windows and saw an old woman bent over a stove in the kitchen. He continued to walk around the house looking in windows hoping to spot his target.

Wolfsangel caught a sound coming from one of the smaller barns just beyond the house. He edged closer to the barn and found that the door was slightly ajar. He peered in and saw a solidly built man standing by a bench drinking out of a bottle of vodka. He was just standing there, not saying anything. Every few seconds, he brought the bottle to his lips. Wolfsangel smiled humorously. That was definitely Olaf, the husband of Mirre. Still an alcoholic.

Wolfsangel waited patiently for Olaf to finish what he was doing and exit the barn. He positioned himself by the door ready to soak his towel with chloroform. Soon enough, Olaf made his way back to the house. Wolfsangel was young, strong and trained, but had learned never to underestimate opponents. TV and movies made it seem so easy to knock somebody out with a few drops of chloroform. Nothing could be further from the truth. He jumped from behind and pressed the chloroform-soaked cloth onto the man's mouth and nose. He held it there with one hand while trying to pin Olaf's arms down with his other hand. But it was as if he was riding a 600 kg rodeo bull. The old man turned out to be tenacious. After his initial shock and surprise, he furiously tried to shake off Wolfsangel. Olaf managed to half turn around and grabbed Wolfsangel's face, which was leaning on his right shoulder, and squeezed hard.

Wolfsangel desperately needed to make sure the cloth did not leave Olaf's mouth and nose. He knew if Olaf managed to gasp fresh air, this would be over. Wolfsangel concentrated his strength on keeping the cloth on Olaf's face. With great difficulty, Wolfsangel managed to tear his face out of his opponent's hands. Olaf was getting weaker and made one more attempt to free himself. He leaned over and swung the weight on his back around and rammed his assailant into the door post. Wolfsangel felt a stab of pain running down his shoulder and through his rib cage. With one hand still pressing the towel to Olaf's face, he grabbed the door post and managed to pin the strong man. Olaf ceased struggling but Wolfsangel didn't relax his hold. He was too smart to assume anything. After half a minute or so, Olaf's body went limp. Wolfsangel continued to press the towel to his face for a while longer. When he finally let go, Olaf collapsed to the ground.

Wolfsangel needed some time to recuperate. He checked for broken ribs and fortunately didn't find any. The pain was still there, though. He could feel his nose starting to swell. Despite the pain, Wolfsangel felt elated. He was successful in bringing Olaf down without a hitch. He glanced at the farm house, but nothing seemed untoward. By now, it was completely dark outside. Using a wrestler's trick he hoisted Olaf's 115 kg onto his back and walked past the houses to his car.

It wasn't much later when the bunker got another resident. Fortunately, the old one didn't even have to move out to make room. In one corner of the bunker sat old Mikkel. Here in front of him was Olaf. Wolfsangel had two of the three right where he wanted them. He felt more confident than ever he was finally moving forward on the right path.

Wolfsangel chained up Olaf's unconscious body very tightly. Years ago, Robert and his mother had room to move, but that luxury was not afforded to Olaf. After a few hours, the big man opened his eyes. It took him a moment or two to figure out he was no longer in his barn swilling vodka. As his eyes focussed on Wolfsangel, puzzlement was written all over his face. When Wolfsangel told him he represented Eirik, son of Anna, Olaf's mouth turned to a sneer. "Oh, him." Wolfsangel watched bemused as Olaf finally realised he was securely bound to a wooden bench in a dank, musty hovel. Olaf growled like a bear demanding to be released immediately.

Wolfsangel looked at him unperturbed. Without saying a word, he grabbed a briefcase from the floor and put it on the table. He took a roll of duct tape out of the case and wrapped it tightly around Olaf's head and jaw. "So, Olaf Andersen, you have to listen now. Hard huh?"

Olaf slowly turned his head away. It was a symbolic gesture of defiance.

Wolfsangel grabbed Olaf's face and twisted it back. "You know what all this means, don't you? This is your final destination. You're going to die. Here in this room." Olaf tried to shake his head.

"Yes, you will die. Have absolutely no doubt about that. However, I will give you the choice on how you will die. Yes, I know you want to say something? Not yet, first you must listen to me."

He forced Olaf's head towards the briefcase on the table and said softly, "That is full of instruments and chemicals for inflicting pain. Intense pain. Pain like you have never experienced before. You have no idea now what I can do to you. You will be subjected to wave after wave of total and absolute pain. I will spread this over a long period of time. You will want to die, but I won't let you until I am ready. Hell itself will be preferable to what I am going to do to you."

He saw that he had Olaf's attention. Obviously a dullard, it took a bit of time for him to finally realise how serious a predicament he was in. The defiant and sneering look in his eyes was replaced with a small hint of consternation. Olaf finally became attentive and Wolfsangel was able to release his hands from Olaf's face.

"However, there is a way to avoid this path to your death, if you so choose." Wolfsangel paused and stared straight into the eyes of Olaf. The man looked back at his captor with a certain curiosity. Olaf was not a man who gave into fear, even in the face of death. Wolfsangel had to admire that.

"How, you ask? I want a total and complete confession of your every thought, word, and deed regarding Eirik Tijsker. You can take your time, but nothing must be hidden and untold. I must be completely satisfied. If I am, I will give you three bottles of vodka and a last meal of whatever you want. You'll have three hours to eat and drink and enjoy your last moments of life on earth. After that, I will ensure you have a very quick and painless death."

Wolfsangel paused to give time for Olaf to absorb all this. "You need to understand two things very clearly. First, I will get your confession one way or the other. Second, you are never leaving this bunker. You will die here. Make no mistake about that. How you die is your choice and you only get one opportunity to make that choice. So, you will either confess without any suffering or you will confess in the midst of pain and torture."

Wolfsangel grabbed Olaf's face again with both hands and leaned in. "Do. You. Understand?"

Olaf stared back and after a moment slowly nodded his head.

Wolfsangel grinned and opened the briefcase. He positioned it so that Olaf could see the contents and know that his captor was not bluffing. To his credit, Olaf's eyes remained impassive.

"It's late. I will give you the night to think about this and make your choice." Wolfsangel decided to leave the duct tape on Olaf's mouth. He gathered his things and walked out the bunker.

He was pleased. Olaf was going to spend the night tightly bound on a hard, wooden bench in a dark and freezing cold bunker. Wolfsangel was going to spend the night in a hotel room in Jessheim, sleeping fitfully in a warm bed.

The next morning, Wolfsangel returned to the bunker and threw his briefcase on the table. He smiled, satisfied that Olaf seemed to have lost most of his defiance and smugness, although there was still a trace lurking in his eyes. Wolfsangel looked at him calmly and then suddenly ripped the duct tape off Olaf's mouth. Olaf grimaced but remained silent.

"So, what's your choice?" Wolfsangel asked.

Olaf smirked. "You know. I'll give what you want quite voluntarily. You won't have to use those things", he said pointing to the briefcase. "The truth is, I have quite forgotten about Eirik. It's been a long time since our paths crossed."

Wolfsangel chuckled without humour. He reached into his briefcase and took out a small handheld audio recorder and at same time handed him one of Robert's reports. "Here, read this. Maybe that will help refresh your memory."

Olaf shrugged and started reading. After a few minutes Wolfsangel was astonished when he saw Olaf sporting a huge grin on his face.

"You think this is funny?" He asked. Olaf smiled and laughed as if the two of them were sharing a joke.

"Man, what a softie. Such a pussy, that guy!" There was obvious disdain in his voice. "Show off, right?"

Wolfsangel shook his head, his rage smouldering. "That's what you think?"

"Yes, a weakling. Imagine being in my position: I see a young man step out of my house early in the morning. My wife is at the door with him, saying good-bye. And you know, I immediately feel like I know that guy. I quickly duck behind a tree and watch. He waved so warmly to Mirre, so happy. Mirre went back into the house and I followed him unseen.

"I was fifty-seven years old at the time and still strong as an ox. I was not afraid of that weenie. He was so deep in thought that he never noticed anything going on around him. He got to his car, opened the door, threw his bag in the back seat and got in. I slipped in the passenger side.

"When he finally noticed me, he looked at me wide-eyed. He was speechless. Not a sound, other than a groan, came out of his mouth. Ha, loser. I recognized in him the same traits as his mother. I asked him if he was Eirik, the Tyskerbarn. When he nodded, I shoved the blade of my pocketknife against his rib cage. I said to him, 'Listen to me or I will bury this knife in your ribcage. Now drive away to Hurdal Verk. You know where that is, right, Tyskerbarn?'

"We drove to the grounds of Hurdal Verk. I forced him to drive to the back of the building, where there was a shed. I pushed him in, left him on a bench, and put a bottle of booze on the table. I filled two glasses and ordered him to drink. 'Have that drink, right now, then I can pour another one. Now tell me, what are you doing here in Hurdal?'

"Eirik seemed scared at first, although he physically looked strong. The drink gave him more confidence. He started telling me about his mission to reconstruct his memories and looked at me hesitantly. So honest, so naive. At one point his face brightened, he seemed to regain his memories while talking. He didn't notice that I really couldn't give a shit. I interrupted him and told him some facts about his life, but nothing special. He said Mirre had already told him that and wanted me to tell him more about his mother Anna and his sister. I started to laugh.

"'What's the matter, you lost all those beautiful memories? Come on, let's have another drink and I'll tell you something. You were that blonde bastard who lived in the same house as my wife. You were that piece of shit, vermin, the sludge worm that contaminated our Norwegian pedigree. You are one of those products from that Nazi breeding farm. Lebensborn, born guilty. You. You should never have existed!'

"I hit the mark. He finally figured out that I never intended to be helpful. He got up, angry and confused. He could hardly stand, he was so drunk. He waved back and forth and then bent over and puked all over the floor. What a loser, can't handle a bit of alcohol. When he was still bent over, I booted him in the ass. He went flying and got the wind knocked out of him. He was completely disoriented for a few seconds.

"I roared with pleasure, grabbed the bottle and sat on top of him. I shoved the bottle into his mouth and tipped it up so that the booze flowed into his mouth. He was coughing, spluttering, and gulping - almost drowning in the booze.

"I had so much fun. 'Drink, Tyskerbarn, drink, and remember.' I laughed in his face.

"He panicked and tried to push me away, but he was too weak. When the bottle was finally empty, I threw it on the floor. It took a bit, but eventually he found his voice. He begged me to let him go. I spat in his face. 'Listen, stinking disease, I've always hated you, you're not worth the living air of Norway. I fucked your mom because she deserved it and I would do it again and again. You want to reconstruct your past? Ha, let's start with your dad, that arrogant piece of German shit. I remember him; I still see him strutting around with that whore. Oh, how much fun they had together here on the Norwegian grounds.'

"Or was it all fantasy? I taunted him. I laughed at him. Oh, I'm losing my memory too! I drummed his skull with my fists.

"Suddenly he screamed like a madman and the adrenaline must have finally kicked in. With superhuman powers, he threw me off. As I was getting up, he pushed me so that I ended up hitting my head on the radiator.

"Eirik tore off as if the devil was chasing him. He got in his car and took off. I watched him navigate around the students' main building and sleeping quarters and race down the Hurdal Verk grounds.

"I didn't care. He wouldn't come back. Too bad the booze bottle was empty. I needed another drink.

"I can look my old man straight in the eye. I did what I did and don't care what others think of me. It was my life, I don't regret anything. In case there is hell, I will curse forever and curse everything there is, but my pride will remain." With that, Olaf's face broke into a wide grin again.

Wolfsangel sat there in silence. The only sound in the bunker was a gas heater that Wolfsangel had started up when he arrived. The bunker was warming up and Mikkel's body started to give off an odour.

The grin slowly disappeared as Olaf sniffed the air. "Hey! What the hell is rotting here?"

Wolfsangel continued to sit, his face impassive but his rage very nearly to the tipping point. Determined not to make the same mistake twice, he pushed down that rage. "I'm glad you can remember Eirik so well. Now tell me the background, the context."

Over the next couple of days, Olaf told his story to Wolfsangel. Olaf seemed to greatly enjoy those parts where he could graphically outline his utter contempt for Eirik. After those sessions, Olaf had confessed his story. There was no more for him to say. The audio recorder eagerly accepted every word.

When Wolfsangel asked if he had any last words for his wife, Olaf looked at him contemptuously and sniffed. "No, I have no message for Mirre. I'm ready to eat. You're not going to break your promise, are you? I'll have a steak dinner with all the trimmings. Don't forget my three bottles of your finest Vodka."

Wolfsangel packed up his briefcase and headed into town to get Olaf's last meal. He felt nothing but contempt and anger for Olaf. It wasn't easy listening to all those stories. But the world will soon know.

When Wolfsangel returned with the food and drink, he put it on the table in front of Olaf. The smell of steak made him drool. After three days of just bread and water, Olaf was ready for a real meal.

"Untie my hand so I can eat," Olaf demanded.

Wolfsangel paused. There was one question that he needed to ask. If he could get an answer to that, he could sleep well tonight.

"Have you ever seen Eirik or heard from him?"

Olaf's eyes narrowed. "Why?"

"At some point, he returned to Fylke and disappeared from there. I want to know what happened to him. You have nothing to lose. Tell me and then you can eat."

Olaf paused, and then spat on the ground. "That son of a bitch is probably living as a mangy stray dog in a dump. That bitch Rannveigh once told Mirre that she had seen Eirik in Jessheim."

Wolfangel's heart leapt. Maybe there is hope of him finding Eirik "Jessheim? What was that?"

Olaf laughed as Wolfsangel cursed himself for coming across too eager. "Ooh la la, you want to know so much, don't you?" Olaf paused and held up his hands. "I'll tell you, but then you have to let me live."

Wolfsangel thought about the possibility for a moment, then shook his head. "They're both still alive, Mirre and Rannveigh. I'll find out from them."

Olaf laughed at him. "I almost caught you there. Now, are you going to keep your promise? I have kept my side of the bargain. Give me my vodka and food so I can die a happy man."

Wolfsangel kept his word. He untied one of Olaf's hands and watched him as he dug into his food. He had to restrain himself from beating the living crap out of Olaf. Why should he keep his word to this waste of skin? After all he did to make life an absolute hell for Eirik?

Wolfsangel had to get out before he lost it. He escaped to the outside. He gazed at the starry sky hoping they would provide a clue about Eirik's whereabouts. He then pulled out a cigar and waited until he felt calm again. When he returned, he saw two empty vodka bottles sitting on the table. Olaf drank hard. An hour later, the third bottle was pretty well empty. Olaf had had enough.

He took his last glass, raised it trembling into the air. Speaking with a heavy tongue, "Death! Ha, Eirik the Tyskerbarn. I hope you are dead."

When Wolfsangel gave him an injection of air, he was still mumbling about the Tyskerbarn. Eventually, an air embolism lodged in his brain silenced him for good.

Before Olaf's corpse was rigid, Wolfsangel sat him on the bench right next to Mikkel, the thinker. However, he made sure Olaf's posture was quite different. Using pieces of wood, iron wire, screws and rope, Wolfsangel set him upright. He put the chest forward, arms folded, fists under the biceps so that his muscles were clearly visible.

Olaf looked arrogant, his cruel thick lips slightly apart. This was an exact impression of the man he had been: a hard and cruel brute. Eirik dared to reappear deep in Wolfsangel. He gazed through Wolfsangel's eyes at Olaf and felt relieved. Olaf had spoken, explained and confessed everything.

When he had finished coating the body with fibreglass, Wolfsangel left the bunker behind. The residual heat from the stove hardened the fibreglass layer, and when it cooled in the bunker after several hours, both bodies froze to the marrow.

Back at his hotel, Wolfsangel typed out and organised Olaf's confession on his computer. When he finished, he put the Olaf papers along with the ones from Mikkel Thomason in his portfolio. It definitely was a couple of hard days being in the company of Olaf. Yet, he was extremely pleased at how well things turned out. He now possessed the full confession of two out of the three. He considered visiting Finn Undredal the next morning and finishing the job.

However, that evening, an email from Blackwater popped on his screen. He and Hellmuth were asked to sign up for an underwater training course in Florida in preparation for a special mission. Wolfsangel called up Hellmuth and, to his delight, found out he was by himself in a hotel room in Berlin bored out of his mind. Apparently, all of his lady friends had deserted him. Wolfsangel laughed and the two of them made preparations that evening to fly out to Florida.

Shortly after undergoing the training, the two of them were assigned a special protection mission in Baghdad that involved a secret underwater channel in the Tigris River. When that was completed, they were immediately assigned a mission in Colombia where they were hired to destroy drug labs. The two of them lived on adrenaline, danger and a big salary! Eirik seemed to have disappeared again.

1999, Hurdal, Norway

It was 1999, nearly two and a half years since Olaf's last meal. He and Mikkel sat unmoved on the bench, waiting patiently for the day when their testimony would be revealed to the world.

During those two and a half years, Wolfsangel never worried about himself. He threw himself into his work. Really, life mattered nothing, death even less. But now, as his job in Afghanistan came to an end, he was like an animal who instinctively knew a thunderstorm was coming long before it was portended in the skies. He again found his thoughts increasingly being invaded by Eirik. Eventually, he had trouble ignoring the weight of the backpack of guilt that was harnessed to his shoulders. He had to face reality: He needed to go back to Hurdal and finish what he started. It took him a couple of days to make the arrangements and prepare to leave Afghanistan.

It took him less time than he expected, after arriving in Norway, to find the third person. The day after his arrival, the third and last occupant of the bunker walked in and sat down on the bench by the table. When Wolfsangel first spotted him, he knew a different plan was needed for this guy. Chloroforming him and swinging him over his shoulder was simply not an option. He weighed over 185 kg. He had to get this guy to the bunker under his own steam. There was no other way. Using a cattle prod as an incentive, Wolfsangel got the guy into his car and drove him to the bunker. That was the easy part. The hard part was getting that adiposity of blubber the three hundred and fifty or so meters from the car to the bunker.

Wolfsangel concluded that, as physically challenging as it was to haul Olaf over his shoulders, it was far easier and less taxing on his patience than getting Sir Circumference to walk the same distance. Several times, Wolfsangel was ready to kill the guy. After every half dozen steps or so, the obese man wanted to rest. It took an electric shock from the cattle prod to keep him moving. Sometimes it took several prods. It took them an exhausting twenty-five minutes to traverse the distance between the car and the bunker. When they finally arrived, Finn was breathing heavily with exhaustion. Wolfsangel was breathing heavily from his herculean effort to keep his rage from exploding.

Wolfsangel shoved him through the door. “Sit down, Finn Undredal, you fat bastard. Don’t worry, it’ll hold your weight.” Wolfsangel chained the corpulent man to the bench and offered him exactly the same deal as he did with Olaf. Without hesitation, Finn agreed to talk. Wolfsangel got the audio-recorder ready to go.

"Okay, Doughboy, listen carefully. You had a visit from Eirik Tijsker - son of Hellmuth Reinhard and Anna Pederson - some twenty-two years ago. He was a German war child, and he came to you for some clarification. He had lost a piece of memory and wanted to know what he was missing. His sister had drowned and he discovered that you were on duty that night and reported the incident at the time. Do you remember the incident he was referring to?"

For a large man, Finn had a falsetto voice. "Yes, I believe so. A group of teens had driven a car on the ice of the lake. They were stunting with the car and eventually the ice cracked and the car fell through a hole. They were about fifteen or so meters from the shore, directly on the school side." The man looked at him benevolently. Despite the presence of two stuffed dead men, clearly this idiot believed he would be allowed to leave if he cooperated.

Wolfsangel did nothing to dispel that belief and encouraged him to continue. "What about the visit? You lived in the same trailer you live in now. He came to your place, knocked on your door, and you opened the door. Is that right? Do you remember?"

"Yes, yes. I can still see it all happen in my mind. He asked if I could remember his sister's drowning. I said I could remember and I explained everything. I could see that I was very helpful to him because he thanked me profusely and left. Isn't that sad, such a young girl? Can I go home now? My dear wife is probably getting very worried." He looked so convincingly compassionate.

Wolfsangel picked up one of Robert's reports and started to read out loud,

"March 20, 1978, Fylke Psychiatric Hospital, Oslo, Client: Eirik Tijsker (1943), Dr. R. Thomassen, Conversation # 9: Confrontation past. And now it comes: Finn Undredal."

Finn's eyes darted back and forth and he murmured softly, "No, no, no." Wolfsangel put it in front of him and told him to read it out loud. Finn didn't laugh the way Olaf had. In fact he read everything quite seriously.

When he was done, he looked up with tears forming in his eyes. "I am really sorry. I'm not that person anymore. I've changed."

Wolfsangel stared at him, shaking his head. "You are going to die, just like the others. Finn, confess everything. You have no choice."

The man considered the words, but Wolfsangel could see that the man still had hope that he would be released. Apparently, he just couldn't accept the fact that he was at the end of his life.

Wolfsangel started the recorder. "I'm Finn Undredal …" For about half an hour, Finn went on about things that Wolfsangel already knew from Eirik's journal. Finn evaded answering the question about whether or not he deliberately refrained from saving Esther. When he was done talking, he asked again if he could go.

Wolfsangel said nothing but bore his eyes into Finn's. Finn started to shift his hefty buttocks, unsure of what to do. Finally, Wolfsangel asked flatly, "You have nothing more to say?"

Wolfsangel watched Finn's face melt as he began to realise the seriousness of his predicament. "Let me go, okay? Please? I won't tell anyone."

Wolfsangel stood up and towered over Finn. "You fat fuck. Do you honestly believe that I am going to let you walk out of here after what you did to Anna and Esther?"

Finn closed his eyes and started to shake. Wolfsangel put his face right up to Finn and grabbed his chin. "You haven't changed one bit. You're still the same slimy bastard you always were."

Like a smouldering volcano, Finn finally exploded. "That whore bitch. I wasn't good enough for her. She wanted the cock of German Nazi. Well, fuck her and her bastard son. I may have been humiliated that night. But, I got them back. When that sassy bitch fell into the water, I watched and laughed."

By this time, spittle was flying out of Finn's mouth and he was shaking so much that Wolfsangel was sure the bench was going to collapse. Wolfsangel's rage overwhelmed him and he grabbed some piano wire out of his briefcase and wrapped it around Finn's plump neck. It took a moment for Finn to realise what was happening and he started to flay his arms violently. Wolfsangel gritted his teeth and pulled the string harder and harder. He could feel it cut through the flesh until it reached the spinal cord. By this time, blood was gushing all over the place. With one final pull and a loud yell, the cord severed the spinal cord and Finn's lifeless body fell to the ground.

Wolfsangel continued to yell as his face became damp with tears of rage. He calmed down as he felt Eirik's hand on his shoulders. Sobbing, he whispered, "Eirik, I couldn't help it. I didn't get a full confession … Please forgive me."

1999, Drammen, Norway

Olaf had obviously lied. He had asked around in Jessheim and driven around to other places where he knew Eirik had been, but he was no closer to finding any leads. It was now more than twenty-one years ago that Eirik disappeared without a trace! The three on the bench could not help him. Deep down, he knew that he did not have the detective skills to find Eirik or his body. On top of that, he was worried that his poking around would get him noticed and people might start making connections between him and the disappearance of the three people.

Maybe he should see if the police could take over the investigation. He knew a police officer in Oslo that would be perfect for the job. He just didn't feel ready to pass on the search just yet.

Besides the fact that he could not find Eirik, not even a body, Wolfsangel was also frustrated about his lack of planning how to make Eirik's story known to the nation. The temptation was to just call the press, but what would happen then? When confronted with the fact that somebody killed three men, covered their bodies with fibreglass to prevent decay, and arranged them on a wooden bench, would Norwegians accept this as a symbolic judgment on them or would they see this as the work of a mentally deranged serial killer? Wolfsangel was pretty sure he knew the answer.

Immediately after the death of Finn Undredal, Wolfsangel was on a high. He completed the "Hurdal Three" shrine and was ready for the next step. He just wasn't sure what that next step was supposed to be. Somewhere along the way of trying to figure that out, his impetus waned. He drove around for days, more or less aimlessly, staying in different hotels every night. He visited libraries in Oslo and Hurdal, interested in everything that had happened during WW2. He wanted to go deeper and interview people for more information, but was afraid of getting noticed. In the meantime, the three dead guys continued to wait patiently in Hurdal's hidden bunker for the big reveal of their judgment.

He needed a plan that would force Norway to confront their past. He had often discussed this with the old Hellmuth. Together they had constructed many alternative solutions, but none of them were viable. So here he was, after four days of aimless wandering, stranded in Drammen at the Scandic Park hotel. He had to face the hard truth that he was stuck.

He decided to take a hike through the hills to shrug off his feeling of doom and gloom. About halfway through the hike, out of the blue, it finally hit him. Stein! Of course, why didn't he think of him before. He is a student of history. He thinks in grand pictures. He might have some ideas.

When he got back to his hotel room, he found Stein's phone number and called him.

Stein was clearly pleased to finally connect. "Hey, my saviour, my hero! Is the wolf still hunting, or have you already found what you were looking for?"

"Still hunting, I'm glad you remember me because I need to pick your brain."

"How can I forget you? I'd love to return the favour and do what I can to help. Tell me more."

"I need your advice. I have done some research on an important topic of national interest but I'm not sure about the best way to get that information out." Without going into too much detail, Wolfsangel sketched out his situation.

"I have a master's degree in History, man. It sounds like you need a media relations expert or something like that to get your information out into the public."

Wolfsangel knew he made the right decision in calling Stein. "Right, that's exactly what I need. Do you know anybody?"

"Well, I know there are professionals out there who do this kind of work. But I don't know any of them personally and wouldn't be able to recommend anybody in particular. However, I do know a journalist who is good at digging up interesting stories and putting them on the internet."

Wolfsangel thought about that. He wasn't up to speed on 'the internet' and wasn't quite sure if that would be the best way to get out the story he wanted all of Norway to hear.

Stein must have sensed Wolfsangel's hesitation. "Look, she is a young reporter, but she is completely comfortable with new methods of presenting news. Newspapers, TV, and radio are fast becoming obsolete when it comes to breaking news stories. The internet is where it is at these days."

Wolfsangel still was unsure. Media relations expert sounded much better to him than a young journalist.

"Listen," said Stein. "She is smart, she can do much more than reporting. Man, this girl is a researcher, a detective, and a writer. She will be able to take your information and do something spectacular with it. If she can't, she will know somebody who can. What do you have to lose?"

Wolfsangel nodded, convicted that he really needed to do something sooner than later. What did he have to lose? "Okay, you're right. Do you have her name and contact information?"

"Her name is Zofia. Wait, I'm looking for it. Yes, Zofia. Zofia Hurum from Trondheim and her number is 49 32 66 91. You can tell her you got it from me."

"Thanks. I really appreciate it."

"Anytime, man. If I can do anything else for you, just tell me."

"Well, actually, I know that you are a History student. Do you know anything more about Holmestrand during the Second World War? It seems that Quisling has been there once, visiting a training camp for SS-soldiers in Grefsrud."

There was a pause on the other end. "Not off-hand, but I'll look into it and get back to you."

After hanging up and going for a short walk, Wolfsangel felt a little better. He decided that a coffee at the Nedre Storgate Starbucks would help him feel even better. And it did. But what really made him feel better was his phone call to Zofia.

A friendly female voice answered his call on the third ring.

Wolfsangel jumped right in. "Hi there. My name is Wulfric Engel. You can call me Wulf - I got your name and number from a mutual acquaintance, Stein Bratt. He suggested I contact you for some advice on dealing with the media."

There was a slight pause and then a tinkle of laughter. "Oh. Wulf. Engel. That makes sense. Yes. I heard about you from Stein. Although, the way he said your name, I thought it was Wolfsangel - as in the Nazi SS symbol. Which, of course, nobody would want to use in this day and age."

Wolfsangel gave a slight cough. Obviously Stein had called Zofia immediately after hanging up with him. "Well, you know Stein. Depending on what he is smoking, his brain doesn't always register reality."

Zofia laughed again. "Yep, I couldn't agree more. You have an interesting accent. Kind of sounds German. Where are you from?"

Wolfsangel decided to move on and pretend he didn't hear her question. "Well, thanks for taking my call. I have done some research on a fairly sensitive topic which would be of interest to a very large group of people. How would I go about engaging this large group of people in this topic?"

She didn't pursue her question. "Well, it all depends on what information you have and who you want to be engaged with. Can you tell me more about your research?"

"I'd rather not at this time. I need to keep that on the down-low. I can tell you that it has something to do with the after-effects of World War II. It is intense and quite personal for a group of people. I do promise, though, that it is of national interest. I think you will be stunned by what it will reveal about the Norwegian people."

There was a pause on the other end. "German, definitely German … Okay. So then, what exactly is it that you want?"

"I'm thinking that the press needs to be involved and the story needs to be central for more than a day or two. The image in my mind is that of a stone thrown in a small pond and how the initial stone causes a ripple effect. You know, a series of waves that hit the public several times over the course of a month or so."

"All right. Umm. I'd say that you need to launch your story initially in a very big way - as many forms of media as possible need to be involved. But, when the story gets launched, you leave out key details and over time you serve them up one or two at a time."

Wolfsangel considered this and he felt his chest tighten with excitement. "Yes. I see what you mean. The initial launch is the rock. The waves are generated by releasing pertinent details one at a time. Stein said you were good. He was right." There was a hint of admiration in his voice.

There was that laugh again. "Thanks! I appreciate the compliment. The other important aspect is that you connect your story with a face."

"A face?"

"Yes. Especially if your story is intense or abstract, people won't necessarily connect it to their daily lives. How does this story affect me? That's what they'll ask. If you are able to put a face to the story, then suddenly it becomes alive to people - they can relate to it."

"I'm not sure I understand."

"Well, stories need to appeal to people both intellectually and emotionally. By giving a face to your story, you appeal to their emotions as well. Does that make sense?"

"Yes, it does. I really never thought of that before." Wolfsangel could feel his excitement level increasing. This was great information. He could really do something with this.

"Consider, Wulf, how this story primarily affects you. Are you affected by it intellectually? In other words, does the story hit your mind? Or, are you primarily affected by it emotionally? Does the story hit your heart? If you want to keep this story alive, you need to ensure it does both."

"Great stuff. Thanks very much for your help. You have no idea."

Zofia laughed. "You're welcome. So, do you think I might be able to get an exclusive?"

Wolfsangel paused, not sure how to answer that. "Maybe. If I am ready, you will be one of the first people I talk to."

"One of the first? Why not the first?"

Wolfsangel smiled. She was a bit tenacious. He supposed that was one of the qualities that made her as good as she is. "I need to leave it at that."

"For Pete's sake, Wulf. Now you have me terribly curious. Now much more than before. Can't you give me any more?"

Wolfsangel laughed. "Sorry. I promise that you will hear from me again. Thanks very much for your help." He hung up feeling a lot more energised now. Yes, he could do something with this. A plan started to form in his head. He walked briskly to his hotel room, picked up a pen and paper and attempted to sketched it out. When would he start? How would he start? How much time should this all take? He designed several plans until the wee hours of the morning. When he went to bed, he still did not have a well-defined plan; nevertheless he felt he was on the right track.

1999 - 2001, Obersalzberg, Germany

It was the story of his life. Lots of plans, but no time to put them into action. At least, that's what he told himself. There was no shortage of work at Blackwater for him and Hellmuth. At the end of August 1999, they were hired by a rich company to strengthen the Macedonian-government army to deal with the Albanian rebels of the so-called Macedonian National Liberation Army. It took up more than two years of their lives, but it was a wild experience for them. They pretty much had free reign from the government on deciding how to deal with the rebels. They flew Mi-17 helicopters and purged several villages of Albanian terrorists. They organised and executed a covert operation to rescue a captured soldier near Tetovo and nearly lost their lives in a major counterattack. Unfortunately, eight of their fellow mercenaries were shot in this operation. They became accustomed to the fury of the husky Macedonians and made friends with the harshest soldiers. The situation there never did escalate into a full-scale war and by the middle of August, 2001, all was under control. A treaty was signed in Ohrid, under the auspices of NATO Secretary-General

George Robertson and the representative of the European Union, Javier Solana. That ended the contract Blackwater had with the Macedonian government.

This meant Hellmuth and Wolfsangel needed to be reassigned. They were offered jobs working on A.P. Moller–Maersk ships as anti-piracy security personnel. As much as Wolfsangel would have enjoyed the excitement of dealing with pirates, he had spent enough time on boats as a young boy. Hellmuth, on the other hand, was highly intrigued by the prospect of taking on Somali pirates. Wolfsangel and Hellmuth parted ways. Wolfsangel went west back to his home in the US; Hellmuth headed south for the Arabian Sea. They both knew it wasn't going to be permanent. They were a great team and they would be back together someday in the near future.

Shortly after arriving back home in Chesapeake, Wolfsangel checked his email. What he saw on the screen shocked him. It was an email from old Hellmuth with the word Dringlichkeitsantrag in the subject line! The two of them had devised a system where they could communicate somewhat privately through Microsoft Hotmail. They also used that platform to archive documents, such as the confessions of Olaf and Finn as well as information about the Lebensborn. Wolfsangel had digitally scanned in Eirik's journal as well as the reports from Robert. Hellmuth had also scanned all his confidential papers and stored them there too. The two of them hadn't communicated much over the past four or five years, so when Wolfsangel checked the date the email was sent, another wave of panic hit him. The email was nearly a month old.

He immediately took out his cell phone and called.

"Hellmuth, what the hell is going on? I've just read your email. You're not serious, are you?"

There was a lengthy pause and Wolfsangel thought for a moment he had lost the connection. Finally, the voice of Hellmuth came on. It was extremely hoarse. "Yes. I am serious. I need you to accompany me to my final destination."

"You want to kill yourself and you want me to come over there and watch you do it. You are out of your freaking mind. Why would you do that to yourself?"

"Listen, you come down and I'll explain it to you. Come when it suits you, but do not wait too long."

Wolfsangel realised that the old man was indeed serious. "Okay. Do not do anything until I can get there and talk to you. Promise? I'll be there in a couple of days."

Hellmuth was silent for a moment, Wolfsangel heard him breathing heavily. Then Hellmuth whispered, "I promise. Come soon, okay?"

"Great friend, do not be afraid, I am on my way. Auf wiedersehen!"

As soon as he got off the phone with old Hellmuth, he called up a travel agency to see if he could get a flight to Germany. After an hour of waiting for the agent to find the best flight, he paid for a flight that left Norfolk International Airport at 7:00 in the morning and landed in Frankfurt that afternoon at 7:00 pm with a short stop in Chicago. All through the flight, Wolfsangel was worried about his old friend. Why on earth did he want to end his life? Why did he need me to be there?

By the time he arrived at Hellmuth's place in Bochum, it was nearly 10:00 at night. When he knocked at the door, a nurse opened and let him in. Hellmuth lay on the couch, covered with a woollen blanket. Wolfsangel was in shock after seeing his old friend again. His face was jaundiced, his eyes were hollow and sunken. He had clearly lost a lot of weight.

Wolfsangel said gently, "Hey there. In the name of Eirich, the son of your whore Anna, I'm here as promised."

It took a moment for the old man to realise who he was. A brief smile flitted across his face only to be replaced by a wince of pain as he tried to sit up. He was rewarded for his efforts with a coughing fit that lasted nearly three minutes. The nurse tried to fit his oxygen mask on, but the coughing turned into a brief choking fit. Wolfsangel never felt so helpless. He sat down on a chair beside the bed and watched as the nurse finally was able to give him some oxygen. After a few deep breaths, the old man was able to sit up and breathe on his own.

He managed a weak smile. "You little shit. You made it."

"Meine Ehre heißt Treue," Wolfsangel said solemnly.

Hellmuth grunted an agreement and turned to the nurse. "Elfrida, thank you very much. You can go now, I will manage, together with this young man."

Elfrida gave him the stink eye, but since it was quite late, she protested no further. She showed Wolfsangel how the oxygen mask worked and left.

"So, you want to end it?" Wolfsangel leaned forward to hear the soft-spoken reply.

"Yes, it has been enough. I am 90 years old, I'm in a lot of pain, constant pain. It's that damn cancer."

"Ending your own life? Are you sure?"

"Very sure."

"A Nazi does not do something like that, does he? That doesn't fit with your creed. Even an animal doesn't do that, and …"

But Hellmuth raised his hand. "Just be quiet, my friend. I'm glad you want to stop me, but I made my decision. Like Goebbels and the Fuehrer, Hitler, I want to end my life on my terms."

"What about me?"

Hellmuth grasped Wolfsangel's hands in a rare display of emotion. "You still have a mission to accomplish. You need to finish it, also for me. I, too, want justice for my son Erich. That's your reason to stay alive. I know in my heart of hearts that you will accomplish this mission."

Wolfsangel was at a loss for words. Over the years, he had grown fond of the old man. It wasn't until now that he truly realised the depth of that fondness.

The old man, also not really an emotional person, continued as his eyes brimmed with tears. "I have fought the good fight. I have slayed all the dragons I needed to. I'm ready to depart. Let me go."

Wolfsangel nodded.

Hellmuth reached for a small box from a side table. "Here, this is for you." Wolfsangel took it, and when he opened it, he immediately recognised what it was and the significance of the gift. It was an SS-Ehrenring, a ring of SS honour, also called a Totenkopfring. The centrepiece was a skull. The ring encouraged the wearers to be prepared to risk their lives at any time for the great purpose. There was a signature on the inside. It was the signature of Himmler himself.

Wolfsangel studied the runes on the side. The old man told him that they signify a redemption from the past. Hellmuth looked at him intently as he struggled for words. "Only then is there room for your future."

Wolfsangel felt this one land deeply. This gift, he knew, was Hellmuth's way of symbolically representing their close bond. "Thank you, Hellmuth. You know I'm not Nazi; still I'm so happy with your gift."

Hellmuth nodded and gave Wolfsangel's hands a final squeeze.

Wolfsangel stuffed his emotions back deep inside his heart. "So, have you already said goodbye to your children and family?"

"Yes, ten days ago we had a family gathering. There I said my goodbyes and divided the inheritance. And, just so you know, I did make a trip out to Norway to the graves of my Anna and my Esther. I was able to say my goodbyes to them as well."

Wolfsangel felt moved inside, he would miss the old one. He put the ring on one of his fingers and thanked him. After a few fresh breaths from the oxygen tank, Hellmuth spoke up again. "Let's leave tomorrow in my Mercedes. I have it parked in a garage close to here. We will drive to Obersalzberg, where Hitler's beloved retreat once was."

Despite the admonition of Elfrida, Wolfsangel poured the two of them a generous portion of cognac. They raised a toast. "To a good death! A person must know how to live and how to die, both with dignity and pride."

Hellmuth was exhausted and fell asleep on his couch. Wolfsangel was too wired to sleep. He sat out on the balcony for a while, deep in thought about Norway and his mission. It seemed like ages ago he had felt energised by the conversation he had with Zofia. That energy had flitted away, unable to be sustained, unable to move Wolfsangel along the journey. Now, it was already 2001. There were three witnesses waiting for a verdict, but he just could not seem to get it finished. He felt lost, floating on an endless ocean, seemingly unable to move him anywhere. He glanced at the sleeping Hellmuth. Had he even a milliliter of Hellmuth's tenacity and resolution, he would have accomplished his mission years ago. His fingers unconsciously began playing with the ring on his finger. He looked down at the ring and felt a sting of shame.

The next morning, a light rain was sprinkling the city when Wolfsangel woke up after a listless sleep. He decided that his first task was to get that car running and pack in all the items they would need for the day. He located the garage where Hellmuth's old Mercedes 450 SEL was sitting there waiting to be driven again. It took a moment to get that thing started, but once it did, it purred like a kitten. "They don't make cars like that anymore," Wolfsangel thought in wonderment. He tossed a shovel in the boot and took off to pick up Hellmeth.

For a man who knew that today was going to be his last day on earth, Hellmuth actually looked much better than yesterday. "Slept like a baby," he said proudly.

Elfrida made sure there was a full bottle of oxygen ready as well as a wheelchair. She likely has no idea what is going to happen today, thought Wolfsangel. As if reading his mind, Hellmuth said, "Don't worry. I told her yesterday that her work was done here because I would be going to a palliative care home to spend the last few months of my life."

Wolfsangel set course for Munich. He should have checked his windscreen wiper blades because the years of disuse had made the rubber brittle. It didn't take long before the blades were totally useless and Wolfsangel was struggling to peer through the watery mist in front of him. He had to make a detour to a petrol station off the Autobahn to find new ones. After a twenty-minute delay, he got back on the road and arrived in Frankfurt just over two hours later. After a quick stop in Frankfurt, they headed out to Nuremberg and finally to Munich.

It felt weird taking this trip. Wolfsangel never imagined that the incredible life journey of this man would end after a seven hour trip down the German Autobahn. It didn't seem to bother Hellmuth, though. He managed to sleep through most of the drive. After a brief stop in Munich, they started their final leg of the trip. Hellmuth had enough sleep by then and became quite chatty. He talked a lot about his personal beliefs and how he was able to reconcile them with Nazi ideology.

By eight o'clock in the evening, they reached a luxury restaurant close to the Eagle's Nest. Hellmuth insisted on eating his last meal here. Wolfsangel parked the car near the door of the Intercontinental Berchtesgaden Resort, realising it was only eight kilometres from Hitler's retreat. It was a good thing Elfrida packed a wheelchair. Hellmuth was too exhausted and weak to walk from the car to the restaurant. Hellmuth's last meal was a traditional German meal - Schweinshaxe with potatoes and cabbage. Wolfsangel wasn't quite sure why Hellmuth wanted Schweinshaxe. It wouldn't have been his choice for a last meal. The old man could hardly get the meat off the bone. Wolfsangel figured there must be some sentimental reason for that particular restaurant and that particular meal.

The sun had fully set when Hellmuth wiped his mouth with his napkin and announced, "It's time." They went back to the car and drove on. It was clear that Hellmuth knew what he wanted and he knew where he wanted it. He was unusually alert and was able to deftly guide Wolfsangel to the right spot. Turning off a main road onto a smaller, narrower road, Hellmuth smiled. "We are nearly there." A moment later he said, "Stop here, on the side, right here. Now take that shovel out of the trunk and dig there, you see, there at that tree. Dig me a grave."

Wolfsangel peered into the darkness but couldn't see the tree Hellmuth was referring to. Hellmuth found a flashlight, opened the window, and directed the beam of light to a solitary tree. "There, now do you see it?"

Wolfsangel nodded. He leaned over to Hellmuth and asked again, "Is this really what you want?" Hellmuth nodded. "Okay, I'll do it for you, but …"

Stepping out of the car, he rummaged in the boot. "…Here, let's have another drink and a cigar."

Hellmuth grinned. "Yah! Good job. Help me open the bottle, yes … okay, light the cigar …"

He gasped and coughed but was clearly enjoying it. He muttered between coughs, "I will not die from smoking this cigar."

While Hellmuth sat and smoked his cigar, Wolfsangel begun the task of digging a grave in front of him, guided only by the red light of the Mercedes backlights. Just after he was finished, they sat together, not saying a word, just enjoying each other's company. When the bottle yielded its last drop and the cigars were reduced to ashes in the wind, Hellmuth raised his hand. "Now, help me up." As Wolfsangel grasped his arm, pulling him off the ground, Hellmuth groaned in pain. His voice, hoarse, "I did my best. I did what was ordered. I regret nothing." There was a pause. "Well, maybe I do have regrets about Anna and our children. I should have done much more to get her and the children from Norway." Turning to Wolfsangel, "Now, help me to end my life with dignity."

Wolfsangel helped Hellmuth step into his own grave. With one last pat on his shoulder, Wolfsangel left the old man standing there. There was a pit in his stomach as he stared down. Hellmuth, a little unsteady on his feet, but refusing to sit down, put his hand on his heart and spoke into the darkness. "It cannot be that a pure Aryan soul forever disappears into nothing." Proudly he raised his old fist in the air. "I will see my SS comrades again, where pure blood flows." He looked up at Wolfsangel. "Goodbye, my comrade. May your journey go well for you."

Wolfsangel stood at attention as Hellmuth straightened up with his last strength. He held up his hand in the familiar Nazi greeting and said, "Heil Hitler!" With a steady hand, he took his pistol, the Walther, out of his pocket, and brought it to his temple. He lifted his right arm once more to give the Hitler salute, and shouted hoarsely, "Sieg heil, Sieg heil, Sieg heil!" Then he pulled the trigger, the sound ripping through the silence and the bullet ripping through his skull. Wolfsangel didn't realise that he had closed his eyes. When he opened them, he saw the body of the notorious Gestapo chief of Norway lying lifeless in the pit he had just dug.

Wolfsangel pushed aside his sadness and with steady and even shovel strokes buried Hellmuth. When he was finished, he covered the grave of Eirik's father with leaves. With his sharp pocket knife, he carved a wolf's hook into the bark of the solitary oak tree standing guard near the grave site. He wondered if his body would ever be found.

He wondered the same about Eirik, the son. Wolfsangel had seen the old one die. He had buried him, marked his grave, and called his name as he finished carving the wolf's hook. But where was Eirik's grave? You only bury a corpse. Maybe there is no corpse.

Wolfsangel got inside the car. The rain, having been in abeyance the last couple of hours, started up again and large drops assaulted the windscreen. The new blades had difficulty keeping up. It was only for a split second, just after the blade made its sweep, that Wolfsangel was able to get a glimpse through the murky darkness. He was journeying on without any markers guiding the way.

He suddenly gasped. A vivid image flashed into his mind, an image that had been buried deep in the recesses of his subconscious. He hit the brakes and the car stopped, throwing Wolfsangel against the restraint of the seatbelt. His mother was standing by a lighthouse. His mother? How did that happen? He hadn't thought of her in a few years. The image was gone. He put the car in gear and headed back to Frankfurt.

At a kiosk there he bought three postcards and three first-class stamps. He sent one to the midwife in Norway, the second to the family of Hellmuth in Germany, the third to his mother in the Netherlands.

2003 – 2007, Bangui, Central African Republic

In the years following the death of old Hellmuth, Wolfsangel continued to be frustrated with his inability to penetrate through the murky darkness of his mission. That bullet made him feel abandoned and lonely with a deep-seated need to connect with young Hellmuth. After returning to Bocham, Wolfsangel managed to convince Hellmuth to seek reassignment from his mission off the coast of Africa and the two of them headed out to the Central African Republic to provide a Canadian diamond mining company with security services.

Over the next six years, the bond between the two men grew stronger. They fought together against both government and rebel groups seeking to either appropriate their clients' diamond minds or sow discontent among the people. They became bonded like brothers and Wolfsangel was able to share his story about Eirik. He told Hellmuth about the first action he undertook when he started his mission, and the three dead people sitting in a bunker in Hurdal. It never crossed Wolfsangel's mind to question his trust in Hellmuth. He knew that this man would lock up Wolfsangel's secrets in a tight vault in his mind. Hellmuth was the only person he fully and unconditionally trusted. He trusted no one else - no one, no woman, no relationship. Wolfangel believed that as far as women were concerned, his heart was cursed.

"Damn, it's warm here," Wolfsangel rubbed the sweat off his forehead and took another sip of his beer. "We are down to the wire on our assignment. Hopefully we can deal with that convoy and wrap things up by the end of the week. I'm looking forward to some R & R back home in Virginia."

They had arrived earlier in the day at M'Poko International airport in Bangui. Their first order of business was finding a place to have a beer. They ended up in a small, musty cafe. Its concrete walls were dusty from the sand floor and smudged with various shades of brown. Yet, for all its defects, there was something comfortable about it. Salsa music belted out from the loudspeaker boxes and ceiling fans rotated above their heads. Young Hellmuth Patzschke - although the description 'young' was no longer applicable - sat with his back against one of the walls and took in the scenery. The big black man behind the bar, dressed in a T-shirt that flaunted a kaleidoscope of vivid colours, came over to give them two new bottles of Heineken and to clean up the previous four.

Wolfsangel took a sip and studied the bottle. "This still surprises me. Anywhere in the world, even here in the remotest part of Africa they can provide good Dutch beer." They spoke German to each other, a language that no one around them understood. Two meters away, at the bar, a young sensual woman with a deep cleavage stared at them. Well, Wolfsangel believed that she was actually staring at the fair-haired Hellmuth whose trained body, open face and long blonde hair always gave the impression that he was a kind of movie star. Wolfsangel wouldn't know what to do if she was staring at him. He himself felt better in his cocoon.

The light blue eyes of Hellmuth danced with excitement. He knew he was being eyed. He ignored her and concentrated his attention on Wolfsangel. "And we drank our fair share of Heineken during the last fifteen, sixteen years that we have known each other. Come, let us toast again to that SS uncle of mine." They raised their bottles and took a huge draught.

Hellmuth continued. "And a toast to Norway!" Another huge draught. Both finished their bottles at the same time and slammed them on the bar.

"So, my friend, what are you going to do with that Hurdal stunt of yours? You had a plan?"

"Well, plan? Not really. That's been my problem all along. I don't have a plan. And then, just when I was close to figuring out my next step, the court case came up."

"What court case are you talking about?"

"The Norwegian Lebensborn, the Tyskerbarn themselves, brought their case to the European Court of Human Rights in Strasbourg!"

Wolfsangel had done a fair bit reading up on this case. A group of seven Norwegian Lebensborn, headed by Werner Hermann Thiermann, brought their case to the European Court of Human Rights. Previously, this group had tried to make their case in the Oslo City Court, arguing that the State had failed to protect them against the horrible abuse they suffered. The group sought compensation in the amount of two million Krones. Oslo City Court dismissed their claim on the grounds that the present-day State cannot be held liable for any actions or omissions of the government in power after World War II. Furthermore, the court dismissed any compensation claim arguing that a statute-of-limitations places a three-year window on any such claims. Disappointed with this ruling, the group eventually took their fight to the European Court of Human Rights. Unfortunately, the European Court declined to hear the case because they argued that the Norwegian Lebensborn did not exhaust all avenues of appeal in their own domestic judicial system.

Hellmuth nodded. "I've heard bits and pieces of this case. What does this have to do with your plans?"

Wolfsangel thought for a moment, trying to figure out the best way to explain it. "Well, my plan was to bring the plight of the Tyskerbarn to the forefront of the Norwegian public. They need to be judged for their actions and held accountable. The court case shifted the whole conversation from the plight of the Tyskerbarn to a legal struggle over the statute of limitations. That's a much safer conversation because it removes people from the responsibility of what happened."

"Ah yes, I see what you mean. People don't feel convicted. Now it is more of a 'tsk, tsk - oh well, what's done is done and it can't be undone, so let's move on.'"

"Exactly."

"So? Why don't you move on?" Hellmuth asked.

"I can't. Eirik can't let it go. He can't let me go. There must be revenge - punishment - true justice for what they did to Eirik. What they did to their own people. I can't walk away."

"Yet, here you are. How many years has it been since you started your mission?"

Wolfsangel looked pained. "I know. I'm an idiot. I'm a weakling that just can't get his shit together."

Hellmuth took a huge gulp of his beer and banged the bottle on the bar. "You know, my friend, this reminds me of a well-known story of revenge and procrastination. It takes place in Denmark, although it was written by an Englishman - Shakespeare. You remind me of Hamlet."

Wolfsangel raised his eyebrows and scoffed. "Shakespeare? Since when are you into English literature?"

Hellmuth shrugged, pointed to his face and biceps. "It's not all looks and muscle, you know. Although, clearly, I have been abundantly blessed in those areas. I do also have a brain. I went to the University of Hamburg for a bit and took an English literature course."

"Okay. Tell me about this Hamlet guy. How am I like him?"

"Well. Hamlet was given a mission by the ghost of his dead father to take vengeance on the man - who happened to be his brother - who killed him and married his wife. Hamlet was hyped up for the task but kept procrastinating - kept making excuses. He just couldn't do it."

Wolfsangel grunted.

Hellmuth mused, "I think the heart of his struggle was his question about whether or not he had the moral authority to take another man's life."

Wolfsangel swigged some of his beer. "That hasn't been a problem with me. I don't have that struggle. It comes with the territory in our line of work."

"True, but at some point, Hamlet realised that if he took the life of another person - let's call it for what it is, murder - he has eternally damned his soul. He had to weigh out the need for revenge over the consequence of losing his soul."

Wolfsangel guffawed. "That's certainly not something I think about or weigh out. I don't believe in that heaven and hell stuff anymore."

"Oh, but I think that deep down, you might have some doubts. Weren't you raised in a deeply religious family? That's got to have affected you. If it didn't, why haven't you finished your mission by now?"

Wolfsangel was silent.

"Listen, Kamerad, you killed three men and their bodies are waiting for you to make the next move. What move are you going to make that won't end up with you being on trial for murder? Sure, Eirik can't let this go, but it's not Eirik that is going to suffer the consequence of being charged with murder. You must have thought about this? You can walk away from all this. Leave the bodies in that bunker, walk away in the knowledge that they have paid the price for their sins. Why is it your job to seek justice?"

Wolfsangel considered those words. It must be the combination of too much Heineken and the weird salsa music, but Hellmuth had never before questioned Wolfsangel's mission. Wolfsangel was okay with that because it made him circumspect. He looked up at Hellmuth. "Have I ever told you about Odd Gripar?"

"I don't think so. Who is he?"

"He is a police inspector now, about five years younger than me. However, the first time I met him was when he was about fourteen years old. It was near Lillehammer, late at night. He was in the middle of the road and I almost ran him down. Of course, I stopped, got out of the car, grabbed a flashlight, shone it in his face and was ready to give him hell. He looked up at me with these intense green eyes. I'll never forget those eyes and what he said. He told me that three nights ago he lost his parents and his brother in a car accident at this very spot."

"Holy cow! He lost his entire family in a car accident? That's quite a burden for such a young guy."

"He told me that officially the police called it an accident - driver's error. But, unofficially, they were convinced that there was another driver involved that ran his parents car off the road. A hit and run. I thought he might be looking for clues so that he could find the asshole who did that and take revenge. But that's not what he wanted."

"What did he want? I would have been pissed at the police for giving up, at the other driver for causing it, and probably at myself for not preventing it."

"Yeah, you'd think. He wanted the perpetrators found and brought to trial. He wanted them judged and punished according to the law. He wasn't interested in revenge."

"Even though somebody completely destroyed his life."

"Yes. Justice must be done, he said, but ultimately it is in God's hands. This guy, who is fourteen years old, tells me that the law is God's instrument in carrying out justice. We probably talked for half an hour and then I dropped him off at his aunt's place. That's where he was living at the time."

Hellmuth seemed impressed. "Wow, someone as young as him who really believes in law and justice. I guess that's why he became a police officer. So, why are you telling me this story?"

Wolfsangel smiled. "You got me thinking, old friend, about what drives us to seek justice and revenge." He looked straight at Hellmuth. "I met Gripar the same night I was on my way to get Mikkel Thomassen."

Hellmuth nodded. "Maybe you and Hamlet aren't so different after all."

Wolfsangel shook his head. There was a silence while Hellmuth downed his bottle. He placed his index finger on Wolfsangel's chest. "I think it's time you put that man on your case, somehow."

At that moment, the girl at the bar walked past the two of them and deliberately leaned over and rubbed her chest on Hellmuth's shoulders. Hellmuth managed to lightly slap her on the behind before she got out of range. Provocatively, she turned her head back at him and gave her hips a wiggle. He laughed and made a lewd gesture.

Hellmuth turned to Wolfsangel who was rolling his eyes. "You and women, what about that? You're like a monk around them. Are you not attracted to them?"

"Yeah, I am," he said defensively ."I just don't have your magnetic gift of attracting anything with a pair of boobs."

"Ha. I don't believe you, I don't think you are attracted to women at all. In fact, I think you are one of those boring asexual types. Just tell me, then. Have you ever met a woman that you have been attracted to? One that you just can't get out of your mind?"

Wolfsangel briefly immersed himself in reading the label on his bottle and held two fingers up to the man behind the bar. "As a matter of fact: yes! I once met a woman like that."

"Ahha, jetzt kommt's raus. The mighty Wolfsangel does like women. You had me worried." They laughed and drank. Hellmuth belched. "Tell! I'm all ears."

"No, you're all dick. You probably think the only woman worth being attracted to is a slim, sexy model. The one I'm thinking of is big and coarse, strong muscles, big breasts. Yes, laugh about it, she was not pretty in the conventional sense, yet …" His thoughts often wandered back to that crazy person.

"Go on. Don't leave me hanging. Where did you meet her?"

"I booked a flight to Stavanger, hired a car and found myself driving to that famous pulpit rock. You know, the beautiful flat rock with a view over the Lysefjord. After walking around there a bit, I booked a hotel room in Sandnes, just across the harbour. While looking for a restaurant, I passed by the Sandnes Culture House. I heard some music playing. The doors were open, so I went in …"

"So, you are also an art lover? You keep surprising me."

"Yes, well, I was bored and curious about that place. I just got inside and was looking around at a table full of clay figures when I was run over by a rough built, spectacled woman about my age. She was wearing a strapless black dress. What I remember most, though, were her hands. They were like coal shovels - big and strong. Now, I am a pretty large guy, but she was almost as big as I am. When we collided, it was me that was thrown off balance." Wolfsangel shook his head at the memory.

"Wow and that big woman you can't forget? Unbelievable." Hellmuth laughed and downed half his bottle in one draught.

Wolfsangel took a sip to empty his bottle, put it down and continued. "Yes, it is, isn't it? She doesn't quite fit your stereotype of the perfect curvaceous woman."

Hellmuth laughed and shrugged as he glanced briefly behind Wolfsangel's back to the beautiful, slender woman who was still alone at the bar, presumably waiting for him. "And so, what was she doing there at the Culture House?"

"She's an artist. I was looking at her clay figures. I remember that one of the sculptures she made was a representation of a man with two faces, a cruel one and an innocent one. She sculpted the body to seem trained and healthy, but there were parts that were missing or broken. The broken, the corrupt parts seemed to be overtaking the whole. And the head, well, it was very sinister and cruel."

Hellmuth, with a gaping smile, "You must have really collided. When did you become such an art critic? Did you find yourself looking deeply in her eye? Did some sort of an energy jolt pass through from her to you?"

"Well, something weird did happen. She suddenly asked me in what story do I live?"

"Are you sure you weren't just mesmerized by her cleavage?"

"No. The crazy thing was … no. I told her that I was in the story of Eirik, the son of a whore. It escaped my mouth without me realising it. She asked why I was in his story. I told her that I was looking for the truth.

"We looked at each other for a long time without blinking. It was kind of weird. Then she asked me if I believed in Jesus as truth. Where the heck did that come from? Then she pointed to the sculpture I was looking at and then to the spotlights in the ceiling and told me that if I found Eirik, I needed to put him in the light immediately. The light will witness to the truth."

Hellmuth didn't quite know what to say. He had never known his friend to be so enthralled by a female. He stared at his friend, searching for words.

Wolfsangel continued, “Then she grabbed me firmly on my upper arms, reached in, gave me a kiss on the cheek. After that, she laughed. She did have a great laugh, though.”

Hellmuth finally founds his words. “I can see why you wouldn’t forget her. Kind of a nut job, don’t you think? The truth is in the light and the light will witness to the truth. I don’t understand that completely? Was she sober?”

“I think so. I’m not quite sure I understand it completely either, but her words struck a chord in my heart. Eirik, the light, the truth, the witnesses.”

Hellmuth clapped Wolfsangel on the back. “What heavy-duty conversations we have had tonight. First Odd Gripar and his belief in the law as God’s instrument of justice. Then this female with the amazing laugh who believes that Jesus is the truth. My good man. For somebody who says he doesn’t believe in God, you have taken these two people quite seriously. I hope this helps in your hunt for Eirik. In the meantime, I hear a good time calling me. I’ll catch up with you tomorrow.”

The woman at the bar was still making eyes at Hellmuth and clearly his baser urges finally took over. He got up and the two of them walked out.

That was fine with Wolfsangel. He had a lot on his mind.

Wolfsangel returned to his hotel room. His conversation with Hellmuth was deep and stirred up a lot of conflicting thoughts. He decided to read through another one of Thomassen’s reports.

March 6, 1978 / Psychiatric Hospital ‘Fylke, Oslo / Client: Eirik Tijsker (1943) / Dr. R. Thomassen / Conversation # 7: daughter Anna Esther 1976

In the past, when I thought about my past, I only saw some facts, without emotion. But some dragons lurked deep inside. I have had beautiful years, with my beautiful wife and dear children. The future smiled at me, but if dragons are not defeated, they will wake up some time.

We had children, worked hard to build up something. We believed in God and we rolled up our sleeves. I enjoyed it so much. For years it went better than I could ever have imagined. I loved my children. My oldest was my confidant, only with him I shared my horrible past. All in all, life seemed to cherish us. Not bad for a rat. But then things went wrong, and I sank deeply.

The winter of 1976 was cold, there was a lot of snow, but January 22 was a thawing day. Our beautiful, sweet daughter, Anna Esther was four at that time. She walked away from home unnoticed and delightedly followed other children to the 'singel' as we call it on Urk, some kind of drainage canal, which was covered with ice. The children of Urk 'creaked' the ice, as they called it. With a large group of kids at once, arms entwined, they walked from one side to the other. The ice rippled and creaked and cracked. There was no danger, if someone would fall in, he or she was immediately pulled out by the others.

Many parents watching it were smiling. I imagine her to be like this: beaming, laughing from the laughter of the others. She must have thought, Oh, many children on the ice. Boys and girls have a lot of fun. Look! They are walking on the ice hand in hand. They are all having so much fun, yes, it's nice! Then it must have gone like this: nobody saw Anna Esther stepping on a chunk of broken ice. She was outside the field of action and attention. She sat on the smooth side of the ditch and slid down gently. Then she stepped on the ice, just like the other children. One foot on the side and the other on a piece of ice. The ice floe was stuck to the grass side, frozen to the long grass, but the other side was sinking under her weight. I think she must have tried to climb back, but the ice was wet and very slippery. I can see it in my mind, she slid away from the side, more to the middle where the big floes were, and because of her momentum she slipped and disappeared under the ice. Chunks of ice closed above her. The water must have been very cold for a little while. No one has seen the dark ice mouth open and close. Someone told me that when small children come into water, they keep looking around in amazement. They do not experience it as dangerous, but do you know whether that is really the case?

That afternoon, when it turned dark, all the children returned home. Also ours. Nobody had noticed her! In no time, alarmed neighbours checked the neighbourhood; maybe she had gone to her girlfriend and was playing indoors? But she was nowhere to be found, and more and more people joined the search. They checked a large area of Urk, including of course the canals. These, filled with ice floes, looked like paths in the dark, tiled with uneven pieces of white stone. The street light gave enough light to control the ice surfaces.

No more children playing anywhere, hundreds of people looking for my girl. I was so afraid and continually prayed: Oh God, oh God, save my little girl, save my precious angel. Let her come to me again. I do not want to lose her! God, no.

Old memories together with a lot of pain broke loose, but I could not place them then. The Urker canals are not that deep for a grown man, up to about the belt. I started on one side and walked through it lengthwise. Just like that time in Jessheim with my sister I switched off my sense of cold. Hundreds of women, men, girls and boys watched me. I had to and would find her, even if I had to descend into the realm of the dead.

Suddenly in front of the house of Kees van Zwarte I saw something. I leaned forward and saw Anna Esther looking upwards at me through the transparent ice. She stared through the ice with her brown eyes.

I looked at her, she me. But, she was in the realm of the dead, unreachable. She looked without fear, yes, did she smile a little? What had been her last thought? She was so white, so beautiful, so perfect and so dead. There I stood, huh, the big strong father, bent over. The people thronged together around us in icy silence.

I took her out of the cold water and carried her, her body, to the side. On all sides people were crying. Deep sadness. The people of the village gathered around me and my daughter. It was very quiet, so quiet. A few minutes long nothing moved, there was no sound. Cold people in the light of street lanterns.

I heard a heart-breaking scream! Marianne walked to me through the crowd, grabbed our daughter, held her against her, and cried so intensely sad that everyone who heard it was drawn with her to her bottomless pain.

A little later I took over the cold body again. I had never cried at Urk, but that night I cried endlessly. Nobody could reach me, nobody could get into me, make contact … not even my wife. The doctor finally gave me a sedative, but then I went into a kind of trance, for days. It was horrible! I constantly saw her sweet face, and Esther's, staring from death to his life.

Brain zaps flashed in my head like jolts of electricity. I never became the same again. Why had no one seen our daughter? Oh, it felt like, like, an open dark hole, and dark black cold water flushed up.

The funeral drew many people. The inhabitants of Urk knew what it is to have a loved one drowning. The drowning of my girl ripped open many old wounds. Evil sometimes affects good people. I know, humanity is always in God's hands, but God, oh God, we humans often do not understand You.

/ Robert Thomassen, Fylke, Oslo, 1978

Wolfsangel shut down his laptop. He had read enough. What about the son? Eirik had lost a sister but he never mentioned his son except at the beginning. He went to the mini-bar and opened a can of coke. Wolfsangel smiled grimly. He desperately wanted to forget everything and banish Eirik.

Wolfsangel needed rest, he was both physically and emotionally exhausted. He crawled into bed and fell into a dreamless sleep.

However, a few days later, a terrible event burst his soul. Eirik wasn't forgotten or banished. In fact, Eirik's quest came at him like an oncoming rhino. He could no longer duck, no longer delay.

2007, Bouar, Central African Republic - Oslo, Norway

A convoy of four M923 military cargo trucks lumbered through a treacherous forest road on their way to Bouar in the Central African Republic. Each was laden with provisions and equipment destined for the government's command post based in the old French army base.

It was probably one of the most dangerous missions that Hellmuth and Wolfsangel had ever been on. The South African government had promised François Bozizés some assistance in ensuring the various rebel groups maintained the fragile cease-fire. Wolfsangel was tasked with commanding this mission - a mission that was fraught with the possibilities of attacks from a multitude of disparate rebel groups.

The mercenaries put aside all other thoughts and focused solely on the terrain, constantly on the lookout for signs of an impending ambush. Each of them knew it was not a matter of if there was going to be an attack, it was a matter of when. Nobody spoke. Tensions were high. Danger lurked behind every tree and bush.

Suddenly, the lead truck halted and the group readied themselves for an attack.

Wolfsangel's already taut nerves tightened considerably more as he discovered the reason for the halt. They were swarmed by a pack of hysterical children and their mothers. Within seconds, they had jammed the narrow roadway clamouring to get in the backs of the trucks. There was no way the convoy could continue without running them over. It was a testament to the training the men had undergone in preparation for this mission. Rather than panicking and driving through the occluded path, all eyes turned to Wolfsangel, waiting for his direction. Either this was part of a plan to ambush the convoy, or this was part of a group of refugees displaced by the civil war. Wolfsangel's emotionless grey eyes scanned the group.

He made a quick decision. He nodded at Hellmuth, spat out the rest of his cigar, and shouted, "We'll take them with us to Bouar. Hurry up. We are sitting ducks out here." The group of mercenaries herded the thirty or so women and children onto the trucks, fitting them in amongst the cargo. After about fifteen minutes of frenzied activity, the trucks continued on their journey towards Bouar. As he sat in the passenger seat beside Hellmuth, Wolfsangel reflected on his decision. Was he getting soft? He had placed his men and possibly the mission in a terrible jeopardy. He was ready to pull out another cigar from his breast pocket.

Again, without warning, a small group of rebels appeared from out of the forest. With a war whoop, one of them lobbed a grenade at the first truck. It was surreal moment for Wolfsangel, almost as if time had slowed right down. Frozen in his seat, clutching his cigar, Wolfsangel watched as the grenade rolled under the lead truck. The explosion lifted the front wheels and the vehicle careened off the road, stopping dead in its tracks at the base of a large tree.

Like predators languishing for carrion, the rebels attacked. Their murderous machetes carved a path towards the wrecked truck. Instinct took over as Wolfsangel and his men moved into high gear. Quickly, they organised themselves in a defensive stance and within a relatively short period of time had taken control of the situation. Their training and weapons were no match for the rebels.

When it was over, Wolfsangel and Hellmuth assessed their condition. They lost a few of their men and several women and children were also killed. The cargo in the lead truck was lost – much of it had been damaged in the explosion and crash. They quickly and efficiently re-formed their group into three trucks and continued their journey.

Wolfsangel had arranged to have the cargo loaded into the first two trucks while the women and children were in the last truck. He and one of his South African comrades took the last truck. None of them believed that they had seen the last of the rebels. Now that their location had become obvious, they were exposed. The men pushed the trucks to their limits, vigilantly scanning the landscape searching for any sign of movement. Wolfsangel knew it was going to become increasingly difficult as daylight would soon be dwindling. They had lost valuable time in not only picking up the refugees but also in fending off the attack. In the back of the trucks, tucked among the cargo, Wolfsangel sensed that the women were trying their best to keep their young ones quiet, but every once in a while, a wail escaped.

About an hour after the first attack, the second one came. It was as sudden as the first one. Wolfsangel saw some movement in a huge tree that was slumping towards the road. As it began to descend, the drivers of the trucks immediately understood what was going on and took evasive measures. Wolfsangel instinctively knew that the first two trucks would escape but not the last one – the one he was in. When the tree finally bounced across the road, the first two trucks just managed to escape. His truck wasn't so lucky. The tree formed an impenetrable barrier - there was no going around or through that tree. Wolfsangel hit the brakes, threw the truck in reverse and valiantly attempted to turn around and head back in the opposite direction.

The road was too narrow and the rebels too fast.

Wolfsangel and his comrade in the passenger seat dove out of the truck and fled into the trees. They stopped to watch the horrific scene unfold – the rebels made short work of the women and children. The screams of panic and wails of terror were brutally silenced. Eventually, the rebels realised that some of the mercenaries were gone. They started shouting and pointing to the trees. Wolfsangel fled deeper into the forest, thinking his small, muscled South African comrade was right behind him.

Wolfsangel found out later that the South African veered off in a different direction. He survived by eventually finding a hole in a tree to hide in. The little man waited it out until darkness had completely fallen. Despite being parched and incessantly stung by the myriad of insects that inhabited the trees, he finally was able to crawl out of his hiding place and wander through the forest hoping to find a rescuer. It was a stroke of luck that he eventually bumped into the group. The remaining mercenaries were determined to get the cargo to the destination. After all, there was no payment for them unless they completed the mission. The depreciated group of men loaded what was left on the two remaining trucks and eventually made it to Bouar. They didn't even bother trying to find the Norwegian. So much for 'Semper Fie'.

Fortunately for Wolfsangel, though, Hellmuth was faithful. Most of the next four days were a haze in Wolfsangel's memory. Trauma has a way of blocking memories. Hellmuth later recounted how he retraced his path back into the rebel territory, thinking nothing of his own life, just desperately hoping to find his friend, the Wolfsangel. He followed the tracks, but as the days wore on, he had a growing expectation that he would not find his Norwegian friend alive. He came across the mutilated bodies of young men either chopped to pieces or severely burned, but not that of his friend. One night, after three days of searching, Hellmuth found a good place to get some sleep. He covered himself with a mosquito net and hunkered down for another restless sleep. After a few hours, he woke up to some noises. Something or someone was crawling through the bushes towards him. He grabbed his gun and waited. The pale moonlight illuminated the ferns and the remains of a rotten tree. Something was definitely there.

He cocked his rifle and crouched down. Eventually, the ferns parted and his ears caught the sound of groaning and heavy breathing. In the pale moonlight, he eventually made out a figure crawling slowly on all fours. Hellmuth stepped quietly to the figure and realised that it was a white man. With a soft cry, he recognised the figure as the man who called himself Wolfsangel. Gently speaking in his own language, "It is me, Hellmuth."

"Oh God, Hellmuth, you are here. You haven't abandoned me." Wolfsangel collapsed.

Wolfsangel was in very bad shape. Hellmuth found him naked, covered in blood and in obvious deep pain. Hellmuth checked him over and was appalled to find out that most of the blood had come from his horrendously damaged anus. The rest of the blood came from the various scratches and wounds that covered his arms and torso.

"What the hell happened to you?" Hellmuth couldn't keep the shock and concern out of his voice as he wrapped a blanket around him

"Those motherless whores slaughtered all the women and children. I managed to escape with Bahati but somehow we lost each other. I spent the better part of a day trying to find my way back. Towards nightfall, I got ambushed by five or six of the rebels. I think they were pretty upset that most of the group got away with the cargo. Those bastards tied me to a tree trunk and …" Wolfsangel's voice cracked. He couldn't continue. Hellmuth did something he had never done to Wolfsangel. He threw his arms around him and hugged him tight.

After a long and deep hug, he gave Wolfsangel another bottle of water and some pain killers. Hellmuth had a first aid kit along and patched up the wounds as best he could. The next morning, they began the arduous task of making their way to Bouar's small hospital. It took the better part of the week to make it. If he had not been so incredibly strong, Wolfsangel would have certainly succumbed to his injuries.

It was a source of pride for Blackwater that one of their top men had, in fact, survived the attack. They took care of his hospital stay in Bouar and made arrangements to have him flown back to the United States for further treatment. Initially, Wolfsangel believed this was going to be a minor setback and he would be back in action in a short time. He figured there would be some physical therapy sessions and possibly some psychological therapy as well; but he was not at all prepared to hear what his doctor told him after a three-week stay in the hospital.

"You have Hepatitis C and there is a good chance you also have HIV/AIDS. We can do a blood-test next week to confirm that. Early test results seem to suggest that you do."

Wolfsangel was stunned. "What does this all mean for me?"

The doctor consulted his chart. "At this point, we can't say for certain. Hep C is a viral infection that can cause your liver to be inflamed and could, if left untreated, lead to liver cancer. The good thing is that we caught it right away and we can start a treatment protocol. Usually, people with Hep C don't even know they have it until the symptoms appear several months after infection."

Wolfsangel was relieved. "So, you can treat this, and I should be okay?"

The doctor studied Wolfsangel and gently shook his head. "Well, that's the part we can't say for certain. We can definitely treat it so that it becomes manageable. For some patients, the infection doesn't disappear. It becomes chronic and life-long. We caught this early enough and we can set you up with a treatment protocol that I believe can be highly successful. Probably, the biggest thing for you right now is you need to make some lifestyle decisions."

"Like what?"

"Well, you need to avoid alcohol consumption as that will put a strain on your liver. You should watch your diet and make sure you keep physically active."

Wolfsangel snorted. That wasn't so bad. Other than the alcohol consumption, the rest won't be a problem. "I can manage that. So, as a start, I need to take daily medication for the next several months?"

The doctor nodded. "Yes. I understand that your job takes you all over the world. You might want to take some time off and focus on getting better." He then took a long, hard look at Wolfsangel. "The other thing is the possibility of HIV/AIDS. Given what happened to you and where it happened, there is a high likelihood that you have contracted this as well. Early test results seem to confirm this. It's highly likely this is going to take a lot longer than several months. You need to be prepare for that."

Wolfsangel stopped to consider this. No matter how he looked at it, this was not good. "How will you know for sure?"

"We need to run some additional tests. Again, the good news is that we caught this early. Most people don't get tested until they have had the infection for some time. You will start to show symptoms such as fever, headaches, fatigue, sore muscles, and swollen lymph glands. For the long run, we will need to determine a therapy protocol."

Wolfsangel nodded. "There is no cure for this, is there?"

He appreciated that the doctor didn't try to minimise the situation. "No. There is no known cure. It is something that will be a part of you for the rest of your life. Twenty years ago, this was a death sentence. Not so much today. It can be managed successfully. Somebody will sit down with you before you are discharged and help you sort through all this information and set you up on a treatment protocol for both Hep C and HIV."

Wolfsangel sat back on his bed and processed all this information. Ever since he left home, he was used to being in control. Now, he was at the mercy of a horrible disease that seemed determined to ravage his body. Throughout his discussion with the doctor, he did not show any emotion. But behind his façade, he was fighting an emotional battle that he did not know how to attack: deep-seated anger, denial, grief, and despair. He knew his way around a physical battlefield. He knew all the signs to watch out for. He knew how his enemy moved; he knew his own strengths and limitations. He recognised that now he was really fighting a psychological battle and he felt like a brand-new cadet. Although he never really cared much for life, he had no death wish. He was going to fight this and return to his former life.

Later, in the middle of the night, he got a small taste of what he was in for. The anticipated fever hit like a whirlwind. The disease was trying to assert its control early on. Wolfsangel's body oscillated between bone-numbing chills and sweat-drenching heat. Before he had a chance to call the nurse, Eirik met him in the fog and urged him. *Go on. Do not give up. You have a mission to fulfil. The blood of the Lebensborn screams for judgment.*

He spent the next week in hospital and then was discharged after promising to meet with a nurse who would help him set up his treatment schedule. The first thing he did was follow his own advice given to old Hellmuth. Wolfsangel sent a postcard to his family. The next thing he did was ensure his full diagnosis, all information about his treatments, and everything that was registered about him, was sent to the Ullevaal University Hospital in Oslo. This Norwegian hospital specialized in HIV and AIDS treatment.

He stayed in Chesapeake a few more weeks to get started on his drug regime and ensure he was physically strengthening. His thoughts turned to Norway and finishing the mission he started some years ago.

What choice did he have? It was a cliché, but he was starting to grasp its magnitude: In the blink of an eye, his entire life changed. Blackwater gave him no choice but to take a medical leave. Hellmuth took an assignment in Zimbabwe. For the first time in a long time, he felt truly alone.

It was Eirik that pushed him once again to focus on the mission. He had no excuse now not to put his heart and soul into it. He picked up another report and started reading:

March 13 1978 / Psychiatric Hospital 'Fylke, Oslo / Client: Eirik Tijsker (1943) / Dr. R. Thomassen / Conversation # 8: Confrontation past / Olaf Andersen

I've had nightmares, Doctor. After that horrible winter I did not work anymore. My colleagues brought me home; I did not get my life back on track. I could not do it anymore. I just sat there, at home, did and felt nothing or everything. Sometimes I spoke with Marianne and the children in the languages of my past, Norwegian and German. I had to go away from there. I did not talk to anyone, yes, I'm sorry, but I had to go back to Norway. I took the ferry to Larvik, then to Holmestrand, the city of my mother. I was hoping to find something to hold on to, a fixed anchor to fix all other memories. I visited my mother's sister, my aunt, and some cousins. But no, no, no. They do not remember Anna and me. No one! I was so disappointed.

I called Marianne, she asked me to come back, saying, 'They want to forget their past, come right back to the present!'

I said I loved her, but there was something in my head. She said that I should not go back to my own vomit as a dog. Leave the past, Marianne said, and she cried. I told her, I must know, otherwise I will die. I want to be able to forgive them … I cannot go any further, memory fragments pop up, things that I have forgotten. I hear voices and see strange lights. I cannot get at them and remove them!.

In a small rental car, I travelled through Oslo to the north, to Hurdal. There I visited Mirre. Olaf was not there, he was visiting his brother in Drøbak. Mirre was as friendly as she had always been. She told me about my mother and father, and about myself. Doctor Thomassen, she said something about Fylke and your father. She told me she had visited me in the psychiatric hospital. She said, I was 14 years old at the time. I was not happy there, she said. I trembled a lot and wanted to leave. She wanted to pull me out of there but was not allowed. I poured my heart out with Mirre. This was the first time I was able to talk about the death of my daughter. I shared with her my feelings of impotence and sadness, but also my love for my sons and wife. It felt so good to be with her. Until late at night we talked about my past, present and future. That night I slept in her house in a spare bed.

The next day after a great breakfast, I promised to come back soon. I waved like a laughing child and walked to my car with a smile on my face. The bus from Oslo stopped in the distance. I did not see it, but he got out of it, Mirre's husband, Olaf. Suddenly he was sitting next to me in the car, forcing me to drive to …

I do not remember. All I remember now is that this meeting made me almost insane. I can remember that at one point I stopped my car on a gravel road. Outside it was quiet, outside. But inside my head all hell had broken loose. I bit my hands and scratched my skull. I saw images, small pieces of my life, blending into each other, heard voices, penetrating sounds, felt restrained, tied up. Words, sentences, sighs, screams, jumbled chaotically through each other. Then there was oblivion, I did not know anything anymore and stared into an abyss for hours.

Robert Thomassen, Fylke, Oslo

Wolfsangel felt somewhat better knowing that, despite all that happened to him in the last couple of months, he was going to focus on moving forward with his mission. Like Eirik did so many years ago, Wolfsangel decided to return to Norway.

Immediately upon landing in Oslo, Wolfsangel visited the hospital in Ullevaal. As he walked up to the door, he reflected on the fact that it was thirty-three years ago, on a cold December morning, Eirik had visited this same hospital.

After some challenges trying to find the right department on the right floor, he arrived at the nurse's desk and asked politely if he could get his medication.

"Yah, that's not how it works," said the buxom blonde nurse, not even bothering to look up.

Wolfsangel was genuinely confused. "What do you mean? I was told by my doctor in the States that all my information and medication would be sent here."

"I'm sorry. You'll have to wait here. Please stay calm."

"Why?"

The nurse finally looked up at him. "What exactly are you asking me? Why do you have to wait here or why do you have to stay calm?"

Wolfsangel, exasperated, but keeping his voice level, emphasized each word. "Why. Do. I. Have. To. Wait. Here?"

She gave him an exaggerated eye roll. "There is someone who wants to speak to you." At that, the nurse decided she had enough, got up and walked off.

Wolfsangel took some deep breaths and started pacing around the hallway, waiting for somebody to show up. What seemed like an eternity, he was rewarded by the arrival of a petite woman of Asian descent who approached the desk and beckoned him into a side room. It didn't occur to him to wonder how she knew he was the right person.

She still hadn't spoken a word. She pointed to a seat and Wolfsangel dutifully sat down. She was not dressed in a typical medical uniform but wore dark business-style clothing. She pulled up another chair and sat in front of him. She sized him up and finally spoke. "Good morning, I am Linnea. Your illness is my speciality. I will be your support as you journey through this process." Her eyes never left his as she spoke.

For a moment the memory of the eyes of that artist from Sandnes flashed through his head. He struggled to control the rising tide of rage that was building up, knowing that the best approach was to be friendly. "Thank-you, Linnea. However much I appreciate it, I'm not in need of your support. Please. All I really need is for someone to just give me my medicine and treatments so I can be on my way." He tried to give his best appreciative smile and made like he was going to stand up and be on his way.

Linnea was clear, but not rude. "Unfortunately, it does not work like that. In addition to a treatment for your physical condition, you also really need an emotional support system. Your illness is very serious and will involve a good deal of psychological and emotional stress. It will be very overwhelming."

Wolfsangel sighed deeply. Once more he protested. "I'll be fine. I don't have any questions at the moment and I have money to buy the drugs and supplies. Really. I'll be fine."

"I don't think you understand, sir. We believe in a more holistic treatment. The physical part needs to be treated alongside the emotional part. If you are committed to healing, you need to do both parts." Her voice became a bit softer. "Trust me. You will appreciate talking to me about your personal well-being. You will definitely run into a lot of questions that you'll want answers to."

Linnea's beaming smile belied her unrelenting resolve. He stared at her, quite convinced now that Linnea wasn't going to permit him to just walk away and do this on his own. His biggest concern was how this would put a cramp into his plans. The thought of having to organise his plans around her schedule irked him. What irked him even more was, deep down, he knew she was right. He really had no idea what the disease would do to him and the truth was he was alone in this journey.

Wolfsangel sighed deeply again, this time mostly for histrionics. "Fine. Okay. I get it. This will take some getting used to. I'm not the type of person who likes engaging in very personal conversations."

Linnea nodded, her beaming smile hadn't changed a bit. "That response is quite normal for the male species. I assure you, though, you need not be afraid that I will dig too deeply into your emotions. You will always remain in control and share whatever you are willing to."

He nodded, quite certain that she was just trying to placate him. "Okay. So, how is this going to work?"

"Excellent. So, every time you come here for a treatment, you will also have a short session with me. We'll meet in my office which is just down the hall."

"What? Every time?" He gave her a sly look. "What if I simply forget to drop in for my session?"

She returned the look. "Well, this isn't my first time with people like you. You'll find it impossible to have a treatment without a session with me. Besides, I am willing to bet that after a couple of sessions, you'll look forward to talking with me and you won't want to skip any sessions."

She held his eyes and Wolfsangel had to laugh out loud. He, the strong mercenary, was just expected to obey. He was to talk about his emotions and feelings with some strange woman named Linnea. This could be one of the biggest challenge he has ever faced in his lifetime.

Half an hour later, he was standing outside, mulling over his experience with Linnea. He had survived his first session and grudgingly admitted that she was actually not bad to talk to. He lit a cigar and decided that the forty-five minute walk to his hotel would be good exercise for him.

The chic Radisson Blu Plaza Hotel was going to be Wolfsangel's home for the time being. It was located in the centre of the web he had started spinning so many years ago. Wolfsangel knew what Hellmuth would think of this building. It towered high about the cityscape – almost as if it was giving the middle finger to the world. Well, that's how he felt right now. Fuck you, Aids! Fuck you, Hep C. Fuck you, world! I have a mission to fulfil, and I am going to do it! My web is nearly ready to snare its prey.

An elevator took him up to the thirty-third floor. Despite the recent trauma, he was starting to feel a bit more positive about the future. Ready or not, it was time for the world to meet Wolfsangel. It was time for judgment - a special kind of judgment. As a child he had gone to a Protestant church with his mother. He was quite familiar with the theological concept of a God that judged people. He remembered the Biblical story of God calling Adam out by name in the Garden of Eden after Adam and Eve sinned. Even though he did not feel this faith like his mother did, something still remained deep inside of him. All peoples will be judged and will have to account for what they have done.

He stepped inside his room and went straight to the balcony. The view was quite impressive. A movement below caught his eye. He spied what appeared to be a group of young people animatedly engaged in talking and laughing. Wolfsangel's eyes followed them until the group went around the corner. Suddenly and very unexpectedly, he was hit with a dizzy spell. He became lightheaded and nauseous. He staggered back, searching for a place to sit down.

Breathing deeply, he recalled Linnea saying it was normal for him to be feverish and tired at certain moments. She had also told him that he needed to become more aware of how his emotional state affected his thoughts and actions. This disease - he couldn't bring himself to name it - definitely affected his ability to control or channel his emotions. At this moment, he could feel a familiar rage building up in the pit of his stomach. He knew it wouldn't be easily tamed; he had to find ways to release it before it overwhelmed him. In the past, he would find release in his work. Now, he didn't know where to direct his rage. He was afraid that the next person who pissed him off was going to be in big trouble. He began pacing the balcony, feeling trapped like a lion in a cage. After fifteen or so minutes of pacing and doing some breathing exercises, he felt slightly better.

A tentative action plan had already taken shape in his mind when he was resting in Chesapeake. He had carefully considered the advice of Zofia, given so many years ago. Returning to Norway, he was poised to put that plan into action. The first step necessitated a trip to Hurdal. He glanced at his watch. That would be about an hour's drive from his hotel. Thinking there was no reason to delay, he immediately made his way to a car rental place a couple of blocks away from the hotel.

The next morning, he visited the three dead witnesses in his cold homemade bunker in the hills of Hurdal. It took him the better part of an hour to rearrange the room. In the end, he was quite pleased at the result of his handiwork. He then composed a message on the wall with some carmine coloured paint, deliberately leaving the paint pot open nearby. When he was satisfied that everything was just right, he took some photos.

The next step was selecting a vantage point where he would be able to hide himself and watch the action unfold. It didn't take long to find the perfect spot. From this position, he was able to focus his Leica precision binoculars on the bunker and still remain perfectly camouflaged.

He was immensely pleased with himself. Wolfsangel whispered, "Eirik, are you here as well?"

Deep inside, Eirik's emotions stirred from deep shame to fragile pride. There was fear, powerlessness, and hopelessness mixed with anger. Yes, Eirik was there. He hadn't left since Wolfsangel read one of his last journal entries last night:

20 March 1978 / Psychiatric Hospital 'Fylke, Oslo / Client: EirikTijsker (1943) / Dr. R. Thomassen / Conversation # 9: Confrontation past / Finn Undredal

I found the policeman, Finn, in Jessheim. I straightened my back and walked to the last trailer. A large, dirty rusty Dodge Ram was parked in front of it. I knocked on the window next door and took a step back. The inner door was opened and through the screen door a rough silhouette appeared. The man was fat and unshaven. He only wore black trousers and a shirt. I immediately felt a strong sense of disgust.

I even felt an urge to run away but suppressed it. I should not have done that. 'What do you want?' The man asked in a remarkably high voice as he opened the screen door. I smelled old sweat. I asked him about the drowning of my sister in 1950.

'You want to know what happened, but why? Why would you still bother me after so many years? I did not do it; I did not see her walking. Fuck, I've told everyone I'm not guilty of her death in any way, so why don't you just bugger off from my front door!'

He stepped forward and although I could most likely handle him, I felt fear. I heard something or someone crying inside. Finn Undredal turned and shouted: 'Shut the fuck up, yes?! I'm talking to someone!' He turned back to me; I was standing a little lower than him, on a path of cement blocks. Finn Undredal leaned against the door he had closed behind him, radiating raw power.

'So, you're that brat. Let me refresh your memory,' he said slowly in a nasal way, as if he wanted to scratch my brain.' Your mother was a Norwegian bitch, and your sister is dead, drowned.'

Finn Undredal did not have to become physical to hurt. He did this verbally; his words were like sharp knives. He spit out: 'That sister was just a piece of infected human waste, just like you are, and nobody gave a shit about her death. Now, go away, before I pay you back for what you did to me!'

He did not touch me, but it hit me very hard. Blinded by the hateful remarks I staggered like a zombie in the direction of my car. Finn Undredal shouted to me: 'Do not come here again, dick, or I'll break a beer crate on your bastard skull.'

Again, I just drove into a small road and stopped, staring ahead of me. I now knew what I had forgotten, but was it a blessing? Again, waves of pain, guilt, humiliation washed through my mind. I experienced all those bad things again; my own head tortured me now with memories, until darkness embraced me.

/ Robert Thomassen, Fylke, Oslo, 1978

He looked at his watch. It was time. There was no turning back, now. The familiar sense of anticipation and exhilaration began to percolate in his stomach.

PART 2

BACK TO THE BEGINNING OF THE PRESENT

2010, Gripar & Wolfsangel, Hurdal, Norway

Gripar

Gripar stood outside surveying the crime scene. As his eyes swept over the bunker, he caught a slight movement out of the corner of his eye. He looked around, scanning the hills, trees, and distant pastures. For a moment, he had a strange tingling sensation of being watched. Gripar checked his watch; it was 10:55 AM. He always felt a bit out of balance when travelling north of Oslo, towards Lillehammer. He was in familiar territory here - being relatively close to the area where he grew up with his parents and his little brother. Although it was over twenty years ago, the memory became vivid as the pain darted in unexpectedly. His mother, father, and little brother were ripped out of this world because of an accident. He knew better, though. It was because of some drunk driver. To this day, this driver has never been found and brought to justice.

Gripar focussed his thoughts and took another look around but couldn't see anything out of the ordinary. He shrugged it off, deciding that he was just spooked. He took one last look at the police tape to make sure it was secure and then hoisted his six-foot four inch frame into his truck to await the arrival of either the local police or the local press hounds. He knew that the Crime Scene Investigation team would video the scene, collect blood, hairs and other physical evidence, and then with his help they would try to reconstruct the crime.

Peering through the tinted window at the structure, he went over the few facts he knew so far. Someone had gone through an awful lot of work to build this bunker. Whoever it was, must have had time, strength and a compelling reason to do so. Obviously, whoever this Wolfsangel is, he has a story to tell and, for some reason, he has decided that now was the time to tell it.

So much for what he knew, Gripar thought wryly. There were a good many things he didn't know. Like, for example, how long ago did the Wolfsangel start this? Did all three men die around the same time? Did he kill them or did he find some cadavers? Why is he making this exhibition public? And, the biggest question, who the heck is this Wolfsangel? Gripar was becoming more and more curious. What's with this name 'Wolfsangel'? It was certainly an interesting choice to identify oneself. Gripar was somewhat familiar with the symbol Wolfsangel. He knew it could be a rune, a marker in the forest, or it could be used in connection with werewolves. Or, and at this Gripar felt a slight chill come over him as he considered that its most common reference is a Nazi symbol. Maybe this guy is one of those nutjobs from the Nordic Resistance movement.

Clearly, he had way more questions than answers. Stepping out of his truck for fresh air, a sound caught his ear. He estimated there were about three or four vehicles approaching. It was, no doubt, the press hounds of Norway. He heard them making the turn underneath the power lines and then, breaking through the horizon, they made their appearance. Leading the pack was an NRK van from the television station. Following closely behind were two vehicles attempting to overtake the van. One had the orange logo of the NTB (Norwegian News Agency). Gripar wasn't sure who the other one was but suspected it was from the Verden Gangs newspaper. Gripar smiled as watched a small red car struggle to make its way up the track. The car sounded like it was powered by a chainsaw motor. He admired its tenacity and determination to keep up with the big boys. His smile widened as he recognised the driver. It was a reporter from the Hurdal News, the local press. Triumphantly, after a herculean effort, the car arrived, managing to sneak in ahead of the NTB van. They all came to a stop right behind his truck. They had no choice; the monster completely blocked the road. Within seconds its occupants poured out. Despite all the cameras, microphone extensions, voices, and questions, no one dared to cross the tape and enter the bunker.

Gripar positioned himself in front of the entrance, behind the red and white police tape. Due to the nature of his work, he had been on television several times lately. Norway's normally low crime rate had been increasing recently due to drug trafficking and gang problems. During the past four years Gripar had been assigned the investigation of a number of violent and weapon related crimes. These crimes did not usually occur in rural areas like these, but whenever something did happen in Norway, there was intense media coverage. With his tall, handsome appearance Gripar was often a target for cameras and more than once Gripar's remarkable eyes and firm voice had penetrated the TV screens in Norway. The truth was, he really didn't like being positioned in front of a camera or microphone. He especially didn't enjoy seeing himself on television. Gripar much preferred to stay in the background.

One of the NRK people, a tall, angular woman, decided to take the lead. "Gripar! Silje Skar from the NRK. What do you think of what the Wolfsangel has done?"

Gripar knew from the Wolfsangel's letter that the Press was going to be notified. He was less interested in feeding the Press with information and much more interested in determining how the Wolfsangel was planning to use the Press to achieve his goals. "Well, I made it just scarcely twenty minutes ahead of you and have not started the investigation. I am not really able to tell you all that much. You will have to wait till we know more before I can comment."

Undeterred, she continued. “Three witnesses, he calls them, but what did they witness? Do you have any leads or ideas on which way we need to look for answers?”

Gripar was slightly annoyed at this woman’s attempt to insert the press into the investigation and wanted to make a remark to that effect. However, with the cameras and microphones directed to him, Gripar figured he’d better stick to his media trained methods. He told them their guesses were as good as any. He, unfortunately, was not able to say anything about it.

Another voice piped up. “I am Brekke Dahler from the Hurdal Press. I was wondering whether there is some symbolic meaning to the fact that the Three are staring toward the valley, towards Hurdal Verk. Why do you think he staged his exhibition here, of all places, Gripar?”

Gripar sighed inwardly; what’s with all this symbolism and staged exhibition stuff? Obviously, they have been prepped ahead of time. Usually, the press stuck to the simple how, what, when, where, why, and how. He pulled up his shoulders and measured his response. “I am not sure, Brekke, I really don’t know anything about symbols and staged exhibition.”

Dahler pressed on. “In the letter the Wolfsangel sent me, he refers to ‘judging the living and the dead’. Now, Gripar, we both know that this is a line from a religious document. What do you think is the significance of this statement? Are we dealing with a religious fanatic?”

As Gripar listened intently, he saw how the media was being set up and played with. Dahler no doubt knew, just like him, that the sentence “to judge the living and the dead” came from a religious document called ‘the Apostles Creed’. It was an ancient document that many churches in Norway were very familiar with. Gripar responded, “At this time, it is too early to tell what kind of a person we are dealing with and what his or her intentions are. What is clear, though, is that there are three dead people in this bunker. This investigation will be treated as a homicide investigation, and we will do everything we can to identify the killer and ensure that justice is done.” With that, Gripar hoped to signal the end of the interview.

The reporters weren't ready to be brushed off so easily. They kept peppering him with questions. Gripar eventually noticed out of the corner of eye a solidly built man pushing his way through the gaggle of reporters. Even though the man wasn't wearing a uniform, Gripar could tell that he was a police officer just by the way he carried himself. Since the crime scene was in this district, Gripar was expecting a police officer from the Romerike Police District to eventually arrive. The man, dressed in jeans and a blazer, strode right up to Gripar and stuck out his hand. Gripar was still processing the appearance of this man and wondering who exactly this guy was.

The man, while fifteen or so centimeters shorter than Gripar, was considerably more muscular. He waited with his hand extended. "Hi, I am Aksel Sloss from the PST. You're probably expecting a Politi from Romerike, but I was instructed to come up here and give you a hand." He pointed to the press. "Obviously, you need it." Gripar, realising that he hadn't responded yet, quickly grabbed the man's hand and shook it.

As Gripar was considering whether Sloss' last comment was sarcastic or serious, Silje Skar recognised the new guy and shouted, "Hey, Mr Sloss! Didn't you serve with the Beredskapstroppen (Police Tactical Unit of the Norwegian Police Service)? Why are they involved with this?"

Sloss cleared his throat. Gripar had to take a second look because he was positive that the man's chest swelled a bit as he answered. "Well, madam, you have a good memory. Seven years ago, I led the tact team that rescued a large group of people from the clutches of malicious Albanians. It was quite the event." There was a pause. "Yes, I miss those days, but I am no longer with the Beredskapstroppen. I've been asked to take the lead in this investigation. Now, if you'll please excuse us, we must get started on our investigation."

Gripar, still trying to make sense of why the PST was involved, suggested that the two of them sit in his truck for a moment to talk. As they made their way, Gripar could hear one of the reporters talking to her camera: "The police are at a loss about the bunker behind us. While we can't get a shot of inside the bunker, earlier today we did receive some morbid pictures which show three bodies displayed on a wooden bench. We know for sure that someone took three corpses and arranged them in a very specific way. Whether this person was also the killer, we don't know as yet. We do know the name of the person responsible for the display. He, or she, signed off as The Wolfsangel, but gave no reasons for this display, this exhibition …"

When the truck door was closed and the reporters couldn't hear anything, Gripar turned to Sloss and asked him why the PST was involved in this case.

Sloss looked at him as if he was completely daft. "Well, of course, this whole thing is moving at a fast pace. You probably haven't been briefed on this yet, but the Ministry of Justice is concerned with the implications that the Nordic Resistance Movement may be behind this. I've been asked to take over."

Gripar raised his eyebrows. He already started to dislike this guy. Sloss caught that and shrugged his shoulders. "You might not like that, but that's the way it is. The Wolfsangel logo that accompanied the letter? Well, you do know, don't you, that the precursor of the Nordic Resistance Movement was the White Aryan Resistance Movement and its logo contains the wolfsangel?"

Gripar rubbed his chin thoughtfully. "Nothing about this case is normal and nothing would surprise me. If this is somehow tied to neo-Nazism, we clearly have a bigger problem than I had imagined. At the same time, if these three were killed by the same person, we could have a serial killer on the loose."

Sloss nodded. "Well, that's what we are here to figure out. Now, about you. Why are you specifically involved with this? I understand that you were sent a note outlining the details of this … this … whatever you want to call it?" He waved his hand in the direction of the bunker.

Gripar showed him the note. Sloss read through it. "Go find the three. That seems very strange. It's almost like he is taunting you. How hard can it be to identify three dead people? What's the catch?"

Gripar looked at the pictures again. "I'm not sure, but certainly I am also interested in finding the killer."

"Well, that's fine. You can work that angle and figure out who those three people are. I'll start working on the link to the NRM." Sloss took some pictures of the note with his phone and, stepping out, he made a show of sizing up the truck. Turning to Gripar, "Compensating for something?"

Gripar watched him stride back to his car. That guy really rubbed him the wrong way. As he reached over to start his truck, he spied the envelope with Wolfsangel's message inside. There was a second sheet of paper in it. He was happy he didn't share that message with Sloss. He picked it up and read it again. It contained the following handwritten sentences:

Gripar, if you persist, you'll find the Hurdal Three will answer these three questions:

> Why are the Tyskerbarn demanding justice?
>
> Is Eirik Tijsker still alive?
>
> Who killed your parents?

Wolfsangel

It was all going according to plan. Wolfsangel couldn't keep the smile off his face as he studied the scene from his hiding spot overlooking the bunker. His smile deepened as his binoculars caught Gripar through the truck window reading a hand-written note. He wondered what Gripar was thinking. He was very certain the Inspector had not seen anything like that in all the years he was a police officer and probably would need time to process this whole event. However, as much as Gripar would want to keep all this under wraps in order to minimise any interference, Wolfsangel was not going to let that happen. All the major Norwegian media outlets were on his notification list. There would be no secrets kept from the public.

By the time the forensic team showed up three quarters of an hour later, he had seen enough. It was time to leave. He cleared everything up into his backpack, swung it over his shoulders and leisurely strolled away. Following a faded path, he eventually found his motorcycle safety chained and locked to a hefty tree.

Later that evening, back at the hotel, Wolfsangel caught the tail end of a crime analysis program which contained a segment on the Hurdal Three. The host had a panel of art experts providing their analysis of the three figures on the bench. One of them, a friendly-looking, spectacled man, was saying in a rather high-pitched voice, "It is like a language, from left to right, a penetrating story. Look, the first one is standing upright, with his muscled arms crossed, his fists pumping up his biceps. I feel strongly that he was proud and haughty, like the Biblical Lamech. Those fat lips seem to mock. He was tough, hardcore, and maybe a little psychopathic. After so many years, he seems to be saying, 'I don't care about anything.'"

Wolfsangel nodded, impressed at how his artistic skills accurately conveyed a specific impression. When the second member of the panel was introduced, Wolfsagel's jaw dropped. He found himself staring at the woman from Stavanger. He hadn't thought about her since his conversation with Hellmuth. So, her name is Kjersti Hurum and her specialty was sculpting. He noticed that she still wore those thick glasses. Yes, it was the woman of light! He leaned forward, eager to hear what she had to say.

She agreed with the previous panel member and went on. "The second man, the portly one, seems shocked. See him sitting there, slumped. He keeps his face down, but his bulging eyes seem to look up. Look, one leg is crossed over the other. And then those hands! His hands are raised up to the height of his shoulders, open to the sky, just as if he is saying, 'I couldn't help it; it was also a mystery to me. You would have done the same if you had been in my place. Those things just happen, right? I can hear him saying that.'"

The third expert, an elderly woman dressed in trendy teen-style clothes with spiked bleached hair spoke up. "Top shelf analysis", she said. "That dude definitely has the look of an unscrupulous executioner. He looks capable of slowly inserting a hot needle into the anus of his victim, and then looking at him as if he does not like it either, but yeah, shit happens. So to speak." Wolfsangel cringed at the sound of her laughter. Nobody joined her, though, which slightly disappointed Wolfsangel because he would have loved to hear the sound of Kjersti's laughter again.

The panel anchor brought their attention to the third corpse, which was more difficult to describe. He pointed out that it leaned more forward than the other two. The left arm was on his left knee, hand open upwards. His right hand supported his chin. The lower eyelids hung low and heavy so that the bulged eyes demanded all attention. On the back of his head sat a hat.

The bespectacled man asked, "Is that not a vintage Fedora gray slit hat? See the small brim and notice how typically the hat is placed on the back half of his skull. He looks like the famous Thinker."

Kjersti nodded. "Yes, that thinker is a really creepy version of the original. He looks kind of like a Nazi doctor of Auschwitz."

Wolfsangel felt Eirik's approval. The plan was working. The photographs of the three men of Hurdal went viral as did the accompanying news report. Wolfsangel spent the whole evening surveying the extent to which the story made its way onto major news outlets and internet sites. It had been a long time coming, but he felt a kind of peace in his troubled heart. Eirik's time had come.

"Well, Gripar, unbeknownst to you, another detective journey has started for you," he said aloud. "I will be both your guide and your follower and together we will find him. We will find him either dead or alive." He could feel excitement building inside. He wondered if it was because the day had gone so well or it was because he got the opportunity to see Kjersti again. He decided it was probably both.

He got up and started pacing the room. He felt antsy, like all of his nerve endings were randomly firing. He saw his folder and rummaged through the stack until he found the one he was looking for:

March 27, 1978 / Psychiatric Hospital 'Fylke, Oslo / Client: Eirik Tijsker (1943) / Dr. R. Thomassen / Conversation # 10: How Eirik returned to Fylke

R,T.: I spoke with my client Eirik again. He has opened my eyes to great injustice. Until then I had had a lot of respect for my father, but when I heard these stories and investigated the facts, this disappeared altogether. I regularly visited Eirik in his room when he was in bad shape. He told me why he had gone to Oslo that night, determined to go to Oslo University. I recorded it, he said the following.

Eirik: 'I turned on the car radio for some distraction. I could use that after my conversation with Finn Undredal. It was news time, news from Norway, my country.' I listened to a speech, live, kept in the university and I froze.'

R.T.: I remembered that night, because I had sat there on December 10, 1977, at the University Festival Hall in Oslo. Aase Lionæs, chairman of the Norwegian Nobel Committee, gave a speech because of the Nobel Peace Prize. He spoke of a clear and simple 'Say No' to violence, torture and terrorism, and an equally clear and unconditional 'Yes' for the defence of human dignity and human rights. The core of his story was: 'That we believe in our lives, in human dignity.' I thought it was a good story and said so too. Eirik agreed but said the Lebensborn were apparently a blind spot for Norway.

Eirik: 'The speaker was talking about suffering. At that moment, in despair, I pulled my hair hard, I could not reach anything. Something felt so, so, so unfair. I suddenly made the conclusion that I had to go there; this radio broadcast was live from the university? I knew where that was and drove south in some kind of dream, determined to tell the Nobel Committee about the Lebensborn and the other Tyskerbarn. I felt excited. They would listen to me.

I drove into the city of Oslo on the E6 but missed the Ulven exit and went straight to the heart of the city. I became completely disoriented. I kept going and going, left, right, straight, to the ports, back, to the centre, to the north. In the end, I ran out of fuel when I found myself close to the Ullevaal stadium, not far from the university. I got out of my car, confused, and went for a walk. I knew it was not far, maybe fifteen minutes.

Then I lost my mind. I heard voices, saw appearances of people from my past: saw Olaf lying on my mother, laughing at Finn Undredal, and my sister Esther and daughter Anna Esther looking at me through the ice. Suddenly there was a group of women in front of me. They were bald, with bloody stripes on their skulls. They looked at me, no feeling in their eyes, completely dead. The voices in my head screamed in devilish fear. Then a cold, heartless voice sounded over everything: 'We spat your mother as she buried her child, we pissed on her grave. Nur Abschaum. Will rats ever become pets?'

I collapsed, grabbed my head, covering my ears, but the voice continued: 'Genetically inferior, infected human waste. Kill yourself, then we will not have to see you anymore. You're shit!'

It became too much for me. I rolled aside, shouted my desperation to heaven and felt myself sinking into a hell of self-hatred. I gave up, then, and accepted my guilt. 'Take my life as an offering … '

R.T.: The cold penetrated him deeply, down to his innermost interior. I know how it continued. Early in the morning a few children found him rolled up, as if to protect himself, on the cold corner of Hasselhaug and Prestegårdsveien. They had noticed that he was still alive. They warned the people at the big gray house on the corner, who called the hospital. The ambulance first brought him to the Oslo University Hospital. Their new patient hallucinated and was very scared. The hospital was able to find out who he was from the wallet that Eirik carried with him. Without much difficulty, they found out the phone number of his wife. She and their children came to visit at Christmas when he had just moved to the psychiatric hospital Fylke. Eirik did not have to be told anything … he knew this building. Recently he asked me: 'Am I back in hell, doctor? Who will help me? Who will tell the truth to Norway, the truth of the Lebensborn children?'

Robert Thomassen, Fylke, Oslo

June 28, 2010

Oslo

Gripar

Yesterday was Sunday. Gripar didn't always enjoy Sundays. When he was younger, he saw Sunday as an intrusion into his daily schedule. His parents were quite religious, and Sundays were always fenced in with rules and rituals. The normal day-to-day routines were put on hold and, growing up, Gripar was always impatient for Monday morning to arrive. Now that he was older and more mature, he really enjoyed the day. If he wasn't scheduled to work on the day of the Lord, he would attend a service at the church near his flat and then usually engage in some service work.

Yesterday was one of those days. Gripar's mouth watered as remembered the spicy scents that had floated through the brick church that stood on a hill near Ulven, in the eastern part of Oslo. The sauce had bubbled on the stove. Every Sunday a number of churches organize a kitchen to feed the poor of Oslo. Their food, understandably, was very popular. Yesterday, Christians from different churches had gathered together in the improvised kitchen of the Østre Aker Kirke. This crew had worked hard on the preparation of Norwegian meatballs with seasoned cream sauce.

Gripar had worn a hairnet as a barrier between his dark curly long hair and the food. He and a few others had made the balls, while others had prepared vegetables and cut bread into pieces. At about half past five in the afternoon they were ready to go to various places in the city's core to distribute food. Before they went, they had gathered for a preparation talk, a biblical 'pep talk', and prayer. Gripar had ridden in an old battered van of the intercultural church; together with three others he had managed to squeeze in the back, between the pots and pans. Gripar couldn't imagine his life without the Sunday.

Certainly the death of his parents and his brother brought an enormous existential crisis in his life, but as he continued to work through that event, he came to realise that his faith was a significant anchor he relied on. But, like Mr. John Wemmick in Dickens' *Great Expectations*, Odd Gripar had an emotional drawbridge that kept his work life and his personal life quite separate.

Today was Monday. Gripar was standing in front of the Kripos headquarters at Bryn. He had always thought the building looked, ironically, too much like a jail – with all the bars in front of the rather small windows. He had arrived just before seven o'clock this morning, a half hour prior to his usual arrival time. That's because this morning, Gripar felt particularly refreshed and rather excited for the day to start. He was to meet his supervisor, Chief Inspector Walter Svendsen to go with him what he had learned so far about the case.

He got right down to the business of picking up where he had left off organising the case of the Hurdal Three on a large portable whiteboard. He had originally set this up in his office, but at Svendsen's suggestion, moved the whiteboard into one of the consulting rooms where there would be more space. In addition to the crime scene pictures, Gripar displayed on the board the various media reports that had burst out during the weekend. He also added in some notes that he had drawn up.

"Well, this is not going to be a quiet case. It's going to be a media show. This Wolfsangel guy has obviously taken his time to put this display together for a purpose." Gripar pored over the crime scene photos.

Svendsen glanced at him. "Well, you need to proceed quickly but cautiously because it won't be long before this case becomes very difficult to manage. It's not a bad thing that the PST is involved. It will give us some more resources to work with."

Gripar grunted.

Svendsen seemingly ignored that noise as he continued to pore over the display. "You know, I don't think I've ever seen anything like this. You're right. Everything looks very deliberate and intentional. I don't believe that we are dealing with a serial killer here. I am fairly confident there's nobody else in imminent danger."

Gripar nodded. "Walter. There is something else that is important here. I also received a personal note from the Wolfsangel. I'm not sure what to make of it." He pulled the paper from his pocket and passed it on to Svendsen. Svendsen took a moment to read it, his face expressionless.

"Hmmm. The Tyskerbarn. Justice. Eirik Tijsker. Your parents. What do you make of that?" Svendsen gave back the paper and took off his glasses. He stared at Gripar.

Gripar shrugged. "I don't know. I guess that is something we need to find out."

Svendsen paced back and forth, deep in thought. "Gripar, I must be honest. I'm concerned that you are being dragged personally and deliberately into this mystery. What's all this got to do with your parents?"

Gripar shrugged. "I absolutely have no idea. I think, though, I should follow this through. Carefully, of course. There must be a reason for the personal interest in me."

Svendsen took a moment to consider this. Finally, he nodded. "Okay. I'll agree. For now. Please be careful and keep me up to speed." With that, Svendsen took a final look at the whiteboard and strode out of the office.

Gripar studied the picture of the three men of Hurdal. They stared back at him, defiantly mocking him.

Steinkjergata, Trondheim

Wolfsangel

"Okay, Linnea, you bitch. You're right."

It was early Monday morning and he felt absolutely miserable - emotionally and physically. He had another listless sleep. It consisted of periods where he was tossing and turning, wide awake, punctuated with periods of sleep where he was entombed in horrific nightmares, reliving the rape and humiliation.

At four o'clock, he was finished trying to fool himself into thinking he could fall into a deep, restful sleep. He got up and went to the bathroom to splash some water on his face. He looked in the mirror and saw a stranger staring back at him. The last time he talked with Linnea, she had told him that the disease was doing something with his brain. She warned him that he won't feel normal for a while until the drug protocol starts to kick in. He shook his head, trying to avoid stoking the anger that was on the verge of bursting into flames. Wolfsangel had fought against the odds in many battles over the years and was determined that he was going to win this one too. He slipped on a coat and decided to take a walk.

The sun was already rising at this time of the morning as he walked for an hour through the city. Despite his best efforts to contain it, a fire of rage was still smouldering within him. He found himself hoping that somebody would attempt to rob him so that he could demolish that person. Nobody obliged him and the Wolfsangel had to release the pent-up tiger fury by taking it out on the punching bag in the hotel's training room.

Sufficiently calm, he headed back to his room and surfed the net for the Wolfsangel story. He was pleasantly surprised to come across an article written by Zofia Hurum. He remembered her advice and reflected that really, without her input, none of this would be going as well as it was. He also remembered her laugh and how it just brightened his day. As he glanced through the article, he was handed a second surprise. Another name from the past appeared: Stein Bratt, student of History and Political Science. Wolfsangel was surprised to find out that Stein had become heavily involved with the neo-Nazis. His interest peaked as he read through the article. Stein was hoping to marshal his neo-Nazi troops into holding a massive demonstration in support of the Wolfsangel. He scoffed. A bunch of losers trying to hold a feeble demonstration. They're just like the Norwegian Death Metal bands trying to stir up crowds into a frenzy through cowardly violence.

Wolfsangel paused to consider. This just might be the vehicle he needed to implement the next step of his plan. Maybe he ought to take a trip out to Trondheim and pay the student of history and political science a visit. As he leaned back in his chair to consider this, he felt a wave of fatigue wash over him. He cursed. Loudly.

He had prided himself on keeping in peak physical and mental shape. His body and his mind were one - at least when he was at work. Now, there was this disease ravaging through his body and he felt entirely helpless. He was at the mercy of doctors, nurses, and support counsellors. He closed his eyes. He definitely felt tired as his mind started drifting. A headache was building up, threatening to debilitate him. His body was abandoning him and becoming weaker. Linnea had warned him.

He tried to shrug off the fatigue. Glancing at his watch, he realized that it was high time to take his medication. He stood up, loathing his weakness. He couldn't stand the fact that there were some foreign substances percolating in *his* body. "No!" He shouted and paced back and forth on the soft carpet. "No, you will not take me down. You will not win. Never!" He banged his fist on the desk and his computer jumped a few inches in the air. He felt caged again. As he paced, another sensation asserted itself - his bladder demanded that it be relieved. It was the third time since waking up. It was a side-effect of the medication. On the way to the bathroom, his vision blurred and he had to sit down. What kind of a weakling was he? He had to stop and rest on the way to take a piss.

As he waited a moment for his vision to stabilize, he firmed up his decision to go to Trondheim and talk to Stein. After answering his bladder's call and swallowing his medication, he sat down again at his computer to search for flights leaving Oslo and arriving in Trondheim later today. There was nothing from Oslo to Trondheim that would work, so he widened his search to Sandefjord departures. He breathed a sigh of relief when he found a Wideroe Dash-8 flight arriving in Trondheim later this afternoon. That's okay, he thought, that will give the medication a chance to do its thing.

After laying down for slightly less than an hour, Wolfsangel felt much better - more in control. He found his backpack and grabbed a few things he was going to need. Within fifteen minutes he was headed down the elevator to the hotel's underground garage. There he stored a BMW S1000RR he had just recently rented. Yes, this was a not-so-subtle attempt to assert his manliness in the face of his disease. He didn't care. As he exited the elevator into the dimly lit basement, he caught a glimpse of white and blue and his adrenaline levels started to escalate at the thought of 200 hp of raw power just waiting to be unleashed on the 118 km trip from Oslo to Sandefjord. He took a deep breath, mounted the bike, turned the key, and as the machine roared to life, he felt in control again. He knew who he was.

He made a quick pit-stop at the hospital. He was scheduled to check in with Linnea. He could tell that she wasn't fooled by his insistence that he felt fine - strong as an ox, even. Between the quick visit with Linnea, the road trip, and the flight, he managed to arrive in Trondheim in good time to accomplish what he set out. It was just after two o'clock and so far, the Wolfsangel was feeling great. His plan was unfolding nicely at this point. He walked out the terminal and headed to the seashore. He took in lungful's of fresh sea air. Pulling out his phone, he called Stein Bratt.

"Stein, this is Wolfsangel. I am at the Trondheim airport and would like to speak to you."

A loud noise assaulted his eardrum and Wolfsangel surmised that Stein had dropped his phone. Probably never expected to meet up with me again. After some apparent fumbling, a smiling voice answered, "Cool, dude. Yes. Let's meet. I'll see you in our den at the Steinkjergata. I am on my way bro." Immediately he broke off the conversation. That was weird. It was a pretty short conversation for two people who hadn't seen each other in a while.

He found the taxi queue and requested a ride to downtown Trondheim. It was going to be a thirty-minute drive to the Steinkjergeta on Frostaveien street. He felt fortunate to secure a Sami driver who knew all about the city. Wolfsangel figured this was a good omen – after all, he could relate to the Sami people. They were the reindeer holders of the north. They were survivors in the midst of a country that had turned their backs on them. Yes, we are kindred spirits, the Wolfsangel thought. When he asked about the local Neo Nazis, the driver smirked. "Those guys think too much of themselves. They think they are the original Norwegians! They don't know us, Sami; we are more Nordic than any of them!" The driver became more animated. "They dwell in violence. I have no idea what they really want. All I know about them is negative, they are always fighting. They are intolerant to everyone."

Wolfsangel agreed. "If you ask me, the neo-Nazis are complete morons." He meant what he said. He felt no connection at all to neo-Nazis; no sympathy, no nothing. Nevertheless, he saw an opportunity to use them in his plan. The way he saw it, he could harness their energy, just like a horse. He needed all kinds of energy aimed at the same goal, energy that he might not always have in the future. He knew there were people riding the wave he had caused, but he was the mastermind behind it all. He was in control, not them.

He looked out the window as the driver deftly maneuvered his cab through the streets of downtown Trondheim.

"We're almost there," the driver reported. "If you're looking for the neo-Nazis, their headquarters is indeed at Steinkjergata, just outside the city center." He drove out of the inner city over the Innherredsveien, past the Lamoen church and stopped at a Shell petrol station on the right side of the road. The driver pointed to the other side of the roadway. "Over there. Behind those bushes is their area. There was a building at first, but that was burnt down. There is still a fixed-up remnant of a school or something, some containers, old cars and junk. I don't understand why the police or the city would allow the scum to set up like this. It's kind of a free state, doing whatever they want without impunity. I'm sure they do drugs and a lot more shit. Just be careful."

Wolfsangel nodded. "Thanks. Here is your payment, and if you have time to wait, you can take me back to the airport later. I'll also pay for the time you have to wait. If I'm not back after an hour, you call the police, okay?"

The driver shrugged. "Okay, that's fine. I'll wait here."

Wolfsangel crossed the street and walked around the grounds until he found a dark alley at the back. He started walking down the alley, cautiously, until he came to a structure that looked like a conglomeration of hurriedly constructed buildings leaning next to each other. The walls were covered in graffiti. One of these days he was going to do some research and figure out what that graffiti was all about. He was fascinated that these seemingly random shapes actually held meaning.

At the end of the building, Wolfsangel came across an old bus parked alongside six vintage motorcycles. He looked carefully around the corner and sighed in relief. He was now sure he had the right address. He could see the morons further up the street. Three of them were sitting on old chairs, dressed in faded green military T-shirts and covered with tattoos. A few girls with straight blond hair and faces made up with goth-style black makeup leaned against the wall. Ah yes, the apex of Hitler's Aryan race. They did not talk to each other but looked around with indifferent and bored gazes. Wolfsangel could sense the violence percolating from deep within the scene. The heavily tattooed men shifted around like a pack of feral dogs looking for trouble.

Wolfsangel felt no fear. Years of military training enabled him to quickly assess the situation and move accordingly. Not wanting to draw attention to himself, he withdrew carefully, put on dark sunglasses and flipped his hood over his head. He took a pen and a piece of paper from his backpack and wrote a note. 'I am looking for Stein Bratt. I want to talk to him. Someone who knows who he is, immediately gets a 1000 Crown bill.' He signed with a wolfsangel icon and looked around for someone who could help him deliver that note to the right person.

It did not take long for someone to show up. A girl walked towards him. As she drew nearer, he realised that she was probably a lot younger than she looked. Her face was pockmarked with signs of drug addiction and her skin appeared leathery. She was trying to walk somewhat suggestively but was failing miserably and embarrassingly. She stopped in front of him and stared at her hands. With difficulty she spoke, as if her tongue was too heavy, "Hey, there. You looking for a good time? I'm your woman."

Wolfsangel doubted that. His nose caught the stench of bad breath, body odour, and urine wafting from her body. He took out a 500-crown bill and ripped it in half. He handed her one half with his note and told her, "The only good time I want involves you bringing this note over there and giving it to the smartest-looking neo-Nazi. I know that might be a challenge to find, but do your best. Then walk back here and I'll give you the other half of this bill."

The girl thought about it for a moment, probably deciding whether or not to trust him and then weighing the need for cash versus the potential for getting beat up and abused by that crowd. Wolfsangel watched her and idly wondered how many blow jobs she would have to do in order to make 500 crowns. She took a deep breath, took the half bill and the note, and walked towards the group. She moved quickly and before the heavily tattooed men realized it, she stood in their midst. She quickly scanned the faces; Wolfsangel could see that she was an experienced observer. A man sat next to the doorway on the sidewalk, he seemed a little shorter than the others. The girl apparently felt that he was different, perhaps a bit more intelligent. She gave him the note and ran back to Wolfsangel, ignoring the offers the neo-Nazis hurled at her, promises of a good time. Wolfsangel was mildly impressed at how she managed to evade their attempts to grab her. She arrived slightly out of breath but immediately after Wolfsangel gave her the second half of the bill, she quickly darted away through the alley behind him.

Wolfsangel had shown himself; now it was a matter of time. He walked past the old bus, until he stood between a few garbage containers. There he could see the men and they could see him. He saw the man on the sidewalk reading the note; he read it aloud to the others. They laughed. The biggest one had a bushy dark beard and his bare arms were fully tattooed. He wore some kind of black uniform hat. Wolfsangel's upper lip curled up, he felt carefree. They seemed intimidating; perhaps they thought that their hatred would give them strength, that they would be invincible. But a wolf grown up in the wild always wins against his tame brothers.

Wolfsangel walked back a few steps; they followed him, further between the containers. He turned around and stood still.

"I have an appointment with Stein Bratt," Wolfsangel said. "I just got him on the phone, do you know where he is? We know each other."

"We know who Stein is, but it's you we do not know."

One of the neo-Nazis had walked around and went behind Wolfsangel. He crept closer to him, a tough two-meter piece of steel. Wolfsangel knew that this crowd loved fighting. Probably they love to beat people, hard, painful and bloody. They know how to fight dirty with hard kicks to the testicles and the head. Well, he had also learned to fight that way, with hard muscular strength, giving the opponent no chance. The Foreign Legion had given him a superior education a few years ago. Real fighting, he knew, is not a sport; it is in the first place to ensure the aggressor has absolutely no control over the situation and after that ensure he will never get it.

It must have been his last year in the Legion when Wolfsangel was stationed in an Asian country. At first, he had no interest in Tai Chi, the funny movements that old people made in the park. But then he met an instructor who taught Tai Chi Chuan as a martial arts. Wolfsangel was initially skeptical and asked him to prove the value of that sport by challenging the Tai Chi Chuan fighter. His first shock came when his opponent did not take a special pose for the fight; he stood there, calm and relaxed. His second shock came when Wolfsangel attacked, the man first followed the flow of his offensive energy and then used it to take him back. Wolfsangel was tough and hardened, but the Tai Chi Chuan instructor proved to be a much better fighter, his techniques were superior to the muscle strength of Wolfsangel. This convinced him to take a few lessons from this instructor. His third shock was that he actually had talent for this martial art. Even at the most exciting moments of a fight, mind and muscle were relaxed and during the fight the attackers and audience became usually surprised by the beauty of human agility and the lack of aggression.

That's why he was ready for an attack, although it did not look like that at all. Suddenly the goon behind him leaped forward. He put his arm around Wolfsangel's neck and choked him. Wolfsangel hardly moved, he bowed slightly and grabbed the fingers of his attacker. Then he quickly circled, bent back the fingers, seemingly to startle the attacker. Within a second, the hand, rotated, was on the back of the attacker and his head was forced aside. Wolfsangel handed out a few quick punches and blows with his free hand, focusing on a number of essential points on the body. The strong neo-Nazi transformed into a floppy sack of coffee beans. He collapsed on the street.

Wolfsangel's body relaxed, he acted like he was surprised to see the sudden appearance of the body on the street. Yet he had used a lot of energy and hoped he would not have to fight again. One of the men pulled a knife.

At that moment, the goons were distracted by the sound of a Harley engine rumbling onto the scene. The bike came to a stop and Stein tried to put down the kickstand. He was having a tough time with that and eventually gave up and leaned the bike against the container. He turned around unsteadily, took his helmet off, and looked at Wolfsangel. "Hey wolfman, good to see you again."

Wolfsangel hid his shock at how much Stein had changed. When they last met, Stein looked like a typical preppy student. He was clean-shaven, well-dressed, and had an air about him that bordered on arrogance. The Stein in front of him looked, well ... like a typical neo-Nazi scum. His hair was long and stringy. He looked gaunt in the face. There were a couple of tattoos peeking out from under his shirt sleeve.

He giggled as he glanced at the guy on the ground. He shook his head. "Men, my fault. I ... I was ... had ... used, you know?" Looking at the others, "I should not have agreed to meet with him here, sorry. However, that man there can be trusted. I know him well, leave me alone with him. I will explain it later, seriously." The other men picked up their groggy comrade and threw him on an old mattress.

Stein turned to Wolfsangel. "Good to see you again, Wolfsangel. Cool. Sorry for this stupid mix-up, I wasn't thinking straight. My mistake. Anyway, how the hell are you?"

"I'm doing ok. I'm taking some time off to search for my friend. Remember me talking about him?"

Stein nodded.

"And, do you remember us talking about Holmestrand and Quisling?"

"Uh, yes. Of course. How can I forget."

Wolfsangel was suspicious that Stein had no remembrance of that conversation. "I've come to see you because I have an idea that will help both you and me. You want a demonstration, right? I read that somewhere."

Now colour returned to Stein's face, he brightened up. "Yes, man, I want action. We love action here in Trondheim. Do you know our name, 'Den Norske Motstandsbevegelsen', the Norwegian resistance movement?" At that, Stein pulled out a half-smoked joint, lit it, and took a deep draught. He offered to share with Wolfsangel but was politely rebuffed.

Wolfsangel wondered if he made the right decision in coming here to work with Stein. "Let's go for a walk and let me explain to you how I can help you with organising the biggest demonstration you've ever had."

Stein nodded his head enthusiastically, attempting to take a drag at the same time. "Sounds cool, dude! Let's go for that walk." Then, pointing to one of the guys standing by, "Can I take Fogh here with us. He's great at organising?"

Wolfsangel nodded and the three of them walked down Frostaveien street while Wolfsangel broadened his ideas. After about forty-five minutes or so, Wolfsangel was satisfied that Stein and Fogh understood what he needed them to do. He was pleased that he hadn't misjudged Stein after all. It turned out relatively easy to get him to do what he wanted. All he had to do was stoke Stein's ego.

By the time he arrived back at his starting point, Wolfsangel was utterly relieved to find the Sami and his taxi were still there. Within an hour, Wolfsangel plopped in his seat on the plane back to Oslo. He felt totally wrecked. He clearly had asked too much of his body. "Sorry, Linnea."

But Wolfsangel's connecting motorcycle ride was not as successful an experience as this morning. He slowly and hesitantly drove back to his hotel. During the ride he had to stop regularly to puke. He had a throbbing migraine and mixed feelings about his neo-Nazi improvisation. Neo-Nazis, Black Metal, Odinism, all that damned nonsense. Under the masks of civilization, all people can be leeches.

Deep in the night he arrived back at his hotel room, where he crashed on his bed within seconds.

June 30, 2010

Gripar

The sun was reluctantly completing its journey towards the horizon. In the summer, while the city of Oslo enjoyed the lengthy daylight hours, most generally also welcomed the evening. Gripar, just back from a short jog and a shower, sat behind two screens.

He mulled over the note that the Wolfsangel meant for him personally. Who was Eirik Tijsker? What does he have to do with the Tyskerbarn? And finally, what does the death of his parents have anything to do with this? He had to admit to himself he was troubled by this. Gripar had taken great pains to keep his personal life and work life completely separate. Somebody was trying to meld the two. And for what purpose? He racked his brain trying to figure out a connection between his family and either the Wolfsangel or Eirik Tijsker. He couldn't come up with anything.

He thought about his parents. He held an unwavering belief that justice will eventually be done. He had known that the death of his parents and brother was not simply an accident. He vividly remembered the day a police officer stopped past his aunt's place to let him know that his dad's driving skills were likely not to blame for the accident. They analysed the scene and realised that his parents' car could have been driven off the road by another vehicle whose driver was either drunk or asleep at the wheel.

Gripar knew in his heart of hearts that somebody else was responsible. Some person made the decision to get behind the wheel of a vehicle in spite of the fact they were not capable of driving safely. After the visit of the police officer, Gripar headed out to the scene of the accident. His deepest desire was for that person to come forward, either forcibly or voluntarily, and own their actions. That was the only way justice could be done.

This note from the Wolfsangel brought up some strong, mixed feelings. Gripar leaned back in his chair. Even though it had been so long ago, a deep sadness threatened to overwhelm him at all the losses that came with this event. He was never given the opportunity to grow older with his parents and his brother. There was also guilt in realising that all these years had passed without any justice. What was he waiting for? Was he just expecting that the person responsible would be discovered or turn himself in? Was he just expecting justice to somehow happen? He really never considered until recently that this was a passive way of thinking. Who would find this driver? Who would ensure justice was being done? Maybe he should do some digging into the records - the police report, for starters - to see if there were any clues that were missed.

His reverie was interrupted by the ringing of his phone. He glanced at the screen and groaned. It was Sloss. He was tempted to let it go to voicemail but his conscience wouldn't let him. He probably should work on that.

"Gripar. Intelligence sources have told me that the neo-Nazis in Trondheim are up to something. Has to do with the Wolfsangel and the Tyskerbarn."

"Oh. What have you heard? What are they up to?"

"We're not sure yet. There is an internet-based news journal called *The Foreigner* that put out an article a couple of weeks ago highlighting some background info on the group. It was written by a reporter named Hurum. I guess she got a lot of her information from some guy named Stein Bratt. Bratt is a well-known neo-Nazi."

Gripar wasn't sure why he was being told this. It was made very clear by Sloss that he was going to handle the neo-Nazi end of things. "Ummm … okay. I'm not sure why you are telling me this? Do you want me to do something with this information?"

There was an exasperated sigh on the other end. "Listen, I'm getting to that. So, just this morning, that same news journal had an article written by the same reporter that connected this Wolfsangel guy with the Tyskerbarn and the neo-Nazis."

Gripar was sure he figured out what Sloss was getting at. However, he decided not to make any assumptions. "Okay. I'm still not quite sure where you are going with this. What does this have to do with me? Isn't this a PST operation?"

Gripar rolled his eyes when he heard another sigh at the other end. "Goodness. You are daft, man. This whole Wolfsangel thing is causing some headaches for the King's Council. Now we have this Tyskerbarn stuff rearing its ugly head. They don't want to start a political shit storm and the feeling is that having a high profile PST member like me may get that storm going. I have a meeting with Sverre Lodbrok tomorrow morning. He is working with the Prime Minister to find a way to keep the waters calm. I want you to do a bit of non-intrusive digging and see what you can come up with on the Stein guy."

It's just what he suspected. Of course, Sloss doesn't want to pursue this himself. Much better to have a peon Politi guy like me as a handy scapegoat if things go sideways. Using his best placating tone, "Okay. I understand now. I'll get on it. I assume you want me to keep you updated?"

"Of course." Sloss hung up.

Well, that was that. Gripar stared at his computer screen and decided to dip his toe into the water. He typed 'The Foreigner & Wolfsangel' into a search engine and was rewarded with links to the articles that Sloss referred to. This online newspaper was not unknown to him. *The Foreigner* was considered the preeminent English-language news source of Norway. He noticed that the article was written by a freelance writer named Zofia Hurum from Trondheim. Hmmm … that name sounded familiar. He had this gnawing feeling that he had met her before. He did a quick scan of the article. It was twelve days old, well before the whole Wolfsangel thing had come into the press. She had done some pretty in-depth interviews with the neo-Nazi group in Trondheim. The second article was not as informative, but he noticed that this same group was now using Wolfsangel's name to create some momentum for their cause.

He looked at his watch. It was late, but not too late for him to make a call to this Zofia and get the information straight from the horse's mouth. He found her contact information and took his chance that he would be able to connect.

He was rewarded. After a couple of rings, a soft, melodious voice answered. "Hello. This is Zofia Hurum."

Oh my goodness, that voice hit him right in the heart. Gripar realised immediately where he had met her. Suddenly, he felt nervous and shy. Assuming his 'police' voice - at least he hoped it would come across as such - he said, "Good evening Ms. Hurum, I am Police Inspector Odd Gripar. I hope I am not bothering you. I just want to ask you a few questions."

There was a pause on the other end. Then a tentative, "Oh dear. Am I in trouble, Inspector?"

Ok. Clearly he had overused his 'police' voice. Well done, Gripar. Starting off on the right note, are you? Trying to dial it down a bit, "Oh no. No … No. It's all good. You are not in trouble at all. I'm … I'm investigating the Hurdal Three and I came across your article in the Foreigner in which you do a back story on the neo-Nazis in Trondheim."

Zofia laughed. The memory flooded back and Gripar became a bit flustered again. "Oh good. For a minute I thought I was in deep trouble. So, what can I help you with?"

"Well … ummm," hoping his voice doesn't crack as it is prone to do at the most inopportune times - especially when conversing with females. "I came across your article about the neo-Nazis in Trondheim."

"Okay, yes. You mentioned that. I wrote that a couple of weeks ago."

"Yes. Well, I am interested in Mr. Bratt and the neo-Nazi movement. I am curious as to what led you to do this piece?"

"I've known Bratt for some time now. We first met while attending the same university. Back then, and still now, I think he is a pretty sharp guy, very interested in political history. Very knowledgeable, too. He loves to debate and argue. I happened to run into him recently at a pub and we got to talking. I found out that he got himself involved in the local Nordic Resistance Movement. He is actually one of their leaders."

Gripar thought for a moment. "Were you surprised at that? Surprised that he would be involved in the NRM?"

There was a brief pause. "No, I guess not. I mean, he was very interested in political movements. I just never realised he was passionate about racial purity and Nazism. I've known him as a person who could do a lot of talking, but back then I rarely saw him put his money where his mouth is."

"What about now? Is he still all talk?"

"Hmmm. It's hard to tell. He certainly did a lot of talking. I had prepared a set of questions for the interview, but I really didn't need them. He wasn't ever at a loss of words about how Nazism could work in a social democracy like Norway. Of course, I disagreed. He strongly believed that in order for those ideals to work in our country, we would have to put a stop to immigration. Our resources need to be put towards ensuring the purity of the Nordic race. I have to say, though, he made some pretty convincing arguments."

Gripar found his mind wandering. He was wondering if Zofia still looked the way he remembered her. Suddenly he noticed there was a pause on the other end. Embarrassed at his wandering mind, took this pause as his cue to ask his next question. He cleared his throat. "The article you did this morning. It seems like the NRM is going to use the Wolfsangel and the Tyskerbarn to advance their own agenda?"

"I think so, but also think there is more to it."

Gripar understood now. "That's why you went back to the Bratt's group of gentlemen - to check up on your hunch."

Zofia laughed. "Why, Inspector, your detective skills are out of this world." Gripar felt the earth tremour slightly under his feet. Her laugh was infectious and he couldn't help but laugh along. "You're absolutely correct. I picked up my bike and drove to the Tyholdstraat. When I arrived at his flat, his motorbike was still warm. It was lying on its side, gasoline was dripping out. Stein was inside, lounging on a chair with a bottle of beer in his hands ..."

Gripar stepped in, "Let me guess. Something drastically changed Stein and he wasn't the same person as you used to know him."

Zofia chuckled. "Right again. Excuse my language but Stein was a complete asshole. When I eventually brought that to his attention, he got quite upset. He even threatened to hit me."

Gripar felt his temperature rise. "So, what was his problem? Was he drunk or high on drugs?"

Zofia wasn't sure but suspected he might have been coming off a high.

"Why didn't you leave? You mentioned you thought he might do something to you?" At that moment, Gripar realised that he was straying off the path of professionalism and was getting a bit personal.

She didn't seem to catch on to that. "Yes, I had a certain level of fear, but this wasn't my first rodeo dealing with jerks. I've experienced worse. I felt like I was surrounded by a wall of hatred and violence, yet my intuition told me to stick it out for a bit longer. Fortunately, after a few minutes he calmed down and sat on the couch trying to gather himself together. The television was on and when there was a recap of the news and he saw the images of inside the bunker, I noticed that Stein listened very intensively. The wolfsangel-sign touched him. You could see he loved that symbol; it seemed to heal him, give him strength."

Gripar found this interesting. "What do you mean by that?"

Zofia paused for a moment to gather her thoughts. “Well, at one point, he told me that he thinks the Wolfsangel is trying to teach this country a lesson. And, then, he said something very strange. He figured in the Wolfsangel, there is finally someone who does not want to cover everything with that suffocating mantle of love, but someone who attacks!”

Gripar wondered if this Stein guy was dealing with some mental health issues. He decided not to voice that to Zofia and encouraged her to continue. He heard papers rustling; she was probably looking through her notes. “He laughed and then, all of a sudden out of the blue, blurted out that he met him once a long time ago.”

Gripar was stunned. “What exactly did he say?”

“He said, ‘I’ve met him years ago. As a pure Aryan, he is the true hero of the Norwegian race.’ What do you think of that?”

“I’m not sure. Do you really think he has met him before?”

“With Stein, I wouldn’t bet a lot of money on it. It wouldn’t be the first time he’s stretched the truth with me.”

Gripar considered this and made a mental note to track this guy down. Zofia filled him in with the details of what she knew about his ‘super demonstration’.

When Gripar put down his phone, he was feeling slightly euphoric. First, he got a good lead on this Stein guy. If, in fact, he actually has met this Wolfsangel guy, he could give us some valuable information. Second, he just loved talking with Zofia Hurum. There was something about the huge smile in her voice and her laugh that was intoxicating.

To top all that, he remembered where he had met her before. He felt a wave of exhilaration wash over him - like when you discover your crush finally notices you. Not that he thought she noticed him in that way, but he didn’t think he would ever have an opportunity to connect with her again.

He decided to spend the rest of his evening surfing the net to find as much information as he could about Zofia.

The next morning, Gripar headed out to Hurdal. Yesterday, he had received a phone call from one of the local police officers who felt she may have a lead in identifying one of the three dead people. He was pleased at how quickly this case was moving forward. It's true, as Walter Svendsen pointed out, there was no evidence at the moment to prove that Wolfsangel was the killer. However, if he could determine the identity of the three dead people, there was a good chance that would lead him to identifying the killer. Gripar didn't think it would be too difficult to identify the three bodies. After all, people don't just disappear into thin air. They would have left family or friends behind who would miss them.

After an hour on the road, he arrived in Hurdal. They had arranged to meet at the local Hot Spot restaurant. When he walked in, he wasn't quite sure who he would be looking for. All he knew was that he would be meeting a Sergeant Ullmann. Surveying the place, he eventually spotted a group of people standing around a table near the rear of the restaurant. Seated at the table was a female police officer. She was laughing at the banter that seemed to be going on. As he strode towards the table, the group became silent and turned to look at him. The police officer stood up and beckoned to him- or, at least he thought she stood. It was hard to tell. She had a fairly diminutive stature. He came up and extended his hand. Yep. She was short. He tried hard not to register his surprise. She grasped his hand and shook it a couple of times. What she lacked in stature, she made up in tensile strength.

"Inspector Odd Gripar. Welcome to Hurdal." She had a big smile on her face. "My name is Sergeant Sigrid Ullmann. Have a seat."

The crowd around the table dispersed leaving the two of them standing. Gripar noticed that there was a person standing near the table who didn't move away with the crowd. She was giving him the eye and Gripar started to feel a bit self-conscious. Surreptitiously, he checked to see if his fly was open. It was not.

"Gripar, this is Lena Maria Pichler, one of the owners of the Hot Spot and the best-looking waitress north of Oslo." The way she smiled at Lena made him think that their relationship was a bit more than simply casual. Gripar shook her hand. He did have to agree with Sigrid's assessment of her. She was about forty-five and radiated a healthy lifestyle. She had all the right curves and with her Scandinavian combination of blond hair and blue eyes, she was quite stunning.

Gripar took a chair opposite Sigrid. Lena Maria grabbed a coffee pot and poured him a cup of coffee, all the while not saying a word. After she left, the two of them became business-like. Sigrid grabbed a large folder from her briefcase. "Okay, I believe the forensic team is still working on DNA testing and dental records. I decided to go through the police archives to find missing persons that corresponded roughly to the apparent ages of the victims. Here is a list of missing people that doesn't include females and young males. You'll notice there is still a sizable list of people. Oh … are you hungry?"

Gripar was caught off-guard by this non-sequitur. "Umm. Yes. Sure."

Sigrid beckoned Lena. As she drew near, Gripar wondered if Sigrid was going to slap her behind.

"Lena," said Sigrid, "I think I'll order a Ham and Cheese Panini sandwich." She looked at Gripar expectedly. Gripar nodded. "Sure, I'll have the same."

Over the course of their meal, they worked through that list. Even after eliminating the obviously unconnected, Gripar was still surprised at its length.

"I ran this list past a couple of my colleagues to see if they could find anything that jumped out at them. They came up with some possibilities. For example, a thirty-five-year-old male, officially listed as missing when he ran away from the psychiatric hospital in Oslo. See this note? It seems that the people who knew him think he is dead. There was a farewell letter."

Gripar read the information. "Thirty-five years old? Could he be one of the three? They appear older, although it is hard to tell for sure."

Sigrid agreed. "I think so too. I also think these three people are somehow connected with Hurdal. So, we started poking around hoping that someone here knows something."

Gripar put the list down. "You know, we can't immediately eliminate all possibilities, but do you think that we are looking for a serial killer in the traditional sense?"

"I know what you are saying. Traditionally, a serial murder is considered the unlawful killing of two or more victims by the same offender in separate events. We definitely have two or more victims. I guess we are not entirely sure these are three separate events."

Gripar was familiar with the generally accepted definition of serial killer. Yes, at the outset, this crime scene has the definite attributes of a serial murder. Still, something didn't sit right with him. "Generally, the distinguishing feature of serial murder has to do with the relationship the killer has with the victims. Once we have established the identities of the victims, we'll be in a better position to determine the identity of the killer."

Sigrid nodded and then added, "We also need to identify a timeline of sorts. When were these victims killed? If we can establish both the identity and time of death of the victims, we should be able to narrow down a pool of suspects more effectively."

"Forensics is working on an autopsy. They may be able to shed some light on that as well."

Sigrid looked at Gripar thoughtfully. "You know, I hadn't thought of it until now, but we are assuming that there is only one bunker. Maybe there are more!"

Gripar shook his head. He had considered that possibility, but he was quite certain there wasn't. "This Wolfsangel guy would have indicated that in his note. He wanted us to find that particular bunker and its contents. I am convinced the location is quite significant to his plan."

Sigrid nodded. "I would agree." She paused to order another cup of coffee. Gripar suspected it was as much about the coffee as it was about Lena. Gripar was amused to notice how Sigrid's disposition changed as she was interacting with Lena. As soon as Lena left, Sigrid was back to business. "Okay. So, I have been focussing on identifying the victims. If they are local, it shouldn't be too hard to figure out. After all, this community is not huge. People just can't disappear into thin air without somebody noticing." She pulled out another folder and dumped it on the table in front of Gripar. With a triumphant grin, "Here. Check this one out. This is the one I think is the most promising lead and is right here in Hurdal." Sigrid pointed to a name on the list.

Gripar peered at the name. "Mirre Andersen. Okay. Go on."

"She called this morning in response to our request to the community for information on missing persons. She thought that maybe her husband, Olaf Andersen, was one of the three in the bunker. We checked to see if any police reports were submitted and we found out that in 1992, she filed a missing-persons report. Then, for some reason, five years later, the report was amended to indicate he was deceased. Naturally, this piqued our interest and we wanted to get some more information. An officer from the Eidsvoll and Hurdal police station went to visit her and check it out. We wanted to know if, in 1992, Olaf Andersen was deceased or merely missing. Interestingly enough, when he started questioning her, she became confused and couldn't recall filing a missing report years ago. According to her, she always thought he was dead and thought that's how she initially reported it."

Gripar glanced at the report. "This Mirre Andersen was born in 1919. That makes her …" Gripar paused to do the mental calculation.

"92 years old," Sigrid interjected. "She is a bit aged, wouldn't you say? I suppose it is understandable that she would be confused about specific dates."

Gripar nodded, a little embarrassed that he couldn't do the quick calculation in his head. "Well, that is interesting. If one of the victims is Olaf, then he would have been killed some fifteen years ago. So, why would this Wolfsangel wait until now for the big reveal?"

"That's a good question. I did some digging, but I could not locate a living Olaf Andersen that matched the profile of Mirre's ex-husband. If he simply left his wife and was still alive, you'd think there would be some trace of him in the system somewhere. I suspect he is indeed deceased and a strong candidate as one of the victims."

Gripar nodded. "I think this is worth further investigation. What if we pay a visit to Ms. Andersen right now?'"

After paying their bills and a special good-bye to the restaurant owner, the two of them stepped into Gripar's truck and set course for Mirre's house.

As they drew closer to their destination, Gripar began to notice familiar landmarks. They took the Glassworks Road and turned left at the Oppered Road, which took them up to some power lines. Gripar remembered those power lines. "Her place is remarkably close to the bunker, just a short walk, really."

Sigrid called out, "Here it is. Number 44." As Gripar slowed down and parked along the side, he scanned Sigrid's police report one more time. He looked up at the house and remarked, "So this is the residence of Mirre Andersen, born 1919."

The two of them stood side by side and took a good look at the setting. It was bucolic with a small wood-clad bungalow, judged by Gripar to have been built by some city folks fifty years ago. From where they stood, the place looked well kept. The house sported a covered deck on the front. There were flowers all over, in hanging baskets, boxes and pots, even hanging upside down as bushels. Gripar smiled – the place looked festive and alive. He found it hard to believe a ninety-two-year-old woman lived here by herself. The deck was quite narrow and a screen door gave access to a porch. In the winter this porch probably serves as a perfect buffer between the harsh cold outside and the warm inside. As his eyes swept to the back he noticed a pigsty and a vegetable garden. Surrounding them were a series of fruit trees. Gripar saw a couple of chickens bobbing their heads as they walked among the trees in search of food. Gripar glanced up at Sigrid, "Are you sure this lady was born in 1919?" She shrugged, opened the screen door and stepped inside the porch; Gripar was right behind her.

Once inside, Gripar paused for a moment and swept the area with his eyes. On his left, Gripar saw a small freezer and leaning against that was a snow shovel and a couple of brooms. They were not needed now. Above the freezer, Gripar noticed two layers of shelves loaded with paint pots, terra cotta pots and glass canning jars. At the right of the freezer, he noted the old-fashioned gas and electric meters attached to the wall against the house. Gripar's head swivelled to the right and he saw some garden tools, baskets, some yet half filled with dried apples, a walker, on the floor were shoes and the coat hanger was covered with a variety of coats. Gripar glanced down at Sigrid and saw the smile on her face. "What? What are you smirking at?"

Sigrid smiled and shrugged her shoulders.

"Just trying to read this lady," Gripar said, a little defensively.

"Are you ready, Inspector?" she asked Gripar, heavily emphasizing the last word. "May I knock on the door?" Gripar wasn't sure if she was being sarcastic; probably was. He nodded anyway and Sigrid knocked and carefully opened the door. A clear voice rang out, "Come on in, I am here". They gingerly stepped inside the house. Both felt like trespassers.

A curious smell wafted up Gripar's nostrils. It was a mixture of odours – musty and dank mixed in with a flowery scent. Gripar was immediately transported back in time to his grandparent's house. The smell here was almost identical. It was essentially a feeble attempt to cover the decaying house with a bright, flowery scent. While growing up, he would often visit with his parents on Sundays. Then, for some reason, the visits stopped. Something caused a rift between them and his parents. He felt a twinge of guilt as he considered the loss of his relationship with his grandparents.

His grandfather had passed away shortly after the death of his son, Gripar's dad. His grandmother was in a nursing home battling Alzheimer's. She wouldn't recognise him even if he did drop in.

Gripar continued his visual sweep. There was a wall filled with wood framed windows, a stove, all kinds of knick-knacks, loads of photographs pinned to the walls. Bookshelves on another wall, an old upright piano. On one side an open kitchen, sink, a small counter, pots and pans on shelves. Window above the sink, overlooking the grass field which surrounded the house. The windows allowed streams of light to enter this dwelling place and Gripar saw a few old fashioned chairs, three of them, a wooden coffee table and sitting there was Mirre.

Mirre was not quite what Gripar expected. Yes, she was old and wrinkly, to be expected from a woman of that age, but she seemed, oddly, to exude life. She had been reading a book which she removed from her lap and placed on a small table beside her chair. Gripar saw it was the Bible. She stood up, slightly bent over, peering with kind blue-green eyes through her glasses. Energetic and curious, her head slightly tilted to the right, she welcomed them in the house and asked the reason for the visit. Gripar introduced himself and Sigrid.

"Oh, you're a tiny thing, aren't you?" she said to Sigrid. "I can look you straight in the eye."

Sigrid laughed a deep, rich laugh. "You know what they say. God only lets things grow until they are perfect." Then giving Gripar an exaggerated look over, "Some of us didn't take as long as others to get there."

Mirre laughed. "Yes, I am living proof of that as well, sister. Welcome to my humble dwelling."

Gripar took the lead. "Madam, I understand an officer was here a yesterday asking some questions about a crime scene not far from here. Do you remember this?"

"Young man, I may be ninety-one years old, but I still have my wits about me. Of course, I remember that handsome young police officer," Mirre chided Gripar, with a twinkle in her eye.

Gripar became a bit flustered. "Well, actually, I was referring to the conversation you had with the officer."

"Oh," Mirre smiled, glancing up at Sigrid who gave her a wink. "Yes. Well, I understand that you may have found my husband."

"Possibly. We are just trying to figure out when your husband may have died. Establishing that would narrow down the list of both suspects and the other two victims."

"So why are you here then? Couldn't that handsome policeman come back and question me further?"

Quite the jester, this old lady, thought Gripar. He had a retort on the tip of his tongue but decided to keep things professional. "At this point, we haven't been able to confirm the identity of the three dead men nor the identity of the person who built that bunker. We do suspect, though, that there is a relationship between the location of the bunker, the three dead men, and the way in which the three men were arranged. I noticed that the bunker is actually quite close to here. It is within walking distance." Gripar looked Mirre in the eyes, hoping to catch something.

Mirre looked away. "You think I may be able to help you?" Glancing at Sigrid, she threw up her hands. "Where are my manners? First, let me pour you a cup of tea. I was just about to have one myself. Please, sit down." She gestured at a couple of aged chairs.

She shuffled to a table where a teapot hid in a flowery tea cozy. Gripar and Sigrid watched in an uncomfortable silence through the whole production as Mirre poured tea into three cups and placed all these items, including the teapot, on a tray and came back. Gripar was impressed at her agility. When both had been served tea, she finally sat down. She fixed her look on Gripar. "Well tell me, young man, how can I help you?"

Drawing out a file folder from his briefcase, Gripar scanned the paperwork inside - for effect, of course. "Well, after you called the police about the possibility of one of the victims being your husband, we checked out the police reports. The original report in 1992 indicated that you were filing a missing person's report because you were fairly certain he had simply disappeared. However, about five years later, the police report indicates that he was deceased. Apparently, you changed your mind? When you spoke to 'the handsome young officer' you told him that you were always certain that he met a tragic death." Gripar paused, put the folder down and looked at Mirre. Out of the corner of his eye, he could see Sigrid smirk. Probably impressed with his trenchant interview skills. "I am curious – there seems to be a discrepancy between what you said at first and what you are saying now."

Mirre put her tea cup down and furrowed her brow. After a pause, she shook her head. "Young man - Gripar was the name - right?"

Gripar nodded slightly.

Mirre looked directly into Gripar's eyes. "That was a long time ago. I'm not sure why the police would have understood me to believe my husband had simply disappeared. I know that when I first went to the police, I was fairly certain that my husband had died. I mean, he had disappeared quite suddenly and without any warning or explanation. Perhaps the police didn't quite understand me and assumed I was reporting a simple missing persons situation. When it became quite obvious that he was not coming back, they may have updated their report. I'm really not certain." She picked up her cup and took another sip. "Besides, I'm not sure why this is important. Do you think that one of those three men might be my Olaf?"

Gripar shook his head. "We're not positive, yet. However, you've seen pictures of the three in the media reports. You called the police. You must think there is a good possibility."

Mirre shrugged and continued to sip her tea.

Gripar came to the realization that he had underestimated Mirre. She may have come across as a frail, feeble, confused old lady to the 'young police officer', but there was definitely more to her than meets the eye. Mentally, her mind was sharp. Razor sharp. She's playing a mind game. He glanced up at Sigrid.

She was at the wall studying the pictures. Gripar was slightly irritated to notice a slight smile at the corner of her mouth. She turned around. "Do you happen to have a picture of him? Is he one of these on the wall?"

Gripar perused the pictures from his chair. He wondered what Olaf looked like. He imagined a meek, mild-mannered man with fine features. He could tell there were photos of all kinds of people, from young to old. He got up to take a closer look. Some of them matched Gripar's imagined description. Many did not. He also noticed that there was an abundance of photos of young men and women with babies on their arms. To his astonishment, Gripar even discovered a few photos that had a swastika in the background. Who are these people, he wondered? What connection do they have with Mirre?

"No. There are no pictures of him there." She lifted herself off her chair and shuffled to the windowsill. She grabbed a small frame that had been hiding between some flowerpots.

Gripar, still studying the pictures on the wall, "This is quite a collection of pictures. Who are these people, Mirre? Why do you keep such a collection on your wall?"

Mirre smiled. "I have lived a long time, Gripar, and through the years I have met many people. For a long time, the township was serious about looking after the campground. Sadly, over the last number of years they have abandoned it. I mean, did you see it? What an unkempt jungle it is now! Back in the day, I cleaned the area and even kept the toilets clean. I got a lot of satisfaction in taking care of the place. Another thing I did, back in the day, was look after the children at Hurdal Verk. I developed some strong bonds with many of them - as you can see." Mirre's voice became wistful and Gripar realised that she was probably quite lonely and missed her former life. "I love looking at these pictures. I feel like I have a large family anyway."

She handed the photo frame to Sigrid. "Here is the picture of Olaf, when he was about forty-five or fifty." Gripar peered over Sigrid's shoulder to study the photo. He was not at all what Gripar was expecting. Olaf appeared tough and his eyes were cold as steel as he looked directly into the camera. His chiselled head featured a scraggly patch of hair on the sides and lips slightly twisted into a sneer. A prominent bushy unibrow underscored his deeply receded hairline and drew attention to a square jawline that housed a cleft chin. Gripar glanced up at Mirre who had sat down again, sipping her tea. Boy, was he ever wrong about what he imagined Olaf to look like. How the heck did these two meet? Gripar took out his iPhone and captured a couple of shots of this picture.

Mirre asked, "So, now that you have seen his picture, what do you think? Could one of them be my husband?"

Gripar wasn't sure. There seemed to be a discernible resemblance. The timeframe of Olaf's disappearance as well as his age could fit in with what we know. If that's the case, what is the connection? "I suppose it is possible, but I can't tell for sure based on this picture. We would need to confirm an identity with dental or medical records. I believe the forensic team is working on that." Mirre nodded.

Gripar made his way back to his chair. He could feel his heart beating a bit faster. He took a small notepad out of his pocket and gestured for Mirre and Sigrid to also sit down. "Can you tell me more about your late husband? What kind of man was he, what did he do during his life?"

Mirre thought for a moment and began her story. "We were married in the spring of 1947. We were both locals from here and I have known him since childhood. During the war he worked, as I did, at Hurdal Verk. He was part of the construction crew that built the side wing addition before the war and he was kept on as maintenance man after. As a matter of fact, he had been working there for many years. After retirement he kept on doing some odd jobs there. Like the stone wall at the pond; he built that."

Gripar noticed she hadn't answered his first question. Just as he decided to ask the question again, Sigrid spoke up. "What kind of a man was he? Judging from his picture, Olaf seems like a pretty tough character."

Mirre paused and pursed her lips. Gripar noticed she slightly shook her head. Obviously, she was deciding how to answer his question. After taking another sip of her tea, she continued, "Yes, he always looked tough; I guess he was, in a way. I don't like to tell people, but you are bound to find out. Olaf was a hard man. He was not a nice man at all. In fact, he was a brute roughneck. He had a pent-up rage inside of him, like the world had done him a lot of harm."

Mirre looked away, her face briefly clouded by some memories. The room filled with that uncomfortable silence again. Gripar could hear the clock on the mantle tick, but he resisted the urge to fill in the silence with conversation. He glanced at Sigrid who was busy taking notes.

Mirre finally broke the silence. "Yes. Olaf was a tough character." Then, almost in defiance, she looked Gripar straight into his eyes. Gripar felt a shiver go down his spine as he noticed that her eyes became cold. It just confirmed what he suspected, there was a lot more to this woman than his initial impression. Gripar broke the connection and looked down at his notes. "What happened in 1992?"

Mirre's voice was steady. "About a month or so before he disappeared, he talked constantly about moving away from here to Drøbak. I think this had to do with a visit he made to a former colleague from Hurdal Verk who lived there. He came back from there saying that he was sick of this area and wanted to get away from the people around here. I am not really sure what he meant by this; he always lived in his own little world and he allowed very few people into it. I certainly was not allowed in. I did not want to move – for sure not to Drøbak, but that did not matter to him. He kept telling me that he was going to do it anyway – with or without me. So, one day, when he didn't come home, I just assumed he finally did what he said he was going to do and moved to Drøbak. I waited for a few weeks, thinking that he would return. Eventually, I realised that he really had left me and wasn't coming back."

Sigrid spoke up, "Did you think he had an accident or died?"

"No, at that time, I could not imagine at that time that he had died. He had always been so solid, forceful, and so hardy. That man was like a rock. One meter ninety, muscular, kind of a big head. No, men like him don't just die." Mirre's eyes grew distant. "I was loyal to him. I was faithful to the promise I made at our wedding … but he … he did not love anybody. He just got up and left me with nothing."

Mirre paused as she drained the last of her tea. Gripar waited for Mirre to continue and when she didn't, he asked her, "Just wondering then, why did you go to the police?"

Mirre thought about it for a moment. "Well, after a few months or so, I was running out of money. Olaf's pension checks weren't coming this way and I didn't know what to do. I decided to write a letter to his former colleague asking him if he could put me in contact with Olaf. I never heard back from him. So then I asked his brother Anders if he would be willing to go to Drøbak and take a look to see if he could locate Olaf. Fortunately, we always got along quite well. He is nothing like his brother. He took a trip down there but came back a few days later empty. He had not been able to find Olaf or his colleague. He couldn't even find where Olaf lived. He talked to a lot of people there, but nobody seemed to know anything about these two. I grew more and more concerned that something had happened to him. I just wanted him found. I wanted to ask him why he left me. I wanted to ask him … why. Deep down, I knew he was gone. So I finally went to the police."

Gripar and Sigrid looked at each other. They had clearly opened up a deep wound that the passing years had not been able to fully heal. Mirre's seemingly organised, neat, and tidy, little home belied a messy and dysfunctional inner emotional state. Gripar wondered what truly brought the two of them together. Yes, he had heard the saying that opposites attract, but there had to be something that bonded them together. He just could not imagine what that might have been.

Gripar spoke up, "Please just a couple more questions. It's about the Lebensborn at Hurdal Verk. The two of you worked there during the war. I am assuming, based on all the pictures pinned to the wall, that you had a special relationship with the children that were housed there. Did you run into any conflicts because of that?"

Mirre smiled knowingly and shook her head. "At that time, all the people from around here knew me from birth. Don't forget that they all knew I love children, all children. They also knew I didn't care about politics, war or Nazi's. I love children, I did not care one bit about the Nazi's and their social engineering. Really, for the Nazi's the Lebensborn were supposed to be about creating a pure and clean race, but for me, the Lebensborn were just innocent children caught up in a terrible ideology. All the resentment and hatred toward them was so stupid. Jesus said let all children come to me and do not hinder them. If our Saviour can open up His arms to all of them, so can I."

Gripar glanced at Sigrid and realised she had a question at the tip of her tongue. He nodded and she spoke up. "What about Olaf? Judging from this picture and what you have said about him, he doesn't strike me as the forgiving type and I don't imagine he shared the same love for the children as you. How did he handle the resentment and conflict over the Lebensborn?"

Mirre shrugged. "He was a good worker. The children, and the townsfolk for that matter, learned to steer clear of him."

Gripar picked up the picture of Olaf and studied it. Gripar found it hard to understand the relationship between Olaf and Mirre. Something was not adding up here. For now, something to file away and pursue later. He leaned over to the windowsill to put the picture back.

He took a sip of his tea. Up to this point, he hadn't really delved into the three questions the Wolfsangel specifically posed to him. He wondered if she would know something. "Mirre, do you know an Eirik Tijsker?"

Mirre didn't seem at all surprised at this question. The corners of her mouth lifted slightly. She got off her chair and went to a bookshelf. Gripar watched as her hands swept past some plants and stopped at an odd artefact. It was more or less rectangular in shape. It stood about twenty centimetres tall with the top portion being narrower than the base. Gripar could only see two of the sides, but each side seemed identical. At the top half, a heart shape had been cut out as if by a cookie-cutter. The bottom half had a circle with six pie-shapes cut out. It looked hand-made. Gripar watched as Mirre grabbed a picture that was sitting next to it. She handed it to Gripar.

Gripar was puzzled. "So, what's this? Who is this person? Is this Eirik Tijsker?"

The photo showed a clean-shaven blond-haired man towering next to Mirre. They were standing on the steps to the entrance of the Hurdal Verk. The man appeared to be in his early thirties. He was wearing a blue coat and his arms were folded across his chest as if he was hugging himself. Mirre, slightly bent at the waist, was wearing a checkered coat and a pair of hiking boots.

Mirre smiled again. "No. His name is Sjurd. Read the back of the picture."

Gripar turned over the photo. On the back was written: *Tijsker's Ommelebommelestien*. "I don't understand. What does this mean?"

Mirre shrugged. "I don't know. To be honest, I never really thought much about this picture until you mentioned Tijsker. All I know is that his name is Sjurd Tijsker. Is he related to Eirik Tijsker? I'm sure you can find out, though. You're a detective, aren't you?"

Gripar's pulse quickened. He asked the question hoping that Mirre had at least heard of Eirik Tijsker. He wasn't expecting this level of information. "How did you come to know Sjurd?"

Mirre walked back to her chair. "He sailed in from Holland on his boat about eight or nine years ago. I'm pretty certain he said he was staying in Oslo. In any case, he decided to make a trip out to Hurdal. He wanted to know more about the history of the area, especially the Lebensborn. Somebody local must have told him that I was the person to talk to, and so I spent quite a bit of time with him touring him around and answering his questions. I found him to be a nice man, very friendly." She paused and smiled. "It's kind of a neat picture. He had one of those cameras which delivered pictures immediately, what do you call it, Polaroid? Somebody snapped a picture of us for him and at the end of the day, he gave it to me as a thank-you for answering his questions."

Sigrid gestured for the picture and Gripar handed it to her. "What does this have to do with the case?" Gripar ignored her for now. He would eventually have to explain.

He asked Mirre, "Do you know how I might get in contact with him?"

Mirre wasn't sure. All she knew was that Sjurd came to Norway from Holland on his boat, he was here on a business trip, and he spoke quite decent Norwegian.

Gripar took the picture back to the bookshelf. "What's this artefact here, Mirre?"

Mirre looked up. "That's a porcelain candlestick holder. I believe it was made in a concentration camp."

At that, Sigrid's ears perked up. "Did you say it was made at a concentration camp?"

Mirre nodded. "That's what I was told."

"Can I take a picture of it? I have a keen interest in World War Two history." After getting permission, Sigrid took a variety of pictures with her iPhone.

"Well," said Gripar, as they drove back, "that was a very interesting meeting. I think we have some valuable information to work with. Can you dig a bit deeper into Olaf Andersen and see if something comes up to corroborate her story? I think I am going to explore the Sjurd Tijsker aspect."

Sigrid nodded, distantly. She clearly was deep in thought. "That candlestick holder is intriguing. There is something about her story that doesn't make a lot of sense. I'm quite certain that those type of candlesticks were used in Nazi ceremonies. I noticed that inscribed on the bottom was the double S."

Gripar grunted. He told Sigrid how Mirre seemed to caress that candlestick holder as she reached for that Tijsker picture. It definitely has some sentimental value. So then, why was a picture of a supposedly unknown person placed on the bookshelf beside this artefact and not on the picture wall?' The more they considered it, the more they were convinced that Mirre Andersen knows considerably more than she is letting on.

Wolfsangel

He was having a great morning. After a small breakfast, he completed his daily work-out without getting dizzy. After that, he was still hungry and ordered an extensive brunch which he ate on his balcony. Overlooking the city, he mused about what he would do that day. First an appointment at the hospital, but then? His thoughts returned to Hurdal. How far would they be with the research? Perhaps they already have a suspicion about the identity of the witnesses.

He finished his brunch, poured himself a cup of coffee, and pulled out a cigar. Sitting back in his chair, he took a deep drag and then watched the smoke curl its way lazily into the air. "Linnea, today life is good to me." He really hoped his illness was retreating. Linnea had told him that there was always a very small chance. He put his cigar in the ashtray and made the decision to do some sailing and fishing. Give the police some more time to work this case, he thought.

An hour later he was at the hospital for a quick check-up and an appointment with Linnea. His next appointment wouldn't be a few more days, so it was the perfect time to get away for a while. He went to the Pipervika harbor and rented a Beneteau Oceanis 38 sailing yacht. It was a beautiful boat, with twin sails, small galley, and sleeping quarters.

He set sail for the southern fjords, hoping to do some fishing and possibly a stop in Holmestrand. Two, maybe three days on the water. Let the public chew on this. He sailed away with the wind at his back. He wasn't too worried. If there wasn't enough wind, he knew that the many nice harbour towns along the coast were very suitable and that there were always anchor spots. He loved the good weather, day-long shining sun and clear blue skies. Fortunately, for him, the wind picked up and the sea became alive.

Gripar

Gripar felt the familiar tightness in his chest – he was like a poodle with a plaything. He didn't want to let go, he wanted to continue pursuing the lead. He showed Sigrid the personal note he received from the Wolfsangel. The two of them were convinced that Eirik Tijsker and this Sjurd guy were very likely related. The coincidence with Mirre and her close proximity to the Hurdal Verk was too significant to ignore. Sjurd Tijsker clearly had more than a passing interest in the Lebensborn. There must be some sort of a secret hiding in the depths of Hurdal Verk related to Eirik Tijsker that the Wolfsangel wants us to uncover. If so, how do Sjurd and Mirre fit into this? Assuming that one of the dead men was Olaf Andersen, how does he fit in? The more Gripar thought about this, the more the tightness in his chest convinced him that he needed to talk to Sjurd Tijsker.

Gripar left Hurdal very pleased with the progress he and Sigrid had made. In all honesty, he had come out to Hurdal expecting little, but now, four hours later, they had a very decent lead to pursue. Sigrid went back to the Eidsvoll and Hurdal police station to see what she could come up with regarding Olaf Andersen in Drøbak while Gripar planned to do some research on locating Sjurd Tijsker.

It was getting late in the afternoon when Gripar made his way home on the RV120. The sun was starting its descent behind the hills, its light rays still bouncing off the gently rolling waves on the lake. He eventually hit the roundabout that led him onto the E6. Now he could make some good time because he didn't have to worry about narrow roads. In less than an hour, he found himself coming up to the Oslo old city centre, near the harbour. Right in front of him he saw the towering Radisson Hotel. After spending the day in rural Hurdal, the sight of this tower seemed so incongruous. Gripar thought wryly of how the old Norway is interspersed with the new Norway. Gripar never really considered himself a sentimental person. He was a pragmatist by nature and was generally excited about modernisation and new ideas. However, tonight he was in a reflective mood, probably brought on by his visit to Mirre. Without his own parents, Gripar wasn't really rooted in the past, but his conversation with Mirre reminded him that time is not something that should be taken for granted.

Gripar decided to stop at the Café Celsius on Rådhusgata. He enjoyed eating at this place. He liked to 'people-watch'. With its close proximity to the harbour and all the docked cruise ships, Gripar could usually find some interesting people. Even though it was surrounded by larger brick buildings, the Café wasn't hard to miss with its bright yellow walls and brown trim. He parked his truck in the corner of the Christiania Torv, put his Police Business sign on the dash, and walked into the café. He felt a little guilty using that sign, but he convinced himself that it was okay as long as he was doing some background scouting. He headed straight to the bar, sat down on a stool and ordered a Coke. He glanced around the room and saw that, oddly, it wasn't a very busy evening. A burst of laughter caught his attention and he turned to see the source. At one of the tables, a black woman appeared to be flirting with an older man. His hair was greying and the lights reflected off the pink skin that peaked through the thinning hair on his crown. Her hand gently caressed the man's arm and a wide smile was pasted on his face. The man was obviously from America. Either that, or he was completely brain dead. Gripar couldn't imagine a European or a Norwegian wearing a camouflage-patterned T-shirt with "Gun control means holding it with two hands" emblazoned on the front. Gripar figured that this guy was a passenger on one of the cruise ships that docked in Oslo and the woman was hoping for some company that evening. Gripar wondered if the man realised that prostitution was now illegal in Norway. Quite curious, Gripar turned back to the bar and surreptitiously watched in the mirror for a bit longer to see if anything would happen. He could tell the woman was quite experienced in getting her man. She was very beautiful – to use the language of one of his younger colleagues, she had all the right junk in all the right places. He observed how she constantly smiled at him, caressed his hands with her finger tips, and brushed her lips across his cheeks as she leaned in to whisper in his ear.

Gripar's thoughts were interrupted as he realised someone was speaking to him. He looked beside him and noticed that a grizzled old man was staring at him. "Sorry. Did you say something?"

"I said, that's just disgusting, hey?"

"I'm not sure what you mean," although Gripar was pretty sure he knew exactly what his neighbour meant.

"Well, look at that – a foreign svarting hitting on that Yank. Why can't they just stick with their own kind and their own country? Fysj! No self-respect." The man took another gulp of his beer, and looked over at Gripar, his dull eyes trying to focus on Gripar.

Gripar was rather surprised at his candour, even taking into consideration the amount of beer this man obviously had already consumed. No Mr. Nice Tolerant Norwegian here. "Well, times are a changing." Gripar took a deep draught of his coke.

"Yeah, I know, and that's the problem. Too much change. We're losing our culture and heritage because of those drittsekken in the Lovebakken. I think that Wolfsangel guy is onto something. At that, the old man got up. "I gotta take a piss." As he stumbled to the bathroom, Gripar smiled at his half empty mug.

The next time he glanced in the mirror, he noticed the woman and the man were just walking out the door. She was hanging onto his one arm while his hand strayed over her booty. The corner of Gripar's mouth curled back up into a smile as his thoughts turned to Zofia. Almost immediately, a hot wave of shame washed over his face as he realised what he was doing.

Gripar coughed into his hands, embarrassed at his thoughts. He drained his glass and turning to the bartender, asked for the menu. He decided on Joica, reindeer meat in game sauce with potatoes. While the kitchen was busy preparing his meal, he thought about what happened today. He asked the bartender, who was busy drying some mugs at the other end of the bar, "Other than cruise ship passengers, do you get a lot of European tourists who come in on their own boat?"

"Yah, besides the Yankee cruise people, it's our bread and butter. Many of them love to sail right up to the centre, which is just two blocks away from here."

"So, what are the chances you would come across a 30- to 35-year-old Dutch male sailing in from Holland and docking here."

The bartender stopped what he was doing and walked over to Gripar. "What's with all the questions?"

Gripar took out his police identification. "I'm trying to solve a murder case and a Dutchman who sailed into Oslo several years ago is a person of interest. I'm just trying to figure out if he came for business or pleasure."

The bartender nodded. "Well, if it was for pleasure, we get a good number of people from Europe, including Holland, who sail into the harbour and visit the sights of Oslo."

"And if it was for business?" Gripar asked.

"I would say that if your guy came from Holland by boat for business, there is a good chance he's a fisherman. Probably came here for either repairs on his boat or to install new equipment. There are a couple of Norwegian companies that specialise in new equipment designed specifically for fishing in the North Sea. Here, try this one, the Geir Verkstad shipyard." He wrote the name down on a piece of paper, which Gripar picked up and put away.

A fisherman - Gripar hadn't considered that. It made sense. His mind started churning out possibilities. Mirre said that this Sjurd fellow had docked in Norway. She probably assumed he was docked in Oslo. However, as far as he knew, there were no shipyards near here that specialised in fishing vessels. Those were located more northwest. So, what would draw him to Oslo? It had to be Hurdal.

Gripar arms suddenly felt heavy as he realised how tired he was. He had accomplished a lot.

He had a ten-minute drive home. By this time the sun had set and darkness had crept over the streets. The shop signs and flat lights cast eerie shadows on the sidewalk. Gripar really liked his place, only a few meters away from pulsating Bogstadveien with its wide choice of restaurants, shops and street life. The Frognerparken and central Oslo was just a short walk away. It was his home. He felt settled there.

Before heading to bed, he read through and organised the notes he made during this day. He studied the picture of Sjurd Tijsker and was intrigued by the long Dutch word printed on the back. What the heck is an *Ommelebommelestien*? Typing word as best he could into a search engine, he discovered that this was a reference to a large boulder located off the coast of a Dutch fishing village called Urk. He came across an interesting folktale around that boulder. Apparently, children from the village of Urk don't come from the cabbage patch or aren't brought in by a stork. Rather, they are taken from the Ommelebommelestien. The expectant father rows to this boulder with a midwife and receives his child upon payment of some sort of a fee. Gripar raised his eyebrows as he read that boys cost twice as much as girls. What about the mothers? How do they fit into this story, he wondered? A paragraph later he found out. The expectant mothers were literally confined to their beds by a nail driven through their right foot.

Well, that's intriguing. Gripar stood up and called Sigrid. He wanted to get her advice on what he discovered. Yes, it was late, but he figured she would still be up. If not, he would leave a message on her voice mail. After the fourth ring, Sigrid answered.

"Sigrid, this is Gripar. Sorry for disturbing you so late."

"No. That's okay. I'm still working on the case. What's on your mind?"

Gripar told her about what he found out about Urk and what the bartender said about fishing. "It's pretty consistent. It looks like everything about the Tijskers is pointing to a fisherman from Urk. If this Sjurd is related to Eirik, the connection to the Tyskerbarn and the Wolfsangel is probably found in Urk."

"I'm guessing you are wanting to take a trip there and see what you can find?"

Gripar had been seriously considering that and was glad that Sigrid had brought it up. "Yeah, I've been looking at flights. I'll see if I can get out there tomorrow. Meanwhile, we'll await Forensics to confirm whether one of the bodies does, in fact, belong to Olaf Andersen."

"Sounds good to me." Sigrid then sighed deeply. "I have searched deep and wide for an Olaf Andersen in Drøbak. I came up empty. But here is the interesting part. Didn't Mirre say that Olaf disappeared in 1992?"

Gripar looked at his notes. "Yes. That's what she said. She figured he went to Drøbak because that's where he wanted to move to."

"Well, based on information from government records, Olaf was living in Hurdal until at least 1997. So, I'm thinking he never went to Drøbak."

Gripar pondered that. "Do you think Mirre knew that? I mean, it's not like Hurdal is a bustling metropolis. What are the chances that Olaf would be able to live in Hurdal without Mirre knowing?"

"I'd say zero."

"I'd agree. You said until at least 1997. What happened after that?"

There was a pause on the other end and Gripar could hear the rustling of some paper. "Well, that's where things get really interesting. The trail stops dead. Nothing comes up after that. So, for example, it looks like Olaf got his license suspended for driving under the influence in 1996. He had applied to get his license restored but never followed through. There is no evidence he had ever renewed his license after that date. There is no banking information that is more recent than 1997. No income taxes paid after 1997."

"That suggests he is either dead or he's fled the country. If he's dead, there should be some evidence. Police reports, funerals, medical records."

"So far there's nothing. I checked all those out as well. I'll keep looking, though."

After ending his call with Sigrid, he went on-line and finalized his arrangements to fly out to Amsterdam tomorrow morning. He was exhausted. It had been a long day, but with some good results. Just as he was ready to head to bed, his phone rang. His heart quickened as he hoped it was Zofia. He glanced at the number and it was like somebody had dumped a pail of cold water over his head. It was Aksel Sloss' number. He decided to let it go to voicemail and deal with that later.

He sat back in his chair as his thoughts drifted to the first time he saw her. It was at Walter's wedding. He smiled to himself as he vividly recalled the memory at the bridal parents' home in Trondheim. Walter's family had been there of course as well as those of his lovely bride. The bride was in her long white dress and Walter was in a black tuxedo. The time came when the group formed a procession and headed to the church for the ceremony. Fiddle players led the way, bride and groom followed and after that the parents, ring bearers, flower girls and so on. Somewhere in the back of the procession Zofia was walking just ahead of him with a couple of her friends. They were clearly having a great time – laughing, giggling, and talking animatedly. He became very intrigued with her and was hoping to catch up with her later that evening. Just before they arrived at the church, the procession had to cross a small footbridge. That's where it happened. Zofia lost her balance, shrieked for help, milled her arms hoping to regain her balance, then fell backwards into the muddy creek below. It all happened so fast. All the people behind her, including Gripar, were frozen for one brief moment of time. Zofia got up, her dress was soaking wet with streaks of mud all down her back. Splotches of mud dotted her face and the crowd collectively gasped. Zofia looked down at herself, looked up at her friends, then burst into laughter. It was infectious and a wave of laughter erupted and eventually reached the bride and groom. By this time, Gripar, who had just been too late to catch her, sprang into action and gallantly assisted her out of the water. Her friends took over and brought her back to the house of the bride to dry up and change. He tried to look her up later on to see if she would be interested in having dinner together. However, life got busy and she disappeared from his memory. Until today.

Wolfsangel

Wolfsangel lounged on the deck of his sailboat, soaking up the sun's rays. The heat felt good on his body and for the moment, he was able to forget about the disease. Wolfsangel found himself in the harbour of Moss, a town of 30 000 inhabitants, about sixty kilometres south of Oslo as the crow flies. The sailing had done him good. His body enjoyed the smell of the salt fjord water and that wonderful gentle breeze. To make the day even better, out of the blue, a mermaid came gliding by. His ears caught the sound of a paddle dipping into the water and when he opened his eyes to determine its source, he was nonplussed by the sight. "Hey, what's that? What are you doing?" A young female stood on some kind of floating surfboard and paddled through the marina using a long paddle. She was probably no older than fifteen or sixteen and, well, extremely good looking! She stopped and turned to Wolfsangel. He must have been staring too hard. He felt his face turn red.

"Hi there! Never seen anyone supping?" She laughed at him. She was a beauty. He did the airport scan. She had long, full blond hair that went past her shoulders. Her eyes were a deep blue that seemed to penetrate right into his soul. Her mouth was sensual and her teeth were perfect and white. As his eyes travelled south, he noticed that her bikini top covered a set of pear shaped breasts. There was a soft, cool breeze that was blowing across the water that made her nipples harden. At that moment, a slight wave of shame washed over him. He hoped it wasn't too obvious. For the love of Pete, she's way too young and he's way too sick. He broke his glance from her chest and turned his attention to what she was saying. He was startled to realise that she was speaking English. He responded in English. "Well no. Suppen, you're saying? What do you mean? Or did you say shopping?"

She laughed. "You speak English. Great. Well, all girls love shopping, for sure. But, this is called stand-up paddle boarding or supping! It's really super fun and healthy!"

Wolfsangel would brook no argument with that. She certainly was the poster girl for health. She explained, "You use almost all your muscles and it is a great way to explore your surroundings."

"Well, you've convinced me," he smiled widely. He turned his attention to the paddle board. "That board of yours seems to be inflatable?"

"That's right, that makes it light and easy to use. Look!" The girl did a little dance on the board. Wolfsangel complimented her stability. Much to his delight she apparently either liked him or needed to kill some time because she sat down on her board and started chatting. "I'm staying up there, up that hill, not far from the harbour. I take this board everywhere. Where are you from?"

"Well, that's a long story, actually. I've sailed up here from Oslo. I'm pretty sure, though, you're from America. I can tell from your accent."

She laughed again. "You're right. Can you tell from my accent which part of the U.S. I'm from?"

Wolfsangel smiled inwardly. She had no idea that he was very familiar with that accent. Doing his best impression, "You're from Norfolk, Virginia."

Her mouth dropped and her eyebrows rose. "You're good. Wow. That's dead on. How did you know?"

He reached in a cooler and drew out two cans of iced tea. He would have preferred beer, but he was trying to abide by Linnea's strictures against alcohol. "I used to work there. Would you like one?" She nodded and shyly took one of the cans. Wolfsangel continued. "Yesterday I passed Drøbak; there was a spectacular sunset last night. The colours were stunning." It was an odd feeling, he discovered that he felt like talking. He laughed to himself. That disease has really changed him. There was a comfortable pause as they both took a sip out of their can. Wolfsangel pointed to the row of houses dotting the hills. "Those little houses beyond remind me of my own childhood, I feel at home here."

The girl nodded. "It looks like a nice place to grow up in. I'm not sure I want to live here for the rest of my life, though. So, tell me, what did you do in Norfolk? You must have been with the naval base?"

Wolfsangel smiled. "Yes. I was doing some training there."

She passed him one of her killer smiles. He decided he needed to be careful and not arouse suspicion. Changing the subject, "Well, I did a crazy thing this morning."

The girl chuckled. "You think it is crazy to talk to a strange American girl on a paddle board?"

"Well, it is. I really am enjoying this. But, that's not what I was talking about. This morning, I went to a real estate agency looking for a house to rent in this area. It turns out, they had a special offer on that little house over there." Wolfsangel was pointing to a bright yellow cottage.

"That little yellow house over there?" Wolfsangel nodded. She asked him why was renting.

"I was looking for a temporary place to stay. The owners are going to go to Malawi, Africa for half a year, for a Christian aid project. They decided to rent out their place for a fair price, fully furnished! I only needed a quick glance at the house to love it."

"So, you're going to be living here for a while." She downed the last few sips and handed him her empty can.

He grabbed the can and tossed it on the deck. "Yes. I'm taking a medical leave for a few months. Unfortunately, the sailing boat must go back to Oslo, but for now Moss will be where I call home." He talked for a while longer with the sporty 'supper.' He found out that her father was pretty high up in the Maersk company. She was here with her dad on a business trip. Wolfsangel gathered that either her mother had died or was no longer in the picture. It was just her and her dad. She definitely was a sweet girl, maybe a bit too naïve. After fifteen minutes she got up and wished him a nice day. She clearly was not aware of the impression she made on men.

As she paddled away, she tossed over her shoulder, "Who knows, maybe we'll bump into each other sometime!" He smiled as he watched her paddled away. He suddenly realised that he didn't even know her name. Probably not a bad thing. If she knew who he really was, she'd have paddled in the opposite direction. Nice girl, though. Linnea had told him that his libido might suffer a downward spiral because of all the medication. Boy, was she wrong that count, he grinned to himself.

He needed to refuel, so he headed back to the harbour. After ensuring the boat was safely moored for the night, he went on a short jaunt to find a place to eat. He spent the evening enjoying fine food. For the time being, he was able to enjoy his food and forget about that disease ravaging through his body.

When he was filled and satisfied, he stretched out in a deck chair. It was still early in the evening. He had his coffee, read the local newspaper and his thoughts wandered back to that beautiful girl in the harbour. When was the last time he had scored with a woman? It's been a while, for sure. That damn disease turned his whole life upside down, including his sex life. Although, as Hellmuth would be quick to remind him, he didn't really have much of a sex life before.

Wolfsangel felt melancholic and decided a beer would cheer him up. Who the hell cares what Linnea told him? The Grim Reaper, he was positive, was grinning at him anyway. If the Grim Reaper couldn't take Wolfsangel's life, he certainly was going to try to make it as miserable as he possibly could. Let him come at me. I'll take him on!

Later that night, it was almost as if the Grim Reaper heard and accepted the challenge.

After a brisk walk through the town - and secretly wishing he would bump into that girl again - Wolfsangel landed on a bar stool at the Old Irish Pub. There was a live band playing some Jazz tunes and, while he normally wasn't into Jazz, he ended up sitting next to an older man who had a pretty deep knowledge of that type of music. Wolfsangel had always likened Jazz music to two Tomcats fighting over a Molly cat in heat. His companion, however, explained how specific Jazz sounds were produced and how the musicians worked together to spontaneously create the mood of the song. Wolfsangel gained a new appreciation for something he previously disliked. That brought him nostalgically back to the many conversations he had with young Hellmuth. He really missed him.

Well. He had a long day and was fading fast. Over the past few months, he had learned to read his body and knew that if he didn't listen, he would be in trouble the next day. Wolfsangel jumped off the bar stool and went to the front counter to pay his bill. Much to his dismay, he discovered he was pretty much through all his cash. Counting his bills, he was fortunate to have just enough to pay for his drinks. He definitely needed to fill it again before he left.

Wolfsangel wasn't overly concerned. There were enough cash machines in this port area. He just had to figure out whether he should use his Norwegian bank card or his German one. There was a good chance that the police would first discover his German identity well before his Norwegian one. He thought of the flight, the sailing boat, the motorcycle and car rental, all of which he acquired with his German identification papers. It was even possible that by now the police were sifting through ATM video feeds in an attempt to locate him. He walked outside into a dark corner of the alley and put on a grey beard that he kept in his pocket for this purpose. Wearing mirrored sunglasses and his hood up, he turned back to the illuminated street and turned right. Out of the corner of his eye, he noticed three shadowy figures step out of the same alley. Wolfsangel ignored them and set a course for the bank just down the street. The ATM was located on the outside of the building. As he pulled his card out of his wallet and placed it in the slot, one of the shadows appeared on his left side. He acted as if he was oblivious. In the reflection of the ATM screen he saw a second guy stepping out of the shadows.

He knew that a street fight was decided in a few seconds. Losing was not an option for him and he had a limited supply of energy. He knew he would not get a reset. He carefully considered his next moves. He pretended to take his money and card, but moved sharply to the first guy on his left. He gave him a thunderous head butt. As the second shadow stepped forward, legs stretched, Wolfsangel kicked one of his kneecaps. Wolfsangel could hear it crack. The man screamed in pain and rolled over the stones. The first man was still raddled, flailing about trying to find his bearings. Wolfsangel took advantage of that and gave a right hook so hard the attacker was launched off the ground and fell hard. Wolfsangel stepped quickly towards the man with the broken knee, but suddenly saw a third shadow appearing in the corner of his vision. Turning abruptly about, Wolfsangel found himself facing a beefy man charging toward him with an upraised arm. Wolfsangel caught a glint of light and realised the guy had a knife. As the knife bore down on him, he blocked the chopping hand with his left elbow, his right hand went below and grabbed his left hand. With a quick movement backwards, Wolfsangel had ripped the arm out of the socket. Another scream pierced the night and Wolfsangel watched in satisfaction as the man fell to his knees, wallowing in deep pain.

He paused for a moment to catch his breath and then walked over to the man with the broken knee. The guy was trying to get up on one leg and limp away. Wolfsangel gave him a vicious kick to the side of his head. His attacker blacked out. The third guy, despite a broken right arm, managed to locate a Stanley knife in his pocket and was waving it about with his left arm. After witnessing the relentless elimination of both his companions, he realized that he had little chance against the Wolfsangel. He started to walk away from the scene - walking backwards and waving his little knife with a threatening gesture. It was pretty clear that he was right-handed and the knife posed little danger. Wolfsangel was tempted to let him go, but as the man stepped underneath a streetlight, Wolfsangel saw that he was an Arab. Wolfsangel was suddenly transported back to Germany to the time he defended the honour of Old Hellmuth. The familiar feeling of rage stirred up inside of him and exploded.

He jumped at the man, deftly dodged his hand, then grabbed it and turned it around. The man fell onto his stomach and felt his second arm cranking out of its socket. Then Wolfsangel took the beard with his right hand and turned his head. He quickly changed hands and took the knife from the ground with his now free right hand, and whispered, 'I will let you live, but you will carry my mark for life.'

He carved a stripe deep on the forehead of the man and two slanting smaller scratches on both ends of it. The wolfsangel symbol was engraved in the skull bone. Wolfsangel pulled the beard higher and then smacked the twisted skull down onto the stones. The would-be attacker immediately blacked out.

All together the incident had only lasted a couple of minutes, but Wolfsangel was exhausted; during this ordeal, he was running on pure adrenaline. As his body struggled to return to normal, his head burst with a violent headache. He took his money and bank card out of the ATM and stumbled away. He felt some euphoria. The violence had done him some good, psychologically. The adrenalin rush made him feel like a god, superior and strong. He wished Linnea could see him now.

The feeling didn't last long. He began to crash as waves of exhaustion washed over him. He became confused and disoriented as he struggled to figure out where he was and how to get back to the marina. The disease was clearly not withdrawing and it was only through a stroke of luck that he managed to find his way back. Yeah. He was glad Linnea couldn't see him now. She'd have some choice words for him.

Gripar

It was early morning when Gripar's vivid and slightly lurid dream was interrupted by the ringing of his phone. By the time he had cleared the haze from his head, recognised that his phone was ringing, checked to see who was calling - it was Aksel Sloss - the ringing stopped and a voice mail message popped up. Gripar groaned. It was five thirty in the morning. He was facing the great challenge of transitioning from a blissful dream state - where Zofia took a leading role - to the hard reality of a conversation with Sloss. Gripar groaned again and sat up on the edge of the bed. The voice mail was cryptic: "How come you're not answering the phone? Call me back right away."

Sloss answered on the first ring. "Sloss here."

"Yes, this is Gripar. You rang?"

"I need an update. Any new information on the Wolfsangel?"

Gripar started to fill him in on the conversation he and Sigrid had with Mirre. Sloss interrupted. "I don't really have time for all these details. Tell me, do you know who the Wolfsangel is or not?"

"Not".

There was a pause and Gripar assumed that he was supposed to provide some additional information. He wasn't sure so he decided to wait.

Sloss sounded irritated. "Ok. Thanks for clearing that up. The neo-Nazis are organising an event for Sunday. They are riding the coattails of the Wolfsangel. As you can imagine, the Prime Minister is quite concerned about the contagion effect this is having. I have personally assured him that we are on top of this and that we will have this guy in custody very soon. I will let the media know that as well."

First rule in police work: don't make promises you can't keep. Second rule: Don't involve the media unless you absolutely have to and only if you can control the narrative. Gripar sighed. "Yes, I saw the posts on-line. Do you think it is wise to make a media spectacle of catching the Wolfsangel and putting him in custody? I think that it is going to make things worse because his arrest will become a flashpoint for further violence."

Sloss started a reply, but this time it was Gripar's turn to cut him off. He didn't feel like engaging in a pointless argument. "It's okay, Sloss. It's not my call. We did get a solid lead from Mirre Andersen on the identity of this Wolfsangel and I am planning to pursue it today."

"Good. Keep me informed." Sloss ended the call leaving Gripar sitting on his bed about an hour before he usually got up. Sloss was playing a dangerous game. Wolfsangel, it seemed to him, was using the media to get out his story. An arrest will play right into his hands and will definitely stir up the masses - especially the ultra-right. He decided not to crawl back under the covers and stumbled for the shower instead.

After eating a light breakfast, Gripar called the Geir Verkstad shipyard. He was pleased to find out the name Sjurd Tijsker popped up in their system. That was all he needed to know for now, enough to justify a trip to Urk. He decided to leave his car at home and take the Flytoget shuttle train to the airport. Just as he arrived, he had second thoughts. This guy was a fisherman. He's probably not even going to be home during the week. What a disaster that would be if he travelled to Holland only to find Sjurd unavailable. Getting the number from directory assistance, he called Tijsker's telephone number. A woman picked up the phone. Fortunately, she could speak English. When Gripar asked whether he could speak to Sjurd or not, she said to call back tonight. He'd be home then. Apparently his fishing vessel was up at the wharf for maintenance. Gripar felt relieved he didn't have to face Sigrid's scorn for not double-checking that before leaving.

After getting through security, he had about an hour to kill before his plane left for Schiphol. He looked for a place to get a coffee. Just a short distance away, the American icon coffee place, Starbucks, had just opened up their first coffee house in Norway - at the airport. There was a long line of customers fervently waiting to offer a sacrifice to the goddess of commercial coffee. He decided to forsake that in search of a lesser coffee brand. He found one that was much cheaper and probably tasted as good. As he sat down with his own version of a Verti, his phone rang. His face lit up when he recognised the number.

"Zofia! So good to hear from you again!" Gripar said with a smile. "I wasn't expecting this. How is it in Trondheim, is it raining again?"

She laughed. "Yes, and you know what, I do not care. I live here in a lovely flat. I have the entire first floor of a house on the Rognervegen. Really, the location of this city is great. The low mountains, the harbour, the houses, all so beautiful; it breathes peace and quiet. During the day I have a good view of the harbour! Awesome."

Gripar found a seat by a window overlooking one of the main runways. "So, are you a real estate agent now, calling me to extol the virtues of Trondheim?"

"Well, there is no debate about Trondheim being a nicer place to live than Oslo. So, we won't engage in that discussion. However, earlier I sent you an email about Stein, but something else happened that night, something that has to do with the Tyskerbarn. Rather than emailing you, I thought I would call you. Can I share that with you now? You've got some time?"

"Yes, of course, I'm at the airport waiting for my flight to leave. I have about twenty minutes or so before I can board the plane. You got me curious."

Zofia chuckled. "Perfect timing, then. So last night I ended up in a fairly deep conversation with my landlord. His name is Raiko. He's such a great person. One of the few people in the world who has never told me that I talk too much."

This time it was Gripar's turn to laugh.

"I met him in the entrance way as I was about to head upstairs. Usually when we see each other, we have a quick conversation about the weather or about hockey. We are both hockey fans and deeply disappointed with the folding of the Black Panthers. However, today, he seemed a lot more serious. He told me that he had read my article on the internet and then shared with me that he was a Tyskerbarn from Bergen. I didn't know that. I could tell that he had a lot on his heart and he clearly wanted to talk.

"He asked me if I wanted to come in for a coffee and hear his story. Of course I wanted to. I love listening to people's stories and how that shapes their lives. Well, he had quite the story."

At that, she paused and her voice became softer and Gripar sensed that she was emotionally touched by it - not that he had any particular expertise in assessing female emotional responses - he was just a good detective.

"That Wolfsangel guy, he has struck a nerve, not only with the neo-Nazis. At one point, Raiko told me - and this is word for word - that the Wolfsangel has touched both the living and the dead. At first, I thought that was silly. But, you know, Gripar, I think I am beginning to understand what he actually wants with 'Judging the living and the dead.' The more I think about it, the more I believe that Wolfsangel is not the judge; he wants us to be that! He wants us to judge ourselves, the living, and the previous generation, the dead. He's opened a deep wound that our country has tried to cauterize through silence and disregard."

Gripar wasn't quite following her. "You think he is looking for Norway to ...?" He let the sentence hang, hoping that she would fill in the missing words because he really had no idea and didn't want her to think he was a dullard.

"Yes, he is looking for Norway, our Norway, to feel some responsibility for its past. For the truth."

Gripar wasn't sure what truth she was referring to but was intelligent enough to let her continue uninterrupted. She paused again. "Raiko thinks that this Wolfsangel might be a Tyskerbarn. Someone from his generation."

A Tyskerbarn? Could that be possible? That changes everything. Gripar stood up and started pacing. Something he has always done when he is thinking deeply. If Wolfsangel was, that would mean he would be in his late sixties or early seventies. The amount of energy that it would have required to kill those three men and set up that bunker suggested to Gripar that he was a younger man - fit and athletic. It would be more likely that Wolfsangel is a generation removed. But, if that's true, then how do the neo-Nazis fit into this? "Zofia, I think your landlord may be on to something there. A Tyskerbarn. Hmmm. All along I was thinking that he might be associated with the Nordic Resistance Movement. He certainly has stirred up that group."

"Gripar, there is something else that I need to tell you. I think it was close to eight or nine years ago when I got a phone call from a man who called himself Wulf Engel. I think now that he might be the Wolfsangel."

Gripar nearly dropped his coffee cup. "What are you talking about? How come you never mentioned that to me before?" Gripar was incredulous. He was conscious of the fact that he had to keep his voice down. He caught a few people turning their heads in his direction.

"I don't know. Please don't be upset. I think it is just a reporter's instinct to keep our cards as close to our chest as possible."

"So, what did he want? How did he get your number? What did you tell him?" After his rapid-fire questions, Gripar realised that he was getting aggressive and he really had no right to do so. There was silence on the other end and, for a moment, Gripar thought she had disconnected her call. "I'm sorry," he said, "I had no right to go on like that and you are certainly under no obligation to answer them."

"It's okay. This guy got my number from Stein Bratt. He wanted some advice on media relations and how to get a story out into the public in such a way as to create an impact. I mean, I don't know for absolute certainty, but I have a feeling this is the same guy. Which means, Stein may have been telling the truth when he said he actually met Wolfsangel."

"I'd say there is a good chance you're right. Looks like you must have given him some good advice," Gripar said wryly. "But that certainly lends credibility to the theory that his target audience is not the neo-Nazis but rather the people of Norway in general. He is building a case in the court of public opinion while very deliberately and carefully controlling the narrative."

There was another pause in the conversation as both were deep in thought. Gripar was thinking about social justice and the length to which the Wolfsangel was willing to take to achieve his goal. Zofia was apparently thinking about social justice too, but in a different way. Almost as if she was talking to herself, "He said he wanted to share his personal history with me. He usually hates stories about the Second World War. But the truth is, he has never forgotten what happened to him. The trauma of that affects his life on a daily basis."

Momentarily confused, "Who are you talking about?" Gripar asked.

"Raiko. He told me about the Lebensborn house he came from. It was Bergen Home in Hop, just around the corner from Bergen. His stories were just unbelievable! He remembers when the war was over, how he and the other Lebensborn children were spat on and terribly humiliated. His mother had been called a German whore throughout her life. Imagine that - her whole life. You know, Gripar, when confronted with stories like this, I am actually ashamed of being Norwegian. That's what I'm going to write about today, a good therapy for me. I feel like I have some pull at The Foreigner."

Gripar was touched by her deep empathy. "I think that is a great idea. Hopefully by putting out Raiko's story, something good might come out of all this mess."

"Yes. I'll do that. I think I'll see if he would be willing to work with me and put his story out. You know, I think I might be feeling some sympathy for this Wolfsangel guy - especially if he is a Tyskerbarn."

Gripar grunted noncommittally. He wasn't prepared to go that far, yet. "I'm so glad you called, Zofia. I think you are on to something important here and I'm looking forward to reading about Raiko's story. Perhaps we can get together sometime and bounce some ideas and thoughts off each other?"

Zofia's voice lost some of its serious tone and became bright again. "I've been thinking about spending a few days visiting my sister. She lives in Sandnes and has a new exhibition of her clay sculptures in the Sandnes Cultural Center. I really have to see it, she's been bugging me for the past week to come out."

"Hmmm … Oslo is halfway, so …", Gripar thought aloud.

Zofia laughed. "Well, then we might see each other soon! Bye!" With that, she suddenly broke the connection leaving Gripar with a chagrined look on his face. So, was that a kiss off or did he have a commitment to a date now? Gripar didn't have much time to ponder that because his boarding call was just announced.

After about an hour and half later, he landed at Schiphol. It took some time to arrange for a rental car. It was on trips like this when Gripar seriously considered retiring and setting up a business that assisted travellers with a comprehensive and efficient way to manage vehicle rentals. He was pretty sure there would be a market for that service. He knew he wasn't the only person whose actual flying time was considerably more condensed than the time it took to get a rental car set up and ready to go.

He set out for Urk without really thinking through how he planned to find Sjurd Tijsker and what he was going to say when he did find him. He was fairly certain that he wouldn't be able to pull up to the local pub and simply ask where he lived. When he arrived at the village of Urk - although, it appeared to Gripar that it had outgrown its designation as a village - about an hour later, he still had no clear plan. Somehow he didn't feel like phoning again, so he did what all men would do in this situation, he decided to drive around a bit and scope out the area hoping a plan would magically appear. As he was navigating the narrow streets, he became side-tracked by the fascinating architecture of the local church buildings. There seemed to be a church on every street corner. He also became aware of the children. The place was teeming with them! There were groups playing football in the middle of the street. Many of them were on their bikes weaving in and out on their way to somewhere. Eventually, he spotted a large parking area at the harborside. He decided to stop there and see if someone could offer some advice on locating a residence.

He ambled up to a bench where three grizzled old men were engaged in an animated discussion. They immediately stopped and stared at him when he approached.

Gripar, keenly aware that he was conspicuously a complete outsider, decided to try out his charming side. "So … This is Urk. What a quaint village. I understand it is famous for its fishing industry." Gripar couldn't tell if his charming approach was working. Maybe they don't understand English. He forged on. "So, why do I see so few fishing boats in the harbour?"

The men looked at each other and after several seconds laughed. "Yah. Hello there, stranger. Welcome to Urk." They clearly were having great fun trying out their own bad English on this Norwegian.

"The fish cutters are now at sea, but they do not moor here on Urk anymore. It is too far from the sea. The fish comes here, loaded onto trucks and then brought to the fish auction. The crews take the taxi home every weekend." The old men dragged their cigarettes and studied the foreigner.

Gripar nodded as if he totally understood the fishing industry and was actually a fisherman himself. "Do you know the best way for me to locate a certain Sjurd Tijsker? I was hoping to get some information from him about his family from Norway."

One of them responded, "Yeah, that's one from Eirik the Norwegian and Marianne Weerstand. Of course, we know Sjurd." Another one hocked a brownish loogie on the ground and then volunteered, "His mother lives nearby."

Then the three of them seemed to have a conversation among themselves, completely ignoring Gripar. At least they spoke English, although with a very heavy accent.

"She's a pure 'Urker', isn't she?"

"Yah. Her ancestors have lived here for hundreds of years."

"I'm pretty sure she lives in Ward 4, Number 115."

"I think you're right. That's just around the corner."

Gripar was totally surprised. He interrupted. "How do you know that so fast?"

The men looked at each other and then guffawed. "Urkers are one big family. We know each other," one of them replied.

Gripar was pleasantly surprised at his good fortune in locating Sjurd of Urk so quickly. After profusely thanking the three men, he decided to walk to Marianne's. One of the guys said it was just around the corner. How hard can that be?

It didn't take long for Gripar to find out exactly how hard that could be. There were so many corners that he quickly lost his bearings in the maze of streets and alleys. Quite by accident, he suddenly found himself at Ward 4, Number 115. It was a small two-story traditional house, no front yard. It didn't appear to have a basement as the front door was level with the street. The front windows had a set of laced curtains surrounding a few pots of red-flowered plants which stood at attention on the window sill. Gripar looked up at the second story. It consisted of a severely sloped roof with a two-paned gable window overlooking the street. It looked cosy. Gripar opened the gate and stepped up to the door. He didn't see a doorbell or a knocker. Not quite sure what to do, he made a tentative knock on the door.

'Koem er in!', a sharp voice sounded. Although he did not understand Dutch, he took the chance that was an invitation to enter the home and opened the door. He was met by a sturdy woman with high cheek bones and angular features. Gripar guessed that she would be close to sixty years old. Apparently, she was in the middle of washing up. She was clutching a dish brush which she put down in order to dry her hands. She gave him a handshake that made him wince in pain.

"Good afternoon, Madam. My name is Odd Gripar. I am a police inspector from Norway and I was hoping to be able to speak with Sjurd Tijsker about a case I am working on."

She gave him a hard stare. "Marianne. I not speak good English. So, you find him, yah?"

Gripar was confused. "I'm sorry. Find who?"

"Eirik, of course!" She jerked her chin up.

"Oh. Your husband." Gripar recalled the note from the Wolfsangel. He didn't realise the family believed Eirik may still be alive.

"Yes, my husband. I married that Norwegian. He gone from Fylke. Never come back."

Putting on a dolorous face, he looked her in the eyes. "I promise you, if we locate him, I will let you know."

Her face softened slightly, but still with a deep frown. "So then. If not Eirik, why you here?"

"Well, I want to speak to your son Sjurd about something that may have to do with your husband."

Gripar started to give her a summary of what had happened in Norway, but she waved her arms and interrupted him. "I don't understand English so good. I call Sjurd."

She took the phone and dialled a number. She spoke rapidly in Dutch and Gripar couldn't follow what she was saying. He heard 'Norway' and 'police' and 'father' and surmised she was giving Sjurd a rundown of their meeting. He must have completely shocked her by showing up, although it was hard to tell. Without warning, she thrust the phone in his hand.

"Hello? This is Odd Gripar. I am a police inspector from Norway. Is this Sjurd? I was hoping to talk to Sjurd about some events going on in Norway."

"Okay. I'm Sjurd," the voice on the other end replied with an accent not quite as thick as his mother's.

"I'm calling in regard to a conversation I had with a Mirre Andersen about a case involving the murder of three people. The case has to do with the Tyskerbarn and I understand that there may be a connection with your father, Eirik."

The line was silent. For a moment, Gripar thought the connection was lost. "Hello? Are you still there?"

"Murder, Tyskerbarn, and my father? Well, that is indeed quite something. I think we should talk. What if you come for supper and we can talk after. My mom can tell you where we live."

Gripar was looking forward to this conversation. He handed the phone back to Marianne who obviously then got the low-down from her son before hanging up. The woman looked him straight in his face, expressionless. That kind of freaked Gripar out. "Noorderzand 23' - 6:30", she said and turned her eyes to the door. No chance of misunderstanding that gesture. He thanked her and walked out the door.

Gripar had about half an hour to kill so he decided to take a stroll at the waterfront. His car was still parked there anyway.

At the highest point of the 'island', on the waterfront, the white and red Urk lighthouse was stationed. Gripar stood in front of it and swept his eyes over the lake. The view was spectacular. The lake appeared to be covered in a blanket of gold as the late afternoon sun reflected off it. To the left was a beach full of children laughing and playing in the sand. Many bicycles were parked on the quay at the beach entrance.

"Stunning view, isn't it?" A deep voice startled him. He turned and noticed a man about his height standing next to him. He was speaking to him in English, but Gripar couldn't quite place the accent. It was Dutch, for sure, but not as thick as Marianne's or Sjurd's. The man studied him with a friendly expression - his eyes twinkling and his moustache twitching. "Is this your first time on Urk?"

"Yes. Actually, it is. Is it that obvious?"

The man shrugged, laughing. Well, it wasn't a laugh so much as a guffaw. He put his hands in his pockets and looked out on the lake. "You definitely don't look like an Urker but you also don't look like a tourist. Guessing from your accent, I'd say you're from Scandinavia somewhere, probably on business."

Now it was Gripar's turn to laugh. "You're perceptive. Do you study people for a living?"

"You could say that. During the day, I'm a high school teacher but I'm really a student of life." There was a comfortable silence as the two of them stared ahead. "You saw the statue of the woman looking over her shoulders as she walks away from the sea?"

"Yes, I did. Isn't it over there, behind the houses?" Gripar pointed to the right.

The man nodded. "It's surrounded by a wall of names."

"So what is its significance?" Gripar asked.

The man paused before explaining. "It's a memorial to all those lives claimed by the sea. When the husbands or sons went out to sea, the wives and mothers never knew for sure if that day would be the last they would see of them."

Gripar understood that feeling. It was a sober reminder of the fragility of life. "Urk seems like such an interesting place. Its people must be a special breed, I'm quite certain of that."

"You are not wrong. My father grew up here. While I, myself, don't live here, I still find my soul connected to this place. As fishermen in a small community, Urkers tend to be fiercely independent, family oriented, and intensely proud of their resilience."

Gripar smiled to himself, anticipating his visit with the Tijskers. "They need to be, I suppose. They are a product of this eternal struggle to earn a living from the sea. I suspect they brook no interference from the government. I guess I'll find out since I'm meeting with one of those fiercely independent fishermen in less than an hour."

The man's eyes widened. Stroking his moustache, he remarked, "I think you must study people for a living. I think you have fairly characterised the Urkers. Are you, by chance, an anthropologist?"

Gripar shook his head. "Not professionally. I am a police inspector from Norway. I guess I do, however, study people."

"Well, Mr. Police Inspector from Norway, I wish you the best." Gripar watched as the man made his way up the street.

He made his way to Sjurd's house at the foot of the hump, at Noorderzon. Sjurd's wife greeted him at the door. "Ah, there is our guest from Norway." Gripar was relieved that she spoke good English. She stuck out her hand. "I am the one you talked to on the phone. My name is Jannie. Welcome to our house."

Sjurd took her hand. "I'm Odd Gripar. Thank you very much for having me over."

She guided him to the kitchen table and then got him a mug of coffee. Within moments, five children came into the room to present themselves. Gripar felt like he was at the VonTrapp house as they came up to the table one by one and introduced themselves without a hint of any shyness. They were eager to try out their English. "How do you do?", "Where do you come from?", "Do you have children?", "You're not married?", "Why not?" Gripar discovered that the oldest was a sixteen-year-old boy, the next two were girls, thirteen and ten, and then the last two were boys, six and two.

In the middle of all this, a tall and sturdy man entered with his wife hanging on to his arm. This definitely was the man in Mirre's picture. He had aged somewhat since then. He looked at his children with obvious pride and then honed his friendly blue sailor eyes at Gripar and nodded.

"Hello sir, I am Sjurd. Welcome to my home!" Gripar felt a big work hand enclosing his own and for the second time today a hand-shake made him wince in pain. Sjurd took his seat at the head of the table. It was like a signal. Immediately, all the children scurried to a particular seat and immediately sat down, eyes on their father expectantly waiting. Gripar surmised that it was officially supper time. Sjurd looked at every child around the table, then he said, "Let us pray." They folded their hands and closed their eyes. "Our father who is in heaven …"

After the amen, Gripar was the first served. Jannie put a couple of huge scoops of mashed food on his plate. He wasn't familiar with this dish. It looked like it was carrots, potatoes and onions all mashed together. She dolloped some gravy on it and it tasted delicious. He told them so and they beamed. As he was eating, he brought the family up to speed on the latest news from Norway. The kids peppered him with questions about his country. The eldest boy explained, "We're curious about the land of our grandfather. We've only been there once. We stayed at that boring campsite."

"So, you have been to that Hurdal campsite?" Gripar asked, looking at Sjurd who nodded. "You must have met Mirre Andersen, then?" The kids didn't know what he was talking about. Gripar explained the picture Mirre had shown him. Sjurd laughed and nodded, "That was when I went to Norway by myself. I think it was around 1992 or so. I had taken my boat up to Larsnes at the shipyard there and had it outfitted with some of the latest fishing equipment. Since I had a couple of days to kill, I thought I would drive out to Hurdal and see my family's humble beginnings."

Gripar remembered the words on the back of the photo. "So that's why you wrote that on the back?"

Sjurd raised his eyebrows and looked at him. "I beg your pardon. I am not sure what you are talking about."

Gripar pulled out his phone and showed him a picture. "Right there: *Tijsker's Ommelebommelestien*"

Sjurd stared at it and then rubbed his chin. "That's strange. I know I joked about that, but I don't remember writing that on the picture." Sjurd leaned in closer to study the picture. "I mean, that's not even my handwriting."

That was indeed strange because Gripar was quite certain that Mirre said Sjurd put that on as a thank-you gift. He decided not to pursue it.

"Tell us more about Norway", one of the girls pleaded. Gripar spoke with pleasure about his country: winter skiing, the Sami, the cities and Norwegian cuisine. The children asked him about all kinds of things, they translated and discussed his words in their Urk dialect. Gripar was amused. He looked at Sjurd, who had long since emptied his first full plate and scooped a second from the big pan.

"You were in Norway a fair bit when you were younger, right papa?" One of the boys asked.

Sjurd ruffled his hair. "Yes. Back then, I was only a child. My father was in a hospital there; we visited him there occasionally."

"He was sick, in his head," Sjurd's younger daughter told Gripar.

That made Gripar curious. "Were the two of you close?"

Sjurd glanced at his wife and shook his head. "My father was always so quiet and emotionally flat towards me. I think my father just endured me. He never told me anything, really. Quite different from my older brother. I'm not sure why."

Gripar could sense a touch of melancholy in Sjurd. His own experience with his father was very positive. Gripar doubted he would be the person he was today without the guidance and love from his father. He considered Sjurd's family. It was pretty obvious that Sjurd was determined not to make the same mistake his father did.

The thirteen-year-old piped up. "Grandpa was born in Norway. His father was German and his mother Norwegian. I know what her name was: Anna." She looked proudly at her mother, Jannie.

Jannie smiled politely. "All I know is that that lady had a very difficult life, she was bullied a lot!"

"When I visited Hurdal Verk," Sjurd reflected, "I saw a picture of the class of 1946 and - you know - that's how I discovered my grandmother Anna. I never knew her. Never met her. I also got a chance to actually see the room where my father had lived as a baby. It is still unchanged after all these years. It was great to talk with Mirre. It brought my family history to life."

The six-year-old boy piped up something in Dutch. He had a big grin on his face. Jannie translated. "He says that his papa looks the same as grandpa, he has seen it in the pictures." The boy looked happily at the others. Sjurd nodded to his son and went on to say, "It went horribly wrong with my father. No wonder the poor man had been so psychologically mixed up. He had to deal with two traumatic deaths in his family. First, his sister drowned and then later his own daughter – my sister."

The family around the kitchen table shared a moment of grief. Sjurd broke the silence and directed his attention back to Gripar. "But I still do not quite understand why you have come here to visit us, all the way from Norway."

"We suspect that this Wolfsangel guy knew your father and is somehow connected to the story of the Tyskerbarn."

"Oh", said Sjurd, "any idea what that connection could be?"

"No. We're not sure yet. He could be a German relative because your grandfather likely had other children in Germany. But he could also be one of the German war children, a Tyskerbarn. There are still many of them alive. Or, maybe he's an old friend of the family. We do not know yet. What we do know is that three people are dead, the neo-Nazis in Norway are all stirred up, and the Tyskerbarn are being re-traumatised."

The room fell silent until eventually Jannie jumped up. "Time for the dessert!" She and the girls cleared the table and grabbed some bowls in which they served yogurt with syrup. After that, the meal was officially ended when Sjurd picked up the family Bible and read aloud a passage: "Jesus answered and said unto her, Whosoever drinks of this water shall thirst again: but whosoever drinks of the water that I shall give him, shall never thirst; but the water that I shall give him, shall be in him a well of water springing up into everlasting life. The woman said unto him, Sir, give me this water, that I thirst not, neither come hither to draw."

He looked up at his guest from Norway and added, "That is the only real Lebensborn, the only well of life." After prayer they all helped with supper clean up. Gripar marvelled at how the whole operation was smoothly orchestrated. Once it was completed, all the family members seamlessly moved into other tasks: some had homework, others had to go to church and the little one had to go to bed. Jannie said, "Well, men, how about if I make you some coffee and the two of you can sit in the front room? That would be nice."

Gripar and Sjurd stood up from the kitchen table. Over a few cups of strong Dutch coffee, the two of them compared their life stories. Sjurd was intrigued with Gripar's family and how he dealt with the loss of his entire family in one fell swoop. Sjurd was not immune to dealing with death in the family and Gripar found some solace in their conversation. Sjurd didn't quite understand why Gripar didn't pursue finding out the truth about his parent's car accident. If the police suspected there might be another vehicle involved in the crash, why didn't he do some digging? Gripar had some difficulty in articulating his reasons. "Am I seeking justice or am I seeking revenge", he asked Sjurd.

"What, in your mind, is the difference?" Sjurd wondered.

Gripar paused and searched for the right words to explain what he was thinking. "Well, I think it has to do with motivation. Do I want to find the truth - as you call it - so that I can punish somebody in order to somehow assuage my pain? That's revenge. Do I want to find the truth so that the person responsible comes to a deeper understanding and realisation of how their actions affected other people and owns their actions? That's justice."

Sjurd took a sip of his coffee. His brow was furrowed. "So, maybe that's what this Wolfsangel guy is trying to do. He is seeking justice. Help Norwegians understand how their actions affected other people and somehow propel them to own their actions."

Gripar saw where Sjurd was coming from but disagreed with the method. "You are almost suggesting that the end justifies the means. This Wolfsangel has likely murdered three people. He has stirred up the neo-Nazis which has resulted in some violence. I don't know. I just don't know." He looked at Sjurd and pointed to one of the many Bible verses hanging on the wall.

"Besides, you are a Christian. Doesn't it say somewhere that vengeance is mine, I will repay, says the Lord?"

"Yes," Sjurd slowly nodded. "That is the challenge we all face. Do we passively wait for God to do his work or do we consider ourselves as his instruments in carrying out His work?"

"Or somewhere in between," Gripar added.

They changed topics and Gripar asked Sjurd about his German family. Sjurd had to admit that he actually did not know his German family at all. He had vague memories as a kid of his paternal grandmother. His youth and the language barrier prevented any type of a meaningful relationship with her. He never met his paternal grandfather or even heard any stories about him.

"You mentioned earlier that you have a brother, though, right?" Gripar asked.

Sjurd grew silent and the mood shifted perceptibly. "Yes. An older brother."

The silence grew thick and heavy. Gripar didn't know what to say. "I'm sorry. Where is he now?"

Sjurd shook his head. "We were told he died while on an assignment with the Foreign Legion. My mother received a death notice but there were no remains to be sent home. She was told the body was consumed by fire. My mother has never given up hope that he is still out there somewhere. Certainly, though, growing up he had a much closer relationship with our father than I did. I guess you could say he was daddy's boy and I was mommy's boy."

"I am so sorry," Gripar said softly.

Sjurd nodded his thanks.

Gripar decided to change the focus of the conversation. "Any ideas of why this Wolfsangel is specifically involving your family?"

Sjurd shrugged his shoulders. "No, I don't. That side of the family is still a mystery to me and my guess is there are some deep secrets that may just be starting to bubble up to the surface."

The two of them talked for another hour or so before Gripar rose to take his leave. He came to Urk not sure what to expect but he left with a deeper understanding of Eirik Tijsker. He still wasn't sure of the connection between the Wolfsangel and Eirik, but he had some theories. He was looking forward to bouncing them off Sigrid.

Wolfsangel

He had a dreadful sleep on his rented sailboat that night in the Moss marina. He just couldn't get comfortable at all. His skin felt like it was constantly being pricked with tiny needles. The chemist had warned him one of the side effects of his medication was erratic sleep patterns. He remembered scoffing at that. He was a soldier used to dropping off to sleep almost any time and any place. It was a necessary part of surviving on the job. He wasn't scoffing now.

After realising he wasn't going to fall back asleep, he decided to just get up and start his day. It was half past six anyway. His whole breakfast routine had changed. In addition to preparing his toast and eggs, he had to count out a whole battery of pills and swallow them with his coffee. What a way to waste a good cup of coffee! The only highlight of his breakfast this morning was beholding his beautiful yellow house. He leaned back on his chair, soaking in the lovely warm summer morning. He imagined the medicine's healing touch coursing through his blood as it gave an ass-whooping to the disease. Ass-whooping. Wolfsangel smiled as he savoured the moment when those three Arab assholes tried to rob him and he inscribed the Wolfsangel hook on their forehead. For the rest of their lives, every time they look in the mirror, they will be reminded of the consequences of messing with the Wolfsangel.

He got up to check online how the events he had initiated were progressing. It pleased him immensely that the Hurdal Three and the Tyskerbarn were still making headlines. The plan was working. Finally, the nation was waking up. Very soon, the Three will open their mouths and the world will hear their confessions.

He suddenly became aware of the wind caressing his hair. It was a gentle reminder to get up and make preparations to sail back to Oslo while the wind would be at his back.

Gripar

Gripar was feeling downright grumpy right now. His day started off quite well. He came back from Urk feeling positive that they were on the right track identifying the three victims and even identifying the Wolfsangel. He also enjoyed a good night's sleep in Amsterdam, which was unusual because he rarely had a good sleep in a strange bed. Things, however, started taking a turn for the worse when, upon arriving back in Oslo, his first order of business was taking a call from Aksel Sloss.

No introductions or prelude. Just, "What the hell were you doing in the Netherlands?"

"I was following up on a lead. I met with Sjurd Tijsker - the son of Eirik Tijsker."

Gripar heard a grunt on the other end. "So, obviously you've haven't heard of the latest escapade of the Wolfsangel?"

Gripar's heart sank. He thought he detected a note of glee in Sloss' voice. What now? "Um. No. Tell me."

"Stein Bratt's group found three Arab immigrants with a wolfsangel cross carved in their foreheads. His group is going nuts with their anti-immigrant, anti-Muslim bullshit and claiming that the Wolfsangel is on their side."

Gripar groaned. "I'm guessing this is complicating things a bit."

"No kidding," Sloss snapped. "The last thing our government wants is more fodder to that group. Besides, you seem to think this Wolfsangel thing has only to do with the Lebensborn program. Even if that were true, it's back-firing and stirring up a bunch of wing-nuts. You've got to get your head in the game and catch this guy."

It was a tense exchange; Gripar was under the gun to find this Wolfsangel and bring him to justice.

His mood didn't lighten much with his second order of business - checking his email for an update on what Sloss was referring to. A smile broke open as he noticed that Zofia had sent him an email. His mood temporarily lifted as he imagined her reaching out to set up a time to get together.

However, he quickly discovered it wasn't quite the email he imagined. It was devoid of any personal touches - just the facts. She had emailed him a hyperlink from some shady neo-Nazi website and noted there were many reactions to it on the internet. He clicked on the link and found himself staring at the following message of 'Vargsmål', written by the neo-Nazi Stein.

Vargsmål, 'Speech of the Wolf.' Black Death! Time to pull up together! Let's get together, Norwegian brothers and sisters, let us come together from all sides, in Holmestrand, years ago training grounds for Norwegian Nazis! On Sunday, July 4th, by car, by bus, on foot, by boat! Take wolfhooks along, paint them on your clothes! Sunday, July 4 is our day of the wolf; we will form a new Norwegian Legion. See you at the parking lot at Holmestrand train station! Stein

Gripar scratched the back of his head. Great. He now more fully understood why Sloss was upset. He wondered if the Wolfsangel himself would be checking out Holmestrand on Sunday?

As he walked into his office, a dark cloud hanging over his head, he was slightly put off by the big smile on Sigrid's face. "Okay. You look happy. I suppose you have good news." It came across a little curmudgeonly.

"Okay. You look grumpy. I suppose you have bad news. Your date last night didn't show up?"

Gripar flashed her his best 'drop dead' look. He had to be careful using that look, though. His mother once told him he looked like a constipated warthog in heat when he pulled that face.

His look did not have the desired effect of silencing Sigrid. She just laughed. "I am truly puzzled by the lack of females just clamoring to go out with you."

Gripar cracked a smile. "Please tell me why you are so happy."

Sigrid was coy. "Well, first, the Forensic Science Department has some results they would like to share with us. I told them that we would drop in sometime tomorrow - I wasn't' sure what time you would be back today, otherwise I would have scheduled it for later this afternoon."

Gripar was starting to feel better. "That's okay. This Sjurd guy is definitely the son of Eirik Tijsker. I have some pictures of Sjurd, Eirik, and the rest of the family. They are being printed so I can post them on the board."

Sigrid started pacing around the room. "Good work. We've now established there is a connection between Mirre Andersen and Sjurd Tijsker. We now need to find the connection between the three bodies and Eirik Tijsker. Speaking of which, I believe I have a strong lead on the identity of another one of the three bodies."

Gripar leaned back in his chair, closed his eyes, and listened attentively. He knew by now not to interrupt her with frivolous questions.

"So, if Olaf Andersen is one of the three bodies and he disappears off the face of the earth in 1997, then it made sense to me to look for other missing people around the same time frame. I went through the list we had the other day and found a lead. I discovered that a certain Finn Undredal, born in 1926, a retired policeman, disappeared in 1998. He was 72 years old at the time of his disappearance. He had been married and divorced. His ex-wife, five years younger, is still alive. Her name is Eira Undredal. They have two children.

"I got a hold of Eira to see if she was willing to speak with me. After some cajoling, she agreed to meet me at 11 o'clock at the Jess Kaffebrennerie. I came a bit early, found a seat, and ordered a coffee. Shortly after eleven, this lady walked in and approached me. She had the appearance of a person much than older than she was. Her mind was a sharp as a pin. She told me that she had been married to Finn Undredal for years, but the two of them were divorced for some time already prior to his disappearance. In fact, Eira could not recall when she had last seen him face to face.

"She first met him when he was about twenty-two, in 1948 or 1949. Finn Undredal swept her off her feet. He often took her out. Charmed as she was with him, she fell in love. She told me that she was new in Jessheim and he was her saviour. Eventually, his true colours showed and she found out that he was very possessive of her.

"Well, not surprising, he was a real womanizer, even during their marriage. Eira recalled that she often took phone calls from other women. She eventually had enough, gathered her courage, and gave him the boot. She later learned that there were people who absolutely hated him because of his father, a real dick who apparently was close friends with the Germans during the war. She also found out that he was involved somehow in a case of a drowned girl. She was glad he was gone for good ..."

Gripar suddenly sat up. "Drowned girl? What case are you referring to?"

Sigrid stopped, her train of thought interrupted. "I don't know. I haven't pursued that yet."

Gripar remembered Sjurd talking about how both his sister and his aunt had drowned. He wondered aloud if this was a mere coincidence. Sigrid promised to look into that as she continued her report. "Well, Finn has a pretty sordid past, so if he is somehow involved in a girl drowning, that wouldn't surprise me at all."

"Okay. Continue on," Gripar responded.

"Apparently, one evening her oldest daughter disclosed to Eira that her father had sexually assaulted her. When Eira confronted him with this information, Finn apologized and confessed that he himself had been abused by his mother when he was young. He agreed to some therapy but some ten years later, he abused his younger daughter. He denies that, of course, but the younger daughter's story is pretty convincing."

Gripar shuddered. Over the years, he had seen the results of the worst side of human nature. He never got used to that. This Finn guy was a policeman. Sworn to protect. "How are the daughters doing now?"

"Eira said that they are doing as well as can be expected … after years of therapy." Sigrid paused and they both contemplated the reality of what those girls went through.

"What happened to Finn. Did he ever get arrested for the assault?"

Sigrid shook her head. "The daughter didn't want to testify and because Finn confessed so readily and took therapy, nothing else happened to him. While this was all being sorted out, he stayed on with the police service. They reassigned him to guarding the cells. He finally got fired because of an allegation he tried to sexually assault a female prisoner. That's when he disappeared for a while and eventually came back to Jessheim and lived with a former prostitute for a while in an old trailer parked just outside of the city."

Gripar got up out of his chair and also started pacing. “What makes you so sure that this Finn guy is one of the Hurdal Three? Is there a connection somehow between Wolfsangel and Finn?”

“Good questions”, Sigrid nodded. “I spoke to his current wife and she said that Finn suddenly disappeared in 1998. He never said anything or took anything with him. He just left. A couple of weeks later, she received a postcard from Finn in the mail. It was postmarked as coming from the USA - from Virginia. He had written, ‘I’m sorry’”.

Gripar studied the whiteboard he had set up. “Interesting. If he is one of the three, what is the significance of the postcard? Why was it mailed from the US? Does Finn strike you as the type of person who would be sorry for something?” Turning back to Sigrid, he noticed a look on her face. “Okay. You’re holding something back. What is it?”

With a broad, almost giddy smile, “When I showed her a picture of the three bodies, she was quite certain that the middle person was Finn.”

Gripar’s excitement grew. If they had potentially identified two of the three people, that was good news, indeed. He gave her a high five. “What we need to do now is find the connections between Eirik Tijsker, Olaf Andersen, Finn Undredal, and this Wolfsangel.”

For the next hour or so, the two of them went over the details as they knew them and charted it on the board.

Wolfsangel

That same evening, Wolfsangel arrived back at the Radisson hotel. He had been to the hospital for a treatment as well as a session with Linnea. Originally, he wanted to drive back to Moss but he felt too tired for the drive. Linnea had told him that was to be expected. She also reminded him he would be experiencing not only significant physical symptoms, but also changes in his emotional states. He would experience a roller coaster of emotions. So far, she had been right and he was learning, albeit reluctantly, to navigate through these changes.

On his way through the lobby, he picked up a copy of the Drammen Times. A headline caught his eye: *'Devils on their way to the lake of fire!'* When he arrived in his room, he cupped a couple of pillows at the head of his bed, sat down and read:

No coincidence! What do Black Metal, the Norwegian Legion and the 4th of July have in common?

The Norwegian black metal scene, generally assumed to be responsible for torching several churches in the nineties, seems to be rearing its ugly head again in another deadly form. Under the call of the Wolf, A band of neo-Nazis are looking to gather together on the fourth of July in Holmestrand. That is next Sunday. Why the fourth of July? Are they going to be celebrating American Independence Day with fire and sulphur? Probably not. That particular date and place is actually hugely significant for neo-Nazis in Norway.

It is true that Holmestrand hosted many Germans as guests during the Second World War. There is more to it, though. Consider that our pro-German country produced fifteen thousand Norwegians as volunteers with the Wehrmacht or SS in the years 1940-1945, many fighting on the front lines. Most Norwegians volunteered to join the Waffen SS, some tried their luck in the Luftwaffe, or the German army, Kriegsmarine, NSKK, Organization 'Todt.' The Norwegian SS men and women reported in Gulskogen and received their training in the vicinity of Grefsrud, Holmestrand!

There's more. The Norske Legion, abbreviated as 'DNL' was founded on June 29, 1941 by order of Joseph Terboven. Our own Major Vidkun Quisling from the Nasjonal Samling party was integrally involved in the founding of the legion from the very beginning. Their first recruitment rally was held on July 4, 1941.

So, these neo-Nazis are not celebrating the American Independence Day. They are recreating the founding of the real Norwegian Legion. Harking back to 1941, this Legion was going to be 100% Norwegian, with Norwegian uniforms, weapons, language and officers. The main goal of this formation was to join forces in the fight against the Russian enemies. Thousands of volunteers arrived. The hope is that thousands of volunteers will arrive this coming July 4 and unite to fight against the enemies of Norway.

/ Stein Bratt/ Trondheim

Wolfsangel grinned. "Thanks Zofia, this was based on your ideas and Stein executed it well. We'll see how I feel on July 4. I might even show up."

He got his laptop to check on what Zofia had completed for the Foreigner. He knew she had been interviewing a couple of Muslims about how they felt about the upcoming neo-Nazi rally.

She interviewed two Muslims who only provided their first names: Zahid and Yusuf.

The Foreigner / Zofia: 'What do Muslims generally think of Nazisim?'

Zahid: 'Nazis were wrong, of course.

The Foreigner / Zofia: Ok, but there seems to be several clear similarities between the Nazis and the followers of Islam. For example, both demonize their enemies and sow hatred. I even read that many Bosnian Muslims fought along with the Nazis!

Zahid: That's Zionist banter and it's not true. We don't sow hatred. Islam is love. If all people were Muslim, we would have such a beautiful planet!

Yusuf: We are peaceful model Norwegians; we keep our civil democratic duties and pay taxes. We would never join neo-Nazis. They hate us. They beat us up! Have you heard what happened in Moss? Three of our brothers were attacked by neo-Nazis, they cut a Nazi symbol in their foreheads.

Wolfsangel couldn't help but grin. Attacked by neo-Nazis. Not even close. They were a bunch of thugs intent on robbing him. He glanced through the rest of the interview but there was nothing of substance there. It was all good. The call of the Wolf was starting to polarise the community.

Feeling himself getting sombre, he wanted to pour himself a whiskey and smoke a cigar. A picture of Linnea flashed in his mind. Grumbling to himself, he poured himself a glass of coke instead. The glass trembling in his hand, he opened his balcony door. He surveyed Oslo and said intensely under his breath, "I will grab you by the balls. Intense pain does a great job in bringing people closer to the truth."

Gripar

Thursday morning, Gripar met up with Sigrid in the parking lot of the Kipros building. They walked to the Forensic lab in silence - each deep in their own thoughts. Gripar knew that he should reveal to the rest of the team the separate note he found from the Wolfsangel. For reasons he really couldn't articulate, he was reluctant to let the others know that somehow the death of his parents are all part of this plot.

Terje Kjeldsen was the lead investigator from the lab. Gripar had worked with him quite often through the years and had a deep respect for him. Their standard joke had to do with their difference in size. Terje was shorter than Gripar by at least forty centimetres. He had started losing his hair in his teenage years and decided just to keep it all shaved. You'd think he might suffer from small-man syndrome, but Gripar quickly discovered what Terje lacked in stature, he more than made up with his sharp mind and keen sense of humour. That combination made many a person feel quite small in his presence.

So, it should have, but it didn't stop Gripar from cracking, "Hey Terje, I was going to make a joke about short people, but I decided not to stoop to your level."

Terje and Sigrid looked at each other as if they shared a deep secret together. "Ha. I was going to give you a nasty look, but I see you already have one," said Terje.

As if on cue, Sigrid followed that up with, "Yah, your face would make an onion cry." After giving each other a high five, the two reverted back to a more serious disposition and continue their walk, leaving Gripar wondering what just happened to him.

"Please, come into my office," said Terje. He gestured for Sigrid and Gripar to join him around a TV screen. On the screen was a picture of the three corpses.

"All right." Terje cleared his throat. "Our team has gone through the bunker with a fine tooth comb. Here is what we have learned. First. Let's talk about the time of death. It is very difficult to determine with any accuracy how long these bodies have been dead. I'll get to the reasons why in a minute. But, we are quite confident in saying that the time gap between the death of this first one and this second one consists of close to ten years. However, the time of death between the second one and this third one is closer to two or three years."

Sigrid, busy taking notes, looked up at him. "Any idea when this bunker was constructed? Could we make the assumption that the construction of the bunker coincides with the killing of the first person?"

Terje shrugged. "I don't think we can. We are fairly confident the bunker is around fifteen years old. That would make the time of death of the first person around 1995. However, you have indicated that the second one likely died somewhere around 1997 - the year at which he completely disappeared. That would only be a two-year gap."

Gripar thought that through. He mused, "Even if we allow some variances, I can't see how we can fit the death timelines between the construction of the bunker and the deaths of the last two people. So, I think it is safe to conclude that whoever killed the first person stored the body off-site and brought to the bunker later."

Terje brought up some pictures of the bunker. One of them showed the outside side and the other three were inside pictures, shot from different angles. "The bunker was definitely well insulated and ventilated. Whoever designed and built it did a very effective job of ensuring it would remain a cold storage even during the summer."

"Yet," said Gripar, "something was done to the bodies presumably to prevent decay. Judging from what I initially saw in the bunker and from these pictures, it appears the bodies were coated with some sort of a translucent covering."

Terje got a smug look on his face. "You're absolutely right. Whoever did this had the bodies encased in fibreglass after a thorough treatment with hydrogen peroxide. It definitely wasn't a professional job, but it was effective in slowing the rate of decay. Each of them had their clothes removed, their bodies washed and treated with a solution of paint thinner and ammonia which prepared the body for the application of the resin. He would have had to apply the fibreglass in a warm environment."

"Any idea if the bodies were fibreglassed at the same time?" Sigrid asked.

"Good question," Terje responded. "I would say, based on the evidence, there is a high degree of probability they were fibreglassed at different times. There are enough differences in the preparation of the bodies and manner in which the fibreglass was adhered to the bodies to suggest there was a significant time gap between each one. My best guess is that the fibreglassing was done shortly after their death."

Gripar started pacing around. "I think we can safely make the following assumptions. First, the first person was killed around twenty years ago. Second, the third one was likely killed around ten years ago. Third, the bunker was constructed about fifteen years ago. So, whoever did this, constructed the bunker, fibreglassed three bodies, and arranged them in a specific display and then waited roughly ten years before revealing this to the public." He paused to stare at the other two. "Why?"

"Everything seems to point to a methodical and organised plan," said Sigrid. "So, there probably are reasons for that. This might provide some clues as to the identity of the Wolfsangel."

Gripar was frustrated. "How does a person find three people, kill them, encase them in fibreglass, and construct a bunker without anybody noticing it?"

Terje, still studying his report, slapped it with the back of his hand. "Unfortunately, the truth is, there is absolutely no physical evidence that this Wolfsangel person was responsible for the death of these three people."

"Ok, that's fair," Gripar replied, "but is there evidence that this Wolsangel was the one responsible for gathering these bodies, treating them with fibreglass, and then arranging them in this bunker. We may not be able to prove he killed them, but we should be able to prove that he is responsible for everything else."

Terje nodded in agreement.

"Were you able to determine the cause of death? Was it the same for each of them?" Sigrid asked.

Terje shook his head. "No, we don't think so. We believe that one of them, this one, died from a heart attack. He did have a small skull fracture, but that wouldn't have been sufficient to kill him. On the other hand, the cause of death for this third one was strangulation. His windpipe was cut by a wire. The cause of death of this second one is undetermined. We are still running some additional tests."

Gripar processed this information. It was confusing. "I know we haven't ruled out a serial murder, but serial killers tend to use the same method. This one has three separate methods. I wonder why? Were there any sign of torture or any indication to suggest there was resistance?"

Again, Terje shook his head. “No. There were no signs of bruising or any other classic signs of resistance. Based on that, I would conclude that the three knew their attacker.”

Gripar agreed. “Yet, the strangulation by wire suggests something personal. It is a much more violent death.”

Sigrid wondered if a toxicology screen was done. “Did anything come up? Were these guys drugged before they were killed?”

“Accounting for the length of time the bodies were deceased, the tox report showed no evidence of drugs and chemicals,” Terje replied. “But the interesting thing is that one of them showed an anomalously high concentration of alcohol.”

There was a pause as the three of them considered all this information.

“Do you have any ideas about the identity of any of these three men?” Terje asked.

Sigrid explained their theory of Olaf Andersen and Finn Undredal. When Terje heard that Finn was a retired police officer, he got excited. “Human Resources will have Undredal’s information on file that we can use to make a match to the body. I’ll work on that straight away. Andersen will be a bit trickier. The best we can hope for is using dental records. Can one of you contact his wife and determine which dental office might have his records?” Sigrid volunteered to do that.

“That leaves us with identifying the first body as well as figuring out a connection between the three of them,” Gripar mused.

“The four of them, actually,” Sigrid pointed out. “The three bodies and this Wolfsangel.”

Gripar nodded, not wanting to voice just yet that there is a fifth - his parents. “The common thread in all this is Eirik Tijsker. That’s where we need to start.”

Each of the three went their separate ways. Gripar decided it was time to look into some details regarding the death of his parents. He went down into the records room and after an hour or so of searching, found the file. It wasn't very thick. As he scanned through the documents, he was suddenly hit with a wave of deep melancholy. It almost overwhelmed him. After going through the report, he was glad he did. He stared at the paper and reread the second last paragraph. He had stumbled across something very interesting. Something that he had not known before.

An hour later, he was sitting back in his office staring at the phone. Sloss had just called to inform him that he and Sverre Lodbrok would be stopping by his office later this afternoon to have a discussion on the Wolfsangel case. Gripar found himself with a headache brewing at the back of his head. He tried to massage it away. The situation was complicated enough with the involvement of the PST and Sloss, but now the Royal Family is involved? This was not a meeting he was looking forward to.

Gripar knew Sverre, not necessarily on a deep personal level, but had some discussion with him over the course of the last couple of years. Recently, he and Sverre were part of a panel discussion on a network TV show dealing with the rise in crime in Norway. Sverre was involved in the recently formed Global Dignity Project – a project that was designed to promote the concept of human dignity across the world. It was a noble project, no doubt, but as a police officer, Gripar often found it difficult to see a lot of dignity in the humans who perpetrated horrific violent crimes. It brought a good deal of satisfaction to Gripar when he was able to arrest the offender and bring him – or her – to justice. For him, justice was seeing the criminal locked up behind bars.

Sverre, on the other hand, believed that all humans, regardless of circumstances, have intrinsic worth and value and are capable of being transformed into living dignified lives. As a member of the Royal Family and as well as a personal friend of the prime minister, Gripar had expected Sverre to be distant and full of himself. Sure, Sverre was touted as a man of the common people, as having a deep love for his fellow Norwegians, and as a man who worked hard to ensure justice and liberty for all. Gripar was inherently skeptical of those kinds of people. He figured Sverre would be like a typical celebrity – concerned about carefully cultivating and maintaining a specific public image. However, Gripar had to admit to himself that he was pleasantly surprised to find the thirty-two year-old, red-bearded man humble and sharp-witted. Given that, Gripar was willing to keep an open mind about this case. Hopefully Sverre was genuinely interested in this case for all the right reasons.

Shortly after three o'clock, the receptionist ushered in Sverre Lodbrok and Aksel Sloss. Gripar warmly shook Sverre's hand. Sloss wasn't interested in pleasantries. "Is there some coffee?" He looked around Gripar's office.

"We'll have to go to the cafeteria for that. Follow me." Gripar led the way. As they passed by the various cubicles, Gripar noticed heads turn up and stare at Sverre as they walked past. Gripar could sense the mood in the room change as people looked at each other wondering why Sverre was here in the building. Of course, Sloss was basking in the limelight. He leaned into Sverre a couple of times as if sharing deeply confidential information. Gripar suspected that Sloss' desire for coffee was a deliberate attempt to walk the red carpet.

When they got back to his office, Gripar turned to Sverre. "I must be honest. I was somewhat surprised to hear from you and am very curious about why you are interested in this case. Does this have to do with our last panel discussion about human dignity?" As Gripar's ears filled with a hearty laugh, he added. "You know, I think you are going to see that this case is about the total lack of dignity."

"Gripar, come on, man. You are too pessimistic about the human condition." Sloss snorted an agreement as Sverre continued, "But, besides, I have other interests in this case besides the study of human dignity. I had a conversation, off the record, with the Prime Minister, and he is actually quite concerned about the potential of this case to embarrass the government."

"Ok. I'm not sure I understand. Is it because it has become so public?"

"Partly, I'm sure. The case is public because whoever is responsible for this is making quite a show in the press. But there's more to it than that. The Prime Minister has been briefed by the Ministry of Justice that they have come across some intelligence regarding a fairly sophisticated group of neo-Nazi's who are becoming increasingly more organised in our country."

"Yes, Sloss here has mentioned that to me", Gripar said. "But, I am not sure how this is an issue of national security".

Sverre and Aksel exchanged glances. "Well, if you can keep this conversation between the three of us for now, I can give you some details," Sverre responded.

"Of course, I understand."

"The Ministry of Justice is concerned about the way in which the loosely connected cells of neo-Nazism in the Nordic countries are becoming more organised and centralised. For example, the Swedish Resistance Movement under the leadership of Klas Lund has been attempting to do just that. The Ministry has growing evidence to suggest that neo-Nazi groups in Europe and Russia are providing support, both financial and structural. It is very worrisome, indeed."

Gripar wasn't at all surprised. Like others in the Kripos, he had been noticing a rise in violent criminal activity that has ties with some Right-Wing groups. Not only that, but it seemed to Gripar that there was a growing tide of people who were speaking out loudly against globalism and multi-culturalism. In the past, it was easy to dismiss these people as nut-jobs. Not so any more. "So, what's this got to do with this case which just arrived in our laps?"

"I'm not entirely sure myself. However, the Prime Minister is worried. And, of course, when he becomes worried, that gets passed on down the pipeline. That is why the PST have been asked to check into this and make a determination if these three dead guys and this Wolfsangel are connected with the Swedish Resistance Movement."

Gripar was becoming more and more convinced that there was no real connection, especially after his meeting with Terje. Sigrid did some preliminary investigation and couldn't find any obvious links between Finn and Olaf with any organised neo-Nazi movement. It also appears like Wolfsangel was pretty much working alone. Shaking his head, "Hmm ... what would be the connection?"

At this question, Sloss took over. "Well, the use of the wolfsangel symbol, for one thing. It is connected to the Nazi SS group called the Werwolf. The Werwolf was thought to be a Nazi underground guerrilla group who was tasked by Goebbels to undermine the Allied advances. There were reports, all unconfirmed, that this group continued on after the Germans lost the war. Their mission was to create havoc and confusion while at the same time propagating the supremacy of the Aryan nation."

Gripar connected the dots. "So, the government – sorry, the Prime Minister - is worried that somehow this Wolfsangel is trying to unite the past with the present and continue on in the pursuit of White Aryan supremacy?"

Sverre nodded. Sloss asked Gripar, "Do you know for sure if this Wolfsangel is a single person or if this is actually a front created by a group?"

"That's a good question. We are not completely sure, but so far the evidence seems to support the claim this is the work of a single person. However," Gripar shrugged. "we haven't completely ruled out the possibility that the Wolfsangel is actually part of a larger group." Looking at Sloss, Gripar asked, "Could he be with the Swedish Resistance Movement?"

Sloss shrugged. "I think that is something that you need to leave with the PST. Your job is to focus on catching this guy as soon as possible and charging him with the murder of three people." Pointing to Sverre, "Let us worry about national security. We thought we would stop by to give you the bigger picture so you understand the importance of getting this guy as soon as possible." At that, his phone beeped. Glancing at the screen, he sighed. "Sorry, I need to go. Something's come up. Your Highness, shall we?"

Sverre shook his head, catching Sloss off-guard. "It's okay. You go ahead. I'll call my security detail and they can pick me up in twenty minutes. I just have a few more questions for Inspector Gripar."

Sloss looked nonplussed. His eyes went back and forth between Gripar and Sverre, not quite sure what to say. Gripar faced an enormous struggle to control his facial muscles in not forming a huge, smug grin. Judging from the look on Sloss' face, he probably wasn't as successful as he should have been. Fortunately, Sverre dismissed Sloss with a wave.

Once Sloss had left, Sverre reiterated, "We just want to be cautious. I think the Prime Minister is concerned enough to sit up and take notice of what's been going on. Besides, you know politicians, they always get worried if something comes up that might negatively affect their public image. There may be nothing to this at all. But, I would love to see how your case is progressing."

Gripar brought Sverre to the room where he had set up the whiteboard. Sverre took his time and examined everything. He didn't say anything – just the occasional grunt or throat clearing. Finally, after ten or so minutes, Sverre turned around to face Gripar. "I'm impressed. You have done a lot of work in such a short time. Now, I need your honest opinion. What do you really think? Are we looking at the work of one man with a mental health issue or is this the work of a highly organised group attempting to promote an agenda?"

Gripar cleared his throat. "Well, to be honest, I think the answer lies somewhere in between. I do believe that this is the work of one man. I am not sure, though, that he has a mental health issue. I do think he definitely has an agenda. It is clear these three people have been dead for a long time. This is not a recent killing. Whoever did this has been planning this whole thing for a long, long time. This person has a lot of patience, that's for sure."

Sverre pointed to one of the pictures – one that clearly showed the bunker wall with the words 'judge the living and the dead'. "What do you make of this, then? What sort of symbolic meaning is behind these words?"

Gripar nodded. "When I arrived on the scene in Hurdal, Brekke Dahler from the Hurdal Press made a remark about a possible symbolic meaning of the 'judge the living and the dead' line. This statement is lifted directly from the Church of Norway's theological document called the Apostles Creed."

"I am familiar with this document, but what is its significance to this story? I mean, is this Wolfsangel guy a religious fanatic who believes it is his responsibility to be the judge?"

Gripar looked at Sverre and furrowed his brow. "The judge of what? That's the big question."

"I guess that might become clear once you have determined the identity of the three men. Assuming, of course, these are the three people that are being judged."

"Absolutely. We are close to positively identifying two of the men. The forensics team is still working on their report,"

Sverre took in the board once more. "So, if this is the work of one man, what is the connection between the Tyskerbarn and the upcoming rally at Holmestrand?"

Gripar moved in closer to the board. "Well, that's another great question. What about the fact that the Germans were using Norwegian women in their attempt to create an Aryan super race? Is this the connection between the neo-Nazi concerns and this case? Is the Wolfsangel a Tyskerbarn and the puppet master behind the surge of the neo-Nazis?"

Sverre was clearly puzzled. "But, it has been over sixty-five years since the war ended. Do you really think it would be one of them? If so, why now? Why wait so long?"

Gripar smiled. “Please be assured, Your Highness, that we are doing what we can to find answers to those questions.”

Sverre returned the smile and looked at his watch. “Well, Inspector, I think you are the right man for the job. Thanks very much for taking the time to meet with me.” After shaking hands, Gripar walked Sverre out to his waiting detail, a little uneasy that he was missing something significant in this entire conversation.

Wolfsangel

Wolfsangel was back in Moss inhabiting his newly acquired rental house. Whenever he drove around on his motorbike, he always took a route that included a drive-by the harbour. He was hoping to catch a glimpse of a certain young lady on a SUP board. Despite finding no success in that endeavour, he was still in good spirits. His treatments were going well and his body seemed to be responding positively. Grudgingly, he hated to admit, he looked forward to his sessions with Linnea. She helped him get in touch with his emotional side that, deep down, he knew was something he really needed to work on. While Blackwater had always stressed the need for the body and the mind to be in sync, Wolfsangel focussed more on the body.

His good mood was also buoyed by how well his plan to keep the story in the forefront of the news was working. The morning news on TV had a short clip letting people know that the police were working on identifying the bodies of the three men. The reporter, in addition to mentioning that the lead investigator was Inspector Gripar, also indicated there seems to be a strong connection of this Hurdal Three to the Lebensborn children after World War II. They also included a brief historical overview of the program.

It was all good. Wolfsangel was pleased. Soon, very soon, people will learn of the identities of the three people. Each one of them will play a role in peeling back the layers of truth that will expose Norway to the reality of what happened.

Despite being pleased at the progress, this waiting around drove Wolfsangel crazy. He found himself doing a lot of pacing around his home. He felt like a lab rat, trapped in a cage. He was not used to just sitting around, drinking coffee, waiting for something to happen. He was a man of action. His head was pulsating, he needed to do something to clear his mind.

Just outside the marina was an outfit that rented motorboats. Earlier that day he spied a beauty. It was a Hydrolift F-26 and was calling his name. He decided to finally heed the call and within half an hour, he was behind the wheel speeding across the Oslofjord heading west towards Holmestrand. His last time sailing, he didn't make it to Holmestrand and he really wanted to scope out the city. He could feel the deck planks under his feet vibrate as he pushed the 500 horsepower engines to full throttle. The wind whipped through his hair and the adrenaline coursed through his veins. He could feel a sense of power and control.

He docked at Holmestrand and found a place to eat. Nearby was a public telephone booth. It was time to make those phone calls. He made three calls, each instructing the voice on the other end to release some information.

First the truth, then the light.

It started to drizzle and Wolfsangel decided it was time to head back. However, by the time he pulled back into the Moss harbour, the cloud cover had broken over the city and the evening sun got her chance to warm up the world. It was a good end to the day. He felt that things were finally moving forward in the right direction.

Except, there was still a loose end. Later that evening he picked up a report that was written by Robert Thomassen.

Saturday April 8, 1978 / Psychiatric Hospital 'Fylke, Oslo / Client: Eirik Tijsker (1943) / Dr. R. Thomassen / report # 11

Today, Eirik Tijsker disappeared from the Psychiatric Hospital in Fylke. Earlier this week, on Monday evening, we had a session scheduled. Unfortunately, I had to call it off because of an unexpected priority appointment that I couldn't miss. I found out the next day that Eirik ended up in a crisis that night and needed emergency assistance. I had a chance to drop by and talk to him briefly. He appeared to be doing relatively well. He was looking forward to the visit of his wife and children who were supposed to come later that day. He asked me if he could show them downtown Oslo. I told him that he is not trapped in Fylke. He was our client, not our prisoner, and could go wherever he wanted.

We set up his wife, Marianne, and the boys to sleep in one of the rooms in Fylke. They were grateful because they really wanted to be close to Eirik. Unfortunately, he hardly recognized them and after two days they left again. On Saturday, he disappeared. He wrote a short farewell letter in which he told her that he couldn't cope with life anymore. He asked her to forgive him. The police managed to locate her before they got on the boat and they came back to Fylke. She searched for Eirik for days but eventually had to give up.

Where is he? Is he dead? We suspected that but could not find his body. The police also sought Eirik in Jessheim after receiving a tip, but no trace of my client was found. Will we see him again? No corpse, no death, so no suicide.

I will close my Eirik dossier, for the time being, hoping that he will be back in a short time.

Robert Thomassen, Fylke, Oslo

Where was Eirik Tijsker?

Gripar

The next morning, as part of his ritual ablutions to start the day, Gripar cycled through the port area of the city. Today, he stopped to admire a sailboat in the port of Oslo. The boat sailed silently and gracefully with its jib to the side. Gripar was brought back to his teen years when his father would take him and his brother out on their sailboat. His dad had always promised to teach him the art of sailing but never got the chance to. After the death of his parents, Gripar went to live with his aunt and uncle - his mother's sister. It was all a bit of a dim memory and Gripar realised that he actually never did find out what happened to that boat. It never really bothered him before to compartmentalise his life to pre-accident and post-accident, but reading through the accident report yesterday had triggered an emotional response that he was having trouble pushing back down into the deepest recesses of his mind.

He felt his cell phone vibrate in his pocket. It was Sigrid. She called to give him an update on what she had found out. First, she found the dental office that has records of Olaf Andersen. She passed that info on to Terje. She had also done some background checking on Eirik Tijsker. She managed to connect with the youngest sister of Eirik's mother who was happy to talk to Sigrid. Eirik's mother was Anna Kristen Pederson. She was born in Holmestrand in 1921. It turns out that she had worked for the Gestapo, first at the SS training camp in Holmestrand, then in Oslo, at the head office. Anna had fallen in love with a high-ranking German SS officer named Hellmuth Reinhard. Anna had given birth to two children of his. One of them was Erich, later changed to Eirik. The other was a daughter named Aveline - later changed to Esther - who had drowned when she was a young girl.

This was fascinating news. The more they dug into the story, the more intrigue they found. They found their Tyskerbarn connection.

Sigrid saved the best for last. The station received two calls yesterday evening. First, Mirre had called and wanted to meet. Apparently, she had been contacted by the Wolfsangel. Excited at that news, Gripar agreed that they should meet with her as soon as possible. Second, Finn Undredal's latest girlfriend also called and wanted to meet with the two of them.

"They both called last night?" Gripar asked.

"Yes, I don't think this is a coincidence. Mirre said she had been contacted by the Wolfsangel. Likely Finn's girlfriend – her name is Irene Stromme – had been as well. There is clearly some movement from the Wolfsangel. I've arranged to first meet with Mirre and then we'll head over to Irene's place. I have her address."

Gripar cycled away, forgetting about the sailboat.

An hour and half later, the two of them were sitting at a garden table at Mirre's home. She had served tea and besides them, the company had one more person. Her name was Rannveigh. Gripar was reminded of a phrase he had seen numerous times in the Bible to describe an elderly person: old and advanced in years. Rannveigh was definitely old and advanced in years. She appeared older than Mirre and a bit more physically less mobile. However, like Mirre, she might be advanced in years, but she sure was still sharp and witty.

Perched on the table was a plain, manila envelope. Gripar could see that it had been ripped open like a child unwrapping a Christmas present. Mirre was watching him with a look of consternation. She glanced at Rannveigh who gave a slight nod. "Thank you for coming out. I'm sorry, but I've kept some information from you. It's something I need to share with you now."

She took a deep breath. "Some years ago, a man who called himself Wolfsangel contacted me. He told me there was this envelope in my mailbox that contained, what he called, Olaf's Confession. He read me some excerpts. There was no doubt in my mind that it really was from Olaf. There were details in there that only he and I would know. The man then told me that Olaf would never be coming back. He didn't explain why, but that's why I was fairly certain Olaf was dead. His instructions to me were very clear. I was not to tell anyone about this Confession until he gave me the go ahead. It might be years, he said, but I was under strict orders not to release this envelope to the police until he had given me specific instructions to do so."

Sigrid articulated the obvious. "I am guessing you got specific instructions to do so?"

Mirre nodded. "He called me this morning." She took the envelope from the table and handed it to Gripar. "So, here is Olaf's confession. It has been a few years since I read it, but I still remember everything. Oh yes, something like this, you never forget!"

Gripar pulled out a set of papers from the envelope without saying anything. Sigrid's suspicions about her were correct. Mirre definitely knew Olaf was dead when she called the police station a couple of days ago. He began to read: *I am Olaf Andersen ... there was once a German whore in the house with children.*

And there it was, the whole story of Olaf Andersen, no gory or intimate details were spared. Gripar didn't know what to say. He passed it on to Sigrid. Glancing at Mirre, he noticed that she was looking at her hands. There were tears in her eyes. "You must think I am a complete idiot for marrying him?"

The thought had crossed Gripar's mind. He didn't say anything. Sigrid spoke up softly, "No, Mirre, we don't. I'm sure you had your reasons."

With her eyes still downcast, Mirre went on. "I should have never married him, this hard man. But what did I know? I wanted so desperately to get out from under my parent's roof. I felt that somehow I could soften him, make him more human. I also really wanted to have a family and for years I prayed for children. For many years, I was angry with God that he didn't give me any. Now, as I look back, I am actually glad that God had not answered my prayers. Anna and her children became my family."

There was silence. The soft wind in the fruit trees wafted in soothing scents. Gripar recalled the last line of Olaf's confession: *No, I have no message to Mirre. Now, give me my whiskey, I'm going to die anyway.* Well, that explains the high concentration of alcohol. It wasn't the definitive, incontrovertible proof Gripar was hoping for, but he had no doubt in his mind that this Wolfsangel killed Olaf.

Sigrid broke the silence. "It sounds like Olaf wasn't really bothered by the knowledge he was going to die."

Mirre didn't respond right away. "He never regretted anything. Never! He did what he wanted and felt no guilt. Our marriage was a farce. He didn't love me. If he believed that I got in the way of what he wanted, he would threaten me with violence. He never made good, though, of those threats."

Gripar wondered what became of the young Eirik. When he asked, Mirre didn't say anything. She just shook her head somewhat hesitantly, as if she didn't quite know what to say.

Rannveigh coughed. Both Sigrid and Gripar looked at her expectantly.

She had been silent through the whole visit. Gripar had wondered why she was here and how she fit into the story. Mirre never really introduced her other than to let them know her name. Her voice was gravelly. "I did see him shortly before he went missing. We passed each other walking down a street in Jessheim. I didn't recognise him at first. He had lost a lot of weight. I don't know if he recognised me. He certainly didn't acknowledge me and kept walking. I turned around and called out his name. There was nothing."

That was about as much useful information as Sigrid and Gripar were going to get. Neither of the ladies were of any help in trying to establish Wolfsangel's identity. They didn't know where Eirik might be nor able to provide any clues as to the connection between the Wolfsangel and Eirik.

The next visit was just as interesting. Irene Stromme had lived with Finn Undredal after his divorce. She now lived in a derelict trailer at the end of an unpaved road. It took them a bit to find the place but eventually Gripar parked his vehicle in front of a domicile that was surrounded by a half-broken, mostly white fence. A row of weeds guarded the large gaps in the fence and a dilapidated weathered mailbox marked the beginning of the path to the entrance. The two of them made their way cautiously down the path and towards the trailer. Their presence was announced by the loud cacophonous cries of some magpies who were not happy about the two trespassers. The birds had laid claim to a set of scraggly mountain birch trees whose limbs probably hadn't been pruned in years.

They both had the feeling that someone was watching them, but the grimy windows provided no visual evidence. Gripar knocked on the door. He wished he had taken a pair of gloves from the car, convinced there were a host of parasites, vermin, and bacteria ready to expand their horizons on his body. He shivered at the thought. No one answered. He reluctantly tried the door knob and found it was locked.

Sigrid spoke up. "Irene Stromme. Are you home? I am Sergeant Ullman and this is Inspector Gripar from the police. You called earlier this morning about wanting to meet with us." They found a trail that looked like it might take them to the rear of the place. Cautiously, the two of them made their way down it. Along the way, Gripar hoped to find a window that was relatively clean so he could see inside. No such luck.

The back door was also locked. Sigrid looked at Gripar and shrugged. Gripar knocked on the door. "Irene! I know you are home. You have nothing to worry about." He paused before continuing. "We'll just sit on those plastic chairs and wait for you to come out."

The two of them headed to the dirty chairs, cleaned them with paper handkerchiefs, sat down and waited for the woman to come out of her front door. The place had become quiet again. The magpies, content in having chased away the intruders, seemed to have vanished. All Gripar could hear was the wind rustling through the tree branches and an occasional hum of an insect. After what seemed like an eternity, but according to Sigrid was less than three minutes, he finally heard some movement inside. The two of them were rewarded for their patience when they heard the door unlock and saw the handle move. Eventually the door swung open slowly and a small creature was released from the darkness of the house. Gripar was mildly surprised that the magpies didn't start up again. Standing in the doorway was a sickly, skinny woman, wearing a dress that was much too big for her. Draped around her shoulders was a faded shawl. Sigrid saw it first and gasped. The woman was cradling a shotgun which was, fortunately, not aimed at them. She was squinting at the two of them, sizing them up. Neither of them moved. Gripar recalled the time as a young boy when his father brought home a homeless dog. It, too, was a skinny thing, obviously mistreated and malnourished. This woman had the same look on her face as the dog - absolute mistrust and ready to bolt if things went sideways. Sigrid and Gripar did not move, they remained leaning quietly in order not to cause panic. The woman stood very still and continued to stare at them.

Gripar broke the silence. "Good day, Irene. I hope we are not upsetting you. We know how badly Finn Undredal has treated you. You called this morning because you have something from him to give to us. Please do not be afraid. I can assure you that Finn is indeed dead. We have confirmed that he is one of the three victims in the Hurdal case." That part wasn't quite true, but Gripar felt the white lie was justifiable.

When she heard that, she lowered the gun and spoke with a slight, barely audible voice. "I was hoping you would say that. Dear God, I have been so scared, so afraid. Thirteen years ago, a stranger told me that Finn Undredal was dead, that Finn would never come back. I didn't know whether to believe him or not. Finn was a very evil person. He would hit me - hard, mean, and often. I can still feel the pain in my body. All this time, I kept expecting him to show up once more and pick up where he left off."

Gripar and Sigrid said nothing, they did not move. It took at least a minute before she took a deep breath and spoke. She wasn't looking at them, her eyes had that distant look. She was clearly needing to get this out into the open. "I was often chained, beaten, and raped. I was alone - there was nobody to call. In fact, I never had anyone, only myself. That fucking asshole knew that. He kept me as a toy, an object of ridicule and hatred. He was a terrible, heartless man. A spawn of the devil himself. He picked me up once, over his head, and threw me into a corner. My bones cracked. He left me there. I almost died from the pain. The next day he finally brought me to the hospital, where they fixed me up a little, as cheaply as possible."

Irene Stromme finally stepped completely outside, closed the door and leaned against it. She continued. "When Finn was drunk, which was quite often, he would cursed the mother of that poor girl who drowned. He said it was her own fault. Yes, he said, it is your own fault, you bitch! He looked at me, but I think he was actually seeing the woman he hated. He screamed that she should not have refused him. He would ramble on about how hurting him like that was the stupidest thing she could have done. He would spit out, 'now your little rat child is dead. Foolish! Cursed woman, Nazi slut ...'"

She paused, shook her head, took a deep breath and continued. This time she looked Gripar in the eye. "One day he was gone. I expected him to be back for dinner, but he did not come back. I became more and more afraid. I knew something was going on, but I did not dare to do anything. I made his dinner for the next couple of days, just in case he would suddenly be back again. Then, after three days, very early in the morning, I heard his car drive up. I was so scared but I stepped outside to greet him.

"It was Finn's car, but it wasn't Finn that walked up. It was a stranger who hid his identity behind a black balaclava. He brushed past me and took a seat in the kitchen. He acted as if he knew me.

"He told me it's over. I did not have to fear anything, Finn Undredal would never return, ever! He also said that Finn had told him everything about his life and his actions. One day in the future, he told me, he would contact me again and tell me to contact the police so I could give them this."

At that point, she reached into a front pocket and pulled out a manilla envelope, identical to the one that Mirre had.

"It's Finn's confession, isn't it?" Gripar asked the woman.

Irene nodded. "How did you know?"

Gripar smiled at her. "You are not alone. There are others." The woman took a deep breath and handed him the envelope. In this case, however, the envelope was untouched and still sealed.

As if reading his mind, the woman said, "The stranger told me I could read it if I wanted to, but he strongly advised me not to."

What a difference between the two women - Mirre and Irene. Both had complete assholes for husbands but the one managed to preserve her self-esteem while the other was unable. It was increasingly more difficult for Gripar to have any sort of sympathy for the two men.

Sigrid spoke up. "So, you have never read the confession?"

Irene's shoulders sagged. "I never dared to open it, but now that I know he is really dead … he is dead, yes, dead! Go ahead, open it and read it out loud." She laughed loud and shrill, a laugh of relief, of newly acquired freedom, of new life!

Sigrid took the envelope and hesitated, looking at Gripar for confirmation. Gripar didn't know what to do. He looked to the woman for some insight. She laughed again. "Who cares. He's dead. What can he do to me now? Read it out loud."

Sigrid opened it up and pulled out its contents. She began reading. "I, Finn Undredal, was born in 1926, in Flåm. I can't remember much of my childhood. I don't think I spent much time outside because I cannot remember anything about nature. No mountains, fjord or waterfalls. I really only remember my mother. She killed herself.

"Shortly afterwards we moved to Jessheim because my father got a job there. He remarried there. He got hooked up with an ordinary peasant woman from a small town up north. She tried to be my mother, but I wouldn't let her. Nobody in my family gave a fuck about me anyway.

"I married a tough old lady. Got some daughters who turned out just like their mother. I haven't seen them in years. Don't want to.

"That old lady thought she could set me on the straight and narrow. She smothered me with her demands. She eventually divorced me because I could not commit my manliness exclusively to her. I can't help it. I love women. I'm crazy about them. I can't help it that I look so good. You know, they are totally attracted to how I fire up the beast in them.

"I don't quite know why, but I ended up living with another woman. That was a disaster too. She is the most irritating person I have ever met. She gets on my nerves so badly that the only way I can shut her up is by slapping her up the head. She asks for it! You probably know exactly what I mean. You draw a clear line in the sand - that's your limit. Anybody who crosses over it does so at their peril. Well, her eternal whining crossed over that line many times. She did so knowing that there would be consequences. I do not understand why she never learned. Really, she won't be able to endear herself to me through her incessant whining. She is such a wimp. Oh, I hate her humility, her meekness; she never blames others, just like my mama. She has that puppy's way of looking at me, you know, sort of guilty. Had I known, I would have kept the first woman. But, what the hell, it doesn't matter anymore, does it?"

Sigrid paused and looked at the woman. Her face hadn't changed. She was beyond the point of caring about what Finn said. He was dead and she was alive. Gripar nodded at Sigrid, encouraging her to continue. He wanted to get this part over and done with.

"Yes. Yes. Yes. I'll tell you about that German whore. Yes, whore. That woman had offered herself to a high German cock during the war. She got a free ride - if you know what I mean. Many Norwegians, like me, had to work hard to survive. My father pretended to be their friend so he could earn a penny, of course. Lots of people did that. He sold them Germans everything, repaired their trucks and earned his money by helping them here and there. But he never whored himself to them, never!

"When the war broke out, at first he was so pissed with the Norwegian government because they had not opposed the Germans one little bit. But then later, he got upset that the Norwegian army were pussies by not standing up to the Communists. Ha, by then he thought the Germans were of the right quality. They took on the world and won, they were superior to everyone. No wonder the old man admired them; he thought it was too bad that he was too old; otherwise he would have joined the Norwegian SS. As a hero he would have received the 'Frontkjempermerke', the heroes medal.

"Well, two years after the war he was shot while standing in his doorway. He got liquidated, as they would say now. By whom? I don't know. I have an idea, but no proof. Doesn't matter now anyway.

"What do I know about Eirik? Only that he was a fucking psycho! Okay, I'll tell you exactly what happened, I don't give a damn. I'm going to die, anyway.

"I already told you that ladies seemed to have a thing for me. I awakened their inner beast. The beast they all know exists within but are too afraid of others to show it. Well, I noticed that his mother's inner beast was awakened whenever I was around. I could see it in her eyes. I got to know her real well. I knew where she worked, where she lived, her children and even her history. For fun, I scared them a few times. I love a good practical joke.

"Besides, in the end, it really was my duty to give her a good fuck and teach her a lesson about loyalty. That whore had no problems at all coupling with that German prick. In fact, she spawned two of his bastards. She should have been ashamed of what she did. But, she had no shame. You only have one side of the story - the whore's side. You got to give me a fairing hearing. I was unceremoniously thrown out, literally thrown out. I was so stripped of all dignity and pride. Of course, I swore to avenge myself. Any real man would have done that. You would have, too.

"Then came that dark and cold night, near the lake, opposite the Romerike School. I got sent there to check on what some punk kids were doing with their car on the frozen lake. I found that these kids had made a hole in the ice. Since everything seemed under control, I was about to drive back to the police station when I saw a little girl walking on the ice towards the hole. I recognised her. She seemed to be looking for somebody. Instead of leaving, I decided to sit in my car and watch to see what would happen. I saw her slip and fall just as she got to the hole in the ice. Her head must have hit the ice pretty hard. She slipped into the water. I don't know why, but I couldn't move. For a minute, it looked like she was going to be able to crawl out of the water. Her head bobbed up and her arms were flailing for a hold. She was staring at me the whole time - daring me to do something. Then she sank and never reappeared.

"I was still sitting in the car calling an ambulance when that woman and her bastard son came. Of course, I got the blame. Like I pushed her into the hole. When the ambulance arrived, it was too late. The girl was already dead.

"This has happened more often to me. People die and I get blamed. Of course in this case, people didn't believe me. They believed that whore.

"I always have bad luck. Same thing with that drunken bitch that got thrown in the drunk tank. I could tell that she wanted me. So, when I had the opportunity, I let her have it. I was just about to bring her into heavenly pleasure when the other policeman on duty walked in. She saw him and started screaming! What a bitch! I tried to silence her, but it did not help. She was like a hell-dog with rabies. I was just too late to get my tool safely behind my zipper. Of course, the other guy saw everything and reported me.

"Just bad luck. I lost my job - no law and order anymore and no respect. I lost my dignity and my good name. I never managed to get it back. All because of that whore and her bastards. My gift is bringing out the primal female. They just can't handle that and it all goes to shit for me.

"Stupid woman. I never did get my life back on track; my first wife had left me and I had to survive. I finally got a job in security back in Jessheim. There I heard that Anna had moved away and her bastard son was in a psychiatric hospital in Oslo. I got this new woman who I really hate. I still have her, even if she is so pathetic. But, at least I have something to fuck and hit whenever I need a pick-me-up."

At that Sigrid shook her head and stopped. "That's it. I'm not reading any more. You don't deserve to be talked about that way."

The woman stood there with her shoulders stooped. Tears were streaming down her face. Gripar realised he was angry. Angry at himself for not considering how reading this confession out loud would affect her. Angry that he was party to her humiliation. Angry at this asshole who treated women like they were chattel. He took the papers out of Sigrid's hand and put them back in the envelope.

Before Gripar could respond, with a primal rage which shocked both him and Sigrid, Irene Stromme looked up into the air and shouted, "Oh dear God, let him burn, burn in hell forever!" Slowly, she lowered her head and turned towards Gripar. She locked her eyes with his. Gripar unconsciously shivered. It seemed like an eternity and then she laughed maniacally. "You do understand that Wolfsangel is my hero, don't you? He is no murderer, no monster!" She turned her back to Gripar and started walking towards her front door. Gripar found his voice. "Thank-you for talking with us."

Without turning around, she made a gesture of acknowledgement and walked inside.

Back in the car, Sigrid immediately made a call to a support group for women suffering from domestic violence. As she told Gripar, Irene will need a lot of support and shouldn't be alone tonight.

It was an emotionally exhausting day for Gripar. There was no doubt now that of the three bodies in the bunker, two of them belonged to Olaf Andersen and Finn Undredal. Officially, of course, they would need confirmation either through dental records or DNA tests.

This story isn't rooted in neo-Nazism, Gripar was even more convinced of that now. Wolfsangel was opening up a story about an ordinary family suffering abuse solely because of their connection to the Lebensborn program.

Do the ends justify the means? Is murdering two absolute scumbags in order to seek justice acceptable? Gripar wasn't sure.

Later that evening, Zofia called Gripar at home. Gripar was glad to be able to talk to her. He enjoyed her company, her humour, and her big picture thinking. She updated him on her conversation with Raiko, her landlord.

"He told me that there was a strong German base for the province of Vestfold in Grefsrud. Apparently it was an SS training camp," she told him.

Gripar didn't know that. He realised that he actually didn't know a lot about his country's history with Nazi Germany. He was surprised at how deeply the Germans had set roots in Norway as part of their master plan.

"Apparently, the big house with the banquet hall is still there. I also understand that the Hedevig Rosingschool for deaf children in Holmestrand was also taken over by the Germans and used for a base." Gripar could hear the awe in her voice. She was like him, completely unaware of the German infiltration into Norwegian society.

"You know," Gripar said, "I still don't quite understand how the neo-Nazis fit into all this." Zofia wasn't sure either and had no theories to offer other than a conversation with Stein.

"Which reminds me," said Gripar, "do you know where he is? We've been trying to locate him the last couple of days but haven't been successful."

"No," replied Zofia, "I haven't heard from him in a while. I doubt he'll want to talk to the police anyway. I think the only way you are going to be to meet him is if you can catch him unaware at tomorrow's rally. You are planning to go, aren't you?"

"Absolutely. What about you?"

"Yes. I was hoping to. I am working on a news piece. My sister is also planning to come out."

Gripar asked Zofia about her sister. He found out that Zofia's younger sister was Kjersti and while Zofia went into journalism, Kjersti went into art. When Gripar asked her what her sister was planning to do in Holmestrand, Zofia became even more animated than her usual self. "She made a fairly large clay sculpture of the Hurdal Three. It is absolutely stunning. She sent me some pictures. They all looked different, just like the real ones, but with more life! The first one with his chin up, intimidating and defiant, rough and uncivilized. The second one looked up with his fat chin down, hands up, almost obscene. The last man, seems older, confident, accustomed to exercise power. She has some real talent."

Gripar figured the first one would be Olaf and the second one was Finn. Still not sure about the third one yet. "So, what is she planning to do with that sculpture?"

"She wasn't quite sure. She just felt this inspiration. She has this passion for melding art and history so I think she is caught up in the story as well, just like the rest of the nation. She said she wants to take it to the rally and show it off. You know artists, they need an audience. Knowing her and how trouble seems to follow her around, I think I will need to keep an eye out on her."

Speaking about trouble following someone around, this afternoon he had an interesting conversation with Sloss. Apparently, Sverre Lodbrok was going to show up incognito - unannounced and unscheduled. Sverre had expressed a desire to meet face-to-face with the Wolfsangel. So Sloss made the arrangements through Stein for the two of them to meet. Unbeknownst to Sverre, Sloss had this hair-brained scheme to use this opportunity to nab the Wolfsangel, despite Sverre's wish to keep the meeting private just between the two of them. Gripar wasn't given any details about where and when this meeting was to take place. In fact, Sloss had urged Gripar to take the day off and enjoy it. Sigrid was adamant that the two of be there. After all, it was Sloss who told them initially that arresting the Wolfsangel was their job. Now he was trying to remove them and set himself up as the hero. No way! The two of them did all the leg work leading up to this. If there was going to be an arrest, they earned the right to be there.

After another thirty minutes or so of chit chat, the two said good-byes with the hope they might bump into each other tomorrow.

July 4, 2010, Holmestrand connected with Vidkun Quisling's delusions, the Nordic Legion July 4, 1941

Gripar

The sun had been up for four or so hours before the town of Holmestrand started seeing some activity brewing by the train station and the park across the street. Sigrid and Gripar arrived by train shortly after 8:30 in the morning. The parking lot was filling up with cars and people were already milling about with many of them heading out the park where the main event would take place. It was a motley crowd, Gripar observed. The curious and the press were congregating with the Neo-Nazis. So far, the scene appeared peaceful, which surprised him. Sigrid was impressed with how well the event was organised. "For a bunch of skinheads, they seemed to know what they were doing," she said. Gripar agreed. During the morning the food stalls, with fries, hamburgers, hot dogs and the like, had arrived and was already doing a brisk business. The organisers even thought to set up some mobile toilets, which were also doing a brisk business.

They eventually made their way to the make-shift stage. A man dressed in a long black trench coat was up there to welcome the growing crowd. Gripar figured it was Stein based on the photos he had seen earlier. He was right. Stein introduced himself and told the crowd that the main event would start at around noon. In the meantime, he urged people to enjoy the sun, eat some food, and get to know each other. He quickly disappeared into the crowd. Sigrid agreed to follow Stein and see if he would lead her to the Wolfsangel. Griper decided to see if he could locate Sloss and Sverre.

Sloss and Sverre were certainly not going to be in the middle of the crowd, so Gripar headed to the periphery. He also decided to keep his eyes open for the Wolfsangel. Based on the profile developed by the Forensic lab, he should be looking for a thirty- to forty-year-old Caucasian male, fit - probably a military type guy. All indications suggested that the Wolfsangel worked alone. He had no idea what this Wolfsangel looked like but as he scanned the crowds, he saw that this description really wasn't helpful in narrowing down the pool of potential suspects.

Wolfsangel

Wolfsangel arrived on the scene just shortly before ten o'clock. He managed to rent the same Hydrolift F-26 boat he used on his last outing to Holmestrand. He moored at the jetty by the north-east side of the Holmestrand harbour. He checked himself to make sure everything was in order. He was quite positive nobody knew what he looked like, but just to be on the safe side he wore a fake goatee dyed grey-black. He pulled up the hood on his jacket, put on a pair of mirrored sunglasses and headed towards the park.

Nearing the Bølgebryteren, he caught an interesting sight. A group of men were heading towards the stage. Wolfsangel was too experienced not to recognise these men were part of a security detail. He was pretty sure they weren't hired by Stein's gang.

Feeling a rumble in his stomach, he decided to locate the food stalls. His eyes began scanning the fare, hoping to come across a Go'Grilla stall. He was in the mood for a hamburger and sweet potato fries. When he had just about lost all hope of finding what he was searching for, he spied a promising stall. As he headed towards it, he stopped cold in his tracks. His heart rate increased. Wolfsangel moved in closer and discovered he wasn't seeing things. His first shock was finding himself staring at a clay sculpture of the Hurdal Three. His second shock was seeing Kjersti Hurum sitting on a stool beside the sculpture.

Wolfsangel was doubly glad he altered his appearance. He stepped back, unsure what to do. He shouldn't take the chance she would recognise him here. However, after getting over the shock of seeing her again after all those years, he stepped in again and took an objective look. First, he sized her up. Okay, she still wasn't the most beautiful woman on the planet; the pejorative 'built like a brick shithouse' came to mind. Yet, she possessed a demeanour similar to an African princess. She held her head up proud. She seemed to still have that inner beauty of spirit that really attracted Wolfsangel in the first place. Then, turning his eyes away from her, he focused on the sculpture. Kjersti had made a platform constructed from some wooden pallets. On the top of the platform sat the sculpture. He felt a sense of pride surging through him. It was an impressive resemblance of the real thing; she had managed to capture the arrogance of those three men. There was a sizable number of people at the stall talking about the sculpture. He grinned. What an added bonus! He glanced around the stall. Off to one side, he noticed a large wooden crate with wheels on it sitting off to the side. Next to it, were a couple of boxes of clay as well as some sculpting tools. He surmised that she had just recently completed the project. It must have been a spur of the moment decision to bring it here.

Wolfsangel suddenly became aware that she was talking to him. "Pardon me?"

Kjersti was in the midst of downing a slice of bread with cheese slices layered on top. She was staring at him. "I said, do I know you from somewhere?"

"Maybe," Wolfsangel grinned. "I really like your work; you have the spirit of Edvard Munch!"

"Thank you," she said with an 'awe-shucks' smile. Wolfsangel gave her stall one more glance and decided it would be best to make a hasty retreat. The last thing he needed was for her to figure out who he really was. As he made his way back to the stage, he spotted the mystery person responsible for the surreptitious security detail. His mind churned with possibilities.

There was a reason he was known by his colleagues at Blackwater as a master at improvisation.

When Stein mounted the small stage for the main event an hour later, he called for the crowd to be quiet and listen. Over the next minute or so, the noise level slowly decreased, and people began to focus on Stein. Wolfsangel could see that Stein felt quite important. He took a deep breath and started to speak. "This day, my brothers and sisters, is a day of recovery. Seventy years ago, our country was in mortal danger. Communism was a real threat. We had a cowardly government that did not care about our beautiful free country. It is a shame that this country produces nothing but cowardly leaders, inferior leaders who dare not straighten their backs, who do not believe in justice and dare not fight for the truth, for their own blood and honour!"

"Yeah! Blood and honour, man," agreed someone loudly. Stein made a fist, and continued, "But I say: this day is a day of restoration, of reparation, a day of salvation. A generation ago this country had a courageous man; a man who was smart, strong and above all a Viking! A man with the truth in his veins, with the courage and strength of a lion. His enemies - and they are ours too - his enemies have managed to defile his name, to humiliate him, to destroy our national pride, to drag a real Viking through the mud. We all know about that, even today!"

Three burly men with shaved heads each waved a flag emblazoned with 'White Aryan Resistance'. They looked proudly ahead, almost daring people to challenge them. The crowd was mostly silent but there was a listlessness forming in the crowd. Wolfsangel noticed that there were some people laughing softly at Stein. One of the guys standing next to him leaned over and whispered, "Who does he mean, Odin?" Wolfsangel shrugged.

Stein went on unperturbed. "But today, friends, today is the day of truth, of national pride, a day of Norwegian power. I hereby restore the good name of Vidkun Q, Vidkun Quisling! He never ran away from oppressors, from dangers, from cowardly poison, from the communists, from guilt or injustice. Vidkun Q, a proud Norwegian, who accepted the government powers of this country because … the other parties had run away. While the pacifist weaklings of his time betrayed our country, and parasites weakened and contaminated our true Viking blood, he withstood - despite opposition - the degeneration! While a void, weak, cowardly, and pathetic parliament helped the country into the manure pile, he did not give up! Vidkun Q was his name; his enemies hated him so much that they raped his last name as traitor and inferior. As if he were the traitor! But let me tell you: Vidkun Quisling has not betrayed us, not this noble man, this man of strength and pure blood. It was the communists, the non-white immigrants, the idiotic pacifists who did!

"Why are we here in Holmestrand, why are we close to the old barracks behind me? Let me tell you. Here in Holmestrand, in his time, Vidkun Q started the Norwegian Nazi training grounds, where Norwegian men and women received a superior training and organised regiments of high quality. They were always the best troops, the best soldiers of the Nazis. They fought throughout Europe, shed their blood for what they believed in, and yet, my friends, and yet … how precious is their blood in our eyes?"

By this time, there were some in the crowd who began to fill with religious fervour. Wolfsangel watched as a small group of people, obviously caught up in the rhetoric, were swaying and nodding their heads. One of them made a Hitler salute. A group of tourists cautiously walked away from the middle, clearly afraid of the symbolic power of that gesture. Wolfsangel grinned as they realized this wasn't an ordinary Sunday gathering. Stein was an excellent orator and obviously loving the attention.

Stein took a sip of water and raised his arms high. "The world owes a lot to this Norwegian blood, and I wonder. Have we ever learned to value their resistance, their sacrifice? No! Because our enemies have hidden or soiled their names, made them into traitors and cowards. Our own blood is still portrayed as hostile blood, today! But now, here in Holmestrand, we are making history, and restoring true pride. We remember the men who were trained here, who fought like lions against Communists, and finally sacrificed their lives for our freedom. Do we care? Do we really care about our country, our blood, our history? Would you like to help restore the names of these heroes whose names were smeared? Do we want to restore honour and truth, strength and courage? Yes of course!"

This generated a strong response of agreement from the crowd. Fortunately for the police, everyone remained relatively calm. Wolfsangel smiled and shook his head as he heard Stein speaking with real passion. "The Hurdal Three are symbols of those cowards, idiots and traitors of the real Scandinavian spirit. They committed a mortal sin against our nation."

At that Stein paused, his face seemed to radiate with rapture. "I spoke to the man we call 'Wolfsangel'."

The crowd responded in unbelief, but Stein exclaimed, "Yes, I did! Last Sunday he found me in Trondheim where I live. I tell you that we too - together with Wolfsangel - will judge those rats; we will judge the dead and the living! This is a wolfsangel." He reached out with an iron wolf hook.

"Thanks to him, we are here. Thanks to his judgment, we are brought here together on these historic grounds." A group of neo-Nazis also raised their wolf hooks.

Stein nodded at them. "Where I stand now, just a lifetime ago, a brave group of real Vikings tried to write history. Thousands and thousands were ready to fight our real enemies and restore pride. Unfair was their verdict then, innocent they died. Let us now promise each other with our life, blood and honour, to bring back these courageous heroes into the history of our country and give back to them their honourable places that they did earn."

The people responded with encouragement. A voice in the crowd yelled, "Yeah! Back to the blood!"

Stein nodded and continued his speech in grand style. "And let's promise to restore and protect the freedom they fought for! There is work to be done. No more time to sit on the sidelines, no more time to watch from the couch! Let us rise from these training grounds, as one group, united in history, blood and hope for the future."

Someone began chanting, "Blood and honour". There followed a chorus of "Wolfsangel, Wolfsangel." Stein was not finished yet. Exhilarated by his own performance, he shouted, "May their precious blood be our salvation. Never again will we forget them. Never!"

The crowd was starting to really warm up now with a crescendo of chanting, "Never, Never, Never?" Stein lapped it all up.

Wolfsangel had enough. Glancing beyond the stage, he saw that it was time. He approached the three heavily tattooed bald Aryan flag wavers and briefly spoke to them. After the three nodded enthusiastically, he reached into his pockets and produced a large roll of banknotes. They knew what they had to do and each took a different direction and melted into the crowd. That vain, pompous Stein was the perfect choice. His plan was working better than he expected. Now there was an added bonus. He just hoped the three men were able to carry out their part. As he headed out to his car, he heard Stein call out to the crowd, "I ask you to make a cut in your palms and when you start to bleed, wipe the blood on your face and let it drop on these historical grounds. In this way you unite yourself with the past, with the power to move on! There is a lot of work to be done."

Yes, there is work to be done, agreed Wolfsangel.

Gripar

After the main speech, the atmosphere at the rally was anti-climactic. There was no uproar, no fights, nothing of that sort after Stein's speech. Other than a small group of admirers surrounding Stein, most people simply walked away from the site engaged in animated discussions with each other. There were very few people walking around with blood on their faces. Really, the only disturbance to this relative peaceful assembly was a noisy group of black-clad heavy metal fans carrying a drunken fellow to the beach, presumably to freshen him up with a dip in the cold waters.

Sigrid and Gripar met up and compared notes. If there ever was an event with a huge dissonance between expectations and reality, this was it. Stein spent all of his time between welcoming the crowds and the main speech inside a tent with his skinhead comrades. Gripar wasn't able to locate either the Wolfsangel or Sloss. The two of them were undecided on what to do next when Gripar's phone went off.

It was Sloss. There was panic in his voice; he had trouble getting his words out. "It's Sverre. He is missing."

Gripar's first thought was he was kidding. What did he mean he's missing? Had he not with him the whole time? "What happened?"

"One second, he was at the back of the crowd watching the speech and the next second he was gone. Nobody saw anything."

"What about his security detail?"

He heard Sloss finally take a deep breath. "They didn't see anything either. The two of us were together pretty much the whole time."

"Well, Sigrid and I are actually here at park." He could hear Sloss make a noise. "We'll start looking around and interviewing people. I'm sure we'll find him."

For the next few hours, the two of them joined officers from the local police district on a hunt for the missing Prince. It wasn't long before members of the PST as well as the Royalty Protection Unit showed up. Since most of the crowd had already left the grounds, there weren't a lot of people they could interview yet. Those they did talk to had no idea that the Prince was even there.

Gripar finally managed to locate Stein and talked with him. He was very unhelpful. Not only was he extremely antagonistic towards Gripar, but he was also actually upset that the disappearance of the Prince had crashed his event. He was supposed to be the star of the day. Why did that royal attention seeker have to disappear just at that place and time? The only useful information Gripar got from Stein was an admittance that he had greatly exaggerated his relationship with the Wolfsangel. Despite what he told Sloss, the truth was Stein had never made any arrangements at all with him to meet Sverre Lodbrok.

By the end of the evening, it was clear the Prince hadn't simply wandered off somewhere. Following protocol, the police checked the fjord water, the forests and meadows, and all the streets of Holmestrand including all outgoing traffic. But Sverre Lodbrok did not return to Skaugum that night. At midnight a national warning was issued, but the next morning there was not a single trace of him.

Later that evening, Zofia called Gripar. Her pretence was she needed some information for her news article. "What do you think, Gripar? Is this the work of the Wolfsangel? How could he have known that Sverre was going to be there today?"

Gripar was quite happy to hear her voice again. "I don't know, but it's too coincidental to be just happenstance. From what I understood, the Prince did not want his itinerary public because he was keen on attending the event in order to take in a first-hand account of raw neo-Nazism. I'm not sure how Wolfsangel found out that Sverre was going to be there."

"Do you think that he is behind the disappearance? If so, what's his purpose?"

Gripar thought that was an easy question to answer. "This would definitely bring the whole Tyskerbarn plight into the national spotlight. Isn't that what he wanted in the first place?"

"True, and nothing would bring this topic to the attention of the public more effectively than kidnapping the Crown Prince. However," Zofia cautioned, "Sverre is a pretty popular person. The Wolfsangel could do more harm than good to his cause if something were to happen to the Prince."

Gripar had considered that too. "If we assume that the Wolfsangel is behind Sverre's disappearance, how did he manage to get him out of the event without anybody seeing him?"

"Good question. That would suggest that the Wolfsangel has a fairly sophisticated infrastructure to pull this off. On the other hand, it is entirely possible that there is another party at work here and is using this event as a smokescreen."

Gripar was concerned. There were lots of questions, but no answers. No doubt about it, the disappearance of Sverre elevated this investigation to a new level of seriousness. Zofia couldn't talk longer because she had to get to work on a news report. After she disconnected, Gripar was left with a pit in his stomach. Where was Sverre?

Wolfsangel

Seated on a kitchen chair in his bright yellow house in Moss, Wolfsangel knew perfectly well where Sverre was. He was in his basement. Wolfsangel grinned as he thought about how he would feed the insatiable monster of the press. The fact is he had the ultimate attention grabber of the Norwegian press - the Crown Prince himself. He actually chuckled out loud as he thought about how the public had received the confessions of Olaf and Finn. The third confession would be disclosed in a short time. He had garnered more than enough attention for the time being.

As he got up from his chair, he became aware that his head was throbbing. He was reminded, once again, that his body was fighting an enemy bent on destroying him. He wasn't going to let this get him down. In spite of his health, things were still smoothly moving ahead. Today, his talent for improvisation came in very handy.

Wolfsangel had come across a disguised Sverre leaning against the train station talking on his cell phone. Surreptitiously watching him were the three security guys he spotted earlier. He arranged to have the trio of bald Aryan flag wavers jack Kjersti's sculpture crate and bring it here. They, then, distracted the security detail while Wolfsangel had managed to drug Sverre and dragged him to the crate. He threw the cell phone into the nearest shrub. He had heard that the latest cell phones were equipped with GPS. The last thing he wanted was his movement to be tracked. He put the empty syringe in his pocket, intending to dispose of it later.

Kjersti's sculpture crate was perfect for the job of moving Sverre undetected from the event, right under the noses of the public and the police. For their troubles and silence, Wolfsangel had given each of his assistants 4,000 Norwegian crowns for taking the crate under Kjersti's nose, for distracting the security detail, and for keeping quiet. Not that they could say much. They never asked and Wolfsangel never told him what he was planning to do with the wooden crate.

The hard part was pulling the wooden crate to the first jetty where his boat was moored. He should have hired the three boys to do the heavy lifting, but he couldn't risk attracting the kind of attention three skinheads would have garnered as they carried an obviously heavy box to his boat. It had been laborious work, but he managed. He was fortunate that the jetty was wheelchair-accessible and so the hardest part was wrangling the crate into the boat.

He had left the harbour very slowly, trying to imitate a resident of the city who was just out for a leisurely trip. At this point, there were no alarm bells ringing. He had first sailed south, along the harbour, past the Hydro Aluminium plant, and even past the small local harbour on the Hagemannsveien. Only then did he go straight to the east, to Moss. He was quite certain that no one had seen him cut through the water. Even if they did, so what?

It was smooth sailing, so to speak, until he was completely dumbfounded by the appearance of that woman. Even thinking about it now, his choler increased. He had sailed virtually undetected and was about three-quarters of the way back when he discovered the stowaway in the cabin. Kjersti had secretly crept in and hid under a blanket. He was completely caught off-guard. He tried to jump at her, but a wave of nausea suddenly hit him and he stumbled. He still was not fully recovered from hauling the heavy crate by himself from the train station onto his boat. His powerlessness made him feel even more savage. He took a couple of deep breaths, stopped the boat in the middle of the fjord and grabbed his medication from his backpack. He sat down and stared at her as he swallowed his pills. He took a deep breath.

"What the hell are you doing on my boat? You realise I could have killed you and nobody would be the wiser?" Just as he was finishing his sentence, he spotted the short iron bar in her big hand. He chortled, "Really? You think you can take me with that little piece of metal."

She hadn't moved an inch since she was discovered. Wolfsangel admired her panache. She stared right back at him, raising the iron bar over her head, slightly unnerving Wolfsangel. There was no sign of fear in her eyes as she spoke calmly. "And what the hell are you doing, stealing my wooden crate?"

Wolfsangel was nonplussed. He didn't quite know how to respond. She continued, "I saw your hired goons take my crate as I came back from the bathroom. I figured I would follow it and see where it led me. Well, it led me to your boat." She crossed her arms defiantly. "You could try and kill me, but I am not going to go easily, I can assure you of that. Besides, you are kind of sick, aren't you?"

Wolfsangel felt it coming, winding its way from the pit in his stomach and through his throat. He threw back his head and laughed. He laughed at her defiance. He laughed at her spontaneity. He laughed at his own stupidity and carelessness. She had snuck on board without him even noticing. "How stupid, stupid, stupid, am I!" Then trying to stare her down, "What am I supposed to do with you now?" She had dropped the bar down to her side but continued to stare at him, her eyes like welding rods.

Wolfsangel finally shook his head. He had fought many mighty men, but so far never had to tangle with a mighty woman. He assessed the situation. He was not physically and mentally fit right now; it would not be easy to get her down. He would be wasting what little precious strength he had left. Besides, he was going to need some assistance in getting that crate inside of his house.

"Fine," he had said, as he headed for the controls. He had to accept that Kjersti would be coming along to the other side of the fjord. She seemed to understand that for now she had the advantage. She pointed to the box and said, "I am assuming that this whole thing has to do with you being in the story of Eirik, the son of … a whore?"

Wolfsangel gasped.

"Yes. I knew I had seen you somewhere before. You've changed your outer appearance, but there was something about you that was familiar enough. We met at the Sandnes Culture House."

Wolfsangel didn't quite know how to respond. He quickly gathered his wits and nodded. "Yes. Yes, that was me. You realise, right, that I can't let you go until I have journeyed through the story of Eirik?"

She shrugged. "Just so there is no confusion, this still is my crate and I am expecting it to be returned to me." He stared at her. She stared right back as she added, "In the same condition that you got it in." Then slowly the corners of her mouth started to curve up. His eyes widened. They both burst out laughing.

Then, giving him a piercing stare, "By the way, you can not kill him! I will do everything to prevent his death."

He nodded and waved his hand, dismissing her concern. The death of that aristocratic stinker did not bother him in the least. Who cares? Maybe he would kill him, why not?

Now, as he sat in his house with Sverre in his basement, he shook his head again. Wolfsangel wasn't sure about her. She had told him earnestly that he can trust her. All she asked for is that he not kill him! She definitely had balls, that's for sure.

Gripar

Gripar was in his office glued to his computer. Because Sverre was missing and a massive national hunt was going on, Stein's speech now received a lot of attention. He was looking for links: Stein with Wolfsangel and Wolfsangel with Sverre. Earlier in the day, he made a second attempt to talk with Stein. This time, he was a little more settled and a little more willing to talk to him. He found out that Stein had become heavily involved in Vigrid some years ago even to the point of being part of Tore Tvedt's campaign to be elected to parliament in the Buskerud region. There was some sort of a falling out, which might explain Stein's reason for struggling with alcoholism.

When it came to questioning him about his first meeting with the Wolfsangel, Stein was unable to provide much detail. His memory from those days was fuzzy - probably the heavy use of alcohol and drugs since that time had significantly reduced the number of active brain cells. All Stein could recall was going to a concert in Germany, being robbed, and this Wolfsangel guy driving him back to Norway. He couldn't remember what he looked like other than being tall and blonde-haired.

When Gripar moved into questions about Stein's remarks at the rally, specifically that it was because of the Wolfsangel that they were all here, Stein declined to answer. He became belligerent and ranted about how all the attention focussed on the disappearance of Lodbrok rather than on his speech. Eventually, Gripar realised he wasn't going to get much more and left.

When he turned his attention to finding a connection between Sverre and the Wolfsangel, he got no further ahead. Frustrated, Gripar looked at his watch. He was expecting Sigrid to show up any time now. They had arranged to meet here and compare notes. He got up and went to the cafeteria for a cup of coffee. On the way back he bumped into Sigrid. She seemed in a pretty jolly mood, considering.

"It's too bad our weekend got spoiled by work. Did you have any plans?" Gripar asked as they made their way to his office.

"I did. Lena and I were going to spend the weekend at Hoddevik. We go there quite often to catch the waves. Have you ever been there?"

Gripar hadn't. He wasn't much into water sports. "That's a nice drive up, though, isn't it?"

Sigrid disagreed. "That's the worst part - the drive. Being cooped up in a tiny car for ten hours isn't my idea of fun. I'd rather just get there as quick as I can and enjoy the place."

Gripar laughed. "Ten hours? It doesn't take that long to get there. Do you drive slow or what?"

Sigrid sighed. "Lena always wants to stop at every sight and take pictures. This time it was her turn to drive. When I drive, we get in the car and don't stop until we get to where we want to go."

When they arrived at Gripar's office, the two of them sat in front of his computer screen.

Gripar filled Sigrid in with what he learned from Stein. There wasn't much. "Well," said Sigrid, "in terms of the Hurdal Three, we have identified two of the witnesses. The mysterious Wolfsangel himself did not make it difficult; the link with Eirik is obvious."

"Yes, the link is obvious, the connection to the Wolfsangel is not. The two have very personal connections with Eirik. They were responsible for a lot of misery in his and his family's life. What did you find out about Eirik's background? Is there a connection between him and the Wolfsangel? There has to be some names that we can start to investigate."

Sigrid dug out her notebook from her pocket. "Well, I dug up some more family background information about Eirik this morning. So, it turns out his biological father is actually Hellmuth Patzschke, born on 24 July 1911 in Unterwaesche."

"I thought you said earlier his surname was Reinhard."

"Yes, but from what I just dug up, Patzschke was actually the surname on his birth record. During his time as a German officer, he must have officially used the surname of Reinhard. Shortly after the end of World War II, he changed his surname back to Patzschke.

"I also found out he served as a Gestapo commander; his lowest rank was SS-Sturmbannführer. I found evidence that Himmler had high praise for Reinhard and many German soldiers feared him. Apparently, both Terboven and Quisling saw him as an intelligent and ruthless man who broke any resistance and never doubted his Nazi beliefs. There have been at least three civil lawsuits against him, but he has never been convicted because they could not find him. They were looking for a Hellmuth Reinhard and they probably didn't realise that his German surname was actually Patzschke."

This information confirms what Sjurd had told him in Urk. "So, he was a German Gestapo Commander. This guy undoubtedly had been integral in the deportation of hundreds of Jews. This guy was a real war criminal, wasn't he?"

Sigrid checked her notes. "Absolutely! This man was responsible for the deportation of five hundred and thirty-two Jews to Auschwitz. He also killed civilians during house searches as revenge. When Hellmuth' identity was finally discovered in 1963, he was arrested and during 1964 to 1967 he served a prison sentence."

"Is he still alive?"

Sigrid shrugged. "From what I could tell, the consensus is that Hellmuth Patzschke probably died around 2002. There seems to be no trace of him after that."

"What about Wolfsangel? How does he fit into this?" Gripar was puzzled. "Did Hellmuth marry Eirik's mother, then?"

"No, definitely not. Hellmuth actually was legally married to a German girl named Petra Lorenz. When the war was over, he returned to Bochum where they had set up their home. They had three sons. One became a B-grade actor but he died while on a movie set. Apparently a stunt action had gone horribly wrong and he was killed in a car crash. He was married and had two girls. The other two Patzschke sons became rather successful businessmen. Both are married to sisters and have several children."

Gripar shook his head. This sounded like a soap opera. "What are the chances any of these characters might be the Wolfsangel?"

Sigrid wasn't sure. "Based on our profile of the Wolfsangel, he would be in his thirties. That means he could be one of Hellmuth's grandchildren. I just don't know what the connection would be. Based on what Sjurd told you, Eirik didn't seem to have anything to do with his German side of the family. It's not even clear that he even met them or had any type of a relationship with them. I think it is highly unlikely that this Wolfsangel is from Hellmuth's side of the family."

Gripar wasn't quite ready to accept that. He had been around the block enough times to realise that sometimes the answer lies in the least obvious. "What else did you find out about Eirik's past?"

Sigrid filled him in on the accusations of Werner Hermann Thiermann and other Lebensborn in 2003 at the European Court of Human Rights. She was quite disturbed at what she discovered how the Lebensborn children were treated by the world of psychiatry. It was a strange science. Were the Lebensborn children really mentally ill? Was it necessary that they be loaded up on large doses of medication and subjected to electric shocks? She pointed out in Thiermann's indictment that German war children were often locked up together with dangerous schizophrenic adults; many of the children, according to the report, were tortured with boiling water as well as used as test subjects for experimental medicines.

Gripar and Sigrid stopped and looked at each other. The room went quiet as the two of them processed what they just read.

"I had no idea of the horrible extent the treatment the Lebensborn endured, Gripar. It is really nauseating. I can't believe that our government never intervened."

Gripar got up and stretched his limbs. His temples were starting to throb. He remembered the three questions the Wolfsangel asked him and was beginning to understand why the Tyskerbarn were seeking justice.

A beeping noise interpreted their thoughts. Sigrid checked her cell phone. "I just received a message from an historian friend at the HL-Senteret. He has confirmed that the candlestick holder at Mirre's is a typical Nazi artefact used in their christening ceremonies. And, get this, as far as he can tell, is a match with one that was found a few years ago along with a ceremonial dagger at the bottom of the Nordbytjernet Lake."

Wolfsangel

Late Monday morning he took Sverre to the guest quarters he had constructed in his basement. Using the skills he had acquired over the years working for Blackwater, he had fabricated a special pad for the prince. He welded some heavy duty wire fencing material to steel poles and set up a room that was virtually inescapable. He checked it himself and was pleased with the results. It did take a lot longer than he anticipated. The welding part was particularly excruciating. He ended up with severe, almost debilitating, headaches from both wearing the dark welders glasses and being subjected to the bright light of the welding arc. Up to this point, he wasn't really concerned his health would turn into an insurmountable barrier to complete his mission. Now, experiencing some twinges of worry, he wasn't so sure. What an absolute disaster it would be if he couldn't finish what he started. He could sense an impatience in Eirik. What if Eirik lost faith in him?

Persevering, he pushed through and completed the project. Now, as he stared at the mighty aristocrat sitting on the metal bench, he congratulated himself for a job well-done. He was relieved that the plan was still intact. He glanced at a door that led to another room. Inside was Kjersti. Last night, she watched Wolfsangel secure Sverre with handcuffs. She showed sign of fear or revulsion. She was an interesting one, that one. He wondered what was going on in her head. He didn't take any chances with them. He certainly didn't want them to be in same room together. Fortunately, there was a spare room in the basement which he used to lock her in. He made sure, last night, to double-check that the door and window were secure.

When he released Kjersti from the room to give her some food and water, she did not show any discomfort. She remained very calm. Sverre was awake but was withdrawn. He did not acknowledge his presence. Wolfsangel tried to get him to eat and drink something, but Sverre simply ignored him.

"Need some help?"

Wolfsangel turned around and saw Kjersti sitting on the floor watching him. Was she serious or was this part of her plan to escape? He looked at her intently but he saw no guile in her eyes. He nodded and passed her the food and drink intended for Sverre. He observed her calmly talking to his prisoner, gently encouraging him to drink, sip by sip, and in between she fed him some snacks. Sverre responded well to her help, he ate and drank something, but made no conversation.

Kjersti turned to Wolfsangel. "I want to help you. I really do, but then you cannot kill him! I need you to promise me that?"

She sounded honest and sincere. He did not answer immediately but thought about it. He had to go to Oslo every now and then, and who knows what else would overcome him. Her help could be useful. On the other hand, he did not have the energy or the mental fortitude right now to deal with another problem. In the end, he had a good feeling about her and decided to take a chance. He nodded. "Fine, I promise. But I am not quite ready to trust that you won't escape and try to betray me. So, I have to keep you here, locked …"

"Agreed, it's a deal", she interrupted. To his surprise, she laughed. "Here, if I had wanted …" She produced her cell phone from somewhere under her clothes. "…I could have already told the world."

Son of a bitch! He had not checked her thoroughly enough. He was mortified at himself for slipping so badly. He prided himself on his ability to be thorough and precise. That is how he and young Helmuth lasted so long in the business. He was rattled but had to admit that maybe, just maybe, this woman wanted to help him and wouldn't betray him. He hissed and deep inside him, Eirik became quiet, his eternal distrust of the people was ashamed. Not everyone was against him.

"Okay. It's all good," he said, taking the phone from her hand. "I'll trust you for the time being."

"And, I'll trust you for the time being, too," she responded. "So, you really are the Wolfsangel?"

She gazed at him, eyes opened wider than usual. He held his eyes on hers as if trying to see deep inside her soul. "Are you surprised? Do I meet your expectations?"

Kjersti laughed. It was that laugh that sent shivers down his spine. He couldn't help it, his face split into a wide grin.

"Yes," he said, "Kripos, Gripar and the Norwegian press will soon discover my real identity. But not before Eirik's story is told." At that, he got up. He grabbed Sverre by the arms and made him sit up straight. Sverre was compliant, although did not utter a single word. Wolfsangel took his iPhone and snapped some pictures.

Fifteen minutes later he left her behind. The basement room at the back was completely under the ground, but the front was above the ground. There were a few windows, with bars in front, a toilet and shower. He had taken her cell phone and locked the door. Despite his mercenary intuition, he decided to risk it with Kjersti.

Sverre was in good hands, he grinned. Certainly, in big hands.

Gripar

Gripar was alerted to the existence of some photos of Sverre shortly before they were published by the press. He immediately called Sloss to let him know. He was still in a dour mood. It was a blow to his pride and good name that the Crown Prince had disappeared on his watch. Try as he might, Gripar was unable to muster up much sympathy for the man.

"So, what does the Wolfsangel want with Sverre?" Sloss asked. "Is it simply a publicity stunt?"

Gripar expressed his doubts. "That is quite a risky stunt. So much could have gone wrong. He must have a good reason in his mind for taking such a chance."

Sloss was studying the pictures. Gripar could hear the melancholy in Sloss's voice. "Sverre does not look good, Gripar. Look, he's stuck in a metal cage like an animal." Sloss paused and let out a sigh and said, more to himself, "This is going to upset the people so much. I'm going to get that bastard." After a slight cough, Sloss switched to his 'command voice. "Well, I'll work on seeing if we can use the photos to identify a clue as to his whereabouts. You continue to work on the murder case and identifying the Wolfsangel. Keep me up to date."

After speaking with Sloss, Gripar decided to check in with Sigrid. He found her in the cafeteria, nursing a cup of tea. She was reading through some files from the Fylke psychiatric hospital. She looked up at Gripar,

"Did you know Eirik Tijsker was a patient on and off at that hospital for many years?"

Gripar hadn't realised that. He recalled what he knew about the hospital. It was built in the 1850s and had served as a psychiatric hospital pretty much since that time. He had heard a story that during the second world war, workers at the hospital collected urine from the patients and dumped them on the hot radiators in order to create a stink so bad, the German soldiers refrained from entering the building and exterminating the patients. Eirik Tijsker could not have been a healthy person if he spent that much time there.

The two of them decided their next step should be to call the hospital and make arrangements to meet with somebody regarding Eirik. Gripar was just searching for a contact list when Sigrid's phone rang. When she got off, she burst out, "Well, that was weird. Really weird. That was the receptionist at Fylke. She told me that the two of us have an appointment booked with a Dr. Robert Thomassen at nine o'clock tonight."

"Huh, what? How can there be an appointment?" Gripar looked around the room and whispered, "Do you think there is a hidden camera and microphone here? How could they have known?"

Sigrid laughed. "I'm sure it is pure coincidence. The receptionist was told earlier today by Dr. Thomassen to call us and arrange a meeting at his flat in St. Hanshaugen Park tonight at nine o'clock."

Gripar didn't know what to make of that but had a strong suspicion that, like Mirre Andersen and Irene Stromme, this was connected to the third body and the Wolfsangel was behind this. "Well, there is nothing much we can do but show up tonight and see what he has to say."

Sigrid agreed and suggested that they wrap things up here and then go for some supper. "You pick a place to go," she said."After all, you live here and should know all the best places."

Gripar's choice was the Grilleriet restaurant on the Storgata.

Wolfsangel

When Wolfsangel came home that evening, he discovered to his great relief that everything was the same. Kjersti had stayed put and had not warned anyone. She had taken care of Sverre well. It struck him again that while she might be a bit homely, she definitely has a good heart. Bit by bit, he instinctively increased his trust in her.

"Do you still have to eat?" She asked.

"I'm pretty hungry," he said. She looked at him, raising her eyebrows. Flashing a smile, "Let me go upstairs with you and make you something to eat. I promise I won't poison you."

Without thinking, he nodded. She came upstairs with him and immediately got to work on a meal.

He studied her from behind as she stood by the stove. It was inexplicable to him that he could trust someone so quickly. He supposed that he could blame Eirik for that. Within half an hour, she was ready to serve a meal of hearty burgers, fried potatoes, and a tossed salad.

She took a chair opposite Wolfsangel. "You look good," she said, pushing her thick glasses further up her nose. He laughed as fat dripped down his chin and asked how it had gone with Sverre that day.

"This afternoon he came out of that psychosis. He could move a little. Of course, he has tried to get free, but now resigned himself to being chained and tied down professionally. He first had no idea where he was or what time it was. He only knew that his death had not yet come."

"What is he like?"

"Absent, scared. He asked for a radio, because - he said - he heard so many voices inside him. I thought this was a good idea and after some searching, I found a small radio and switched it on softly. He kept asking me questions, 'Are you Wolfsangel? Why are you keeping me trapped here? What is it about?' He kept talking about the strange sounds and voices in his head."

"Maybe he has some sort of a mental health problem," Wolfsangel mused.

"I hope you are not right." She leaned forward and asked, "Remember Sandnes and how I ran into you! Who would have thought then that our paths would cross again."

Gripar

Sigrid arrived right in time at the Grilleriet restaurant. Gripar had himself just showed up and was looking at the menu posted by the entrance. Even though they were out of uniform, he was feeling a bit conspicuous in this cozy and chic restaurant. He knew this definitely wasn't a date, but yet a flood of embarrassing memories came rushing through Gripar's mind as he recalled the last time he was at a restaurant with an attractive lady. He noticed Sigrid glancing around uneasily and asked her what the matter was. "I'm not sure, Gripar, but I think this is the kind of restaurant that serves great food but in very small portions." Gripar gave her a confused glance.

"I'm hungry. I didn't eat lunch and I had a small breakfast. I'm a growing girl, you know."

"Really? I would have thought you'd have reached your full adult height by now," said Gripar, smirking.

Sigrid had mastered a 'drop-dead' look capable of stopping a charging elephant. She gave him one now. Gripar felt that look. Not quite understanding her dilemma, sheepishly asked, "Why don't you inquire about the portion size?"

Sigrid nodded. Turning to the pert, young hostess, "Would you be able to get me the chef? I have a quick question to ask him. Or, her."

"Him. Of course, no problem, madam. A moment."

As the hostess turned around to head into the kitchen, Gripar gave her the once over and smiled appreciatively at what he saw. He glanced over at Sigrid and to his amusement found she was doing the same thing. Sigrid caught his glance and shrugged her shoulders. "Just because I've ordered, doesn't mean I can't look at the menu."

"Yes," Gripar deadpanned "Unfortunately for you, though, the portions aren't large enough."

Before long, the hostess returned with the chef. When Sigrid explained her reservation about eating here, that the food should not only be delicious but the portion size needs to be commensurate, the chef nodded vigorously. "I will personally ensure that you get enough. I will prepare a couple of delicious and appropriately sized morsels of venison for you. Please, allow the hostess to take you to your seat and be assured we'll take care of the rest."

As they were escorted to their table, Gripar spied a familiar face sitting all alone at one of tables. "Well, Ms. Karen Nygaard, how are you?" He was speaking to a woman who was in her late thirties. She was dressed in a business casual sort of way with a loose fitting beige dress, a vest that covered her arms and a matching shawl. Her hair was in a bun, very discreet lip gloss, and hardly any make-up.

She recognized him right away. "Well, if it isn't Odd Gripar. So good to see you again." They made some small talk and then she abruptly stood up and grabbed her purse. "Well, I'm just leaving. I was waiting for my table partner, but he just called to say that he's held up and won't be able to make it. I guess I'll head home to eat instead."

Gripar waved his arm. "Please, come eat with us. We have room at our table."

Karen laughed nervously while looking at Sigrid for confirmation. Sigrid smiled. "It's okay. We're colleagues here on business."

Karen nodded. "All right then. I would be pleased to join you."

As they sat down, Gripar formally introduced Karen to Sigrid. "You are in for a treat, Sigrid. This is Karen Nygaard from the National Archives of Norway. She is probably the best source of information about German war children. She has written a couple of books and articles on the topic. And she loves red dry wine." He immediately ordered it. Karen seemed pleased at how he was putting himself out there and ordered an appetizer of fish. "For with the wine," she said. The three of them quickly became engrossed in a conversation about her research and their interest in the Lebensborn Tyskerbarn.

"Why was it so horrible after the war with these children?" Sigrid asked Karen.

"I have thought about this a lot. I believe it had to do with how Nazism challenged the whole ideology of the Norwegian male. Hitler's Aryan race concept was built around a physical ideal. Norwegian women became instrumental in achieving that ideal. The males felt threatened and challenged by their Norwegian women. After all, their women chose the enemy, the Germans, over them. In the arena of the primitive tribal code of honour, the women became the war zone.

"Hmmm. So it's all about honour and pride. Typical of the men," Sigrid smiled.

Gripar had the distinct impression that he was expected to be the spokesperson for the Norwegian man and defend their honour. He snorted in derision. The way he startled both Sigrid and Karen, he realized the derision may not have come through the way he had hoped.

Karen continued. “Consider that if a woman becomes sexually involved with the enemy by her own free will, she will be seen as infected or contaminated by her own people.”

Sigrid nodded. “Especially by the males. She is considered unfaithful. An adulterer. It certainly would have been emasculating to the men. I see where you are going.”

“So, after the war, the hatred for the German enemy was transferred to the Tyskerbarn women and their children?” Gripar asked.

Karen took a sip of her wine as she considered the question. “I suppose that’s a good way to look at it. The result was that these women and children bore the brunt of Norway’s collective hatred. Our country was immediately told by the international community to stop the abuse, but the government kept looking away. Then, when an Australian organization announced they were looking for potential immigrants, the Norwegian government offered these children!”

The table became silent for a moment. Gripar tried to wrap his head around the enormity of the lived experience of these children that nobody wanted.

The waiter arrived at their table and the mood lightened. The chef even came up to double-check that everything was perfect. It was. They feasted on delicious deer bolts, cooked to perfection, and much more. The Tyskerbarn were forgotten for an hour; the company enjoyed a great culinary moment.

Even Sigrid had enough to eat.

Wolfsangel

Wolfsangel had no interest whatsoever in developing a social bond with Sverre. He just needed that body alive for a while. He walked into the cellar, disguised as usual. He assured Sverre again he had not kidnapped him to hurt or kill him.

"You are here only to draw attention to my subject, the Lebensborn and the Tyskerbarn." Wolfsangel turned to Kjersti. "And she will make sure you do not die."

That evening Wolfsangel asked Kjersti to join him upstairs. He had a deep need, that evening, for some company. Besides, beer tastes better with a good conversation.

That night she went to her bed in the basement without resistance, as usual. The door was hesitantly locked behind her, but her hands were free to move.

Outside the yellow house, the entire country buzzed with the news of the Prince's disappearance. Wolfsangel imagined the police feverishly searching for traces of him and the nation praying anxiously for his safe return.

Inside the yellow house, however, a completely different emotion searched for a crack in an armour-encased heart.

Gripar

After dinner he and Sigrid decided it was easier to walk to the home of the psychiatrist than waiting on transit schedules. It was a half hour walk and the weather was good. As they walked in silence, Gripar's thoughts went to Zofia. He knew that after the Holmestrand gathering, she had disappeared with that neo-Nazi Stein. He had seen her step into his car with a few of his buddies. He hadn't heard from her since then and was worried. Well, okay, maybe a bit jealous, too. He wanted to hear her voice again, especially her laugh. He grasped his cell phone in his pocket and thought about calling her but really couldn't think of a good excuse. He was conscious of his colleague walking beside him and he suddenly felt like he was a teenager, embarrassed about his feelings for a girl. He went back and forth in his head and finally made the decision to grab his phone and call her. Goodness, he was a police inspector. Why did he feel like he was a floundering fool when it came to Zofia?

Gripar cleared his throat. "I'm just going to make a professional phone call to a news reporter." He took a deep breath and dialled the number. After the first ring, he thought that maybe this was a bad idea, but in for a penny, in for a pound. After the fifth ring, she picked up.

"Zofia here. How are you, Inspector Odd Gripar?"

He was just ready to say, 'Odd Gripar here' but was thrown off for a moment when he realised she already knew who was calling. "Yes. Good. Good. And you? I was a bit worried. You left with Stein after the gathering? Just wanted to make sure you are all right."

There was a pause on the other end. "How did you know I left with Stein? Are you checking up on me, Inspector?"

"Ah. Not really. Well, yes, I suppose," he fumbled, not quite sure how best to answer this question.

To Gripar's relief, Zofia rescued him. "Well, thank-you very much. It is nice to know that there are people in the world that care enough about me. Anyway, I'm fine. A bit creeped out, though."

Gripar, completely forgetting that he was walking next to a colleague, raised the level of concern in his voice. "Oh dear. Where did you go, then, with Stein?"

"I went back to his place. I was hoping to get some more background information on my story. Boy, did I bump into some unhealthy stuff there. I did not know that there could be so much hatred towards immigrants, Christians, Jews, Muslims, the government. The room contained a motley crew of Skinheads, neo-Nazis, devil worshipers and other occultists. My head was spinning after that visit."

"That does not sound good at all. Did you come across any connection with the Wolfsangel?"

"I found out that when Stein just recently met Wolfsangel, in Trondheim, the idea of a Holmestrand demonstration came from him."

That was an interesting tidbit of information. His suspicion that Wolfsangel was the impetus behind the demonstration was at least confirmed. "Any idea whether or not the Wolfsangel was behind the disappearance of Sverre?"

"Not officially, but the general feeling among the group was that he was behind it. Of course, Stein didn't want to talk about that. Stein was completely pissed that his event was overshadowed by the disappearance of Sverre."

Gripar snorted. "So, Stein finally realised he was expertly played by the Wolfsangel. By the way, I tried several times to get a hold of Kjersti to ask her if she had seen anything at the gathering. She never picked up. Her phone just went to voicemail. I left a couple of messages, but she hasn't returned my call. Have you spoken with her?"

"Yes, she called me about an hour ago to let me know that she will be going off the grid for a while. She is heading up north to do some research on her next project. I did tell her that you wanted to …" She was interrupted by Gripar's sudden explosion of an expletive.

Gripar just stepped on a paper cup half filled with a fizzy drink. He got his pant leg full of the sticky fluid and looking down at his partner's leg, realised that she got sprayed too. "Smooth move, there." Sigrid sounded quite annoyed as she check to see what damage had been done to her pants. Gripar profusely apologised and then realised there was a voice coming out of his phone. He put his phone back to his ear. "So sorry." He tried to explain what had just happened. At the end, both he and Zofia were laughing. When Gripar caught Sigrid giving him eyerolls, he could feel his face going red. "Umm … well, I should let you go." Gripar then screwed up his courage and continued, "When's the next time you are planning to be in Oslo? I would love to take you to dinner."

There was a tinkle in her voice, "Are you asking me on a date?"

Gripar fumbled for words. "Yes. No. Well … it would give me an opportunity to pick your brains - professionally, of course."

"Of course. I am hoping to be in Oslo in the very near future. I'll give you a heads up."

They said goodbye and as Gripar put his phone back in his pocket, he caught Sigrid smirking at him. "What?"

"That was one of the most professional phone calls I have heard in a long time," she grinned. "Being a top-notch detective myself, I deduce that you, sir, have feelings for that girl."

Gripar thought about denying it, but decided that he wasn't going to win anyway. Fortunately, for him, they had arrived at their destination. Just before nine o'clock they stood in front of a beautiful Victorian home. According to a sign carved in the brickwork, it was built in 1897. The place stood next to the St. Hanshaugen Park, as if the park belonged to the house. The location was great, only a few minutes' walk from the Royal Park. Gripar rang the bell and the door was opened by a man of about sixty or sixty-five years old. Gripar presented himself and Sigrid; the man stood quiet for a moment. Gripar thought that perhaps this guy was having a mini-seizure.

Then, taking a deep breath, he said, "Finally. Finally, you have no idea how relieved I am. My name is Dr. Robert Thomassen. I know who the third Hurdal corpse is. It is my father."

Sigrid and Gripar looked at each other. They didn't see that coming.

Thomassen invited them into the house. As they made their way through the foyer into a sitting room, Gripar took in the interior of the house. It was the same quality as the outside. It was a beautiful house. Gripar looked around appreciatively. There were several impressionistic paintings on the wall, a mix of old and new furniture and two enormous foreign clay vases.

They were seated in comfortable chairs. Gripar waited for Thomassen to continue.

"Yes, one of the three witnesses is my father. I am the son of Mikkel. He was born in 1910 and I was born in 1946. Mikkel was a psychiatrist at the Oslo hospital, on the Ekebergveien. I followed in his footsteps and am currently there also as a psychiatrist. I am married to Svana, who has just left with our dog for a walk." Leaning back in his chair, he exhaled slowly. "So, I am finally free to share a terrible secret."

Gripar didn't interrupt. He sensed that the man was burdened with a deep and dark secret. Sigrid grabbed her notebook and a pen from her purse.

Thomassen continued by taking them back to 1988. That was the year his father disappeared. He told how he, along with his mother, had been kidnapped five years later by the Wolfsangel and how they had to write the confession of his dead father. "I have it here. Let me read it to you. I realize that this confession will likely be all over the news media very soon, just like the others. Naturally, everyone will think that my father was the author himself."

"They will certainly think so, unless you reveal to the media that you wrote it," Gripar said.

Thomassen shook his head. "I really don't want to do that. You know the truth, so be it. I'm so relieved that you are here and that I can share this with you."

Thomassen took out sheets of paper and started reading aloud:

"The confession of Mikkel Thomassen." There was a pause. Thomassen took a deep breath before he continued. "Permission was not needed, ever. I have never needed permission to tie people up and put them in solitary confinement. Everyone accepted my methods to break the will of my subjects, whether you called them patients, clients or anti-social, did not matter. I never knew anything else than that I could do with people whatever I wanted. I had the absolute right and power, even if needed be, to let someone perish in the name of science. Lives of individuals didn't mean anything and nobody ever questioned me. Before the war I could be completely open and honest about the eugenic ideology, and years later I was still able to play God with human lives. Geneticists encouraged me to experiment, looking for improvement of the Norwegian breed. I am convinced that the Aryan race is superior to all others. That is why the Tyskerbarn, as an Aryan subgroup, were ideal material for experimentation on extracting 'bad' genes or rebuilding the mind.

"Before the war, during my stay in Frankfurt, Germany, in 1938, I was mentored by the eminent professor Otmar Freiherr von Verschuer. This professor worked closely with another very intelligent man with whom I became friends: Josef Mengele. How did I get to know him, you ask? Through music. I like violin and piano music. During a concert at the Berlin concert hall, I discovered that I shared this love with Josef Mengele and the love for our work.

"Too bad, that war. Fortunately, after the war, I heard that Dr. Verschuer had escaped prosecution and was still highly regarded in the field of clinical psychology. I even met my friend Mengele again, in Canada. Imagine, my good friend Josef Mengele knocked at my hotel door, in Montreal during a cold blizzard in 1957. Mengele!

"While we drank at the hotel bar, Josef told me he was invited by McGill University and the MKULTRA project. It was a real reunion, everyone was there! Thanks to the Paperclip project, their ideas had all survived! People die. Ideas live forever. Secret services from every country will agree that wars are won, not on the battlefields, but in the minds of the people.

"They are nothing without us. That is how it was, is and will be, my dear friend Mikkel, Josef Mengele told me. He was right of course! That short period in Canada was really great. Josef Mengele, a man after my own heart!

"However, too many people kept an eye on us; we were not allowed to be noticed. The respected guru, Ernst Rüdin, had survived the war with honours and was respected until his death. I still agree with him that inferior people should not be allowed to produce progeny."

Here Robert Thomassen looked up from his papers, his hand shaking and his face slightly red. "The next relevant piece mother and I found was in dad's pocket agenda. I wrote it down." He passed it on to Gripar.

Gripar read it and then passed it on to Sigrid.

Diary MT 16 March 1955 (transcribed by Robert T.)

- I once again received a large CIA grant for MKULTRA. This means I can continue for many years to come
- Government has been informed of experiments on Tyskerbarn: LSD, Electroshocks, hypnosis, sensory deprivation.
- Great success from the tysker boy, Eirik. We succeeded in dividing his personality! Memories eliminated by Cameron method, reprogramming started.
- After 2 years, Eirik was amazingly strong after total breakdowns, convulsion, and hysteria. Changes seem to be long-lasting in nature.

Sigrid looked up quizzically. Thomassen explained, "My father's agenda mentioned several times how he became an honorary member of prestigious organizations. His work in eugenics was his real passion. When father saw Eirik in the hospital in 1978, twenty years had passed. I believe he was quite disappointed that his work had not turned out as sustainably as he hoped. But, still, twenty years is a success and something he would have liked to share with his old friends. My father was convinced that eugenics would eventually support his DNA research work."

Gripar was fascinated, in a morbid sort of way, how Norwegian scientists supported the work of the Third Reich. He had no idea. He asked Thomassen how his father would have treated a patient like Eirik. Thomassen spoke at length about so-called brain-washing and the methods used to eliminate memories. Gripar got a pretty good idea of the treatment that Eirik would have been subjected to.

Sigrid was pretty quiet through this whole thing. Gripar could see that she was affected by these stories. "So, what about the Wolfsangel? You are the only person we know who has spent time with him and lived to talk about it. How does he fit into this story?" she asked.

Robert figured that the Wolfsangel's true purpose of all this was to find Eirik. That surprised Gripar. He knew, of course, that Wolfsangel was hoping to find Eirik alive, but believed that the primary purpose was about exposing the Norwegian people to this terrible tragedy. "Why, do you think, he wants to find Eirik?"

Thomassen thought about it for a moment. "It is true that the Wolfsangel wants to bring the Lebensborn situation up into the public eye. But, in a very specific way. I feel like we are being set up for a public trial. Evidence is being collected, confessions are being distributed. The judge is ready. The only thing missing is the plaintiff."

"Okay". That made sense to Gripar.

Sigrid pointed to the confession in Thomassen's hand and said to Gripar, "This Wolfsangel must have a very significant personal connection with Eirik Tijsker. There were many Lebensborn children that suffered horrific and despicable things being done to them. Why specifically Eirik? What is he to this Wolfsangel?"

"If Eirik is still alive, we need to find him. He would have some of the answers to these questions," said Gripar.

Sigrid shook her head. "I have not been able to find a trace of him."

"Well, on the other hand, we haven't found a body yet either. So, all we can say for certain is that Eirik Tijsker is missing. Even when I first met his wife in the Netherlands, she thought I might have found her husband. She doesn't believe he is dead."

Sigrid looked up at Thomassen. "You said that your dad disappeared in 1988. Then, you and your mom were held hostage by this Wolfsangel guy in 1993. Your dad's body was in the bunker when you were there, too. I know you assume the Wolfsangel killed your dad, but the forensics report suggests that he died of a heart attack."

Shock registered on Thomassen's face. He spluttered, "I ... I thought that this Wolfsangel killed him. Certainly, that is the impression he left us when he forced us to do the confession."

Sigrid shrugged her shoulders. "Forensics said it was pretty clear that your father died of a heart attack. There was some bruising on his head which we assumed was a result of him falling as he had his attack."

"So, why did my father just vanish? This Wolfsangel had to have been involved with that somehow. So, how did my father's body end up in his bunker?"

"That's a good question," said Gripar. "We, too, think the Wolfsangel was involved somehow in your father's death. I still wonder, then, why he waited five years before he captured you and your mom?"

Sigrid nodded. "I think we need to really explore deeper the connection that Olaf Andersen, Finn Undredal, and Mikkel Thomassen have with Eirik Tijsker. That could give us some clues as to the identity of the Wolfsangel."

Later that evening, as he was walking from the metro station to his flat, Gripar stared into the silent darkness, searching for answers. Robert Thomassen had passed along to him eleven reports, mostly copies of diaries written by Eirik at the request of Mikkel. Robert mentioned that Wolfsangel had found these extremely valuable. He was planning to read it thoroughly; maybe then he would get a deeper understanding of the scope of Wolfsangel's project.

He felt a few drops of rain on his face, but - deep in thought - he didn't notice. The country was still in turmoil; their crown prince was still missing, having been kidnapped by a man with the strange name Wolfsangel; someone who clearly does not shy away from killing people. This was indeed an unusual case. Gripar had always approached his detective work like a jigsaw puzzle, carefully putting together each piece and slowing forming a big picture. With this one, he was taking individual puzzle pieces out of the big picture and examining them to see how they fit together.

Just before he got home and opened the door, he looked around and whispered softly, "I think, Mr. Wolfsangel, the key to solving your identity lies with finding Eirik. I know you want him found. Now, so do I. I will do my best to find him, I can promise you that."

Wolfsangel

The next day started very quietly. Wolfsangel walked downstairs, opened the door, and awoke Kjersti. She had slept wonderfully, she said. Wolfsangel glanced at the cage and noticed that the prisoner was sitting asleep at a strange angle. "Come on upstairs," he said to Kjersti. Together they walked upstairs.

"He slept badly," Kjersti said as she fried some eggs for breakfast. "I think he dreams a lot."

He was glad she didn't ask how well he slept. He would have had to lie to her, which he realised would actually bother him. "Keep him alive, that's all," Wolfsangel shrugged. "I promised you that I will not let his body disappear in the cold fjord waters."

"That's good." She took off her glasses and cleaned them with her handkerchief. He studied her face, untouched by make-up. He watched her big hands handle her glasses. Her face reminded him of his mother's tender face. This woman, like his mom, really had something typically Scandinavian, with high cheekbones and eyes slightly further apart. As he sat quietly opposite from her, he wondered exactly why he took her upstairs? He came to the conclusion, a bit reluctantly, that he wanted to see her. He enjoyed being around her. He felt better about himself when he was around her.

As she tidied up the kitchen, he sat at the table with his laptop. Within a couple of minutes, he had sent the confession of Mikkel to all the major Norwegian media outlets. Kjersti stepped to the door and then called out over her shoulder, "If you're done, come outside. The weather is nice, we can sit outside." She was getting way too comfortable here and he was getting way too lax in watching her. He watched her go outside and realised he needed to make a decision. He had to trust her because the truth was, he needed her. As if to confirm, when he tried to get up, he immediately had to sit down again as a wave of pain and nausea swept over him.

He eventually made it outside. As he sat down, Kjersti handed him a glass. "Here, enjoy a cup of iced tea." He took the glass and smiled appreciatively. She beamed back. "Congratulations, by the way! You're done with your task, right? I read on the internet that the identities of the Hurdal three have been revealed."

He didn't ask how she had access to the internet. He didn't want to know. She was right, though, the three dead have told their stories. Now Norway has been left to steep in the stories of the Tyskerbarn. He felt satisfied. After polishing off his iced tea, sitting in front of his wood-clad house, Wolfsangel pulled out a cigar and revelled in the taste. He closed his eyes and sat back. For the first time in a long time, he felt at peace. He was nearing the finish line.

He felt a hand on his shoulders. He couldn't remember the last time he was touched by a female. "How are you doing?" asked Kjersti. He squeezed his eyes shut and enjoyed the touch.

"Relieved," he said. "Everything has gone according to plan."

"I love the smell of your cigar."

He reached into his pocket. "Do you want one?"

"Oh no. I like the smell. But that's about all." She smiled tentatively. "What are you thinking about?"

That was getting a bit personal. Wolfsangel took a deep drag and slowly exhaled the smoke. "Did you read those confessions I left behind at Sverre?" She nodded. "The psychologist Mikkel was actually the first one. He died before I could get his confession, so his wife and son did it for him."

"How did you make them do that?"

He thought about the bunker. "I didn't have to use force, if that's what you are concerned about. In the end, I think they wanted to. I feel the son was ashamed of what his father had done. He certainly knew a lot about his father and his work."

Kjersti looked Wolfsangel in his eyes, unnerving him. "So, what are you going to do now? Do you really think that Sverre can just return back to normal society?"

He averted her eyes and looked out at the water. "I do not know. I guess we'll have to wait and see. Take good care of that guest, I kind of prefer him to stay alive. By the way, did you take your mobile phone back?"

She looked chagrined. "Yes. You didn't hide it very well. I needed to send a message to my sister that everything is all right."

He shook his head. "Goodness I am definitely losing my touch."

"Wolfsangel. Look at me." She gently turned his head toward her. "You have nothing to worry about. Relax."

He looked at her and believed her. Her presence, this ambience, the accomplished task made him feel that he was alive. He became aware of how locked up he had been living. His life had always been adrift, now it seemed like he was entering a quiet port.

The deep-seated agony, distrust and fear of his illness subsided somewhat. Then he did something that would amaze him for a long time.

He laughed - deeply, from the belly.

Gripar

Gripar sat at his desk staring at the paper in front of him. He had drawn a web of names around Eirik's. Wolfsangel's identity had to be connected somehow to this list of names. Was it an unknown half-brother of Sjurd? Did Hellmuth have children with other women? Maybe a German war child, a relative, friend or an old friend, but Wolfsangel was certainly attached to Eirik. He circled a few names and made his plans to check these men.

His phone rang. He never really understood the expression 'his heart leapt' until he experienced it now. It was Zofia!

"Hey Mr. Policeman, how are you? Have you done your job and caught the bad guy yet?" Then that laugh.

Gripar returned the laugh. "Hey Ms. Journalist, mining for juicy tidbits for your newspaper again? It's really too bad I have nothing for you."

"Well, let me decide that. So, have you made any headway in identifying the Wolfsangel?"

"Nothing solid. I have some ideas. I think he has to be somebody closely associated with a Tyskerbarn."

Zofia's tone turned serious. "I wonder if the Wolfsangel is going to disappear now? After all, the three men in the bunker have been identified and the story about the Lebensborn has been told across the nation. What more does he want?"

He wants to find Eirik Tijsker, thought Gripar. He wasn't sure why he didn't say anything about Dr. Thomassen's theory. He felt a twinge of guilt, but he still didn't quite understand his and Zofia's relationship.

Zofia continued. "Maybe he was hired by the children of a Lebensborn organization. Perhaps he only sees it as a job and will now just disappear."

"That may be, but we can't forget that three people are dead. Even if he does disappear, justice needs to be sought after."

"I suppose," said Zofia, although Gripar wasn't quite sure she was buying into his thinking. For Gripar, it was clear. Just like the Olof Palme situation, justice needs to be sought and the right person must be held accountable. He realised that the two of them were treading carefully through a minefield of controversial topics. He really had no idea where she sat politically. Zofia must have sensed the same thing, and decided to switch to a safer area. "What about the man that is the centre of this whole story? Eirik. I feel that I need to know more about him and write his story!"

"How do you mean?"

"I really would love to dedicate a whole special edition to him! His story needs to be told. He should be front and centre, not the Wolfsangel."

Gripar didn't think that was a bad idea. He could leverage that to his advantage - in more ways than one. "I can help you with that. Next time you're in Oslo, let's get together. We can talk over supper."

"Oh, well. It so happens that I will be in Oslo this evening. What about tonight?"

Gripar was caught off-guard. After previously making a couple of unsuccessful attempts to get together, he wasn't expecting her to acquiesce so quickly this time around. He felt a tide of panic slowly rising. He took a deep breath and stepped into the unknown. "Fantastic. Do you have a favourite restaurant here?"

"No. Surprise me."

Gripar thought of the Klosteret Restaurant on the Fredensborgveien, in the heart of Oslo. Perfect food, fine wine, and most important, a romantic view. "Okay. I know just the place."

"Great. We'll have lots to talk about. I am really looking forward to seeing you."

When they ended the call, Gripar was both elated and apprehensive. He was going on an actual date. This was something he hadn't done for quite some time.

Wolfsangel

The muscular woman sitting across from him had this stunned and surprised look on her face. That made him laugh even harder. She broke into a gargantuan smile and waited for him to compose himself. "So, did you pee yourself?"

Wolfsangel sighed with satisfaction and rubbed his eyes. He thought he felt some moisture in his eyes. His underwear, he was quite confident, was dry. He resisted the impulse to look down and check. He focussed on Kjersti. "No, but I suddenly feel a kind of relief, a feeling of triumph."

"Triumph? What did you accomplish?"

"Maybe it's more like a release. I don't think I have laughed like that in years," he replied as he scratched his head.

"It's about time. Laughing is healthy!"

"I can always use some health, I suppose. What about you? You need some more laughter in your life?"

"I think I might be okay in that department. My sister, on the other hand ..." At that, Kjersti's mood became somber. "After the demonstration in Holmestrand, she went with that neo-Nazi Stein to a Mayhem concert. Lots of laughing there, just not the healthy kind."

Wolfsangel could well imagine. He had nothing but disdain for neo-Nazism, especially when it was people like Stein who represented the best they had to offer. And Mayhem? He had seen some of their material, steeped in Nazi icons and laden with calls for Norway to purify itself of foreigners. He enjoyed heavy metal music himself, but this stuff was highly corrosive black metal. He grunted. "Immersing herself with Stein in that black world. Sure, he is now firmly seen as a kind of hero in that world. But why would she join him there? Just to pursue a story? What does your sister really think of him?"

Kjersti shrugged. "Zofia thinks he is a total loser. According to her, he spent most of his time drinking litres of beer and taking drugs. He was swallowing amphetamines, mushrooms, and even snorting cocaine. The whole time they were there, he never slowed down. She found it both fascinating and scary." Kjersti took her glasses off again and cleaned them with the hem of her shirt. Wolfsangel saw that her eyes were moist. She and her sister clearly are tight. He couldn't relate to that kind of a sibling bond.

Wolfsangel wisely decided not to say anything but waited until she was ready. After putting her glasses back on her face, she continued the story. "After the concert, she went with him to a remote farm somewhere. The party continued there with dark music, more alcohol and drugs, and even a descent into the word of the satanic. Zofia said she saw Stein, still on a high, speaking with corpses, slaughtering a sheep, screaming curses at the underworld. My sister said she had vivid images of blood, yellow teeth and ice-cold screams. Stein became utterly insane. I was happy to hear that she got back home safe and sound."

Wolfsangel doubted that anybody would be able to come out of that experience unchanged. He said as much to Kjersti. She looked worried as she nodded in agreement. He got up and stretched his arms. "Nothing about humans surprises me anymore. I've seen so much evil in my line of work. I suppose this is a result of the fact that human nature is corrupt and we are all inclined to all manner of evil and incapable of doing any good. Well, that's my sermon for the day. Here, let me get you a glass of wine." With that, he stepped into the kitchen.

When he returned, he saw an expression on Kjersti's face that he didn't know how to interpret. "What?" he asked. "Why are you giving me that strange look? Did I say something stupid?"

She seemed at loss for words. Hesitantly, she said, "You just quoted from a religious document - the Heidelberg Catechism. Did you realise that?"

He knew exactly what she was talking about. Those words had slipped out subconsciously as part of the religious socialisation he received from his parents. His upbringing had been steeped in that dogma, but it really wasn't until he started working for Blackwater did he really begin to grasp its significance. He wasn't sure that he fully embraced the belief in the corruption of human nature. There was too much baggage with it. It meant believing in an omnipotent being that was higher than himself. It meant believing there was a master plan for every human being. This belief system caused a lot of dissonance in his worldview. How can what happened to Eirik be part of a grand master plan? How can what happened to him be part of a grand master plan? On the other hand, he had seen so much evil and destruction that it was difficult to satisfactorily explain its existence. He felt a dull pain building up at the back of his head. He didn't really want to engage in a conversation about religion. "What do you mean? The Heidelberg Catechism? That's a couple of words I haven't heard in a long time. That's a type of German beer, isn't it?"

She knew him well enough to figure out he was trying to deflect the conversation. She looked up at him as he stood in the doorway between the kitchen and the sitting room. "I'm curious about your moral principles. What exactly is it that you hope to achieve with your Hurdal display? Overcoming evil? Are you seeking an honest judgment, justice perhaps?"

"Are you suggesting that I am taking on a Jesus complex?" He leaned against the threshold and looked at her, understanding that this conversation had the potential to take him on a metaphysical journey he had been reluctant to take. "A saviour complex. Great. I am Jesus coming to judge the living and the dead of Norway for sins committed but not acknowledged." He chuckled and shook his head. "My father once told me: You may let go of Jesus, but he does not let go of you." He made his way to a chair and sat down. He realised that he was still holding her glass of wine. He handed it to her and the two of them sat in silence sipping their drinks.

Their slightly uncomfortable silence was eventually broken by Kjersti. "You do believe in a better world, don't you?"

Wolfsangel did not answer immediately. It was an intimate question. "That's a difficult question for a mercenary. Let it settle for a while, okay?" Wolfsangel downed his drink and lifted his glass to heaven, chortled. "Hey Jesus, thank you for the angel Kjersti. Let us drink to that."

Kjersti laughed heartily, raised her glass, then downed her wine in one gulp. Wiping her mouth with the back of her hand, she murmured, "Well, I guess I had better not ask whether he believes in God. That would be even more difficult for a mercenary." She gave him a sideways glance and smirked.

Wolfsangel got up and refilled their glasses. He felt a connection with this woman that puzzled him. He was not good with intimacy and trust. Yet, he was becoming completely comfortable with her. It was hard to believe that a day or so ago, he had seriously considered strangling her.

He mused, "A better world? God? Faith brings a lot of good … God? No, I do not know."

"He must be there! Without Him the world is meaningless." She looked at him quizzically.

"I don't know. Maybe we humans have this need to create our own meaning."

"Ah-ha. So you are really an existentialist at heart?"

He raised his eyebrows at her. "What the heck is an existentialist?"

"Well. An existentialist doesn't believe in a higher being. He believes that it is up to each individual to create meaning in a world where there is no meaning. Think about it. All this stuff that you are doing. Are you doing it for yourself or for Eirik and the truth … for God?"

The dull pain at the back of his head was increasing in intensity. Gently massaging the back of his head, Wolfsangel spoke softly to himself, to Kjersti and to someone in his past, "Yes, truth must be served, however faith must be given to you. I longed for it in the past, but it did not come to me."

"Is that what defines your relationship with Eirik?" Kjersti wondered aloud.

Wolfsangel jumped up. "All this heavy duty talk has made me hungry. Just a few minutes away is Pizzeria Campino. Here, take this money, and buy some kebab, BBQ chicken or pizza. And don't forget our guest in the cellar."

Kjersti looked at the money in his hand but didn't take it. "You trust me?"

Wolfsangel put his hand down and looked in her eyes. Yes, he concluded. Bizarrely, he did. He nodded. "Hurry, though, I'd like to eat my food while it is still hot."

Half an hour later, the two of them sat at the table eating the still warm pizzas. Kjersti had ensured that Sverre also was well provided.

Gripar

Gripar was extremely nervous. His last date was a complete and utter disaster. Even though it was over two years ago, the memory of it was etched in his mind. It was with a woman he met while working on a case. She was a material witness and they had worked quite closely together preparing her testimony for the trial. After the trial, the two of them decided to go out on a date. He thought it wouldn't be difficult at all since they had worked so closely together and they knew each other so well. They decided right at the start to refrain from engaging in talk about work-related issues. After about twenty minutes or so, he had run out of things to say. To his dismay, he found himself floundering about, making inane small talk to salvage the dinner. As an introvert, Gripar found spontaneous conversations very challenging to initiate. In order to avoid a repeat, he decided to prepare himself mentally with a bunch of, what he figured, were suitable conversation starters to use when things slowed down and got awkward.

He arrived at the Klosteret Restaurant at Fredensborgveien a few minutes before their agreed time. Across the street he spied her looking for a break in traffic so she could cross. She hadn't changed much since the last time he saw her at Walter's wedding. His anxiety rose sharply and he considered walking away. Taking a deep breath, he chastised himself. Get it together, Gripar, you're going to ruin the date before it even starts. He waited for Zofia to cross the street and approached her.

"Zofia!"

"Gripar, Odd Gripar?"

"Yes. Yes. That's me. Good evening, how are you doing?" He wasn't sure if he should put out his hand for a handshake. He started to extend it and then realised that it would be a bit dorky. He couldn't very well kiss her though, either. What to do? Gripar's panic levels were starting to rise again and he half-hoped his phone would ring and he would be called out. He took a couple of deep breaths.

If she noticed his awkwardness, she didn't show any signs. She grabbed both of his hands and gave her trademark laugh. "So, we finally meet face-to-face. Your clothes, look …! You made the same choices as I did. That's a good sign."

Gripar as well as Zofia had chosen a combination of dark leather and black clothing. Gripar told her that his leather vest was made of buffalo skin.

"Oh," she remarked, "Where did you get that?"

"I bought it a few years ago in Head-Smashed-in-Buffalo-Jump in Canada. And where did you get that beautiful leather jacket?"

"That is made from the skin of an Indian antelope buck. Nice huh?"

"Stunningly beautiful. You look … amazing. That photo of you on the Foreigner website doesn't do any justice." It was true. Zofia looked as beautiful now as she did when he first saw her. Her ebony-coloured hair had a slight curl and hung loose past her shoulders. Her facial skin was flawless and her eyes had a grey / blue tinge.

She giggled and grabbed him by the arm as they headed into the restaurant. Gripar felt good about this evening. As the hostess showed them to their table, they immediately ordered drinks. She ordered a Fernando and Gripar settled on a glass of white wine. A pianist enchanted the space around them. Eventually, the waiter came back and took their dinner order. It seemed to Gripar that the time just flew as they got to know each other better. Eventually, Gripar got the nerve to recount his first memory of her at the wedding. They both laughed and fell into easy conversation about Eirik and the Tyskerbarn.

As the waiter was clearing their dishes, Zofia grabbed Gripar's hands and held them in hers. A tiny jolt of electricity coursed through his fingers. "Gripar, this was a fantastic dinner. Thank you so much for your insight into Eirik. I think I will have a fantastic story to tell."

He said nothing for a moment, looking at their hands, fighting against his rising anxiety that he needed to make the next move. Should he invite her over to his house? So far everything was going perfectly. The piano music was definitely creating the right mood and he became more articulate of his feelings for her. He finally looked up, in her eyes. "Let's take a walk. It is a beautiful evening for a stroll."

"Yes, let's do that. Come on, we're going straight away!" Zofia said.

They paid - Zofia insisted they go Dutch - and went outside. The weather outside was perfect and they started walking and talking. They walked towards Akershusstranda where a large cruise ship was moored. Then along the opera house towards Ekeberg, following the waterside. Lost in their being together and deep in conversation, they did not notice that they crossed the bridge and walked across the cemetery on the Ekebergveien. They walked out again at the side of the Gamlebyen kirke.

"Hey, this is my church!" Gripar said. "Look, there at the corner of the square tower. Look, we come together every Sunday afternoon." They stood on the side of the church under the orange glow of the lamppost and looked into each other's eyes for a moment, after which they both shyly looked away. Zofia noticed a sign.

She pointed at it. "Lovisenberg Diakonale Sykehus, psychiatric department. If I am not mistaken, people with schizophrenia and psychosis are helped here."

"Yes, you're right."

Just as he had screwed his courage to the sticking place - Lady Macbeth would have been proud of him - and was ready to ask her if she wanted to go back to his house, her phone rang. She glanced at the screen. "So sorry, Odd. I don't recognise the number, but I should take it. It might be work-related."

Gripar nodded. He understood; and he understood her need for privacy. He stepped away and watched traffic go by. He was quite pleased at how the evening had gone. It was so different from the last one. He felt like he just climbed the highest mountain and swam the deepest sea. Well, that was a bit clichéd, but he was elated the evening had gone so well. He was brought out of his reverie by a tug at his arm. It was Zofia. Judging from the expression on her face, she didn't have good news.

"I need to head out to the Oslo University Hospital. Stein Bratt was dropped off there. He is in very rough shape."

Gripar was confused. "Okay. Why do you need to go there?"

Zofia started looking out for a taxi. "I was somebody he associates with. I guess Stein gave them my number to call. Stein doesn't have any family here and I'm the only one nearby that knows enough about him to answer the necessary questions to get him admitted into the hospital."

She managed to flag down a taxi and was ready to get in by herself when Gripar made the decision to go with her. "Wait, I'm coming with you."

Zofia flashed him a warm thank-you smile and the two of them got in. Zofia gave instructions to the driver and ten minutes later they pulled up to the hospital.

They found him in one of the rooms. He was lying in a bed connected to a machine providing him an intravenous saline solution. While the nurses gathered some information from Zofia, Gripar walked around the room. Stein seemed unaware of what was happening. Gripar was a little peeved that his date night was ruined by this guy. Gripar sighed and walked out of the room in search of a coffee machine.

By the time he returned, Stein was sitting up in bed and was talking with the nurse and Zofia. He glanced up at Gripar when he entered the room. Gripar extended his hand. "Hi Stein. Of course, you remember me." Stein's bloodshot eyes tried to focus on Gripar. Gripar smiled. "I'm only here because I was with Zofia when she got your call." Stein didn't seem to take to Gripar's charm and without saying anything returned his attention back to Zofia. The nurse had left the room.

"Do you want to go to sleep, Stein, shall we leave?"

"No, no, please stay. I am ... afraid to be alone."

Gripar was inwardly trying his hardest to will Zofia into declining the invitation.

"That's okay, we can stay. Aren't you tired?"

"Very tired, but ..."

"What?" Zofia encouraged Stein. Gripar decided he had no choice but to make the best of this situation and see if he could accrue any more useful information.

Stein seemed to try to smile, something that miserably failed. He shook his head, as if trying to get information straight. Apparently, it was not easy to organize his confused thoughts. That's what you get when you're a druggie, Gripar thought to himself, somewhat judgmentally. It was clear to him that Zofia and Stein had a close relationship and that gave way to some pangs of jealousy.

Stein started talking to himself and then after a minute or so got his bearings straight and began his story. Zofia and Gripar sat down on some chairs and listened.

"I was the star in Holmestrand. How long ago was that? Then, a small white house in the forest; mountains around it, cold and foggy. Someone said that he had a place of great significance but did not say anything about it. We walked up a mountain." Stein paused, a look of confusion on his face. After a minute he continued. "My feet were cold, wet and almost frozen. We followed the long dark-haired man who wore a cape made of horse skin. We walked and walked. At one point we reached the tree line and most of our group did not have the energy and breath to continue. They went back, but I and the tall, dark stranger continued. We did not look back." Stein shuddered and coughed. Zofia gave him a cup of water and he continued his story. "In the end we reached an old house, almost at the top of the mountain. There was an ice-cold valley in a hollow of that stark mountain. The black shadow told me that this hut had been standing here for years, made by his grandfather, he said, who had brought every piece of wood and all the other materials there on foot."

Zofia was quiet up until now. "But where were you, where was this?"

"I have no idea, after a while I discovered that I was alone. The stranger had left me there. I had to go back to the world. I was so hungry and tired. I was scared. I do not know how I got back into the village, more dead than alive."

A nurse came in and gave him an injection right through one of his swastika tattoo. Eventually, Stein relaxed and drifted into a deep sleep. Gripar could see that he was in bad shape, some of his toes were black. His mental health was just as bad, he seemed to tilt to an abyss of insanity.

Gripar couldn't understand why – he really couldn't no matter how hard he tried – but Zofia felt obligated to stay with Stein. Gripar stayed with her at the hospital for an hour or so just talking before deciding it was time to head home. He left the hospital feeling he might be in love.

Wolfsangel

The morning light filtered into his room. Wolfsangel lay in his bed, starting up at the ceiling. He felt good, well-rested. He pushed aside the covers and swung himself onto the side of the bed. Then, a sudden wave of pain hit his nerve centre. Damn. Again, his body had fooled him into thinking that all was good. He reached for some pill bottles on his nightstand. Two pills and a swallow of water later, he felt reasonable. He shuffled off the bed and pulled on his clothes. He became conscious of the sweet smell of bacon wafting from the kitchen and was transported in time back to his glory days with Hellmuth. Those memories seemed like a different era. So much had happened since those days. He pushed the nostalgia aside as he followed the smell to the kitchen.

He stopped in the doorway and surveyed the situation. There was Kjersti, bent over the stove tending to the bacon and eggs. That woman really cared about him; he considered her from the back. Okay, maybe she was not built like a fashion princess, but there was a good deal about her that was very attractive. For a fleeting second, he glimpsed his future. He was startled. The future was something he really hadn't thought about in a long time. His whole focus for the last several years was on the past. Now, his mission was, in a way, accomplished and successful. Why not let Sverre go and disappear from Norway? Maybe his future lies with this woman? He shook his head, concluding his mind had been addled by too much medication.

After eating breakfast with Kjersti, he checked his own personal email as well as his work email. Not much there. He was officially still on sick leave, but one message caught his attention. Xe Services, the company that bought out Blackwater, was looking for someone for a small mission in Central Africa. There was high risk and even higher salary. He thought of Hellmuth again and the adventures the two of them had together. He felt a twinge of envy. Someday he'll able to get back to the work he loved.

He then checked up on what the press had published about Eirik's story. He grinned as he noticed that the Norwegian press had exploded again. The major TV stations, social media and even the international press carried the story about Sverre. The hunt for him was massive and Mikkel's story was known far and wide. Everything came together now. He shared his pleasure with Kjersti.

She read out loud a headline in one of the news sites: "What now, Wolfsangel?" Turning to face him, she asked, "Yes, indeed, what now? Good question!"

"I'm not exactly sure. I certainly don't feel sorry for the three assholes in the bunker. I mean, does a stork feel sorry for the frog he swallows? Do locusts feel remorse for devouring a farmer's livelihood? Life is grim and hopeless."

Wolfsangel could tell that Kjersti did not agree. She planted her hands on her side and pushed her chest forward. "Why do you say that? That's not how you were talking yesterday. You obviously care about Eirik and his truth. You have feelings, don't you?"

Wolfsangel took a big sip of coffee and shrugged. "Eirik gave me no choice, I had to do this. It's a dirty job and someone has got to do it."

Kjersti stood up, there was a flash of anger. "Was killing a kind of redemption for you, for Eirik, for both?"

"No, I hate the idea of salvation, life is just simply miserable. Maybe my life would be easier if I could live by a few real convictions."

"What then, Wolfsangel? All you have is a deep desire to survive, nothing more? Death is the end result of life - rotten humus? So, then. Why do you care about such a lame thing as justice?"

These were good questions. He was reminded of the conversations he used to have with Hellmuth - the back and forth - questions and answers. Unpeeling the meaning of life. He looked out the window and noticed it started to rain; first only a few drops, but soon it poured. The water cycle. The cycle of life. Yes. Why did he do it? Kjersti continued to look at him with those strange blue shining eyes of hers. He stared out and answered the eyes. "Justice must be done. Humanity must always maintain moral principles; otherwise life has no value for living and dying. I want to believe in human dignity and courage."

After a brief silence. "I might agree with you."

He suddenly felt a need to explain something to her. "Kjersti, I'll tell you something about why I do this. The last witness, Mikkel Thomassen, was the first to die in my hands. I was not yet twenty. I was full of Eirik's revenge, but I happened to meet a teenager with striking green eyes who didn't care about punishment and revenge. He had just lost his parents in a senseless car accident. He told me that justice has to be done out of respect for all life. Justice is what he sought for his parents and not revenge.

I thought that through and came to realise that he is right." He leaned forward, his face now close to that of Kjersti. "That is why justice must be done. Because God is not there, it is up to us. We must judge ourselves and seek justice from that starting point."

Kjersti tore her eyes from his face, leaned back, and then shook her head. "There is more between heaven and earth than what your brain can dream of. What you are talking about is godless atheism. Why do you want to pursue that route? Atheism has, as far as I know, only produced death and destruction in forms such as National Socialism, Communism, Pol Pot and Mao."

Wolfsangel smiled. "So, you believe in God?"

"Hell yes." She smiled as she caught the irony of that. "How do we otherwise know what is right and wrong if there is no God? Consider the Tyskerbarn situation? How do you know what is right and just in this jungle? I get the sense that for you it comes down to the right of the strongest."

She was getting a bit feisty and, although Wolfsangel was enjoying this discussion, he figured it would be a good idea to end it before it got too serious. She is on his side right now and the worst thing he could do was alienate her philosophically. That could potentially turn her against him. "Perhaps," he told her. Wolfsangel lapsed into silence, drinking his last bit of coffee. He sighed and finally said, "You are quite a smart … well, actually, a wise lady. Give me some time to reflect on what you're saying." He made a move to get up.

Kjersti grabbed his arm. "I really think you need to decide how you will finish it here in Norway. We must release Sverre quickly. There is a nation-wide hunt for his whereabouts. His family misses him. The truth is, he is not guilty of the Tyskerbarn issue."

Wolfsangel nodded. She was absolutely right and told her that.

She took on a serious look. "We need to find a way to release him in such a way that the attention is diverted away from you and on the Tyskerbarn issue."

Wolfsangel agreed but was at a loss as to what that might look like. Wolfsangel was aware of how the disappearance of Sverre had produced a massive hunt. The King of Norway was very upset and his pain was felt by the common people. Kjersti pointed out that the tide was on the verge of turning against the Wolfsangel. She recounted a news story she saw earlier in the day about an ordinary mother who told Vestvold news channel that she was afraid.

'Knowing that a murderer is roaming around in Norway does not make it easy to sleep at night. I always take my dog out in the morning and often look over my shoulder now. You know, I get that feeling that someone is walking around with a drawn pistol or something like that. '

Wolfsangel agreed that it was time to end it. He had accomplished what he set out to do. He recalled how he had sent out some photos of Sverre sitting in a wire cage. It was reminiscent of the scene from Silence of the Lambs - except he had no cannibalistic urges whatsoever. Those pictures had provoked some journalists to investigate deeper and discover the link between Eirik and the Romerike School as well as the drowning of Eirik's sister in the Nordbytjernet lake. In such a short time, having Sverre Lodbrok as a hostage produced more than he expected. Yes, it was time to put an end to this.

He turned to his partner. "We'll need to put our heads together and think of something." He got up and told her that he had to go to the hospital for a check-up and more medication. He left, no longer worried about Kjersti attempting to escape or disclosing to the police his whereabouts. She truly had become his partner and his heart gladdened. It felt good to have a partner again.

When he returned, Wolfsangel had to battle a melancholic mood that usually set in after a visit to the hospital. He would go in hoping for good news that the medications were working and the disease was on the run.

Then the doctor would try to put a good spin on the results. There was nothing different with this visit. It was obvious to Wolfsangel that things were not going as well as his doctor had hoped.

Kjersti came in the room, her thick hair tied behind her head with an elastic band. She pushed her glasses up and gave him the once-over. "Are you okay?" She asked with a concerned look on her face.

Wolfsangel wasn't ready to talk about that part of his life, so he nodded.

Kjersti didn't appear to be convinced, but she didn't pursue it. "I have an idea to run past you. I think I found a good ending for your actions here in Norway. It comes from the Bible." She grabbed his laptop and opened it.

He hesitated. "From the Bible? Those events happened a long time ago. How will that be relevant to me now?"

She had a shit-eating grin on her face. "Here comes the ugliest of all Bible stories. It is about a person who is cut into pieces and those pieces are then shown to all. Shall I read it?"

When she was finished, she outlined her idea. It was mind boggling yet hilarious! Wolfsangel's melancholy melted away. The two of them developed a plan to bring this all to the end. Wolfsangel was satisfied. It was going to be the clapper, the final big bang - so to speak.

Later that afternoon, Kjersti and Wolfsangel cleaned Sverre's home away from home. They gave him some sandwiches and a bottle of water. Sverre was silent through this whole process. His eyes followed their every move and radiated defiance. Wolfsangel laughed at him. "You want to go home, right?"

Sverre nodded. "How long? How long will you keep me here? I have a wife and children who are worried sick about me. Have you no compassion?"

Wolfsangel's eyes bore deeply into Sverre's. "Do not talk to me about compassion." Waving his arms at the cell, "This is but a small thing compared to how the Tyskerbarn were treated. Where was the compassion then that you desire now?" Wolfsangel paused, his eyes still boring into Sverre's. Sverre broke the connection and looked away. "Do not worry," Wolfsangel continued, "you will be going home soon as long as you cooperate."

He picked up his cell phone and let Sverre leave a one-minute message. At the end, Sverre had to hold up a piece of paper to the camera. Written on it with a black felt marker was R1916230. It was clear that Sverre did not understand but he knew better than to ask. Wolfsangel checked his prisoner again, even though he was very certain the prince could not get away at all. He headed up the stairs to his laptop and went to Tor's underworld. An hour later, he confirmed the message surfaced somewhere in Norway.

In the meantime, Kjersti went to the shops in search of the right materials she would need for her part. It took some scrounging around, but she returned with some paper and a calligraphy pen. She found what she was looking for on the internet and spent the next hour or so working on her project.

Wolfsangel was pleased. He felt a sense of satisfaction. The video clip and the mysterious code had gone viral. There was relief that the prince was okay, anger that he had been abducted and held in an animal cage, and consternation over the meaning of the secret code. One last time he had carried out Eirik's order with another melodramatic warning to the country.

Gripar

Something strange had happened at HL-Senteret. Sigrid received another call from her historian friend at the Centre who strongly urged her to come down because he had something very important to show her. As she was tied up with something else, she asked Gripar to make the trip.

Shortly before noon he arrived at the front entrance. It was his first time actually being here since The Norwegian Centre for Studies of the Holocaust and Religious Minoritie moved from the University of Oslo to its current location. Sigrid was a dilettante in post-World War II history and had informed him that this new location was established in the former Villa Grande. When Gripar had raised his eyebrows and shrugged, she reminded him what George Santayana said about people who don't know their history. Villa Grande was the residence of the Norwegian Nazi leader, Vidkun Quisling, during the Second World War. Gripar had to acknowledge that this current case had certainly broadened his understanding of the historical significance of Nazism in Norway.

He met with two historians from the Center, Terje Emberland and Sigurd Sørlie, in Emberland's office. Gripar briefly discussed with Emberland the significance of the SS candle stick holder he and Sigrid had found in Mirre Andersen's home.

"That was quite a find. This most likely means that one of the Lebensborn at Hurdal Verk was a child of a high-ranking German official. Was there a dagger there as well?" Emberland asked.

"I didn't see one," Gripar replied, his mind trying to put a context to this information. Why would Mirre have these accoutrements? His musing was interrupted by somebody clearing his throat. Sørlie was smiling at him. "Ah, yes. The real reason I am here. Please tell me why you called Sigrid."

The two historians recounted how a Dutch student from Oslo University came to the Centre with an envelope. She claimed that it was mistakenly delivered to her home and wondered if the receptionist could pass it onto the right people. They showed Gripar the envelope. It was an ordinary brown envelope that was addressed to both Emberland and Sørlie.

"Mistakenly delivered to her home?" Gripar remarked. "That seems odd."

Emberland nodded. "That's what we thought right away. We called security and they went through the CCTV footage." He handed Gripar a couple of screenshots of the woman.

Gripar studied the pictures. It showed a relatively robust woman with a hand bag standing at the counter. The details were fuzzy and her face was hidden by a large floppy hat. She never looked up. She looked vaguely familiar. He couldn't quite place it, but he had a feeling that he had seen her somewhere before.

Sørlie spoke up. "Here is the real reason we called the Police." He handed the Gripar the contents of the envelope.

It consisted of a couple of sheets of parchment paper that contained neatly scripted handwriting. The writing was not in Norwegian or English. The layout reminded Gripar of an ancient Bible.

Gripar looked up at Emberland, eyebrows raised and shrugged. What was he supposed to take from this?

"Look over here," Emberland pointed. Written at the top left of the first page was "Oslo. Tomorrow. R191630."

Gripar was still missing the significance of the note. What was so special about this that the police were called. Sørlie was beaming as if they had just solved the Egyptian pyramid mystery. Emberland was practically standing on his tippy toes, bouncing up and down.

Sørlie couldn't contain himself. "This calligraphy is copied from the Statenvertaling - a Dutch Bible, like the King James. The passage is from Judges 19."

Gripar remained as confused and puzzled as ever. Emberland continued. "The code that appears in the video and on the top of this parchment is R1916230. Richteren is Judges. The passage is from Judges 19 verses 16 to 30. When you read it, you'll understand our concern and why we felt we had to call in the police."

While Emberland was talking, Sørlie located a Norwegian Bible from one of his book shelves and found the passage. He read it aloud:

"That evening an old man from the hill country of Ephraim, who was living in Gibeah came in from his work in the fields. He saw travellers in the city square. The old man invited them in. But while they were enjoying themselves, some of the wicked men of the city surrounded the house. Pounding on the door, they shouted to the old man who owned the house, 'Bring out the man who came to your house so we can have sex with him.' The owner of the house refused and gave them his concubine. They raped her and abused her throughout the night, and at dawn they let her go. At daybreak the woman went back to the house, fell down at the door and lay there until daylight. Then the visitor put her on his donkey and set out for home. When he reached home, he took a knife and cut up the concubine, limb by limb, into twelve parts and sent them into all the areas of Israel. Everyone who saw it was saying to one another, 'Such a thing has never been seen or done'."

Gripar started pacing, the significance slowly dawning on him. "Someone will be cut up and divided? Is that the message he wants to send out?" Then a chilling thought struck him. "Is he talking about Sverre?"

"That's what went through our minds and why we thought we needed to call in the Police," Sørlie said.

Emberland added, "We're not even sure, in the first place, why this message got sent to us rather than to you."

Gripar had an idea about that. "I think he is trying to make very public symbolic connections between the Norwegian Lebensborn, the holocaust, and Nazi Germany. You can be sure you'll be contacted by the media asking for your take on all this." Recalling what Sigrid told him earlier, "Besides, who understands better than this institution that those who don't know their history are doomed to repeat it."

As Gripar suspected, it didn't take long before this story found its way into the mainstream press. The Wolfsangel was a master media manipulator, that's for sure. The irony was not lost on Gripar how Wolfsangel made sure that the Old Testament was well read for a few hours. No evangelist could compete with that. This Biblical story was definitely strange, incomprehensible, but extremely fascinating. Gripar wasn't expecting anybody to get converted by this story, of course, but that was not the intention. Terror and sexual violence are timeless themes and this particular story contained both elements. At the end of the day, Gripar, like everyone else, understood the message that sometime tomorrow a body would be cut into pieces.

The police were on high alert and intensified their search for Sverre. The nation was on edge.

Wolfsangel

That same afternoon, a coach filled with tourists wended its way slowly through the park at the Royal Palace in Oslo. Mashed against the widows of the bus were the faces of tourists hoping to catch a glimpse of the grieving king. Following close behind was a light-blue Ford Ranger with the logo of a construction company pasted on the door. Inside, the driver was having a conversation with the passenger.

"Look there, the statue!" Kjersti pointed with her finger. She parked the truck next to the Statue of Maud and the two of them got out. She, as well as the Wolfsangel were dressed in fluorescent orange and yellow coats with matching hard-hats. Wolfsangel knew from experience that fortune really does favour the bold. They placed traffic cones around the statue and each grabbed a shovel from the back of the truck.

Security was a bit tighter than normal but nobody bothered the two workers. They quickly dug a hole and buried a package. Once they were done, they took up the cones, and drove off to a parking spot on the Kronprinsens, where it intersects with the Ibsens, on the side of the National Theater. There they waited for the next step of the plan.

Gripar

Although tension was high and the sense of urgency was almost overwhelming, Gripar and Sigrid were ready for a break. They were in Gripar's office poring through their notes taken since the beginning of the case. They were trying to find connections between the story in Judges, the Hurdal Three, and the Netherlands. "Assuming that Wolfsangel was responsible for the message to HL-Senteret, why use the Dutch version of the Bible passage?" Sigrid asked with an exasperated tone.

"The obvious connection of the Hurdal Three to Holland lies with the Tijsker family," noted Gripar.

"Okay. Now, what about the story in Judges? What's up with that? I'm having trouble believing that this Wolfsangel is actually planning to cut up Sverre. That just doesn't fit with what he is trying to accomplish."

Gripar nodded. He had thought the same thing. "If it doesn't refer to Sverre, then who does it refer to?" At that moment, before Sigrid could respond, Aksel Sloss strode in demanding an update. Gripar marvelled at the complete absence of humility Sloss was exhibiting, especially after the embarrassing failure of his ability to keep Sverre safe. Both Sigrid and Gripar filled him in on what they have discovered so far.

When they were done, Sigrid mouthed to Gripar, "Do we tell him about the dagger and candle stand?" When Gripar nodded, she turned to Sloss. "We discovered that some years ago a diving team had found a dagger and a candle stand in Lake Nordbytjernet." Noticing Sloss' quizzical look added, "The lake where Eirik's sister had drowned?"

Sloss shook his head. "What does that have to do with the case?"

Gripar was ready to explain, but Sigrid took the question. "A historian recently has identified them as a ceremonial dagger and candle stand of high-ranking German SS officers. He surmised that these artefacts were most likely used in a christening ceremony of a Lebensborn child."

"So?"

Gripar glanced at Sigrid and shrugged. "These ceremonies were usually performed only for top SS officials."

"How does this help us with discovering the identity of the Wolfsangel?" Sloss asked, clearly irritated.

Gripar explained, "It's circumstantial evidence, for sure. But everything of significance that ties Wolfsangel to Eirik is around the Tyskerbarn children. We know that Eirik and Mirre Andersen are directly connected to the Lebensborn program at Hurdal. We suspect that the Wolfsangel is as well. We are hoping that this candle stick and dagger will be one of many dots that we can connect the three of them and eventually lead us directly to his identity."

Sloss nodded, somewhat placated. "Well, keep at it. I want him in custody as soon as possible." He headed for the door, pausing before he opened it. "By the way, I understand that the Wolfsangel is supposed to give instructions at 6:00 pm as to where his next event will be. Once we know, we'll send a patrol team to see if we can get him. If you figure anything out before that time, let me know." Without waiting for a reply, he stepped outside and was gone.

"Didn't Muhammed Ali once say that it is hard to be humble when you are great?" Sigrid remarked with an exaggerated eyeroll. Gripar smiled and nodded. "Evidence of the effects of too many hits to the head. Let's take a break and head out for a drink at the lounge of Hotel Continental. It's close to the Royal palace, near the centre. It's just about five o'clock right now. We have a bit of time before the big six o'clock announcement."

The two of them decided to walk. They both wanted to stretch their legs after sitting at a desk for the past couple of hours.

On the way to the pub, Gripar got a text message from Zofia. Gripar still found it a heck of a lot easier to call than fumble around with his fat fingers trying to hit the right letters, but he didn't want to be seen as 'old fashioned' or 'out of touch'. While Sigrid tried to keep a smile off her face, the two of them briefly texted. After a minute or two, Gripar paused his conversation to ask Sigrid, "Is it okay if Zofia joins us? She is working on a story and this would give her a front seat to all the action." Sigrid didn't have any objections so Zofia agreed to meet them at the lounge and go with the three of them to the Palace Park.

Zofia must have been fairly close because the waitress hadn't even brought them the drinks they ordered before she showed up. The three of them sat at the outside tables, enjoying the rays and the heat.

"So," said Sigrid, "I hear that you are a journalist living in Trondheim who has come here to pursue a special interest in this case." Gripar groaned inwardly. Sigrid had this way of emphasizing certain words to create some sexual innuendo. Sigrid flashed him a smile, confirming that the 'special interest' had something to do with him.

Zofia either didn't catch it or decided to let that pass by unnoticed and nodded. "I would like to write a special edition about Eirik, I'm quite interested in his life story."

"Well, you've come to the right city. Apparently, we are not too far from the place where Eirik's parents, Hellmuth and Anna, fell in love with each other." Again, that smirk on Sigrid's face.

Gripar decided to change the tone. "Yes," he said. "It was in the fall of 1942, the day the Gestapo headquarters was bombed. According to Mirre, the two met there while helping out at the scene."

Zofia was interested in that point. "That was at the Victoria Terrasse. That's an interesting building. I remember in school reading about that botched attempt by the allies to bomb the building. The Mosquito Raid, wasn't it?"

Gripar nodded. "Yes. I can't quite imagine it. A German soldier meeting up with a Norwegian woman and falling in love during that raid."

"There is total irony in that situation," Sigrid agreed. "I mean, we have a bombing raid on a Gestapo headquarters located right here in Norway. This raid was scheduled at the time of the Quisling Rally - supposedly designed to disrupt the Norwegian Nazi collaborators. And during this whole thing, two people - a German Nazi and a Norwegian Collaborator fall in love."

"You think Anna was a collaborator?" Zofia asked.

"Well, strictly speaking, she was. I mean, I am the last person to judge another person on the basis of who they fall in love with, but I am curious what drew the two of them together."

"Why not just love - pure and simple? Do you think Anna deserved to be treated shamefully because of that?" There was no hint of accusation in Zofia's voice.

Sigrid shook her head vigorously. "Oh no. Certainly not. At the same time, I don't believe it was pure and simple love. German soldiers had a mission to accomplish and Anna was likely a pawn in this mission." Sigrid put her glass down and leaned forward with a serious look on her face. Gripar saw this as a sign that Zofia was in for a history lesson. "Did you know that the Quisling collaborationist government worked closely with the Nazi government to pass laws forbidding underaged daughters to marry or leave home without parental permission. Children born to Norwegian women and German fathers could receive German—instead of Norwegian—citizenship under the new laws. This ensured that the infants could be easily removed to Germany for adoption, with or without their mothers' consent. In fact, Norwegian women, especially those who were blonde and blue-eyed were encouraged to relocate to Germany and bear more children."

"And you think Anna was a willing accomplice to all this?" Gripar asked.

"I don't know. I guess that's the whole crux of the matter. Certainly, many Norwegian people after the war thought so. I guess it is hard to believe that many of them were unwilling. Nobody forced them to marry German soldiers. The Lebensborn program wasn't a big secret. Certainly, those who worked, for example, at Hurdal Verk, knew what they were doing. Based on the confessions of both Olaf and Finn, there is a good deal of evidence to suggest that Anna knew exactly what she was getting into."

Zofia was silent through this, deep in thought. Gripar felt bad because he certainly had no intention of bringing her into this deep historical debate. He really didn't know where she stood on this. "Okay," she said, "If we leave Anna aside for the moment, Eirik doesn't deserve to be treated like a pariah. Isn't that what the Wolfsangel is trying to bring to our attention? I mean, I think he put the Hurdal Three on display to make this country aware that they chose not to hear the crying of the German war children. These children were abused in front of the Norwegians, but Norway closed its ears and pretended to be asleep."

Gripar nodded. "He certainly forced Norway to look in the mirror of their past. Maybe that's the significance of the Biblical story in Judges."

Zofia became more animated and passionate. "The man in the Bible story did not see his wife as a human being but rather as a lower species. It's the same thing here. Not once has Norway ever considered the Tyskerbarn as fellow humans. The Norwegians closed their ears and eyes to their abuse, to their suicide, to their death. Then they advised the survivors to keep quiet and just keep on living."

There was a lull in the conversation as each pondered the situation. Gripar caught the sound of children laughing. It was incongruous to the mood they had lapsed into. He thought about Sverre. Here was an innocent man in a horrible situation. Gripar didn't want to think about what could possibly happen.

Sigrid broke the silence by asking Gripar if she should show Zofia the screen shot of the woman who delivered the note. "You never know, perhaps she has come across this person on her travels." Gripar nodded.

Zofia studied the picture for several seconds then shook her head. "No. I don't recognize her. I mean, her face is concealed under that hat, but she doesn't look familiar." She studied the picture a bit more and then passed it back to Sigrid. "So, she walked into the Centre and simply passed it on to the receptionist? Did she say anything?"

"Well," said Gripar, "she gave some cock and bull story about being a Dutch student who found this letter in her mailbox and was hoping to pass it on to its rightful recipient."

Zofia laughed at that one. "Cock and bull story? What do you mean?"

"Clearly, she was lying. She claimed the postal service delivered it to her address. There wasn't a cancelled stamp on the envelope. And the receptionist, herself an immigrant from Holland, said there was no way she was Dutch."

"Hmmm. Does that mean she is working with the Wolfsangel?"

"Not necessarily," Gripar replied. "She could have been hired to drop off a letter. Kind of like a courier of sorts."

The table fell silent for a moment while they polished off their drinks. Gripar had just suggested that he order refills when Zofia's phone rang. When she found out who was on the other end, she stood up and walked around the corner for some privacy. At that moment, Gripar's phone rang as well. It was Sloss. He had been given the location of the Wolfsangel's next move. By the time he got off the phone, Zofia was back. They both spoke at once. "We need to get to the Statue of Maud."

On the way out he quickly paid the bill and they ran across the street through the Slottsplassen towards the statue.

Gripar noticed right away that despite the huge police presence, the atmosphere in the park around the statue of Maud was a strange mixture of excitement and relaxation. It seemed like the beautiful weather gave everyone a good feeling.

Sigrid pointed out the Victoria Terrasse across the Hendrik Ibsens. "Weren't we just talking about that place and the attempted bombing? Ironic, isn't it. Do you think this site was deliberately chosen by Wolfsangel?"

Gripar didn't answer. He suddenly noticed that Zofia had disappeared and was searching for her in the gathering crowds.

Wolfsangel

The two of them had been sitting in the pickup truck watching their plan slowly take shape. It was like an old steam locomotive - agonisingly slow out the starting gate but once moving, there would be no stopping. Wolfsangel had pushed the throttle by alerting the press to the location of this event. The next step should occur any minute now.

It was Kjersti who had seen them first. A group of pizza delivery guys had arrived on mopeds. Wolfsangel and Kjersti stepped out of the truck and walked across the street for a closer look. As previously arranged, they drove in from all sides and converged at the statue. Wolfsangel and Kjersti observed them briskly taking boxes from the carrier racks and arranging them around the statue. In less than forty-five seconds, they were speeding off. Wolfsangel spotted the arrival of the police. The timing was impeccable. Their plan was gaining steam.

Wolfsangel sat down on the grass and laid back. He closed his eyes and took a deep breath. He was relieved but tired. Exhausted, really. He knew he was pushing himself; his body was starting to resist. He hadn't eaten anything since noon and his medication required him to have a full stomach in order to be the most effective. There just wasn't time. He and Kjersti had agreed to push themselves out of bed bright and early this morning and had been working hard pretty much all day.

Of course, it was kind of their own fault they had to push themselves this hard today. Yesterday had not been as productive as they had originally planned. After renting an industrial jigsaw from a Ramirent and buying some sturdy moving boxes, they decided to combine business with pleasure. It had been absolutely a gorgeous day. For a few hours, it felt like a holiday. Wolfsangel had made the decision to go, not north to Oslo, but a few miles south to a more scenic area. He drove while Kjersti closed her eyes, soaking in the sun rays. In Gressvik near Rapp Hydema they 'borrowed' without notifying the owner, a small truck with a crane, after which they drove back to Moss. Kjersti insisted on driving the crane truck.

He enjoyed that day, but today he found himself worrying and fretting. These days, he was doing that more than usual. When he was with Blackwater, he took the missions in stride - confident that his training and background would bring him back safe and sound. Now, he found himself fretting at each detail. In his mind, he replayed the scene last night in Moss through the eyes of a casual passer-by. On a regular weekday, a maintenance truck with a crane, equipped with hoist and chains, appeared. So what? It was only eight o'clock in the evening. A truck did not turn to the ferry, like the other vehicles, but crossed the bridge and then turned to the park. He, in orange work clothes, got out. On the passenger side, a sturdy woman, dressed as a maintenance worker, also got out. They placed a few orange cones around the statute. No big deal. A chilly wind from the fjord had chased most of the inhabitants indoors. He was confident, however, that the few people who might have witnessed the event would later say that they had found nothing out of the ordinary. Sure, in the end, the truck was used for nefarious purposes and Moss was without her wife; but nobody was really going to care. He laughed to himself and sat up to look toward the plaza. He felt reassured. Things were going exactly as planned.

"What were you laughing at?" Kjersti's voice broke his reverie. He looked at her blankly before realising what she was referring to.

"Nothing. I was just thinking about our plan and how you came up with a real beauty. What made you think of the Norwegian Lady at Moss?"

"You told me you came from Virginia in the United States. I did some research. The Lady is from the figurehead of a ship that crashed off the coast in the late 1800's. It is a symbol of friendship between Moss, Norway, and Virginia Beach, USA. Did you know that?"

Wolfsangel shook his head "Tell me."

"A Norwegian ship, I think called the Dictator, crashed off the coast of Virginia. The locals tried to save the ship and the crew, but the ship broke. Nine men of the crew were rescued; the other members lost their lives. The beautiful figurehead of that ship was placed on the coast with a view of the sea, as a memorial to the shipwreck and those who perished. It stood until destroyed by a hurricane in the 1950s."

"What does that have to do with Moss?"

She told him that the ship was from Moss. Years later, an artist was commissioned to produce two bronze replicas of the original figurehead. In 1962, the unveiling of both 'Ladies' took place simultaneously, here in Norway and in Virginia Beach. "They wave to each other, this one and her twin sister in Virginia. So, of course, I thought about you and how you have one foot in Virginia and one foot in Moss."

Wolfsangel laughed again, astounded at her eye for detail. "I do know that statue. I've seen her wave there without knowing any of this background information. As soon as I get back home to Virginia, I'll stand next to her waving at you."

Kjersti shook her head solemnly. "That won't be possible."

"Why not?"

"Because if you are back home, I'll be standing next to you and not separated by an ocean."

"Oh." He paused, surprised, not sure what to say next.

She grabbed his arm and drew herself closer. "No more deaths, though. Not Sverre. And not any more statues." He knew the Judges story had upset her and the thought of cutting people up in pieces horrified her, even if those people were wooden, bronze, or stone. She was a person who celebrated life.

Their mood was interrupted by the Kjersti's cell phone beeping. Before she could retrieve it out of her pocket, it had sounded off three more times in rapid succession. She glanced at it and her face blanched.

Wolfsangel sat up. "What's wrong?"

"It's my sister. She's here somewhere."

"So? She is part of the press. It would be natural for her to be here."

"No, you don't understand." Kjersti stared at her screen and then stared at Wolfsangel. He could see terror in her eyes. "She is wondering if I am here. Apparently, she saw a picture of me when I was at the HL-Senteret. She asked me if I am working with you."

Wolfsangel grabbed her phone and read through the messages. At first, he felt a twinge of panic. Then, realising it was just going to be a matter of time before people realise that Kjersti is connected with him, he calmed down. "Just tell her that you are fine and that you are resting on the beach at Moss. Ask her if she is here in the area." Wolfsangel marvelled at how quickly she was able to get off that message.

Her phone made a sound and Kjersti read the text. "Okay. She is here with the policeman Gripar. I'll have to watch my step. Last thing I need is for her to spot me here." The two of them walked back to the truck.

Many years ago, bombs were dropped here. Many people died from the deadly act of the British. Human bodies were torn apart. Because of that event, two people encountered each other – a well-known Gestapo leader and a beautiful Norwegian young woman. Today, because of them, people were gathering again. Eirik revived.

Gripar

The crowds were congregating in the plaza. The palace windows depicted a collage of faces peering in consternation at the scene below. Everybody was waiting for something to happen. The police had set up barriers around the statue and were slowly forcing the crowds to back away. Officers with a large piece of tarpaulin made a circle around the boxes. If this was Sverre's carved corpse, it was not going to be shown visibly to the hundreds of people present. The boxes disappeared from view. People became silent and waited. Hundreds of others arrived and walked to the waiting crowd without making a sound. Whatever good feeling existed earlier, there was a tension building that was felt far beyond the circle of people. Milling about the crowd were police in tactical uniforms. Emergency vehicles with their lights flashing and sirens blaring arrived on the scene.

Gripar was stationed close to the statue along with Sloss. The two of them were certain the Wolfsangel would be at the scene watching events unfold. Gripar kept scanning the crowds hoping to spot something that would give him away. Sigrid was mingling in the crowds hoping, as well, to spot something that would point to the Wolfsangel. Gripar's mind drifted to that passage in the Bible that portended this event. It was really the ugliest of all Bible stories. Awful. What was the point of this story? Cutting up a raped woman and distributing her body parts across the country? A man who gave his own wife to be gang-raped? It was haunting his mind that there must have been people who had heard her cries in the night, but that no one came to save her, even afterwards, when she cried in front of the closed door in the morning, moaning and bleeding to death. Nobody cared about her.

Sigrid called him on his two-way. "Anything?"

"No. I think it would be difficult to spot him at this point. Everybody is just milling around checking to see if there is any action. I am assuming there will be some sort of an event happening and then I think he will be a little less transparent."

“What’s going on by the statute?” Sigrid asked.

“Right now, it is roped off. The Explosive Disposal Unit just arrived and are checking out the packages to make sure they are not bombs.”

“Would he really have cut up Sverre? I can hardly believe it.”

“Neither do I, but you never know. This Wolfsangel has already killed people to achieve his goals. No reason to believe that he wouldn’t in this situation. Symbolically, this is a unique set-up. Right in front of the statue of Maud, Queen of Norway - Sverre’s great-grandmother.”

Suddenly, one of the members of the bomb squad stood up and gave a thumbs up symbol. Gripar asked what was going on. One of the officers told him that there was no bomb, just a bunch of bronze pieces. “Hang on, Sigrid, looks like there is no bomb.”

Gripar walked over to the boxes and looked inside. It took him a minute to figure it out. The boxes contained the sawn-up pieces of a bronze statue. Within a couple of minutes, a group of police officers put them together and before long the word was out that it was The Norwegian Lady statue from Moss.

“It’s not Sverre.” Gripar told Sigrid, awash in relief. He had no idea what they would do if it actually was. He didn’t want to think about it. “It’s the image of Moss’s wife, but just like in the Bible, a woman cut to pieces!”

“I doubt this is the main event. There is more coming.”

Gripar agreed and kept scanning the crowds. They were milling about, not sure what to do. It felt like an amateur magic show and the crowd was feeling let down. Suddenly, the air was filled with a booming voice. “Hey Wolfsangel, you coward. Why don’t you reveal yourself? You have our attention now. Release Sverre and talk to us like a man.”

Gripar’s two-way crackled. “That isn’t Aksel Sloss, by chance, is it?” Sigrid asked dryly.

It was. He had taken a megaphone and was standing on the concrete pedestal of the Statue of Maud. His taunting voice had caught the attention of the crowds and they drew as close as they could to the statue. Sloss went on and the crowds started to nod and shout encouragement to him. Gripar could see that he was basking in the limelight.

A sudden explosion killed that limelight in a hurry. It wasn't really an explosion. It was more of a large popping sound. It caught everyone off guard and the air was filled with screams and shouts as people tried to get as far away from the statue as possible. In his haste to get away, Sloss tripped and fell face-first to the ground. Gripar was amused to see the mighty Sloss was having trouble getting distance from the statute. Gripar glanced up at the statue and noticed that her head was gone.

It happened so quickly. The initial explosion was followed by a series of smaller ones as colourful fireballs erupted out of the headless statue. Gripar stared at the sight. Fireworks. It was nothing more than fireworks. The panic slowly turned into wonder as the crowd realised what was going on. Sloss was finally able to pick himself up, his mouth wide open as his mind registered what he was seeing. An alert media photographer captured the moment.

A nervous twitter started to replace the screams and there were many embarrassed people as they realised their preoccupation with their own vulnerability. Gripar could appreciate how Wolfsangel had designed a very symbolic, very creative event. There was almost a collective sigh of relief as people realised that the world didn't end. No machine gun bursts, just red paper streamers raining down on the astonished people. Laughing, somewhat ashamed, people rose again.

Gripar grabbed his phone. Zofia. He had momentarily forgotten about her. He had to make sure that Zofia was okay. She picked up on the first ring. "Don't worry. I'm okay. Can't talk now. Right in the middle of something." Gripar breathed a sigh of relief just as he heard Sigrid's voice in his earpiece. "Hey. Got something. Southeast of the statue. In the bushes."

Gripar turned around and scanned the bushes. He caught some movement. He started running towards it. There was a footpath that led to the plaza to the north and to Henrik Ibsens Gate to the south. When he hit the footpath, he looked in both directions. The crowd was dispersing along this path but to his right, he saw the back of a person who looked very familiar.

Wolfsangel

Wolfsangel was still parked across the road by Ibsen's Gate 27. He had gone back to his vehicle, but found that the trees between the statue and the gatehouse prevented him from seeing anything. Of course, he would have preferred to be right there and watch but considering his health and the intense desire of the police to find and arrest him, he knew that was not a good idea. He was too far away to hear the explosion, but when he caught sight of the fireworks, he grinned. He was now quite sure everything had gone off just as planned. He wanted to get going now, but Kjersti had gone in for a closer look. He was proud of what he and Kjersti had accomplished. Yes, he recognised Kjersti as a full partner. He couldn't have pulled this off without her. Eirik would be proud of their team effort.

He caught a movement down the path. He saw Kjersti emerge from the tree grove about three hundred meters away. He started his truck ready to make their escape back to Moss. As he was willing her to move a bit faster, suddenly a man came into view further down the path. There was something familiar about this man. His throat caught when he realised it was Gripar trying to catch up to Kjersti.

Gripar

Gripar broke into a run to chase after the woman. She was solidly built, dressed in loose clothing, and wearing a cap and glasses. He was pretty sure that was the woman who had dropped off the note to the historians at the Holocaust Center. She had a head start on him, and when she realised she was being chased, she broke into a run. Clearing the footpath, she darted across the street and threw herself into the cab of a light-blue Ford Ranger pickup truck. It must have been parked by the gatehouse waiting for her. He could make out the driver who just caught sight of him. The two locked eyes for the briefest of seconds. Gripar knew instinctively that he was looking at the Wolfsangel. He radioed Sigrid and gave her the details.

Wolfsangel

Wolfsangel turned into the driving lane and sped up. Those green eyes locked with his. Despite his disguise, he knew that he had been made. His mind started racing ahead - assessing his situation, evaluating possible alternatives, and then making a decision. Even though things didn't end as well as he had planned, he still felt good about the day. He had been in this situation many times and he did not panic. For the briefest of moments, he felt alive. He felt Eirik giving him the high five.

"Wow!" Kjersti was excited as she banged her fist on the dashboard and laughed hard. "We did it! You should have seen Maud explode! You should have seen that fool police guy tumble in fright. This is going to hit the international news media, for sure."

Her enthusiasm was infectious and Wolfsangel laughed with her. He loved her laughter. It was raw, unpretentious, and authentic. It was a window into her soul. "You did it so cool, so controlled. Just like a good mercenary in a war situation."

She grabbed his arm "Is that your way of saying that you love me?" He turned to look at her, eyes wide open and jaw hanging low, his mind registering shock. Kjersti raised her eyebrows and then roared with laughter. She leaned over to kiss him on the cheek.

Wolfsangel was left with deciphering what just happened. The past came crashing head-first into the future. He shook his head, his mouth struggling to find words. He was brought into the present by a loud yell from Kjersti.

Wolfsangel saw the car ahead of him break suddenly and he swerved into the other lane. “Don’t worry,” he said. “There’s a roundabout just ahead. We’ll keep left and head to the Radisson Hotel and ditch this truck. I’m certain the police have been alerted and we don’t have much time.”

Within a couple of minutes, he was able to navigate through the heavier than usual traffic and pulled into the parking lot under the hotel. He shut the engine off and the two of them did a quick, but thorough, sweep of the interior to ensure they didn’t leave anything incriminating behind. Removing his fake beard, he grabbed Kjersti’s hand and the two of them strolled through the hotel to the Holbergs Plass.

Gripar

Disappointed, but not surprised, that he couldn’t catch up to the woman, Gripar made his way back towards the statue. Just before he got there, a beige Passat came towards him and stopped. Sloss’ head drew near the open window on the passenger side. “Hey, get in. They saw the truck pull into the Radisson parking lot.” Gripar got in. Before he could get his seatbelt on, Sloss was tearing down Henrik Ibsens Gate.

“I knew, just knew, that prick would be watching the whole thing. I just about had him, too,” Sloss told Gripar. Gripar decided that it would be unwise to bring up the point that the exploding head likely left brown-stains in Sloss’ underwear and at no time was Sloss even remotely near the Wolfsangel. Gripar made a sound that could be interpreted as agreement.

He heard Sigrid calling him through his ear-piece. “Gripar. The plates of the truck are registered to Hertz Car Rental. There is an outlet right by the hotel on Holsberg Gate.”

Gripar relayed that information to Sloss. Within minutes they had pulled up to the place. They walked up to the reception desk where they confronted a middle-aged, heavily made-up woman reading a magazine.

The two of them showed her their police identification. She seemed totally unimpressed.

"Madam," Sloss said in the most authoritative voice possible, "apparently your place has a vehicle with license plate number EJ26190. Would you be able to check to see who rented this vehicle?"

The lady, with a completely bored expression on her face, asked to see their identification once more. She made a show of going carefully through the information, even glancing several times between the ID pictures and their faces. Sloss was annoyed. "Listen, we don't have a lot of time. A major crime has been committed and there is a good chance your vehicle was involved."

"Good heavens. Really?" the woman responded, her voice still expressionless. "What is this world coming to. You really think one of our vehicles may be involved?" When Gripar nodded, she said more to herself, "I wonder if I should call Magnus. He should be the one taking care of this."

Gripar had the distinct impression she was deliberately being obtuse. He suspected the Wolfsangel had paid her off to delay them. "Listen, madam, all we need to know is if this plate belongs to one of your vehicles and if so, the identity of the person who rented the vehicle. As my partner said, this truck may have been involved in a major crime - possibly involving the abduction of Sverre. We really need your cooperation quite quickly."

At that, the woman's eyes widened. "Seriously? Well, let me get on that." Gripar caught Sloss' eye and gave him an eye roll. His suspicions were dead on. Within twenty seconds, she had the answer to the first question - yes - and was working on the answer to the second one.

A couple of keystrokes later, "Hmm, that truck was rented by a man who identified himself with his passport as Gunnar Patzschke."

Gripar felt a current go through his body. "Patzschke? Are you sure?"

"Yes. It says here that he used his passport to confirm his identity. Apparently, he is a good customer. He has a platinum membership card."

Gripar must have had a look on his face because Sloss turned to him and asked, "What's the matter? Do you recognise this name?"

Gripar decided to keep his cards close to his chest for now. "No, I was just surprised at the German name."

Sloss asked the woman if she had more information such as a phone number or an address. She studied her screen. "He presented a German passport with a Berlin address." She wrote the address and phone number on a sticky-note and handed it to Sloss. Gripar took out his phone and snapped a picture and sent it to Sigrid to check out.

Sloss was ready to leave when Gripar, as an after-thought asked, "Does this Patzschke guy have any of your other vehicles on rental?"

After a couple of mouse clicks, she smiled and said there was. He currently has a BMW S1000RR out on a month-by-month rental basis. Gripar got a description of that bike and sent it off to Sigrid as well.

Sigrid got back to Gripar. "Are you kidding me. Patzschke? Doesn't Eirik's family have relatives with that last name?"

Gripar grunted non-committally hoping that Sigrid would catch on that he can't talk openly right now. She caught on immediately. "Well, that address in Germany is connected to a corporation called Xe Services. As far as I can tell, that's a private international security company. I couldn't get any information out of them on a Gunnar Patzschke." Gripar could hear someone speaking in the background. "Just hang on a second, we found something out." After a brief pause, she came back. "They found that truck in the hotel parking lot. It is abandoned. I'll get them to check to see if there is a Patzschke registered as a guest in the hotel."

Gripar thanked her.

Wolfsangel

The two of them made their way from the hotel parking lot to Oslo Central Station. Wolfsangel collected his thoughts and focussed on a plan. Clearly, they need to leave this place as quickly as possible. The policeman was on to both him and Kjersti. It wouldn't take long for them to determine where that truck was rented from and who rented it. Wolfsangel had to assume that his German identity, Patzschke, was now making the rounds around the Norwegian police service. He also had to assume that the police were looking for a couple.

Looking at Kjersti and grabbing her hand, he told her, "I used my German passport to rent the vehicles. I expected that my identity would be revealed at some point, not just yet. So…," extending his hand, "…my German name is Gunnar Patzschke. It's my pleasure to know you."

Kjersti smiled widely. Grasping his hand and giving it a vigorous shake. "Gunnar! Well, nice to know that your mom and dad didn't christen you as Wolfsangel. Shall I continue to call you that? Or, do you prefer your real name?"

Wolfsangel stared at her, mouth agap. Nothing seemed to faze her. She truly was an amazing woman. When he first saw her, he was greatly intrigued by her. He recalled his conversation with Hellmuth. Then, when she first came into his life as a stowaway, he saw her as an annoying, unnecessary burden. In fact, he wanted to strangle her. Now? What the two of them have been through? Amazing.

She lightly tapped him on the head. "Hello? Hello? Anybody home?"

He blinked and then laughed. "Fine. You may call me whatever you want." He looked around and became aware that the crowds were thinning. Rush hour was long over. "They probably are right on our heels. I have to get rid of them, Kjersti, and I definitely do not want to lead them to Moss."

"Understood. Once we get to Central Station, I'll head to Moss by train and keep our guest company. I'll do what I can to prepare for your big escape and wait until you come. Let's keep in touch, okay?"

They walked the rest of the way in silence, the weight of parting was tugging at their hearts. They stopped in front of the train platforms. He wrapped his arms around Kjersti. He could feel a lump in his throat - a feeling he hadn't experienced for some time. "Thanks." His voice cracked a bit. Swallowing, he tried to gain his composure. "Thanks for everything. Thanks for your help in planning and executing this event today. It was so well done. It was amazing. And nobody died."

She stepped back to look at the Wolfsangel. Her eyes were misty. She slapped him on his thigh. "You know, I think I'm going to miss you. You take care of yourself. Make sure you don't forget your medication. God bless." Abruptly she got up and started walking off.

"Kjersti!" She turned to him and waited. "We will soon meet again. Count on it!"

She nodded and left in search of a ticket machine.

The safest option for him to get to Hurdal would be the bus. The more exhilarating option, of course, would be taking a motorbike. However, that option was too dangerous and risky. By now the police would have located both the truck and the motorbike. All he had on him right now was his Patzschke identification. The moment he used it, the police would be on him. He was lucky he had some cash to buy a one-way bus ticket. He headed to the bus terminal and purchased a ticket for the 7:15 pm bus out to Hurdal.

It was an uneventful trip. He arrived in Hurdal just before 9:00 pm. Stepping off the bus, he decided the safest way to get to Hurdal Verk was walking. What normally would have been a short twenty minute trek turned out to be much more exhausting than Wolfsangel had expected. Forty minutes later, sporting a migraine headache, he reached Hurdal Verk.

He expected the place would be relatively devoid of people at this time of the year. The new batch of pupils would be arriving in a few weeks. He broke into one of the residential buildings at the beginning of the site. He probably should eat something but he desperately needed to take his medication and rest. In addition to his migraine, he felt feverish and sweat was dripping from his forehead. He took a cold shower, swallowed a myriad of pills and lay down on one of the beds. He glanced at his watch. It was 10:37. He closed his eyes but to his dismay, he didn't immediately fall asleep. His mind kept churning through images of Eirik, Hellmuth Sr., Hellmuth Jr., Gripar, and Kjersti. After a listless hour or so, his mind slowed down and he felt warm waves of sleep washing over him.

Gripar

Gripar and Sloss drove back to the Kripos headquarters. Gripar wanted to meet up with Sigrid and plan their next move. Fortunately, Sloss declined to join them. When Gripar walked into his office, Sigrid met him with an enormous grin on her face. She still had a good day, despite Wolfsangel slipping through their fingers. Sloss had been publicly embarrassed, and she had discovered some useful background information.

"Okay, so we haven't been able to conclusively determine whether the Wolfsangel was using a stolen identity or the Wolfsangel is Gunnar Patzschke. But, certainly, we have been able to trace the path of Gunnar Patzschke over the past couple of weeks. His identity was used to rent a sailboat from the Pepervika harbour that ended up in the Moss harbour. And get this, Moss was also the place where the Norwegian Lady statue was originally located."

Gripar felt a rush of excitement. "Moss. Wasn't that also the city where three men had their foreheads carved with a wolfsangel rune?"

Sigrid nodded. "A team has been sent to Moss to see if they can find anything."

"Good. They need to check to see if that identity was used anywhere else in the city. Have you been able to determine if a credit card under that name had been used?"

Sigrid went through some of her notes. "Forensics is looking into it. So far nothing relating to Patzschke has come up. To accomplish what he did, this Wolfsangel certainly needed a source of funding."

"What about an accomplice? Have we found anything out about that woman that came to the HL-Senteret? I am positive that was the same woman that I saw in the truck with this guy."

Sigrid raised her hand and looked up. "Right. Thanks for mentioning that. I had almost forgotten. I had some colleagues check to see if there were any other CCTV cameras in the area. I was thinking that maybe we could get a clearer shot of her."

"Good thinking. You're on the ball." Gripar smiled, then added, "If you found something, that is."

Sigrid drew a circle around her face with her finger. "This isn't just good looks, you know…" Then working through a stack of papers, found what she was looking for. "…Here. I did find something. Look at this. It's a pretty good shot from a camera at the Global Assets and Trading building just down the street."

Gripar took the picture. He was staring at the woman he saw hop into the truck with the Wolfsangel. Excited, he nodded vigorously. "Yes. That is definitely the same woman who was at the park and hopped into the truck with the Wolfsangel. Any idea who she is?"

Sigrid hesitated before she answered slowly. "Yes. We think her name is Kjersti Hurum. She is the sister of Zofia."

Wolfsangel

Wolfsangel shot up in his bed. Years of training and experience prepared him to be subconsciously alert for any danger. He had to momentarily fight through the haze created by the medication, but he had the distinct feeling something was amiss. He never dismissed his instinct about such things. He glanced at his watch. It was 03:18. He slowly got out of bed and crept up to the front window. He kept to the shadows so that nobody outside would see his silhouette moving. He peeked through the curtains and was confronted by a solid wall of blackness. He remembered earlier this evening, as he came in, there was a fairly dense cloud cover. This was still preventing any moonlight from reaching the deep darkness around him. He was pretty sure there was someone out there. He could feel it even stronger now. He had to get out of here.

After making sure there was absolutely no light inside of the building, he drew up a plan in his head. He knew he would be vulnerable as soon as he was outside, but the alternative of being trapped inside was not an option. As he paced around the room, he made up his mind about what he needed to do. If the police aren't already here, they soon will be. He had to get away, not only from this house, but also from this country and quickly. He had accomplished what he had set out to do. To stay any longer would invite capture and a fate that he didn't want to think about. He thought about Kjersti and the position she was in. It couldn't be helped.

Determined, he took a deep breath. He knew that he first had to cross an open space behind the house, then a few meters of bushes and last the road behind it. After that, a lot of space, running to the village of Hurdal. He felt an adrenaline rush. He was strong. He was fast. He will make it…

The window shattered in a million pieces and a flash grenade fell on the floor.

Wolfsangel

The explosion just about lifted him off his feet. Fortunately, he had anticipated something like this and was through the kitchen and almost to the back door when this happened.

He tore open the back door and rolled out on the grass. He headed straight for the grove of bushes. Just before he reached them, a large man loomed up and blocked him. The man shouted some sort of a warning about stop or else. Wolfsangel moved like a hell-acrobat and jumped up, hammered his two elbows into his opponent's skull, dodged the falling body and kept moving. He dived, rolled and slid until he was through the bushes. Once he was through, he ran like a cheetah.

After about five minutes of hard running, Wolfsangel stopped for a moment to catch his breath. He filled his lungs with fresh air and at the same time slowly pushed down his anger at nearly getting caught. That disease had dulled his senses and weakened his body. Once he got his breathing and emotions under control, he cocked his head trying to catch any sounds that would indicate whether his pursuer had managed to follow him. There was a slight breeze that rustled the leaves, but he was pretty sure he heard something. He peered through the darkness, hoping to penetrate it. He caught a movement in the corner of his eye. He turned and focussed his attention in that direction. Yes, he caught the sight of a silhouette of a man. He definitely was being followed. It looked like that policeman he had seen with Gripar and Sverre in Holmestrand. He hoped there was only one of them, but the chances were high there were more. He continued on, careful to make as little sound as possible.

When he reached the open road, he realised immediately his risk of exposure. Not only was the sky beginning to lighten with the impending sunrise, but there was also no way to cross the road without making a sound. His original plan was to make it into town undetected under the cover of darkness. That was no longer possible. With his pursuer still behind him, waiting for him to reveal himself, he had to make a stand and take care of this situation sooner than later. A plan quickly formed in his mind. He raced across the road and immediately turned sharply to the right. He was close to the hydro lines which led to Hurdal. He found the path he was looking for and made his way up the hill.

Near the top, Wolfsangel found the large rock he knew was sitting there and ducked behind it. He heard his adversary coming closer. From what he could detect, he became confident there was only one of them. Wolfsangel relied on his experience and training to keep totally quiet and focussed on the next step. Rummaging around, his hand found a large stone. When he saw the figure pass by, he slowly stood up and raised the stone over his head.

With a sudden speed, the man spun around. Simultaneously throwing the rock and lunging at the man, Wolfsangel used the element of surprise to attack him. He hit the man in several places over strategic spots on his body. However, Wolfsangel realised fairly quickly that this guy wasn't an average opponent.

Several times Wolfsangel found himself in a professional grip, but every time he was able to break free. He used all the tricks he had ever learned on this well-built man. Suddenly he felt his attacker's arms around his neck in a stranglehold which he knew would be almost impossible to get out. He could feel his head swell as the blood circulation was blocked. He became dizzy and through the haze summoned one last effort to break free. He was able to move his body slightly behind the man. With his left elbow he flipped the body over his hip. He was unable to break free from the arms but as they fell, Wolfsangel was able to twist his body and landed backwards on top. That was sufficient enough to knock the wind out of the attacker and his grip relaxed enough for Wolfsangel to suck in a lungful of air and at the same time chop his elbow hard into the man's solar plexus.

Wolfsangel heard the man gasp and felt the arms relax and fall away from his neck. That gave him the opportunity he was looking for. Summoning all his strength, Wolfsangel hit his adversary square on his throat. The fight was all gone out of the man. He lay on the ground struggling to find his breath.

Wolfsangel was on one knee, hunched over. Normally, at this point, Wolfsangel's rage would have taken hold of him and he would have extinguished life with his bare hands. As he stared at the man he definitely now recognised, all he felt was exhaustion. Exhausted physically, of course. But, he was also exhausted emotionally. He literally had no fight left in him. There were fortunately no others, this man had operated on his own. Wolfsangel straightened up, took a minute to catch his breath, then continued along the path to Hurdal.

Gripar

"What the heck were you thinking? You should have called for back-up." Gripar stared at Sloss. Sloss had lost most of his cockiness and nodded. He was obviously in a lot of pain. His face was covered in bruises and the medical staff had wrapped up his chest to stabilize the broken rib.

Gripar had driven up to Hurdal this morning when he got the call. His mind was still reeling from the events of yesterday. He couldn't make sense of Zofia's sister's involvement in all this. He wondered if Zofia knew about this all along. And then there was Eirik Tijsker and Hellmuth Patzschke. Assuming the Wolfsangel is really Gunnar Patzschke, is there a direct relationship between Gunnar Patzschke and Hellmuth Patzschke.

"Well, that's too coincidental for us not to believe that the two Patzschkes are somehow related," mused Gripar.

Sigrid agreed but cautioned him. "We don't know for sure if this Wolfsangel assumed an identity of some Patzschke guy or if he really is that Patzschke guy. I'll have to keep digging."

Gripar glanced at Sloss. He looked a mess although Gripar wasn't feeling any particular amount of sympathy. Why would he recklessly pursue the Wolfsangel by himself without telling anyone about his plans? That was against normal police procedure. "How did you know he was at Hurdal Verk?" Gripar asked.

Some of Sloss' smugness came back. "I knew that at some point he would return back to the place where he started from. I had some people living there keep an eye out and alert me if they found something suspicious. The custodian at the Hurdal Verk called me at around 9:30 in the evening that a strange man had showed up. I was pretty sure that it was the Wolfsangel so I took the chance and went out there."

"Well, I can tell you that he definitely is not around now. We set up a perimeter and tried to contain him. We did a complete search of the town. We even had a canine team come in. Nothing. Somehow he slipped through."

Gripar was suspicious that Sloss was up to something. For the time being, he put that on the backburner. He needed to touch base with somebody else first. Gripar left the medical clinic and went back to his car. It took him some time to connect, but fortunately, the tough Dutch fisherman from Urk was on his boat still within cell range.

"Good afternoon, Sjurd. This is Inspector Odd Gripar from Norway. I hope you're fine." Gripar could hear the noise of the wind and sea through Sjurd's phone.

"I'm fine. Why? Were you worrying about me?"

"Me worry about a hardy fisherman like yourself? Not likely. You can take care of yourself. So, how is fishing? Is that sea not empty yet?"

The connection wasn't super, but it was good enough to hear the derision in Sjurd's voice. "The North Sea is the best sea in the world, full of fish. Still, that darn GreenPeace keeps spreading misinformation that we are emptying it."

Gripar knew what Sjurd thought of GreenPeace and Brussels. He decided not to engage. "Well, my reason for calling: Does the name Gunnar Patzschke mean anything to you?"

There was a slight pause. Gripar wasn't sure if that was because he caught Sjurd off guard or if it was due to a poor connection. "No." Pause. "Well, Gunnar is, or was, the name of my brother. Patzschke? I don't know anybody by that surname. Why do you ask?"

"How about Hellmuth Patzschke? Does that name ring a bell?"

Again a pause. "Well, it is interesting that Hellmuth is the first name of a German soldier that my grandmother had a relationship with during the war. I believe that my father was one of his biological sons. His last name, though, wasn't Patzschke, it was Reinhard. What's with all these questions?"

"Well, we almost caught Wolfsangel, but he escaped. However, we did discover some of the paperwork he had been using. It was all under the name of a Gunnar Patzschke."

"Okay. I'm still not quite understanding where you are coming from. There must be hundreds of Patzschkes and thousands of Gunnars in the world."

"Yes, that's true. However, Hellmuth Reinhard's real name is Hellmuth Patzschke. He kept that name hidden because of his past with the Gestapo."

There was a lengthy silence. If it wasn't for the sound of the wind coming through the phone, Gripar would have thought Sjurd hung up on him. When he did finally speak, Sjurd's words seemed to reflect his genuine confusion. "Are you sure about this? Are you saying my biological grandfather is a Patzschke? That would mean … My father is … No, that's not true. He is a Tijsker."

Gripar remained silent as Sjurd processed that. Sjurd seemed genuine. "You're not joking, are you?" Sjurd asked. Gripar assured Sjurd he wasn't.

"I keep thinking about how you got on to my name in the first place. It was due to a picture that some elderly lady gave you with a note allegedly written from me on the back. None of this makes any sense," Sjurd said.

Gripar agreed. It doesn't make sense. "Is there a possibility that your father had other half-siblings - Patzschke family members … that might be involved with this Wolfsangel?" His voice trailed off. He was grasping at straws, he knew that.

"All this is awfully coincidental," Sjurd said. "I can see why you called me. I am not aware of any family members that could possibly be involved. Could it be that somebody with a bit of background knowledge is using these particular names to keep his identity hidden by throwing you on a wild goose chase?"

Gripar had not discounted that. "It is definitely possible. Why, though, would someone want to use your brother's name? It seems very specific and not random. Did your brother have any friends or close associates that might be responsible?"

There was a lengthy pause. Finally, "I honestly don't know. I guess I should be ashamed, but I really wasn't close to my brother. When my mom got the notification of death, I didn't even know he was working for the Foreign Legion."

Despite not seeing his face, Gripar could sense Sjurd's deep and profound pain. Gripar called Sigrid to fill her in on his conversation with Sjurd.

After talking with Sigrid, Gripar checked, double-checked, and even triple checked his voice-mail to see if Zofia had left a message. He had left three or four messages already and no response. He dialled her number again but it went to voice-mail after several rings. Either she is missing or she is avoiding talking to him. He suspected that she knows he knows and is avoiding him.

Wolfsangel

The next morning was a quiet one. Both humans and animals seemed to be busy with their own lives. People were walking down the street on their way to do their shopping. The sound of laughing children filtered through the cacophony of birds squawking at each other. Indeed, it seemed like just another ordinary day. There was no indication there was a national hunt for the murderer of three men and the kidnapper of the Crown Prince.

A taxi pulled up in front of Mirre's place. Out stepped an aged but very spry Rannveigh who instructed the driver to place the boxes of produce loaded in the back into Mirre's twenty-year old Renault. The back seat of Mirre's car had been removed years ago so that she could have space to take her garden produce to the farmer's market in Jessheim. The Farmer's Market gave something for Mirre and Rannveigh to do in the summer months. The car was already quite full when Rannveigh arrived, but the taxi driver also managed to stuff Rannveigh's boxes of potatoes, tomatoes and beans into the old vehicle. It was now completely full; the car sank, but did not break through its shock absorbers.

For the two ladies, the Farmer's Market wasn't just a destination. The two of them always made the journey a very integral part of the experience. Mirre never pushed her car past the 45 km/h mark and the two of them had great conversations along the way. They always made sure they had a thermos full of coffee and a bag-full of fresh, home-made cookies.

They each climbed in the car with some difficulty - stiff muscles and aging bones had that effect. Their first stop was a petrol station where an attendant filled the fuel tank and checked the oil, despite it being a self-serve station. Before the two ladies left, the attendant warned her not to speed because there are a lot of police on the road right now.

"Oh dear," said Rannveigh looking at Mirre. "You are going to have to watch your heavy foot today."

Mirre giggled. "Why are there so many police on the road?"

The attendant told them what she knew. "They're looking for someone. There are various check stops on all the main roads!"

The two ladies didn't seem worried. "As long as we are allowed to pass and get through. After all, the market closes in the afternoon." When they drove away, they tossed out a friendly wave to the young lady and headed for Jessheim.

On route they hit two check stops. At each one, they nibbled on their homemade cookies and chatted away while the police officers checked her car. The ladies were both very polite when they were cleared to go. "Thank you, dearies", they would say, and one would add, "Here, take a nice cookie and good luck in finding your fugitive."

It was close to an hour later when they finally arrived at Jessheim. Rannveigh expressed surprise when Mirre did not turn at the Skogmotoppen, but kept going straight to the train station. "Mirre, I know my eyesight isn't what it used to be, but I believe you are going in the wrong direction for the Market."

Mirre, concentrating on the traffic, explained. "We're going to the train station. You'll see why in a minute. It's okay, dear, I'm not losing my mind." She drove to the old brick building and found a spot to park between the building and a clump of trees. She got out and opened the back of the car, taking one look at the stack of produce. "Rannveigh, come out, help me."

Rannveigh struggled out of the car, muttering the whole time about being kidnapped by some senile old lady. "Why? We are in the wrong place. Tell me your secret first."

"It'll become obvious in a minute, dearie, now come on, help me. Here, we need to take these middle rows of stuff out and set it on this picnic table." It wasn't an easy task for the two of them. They couldn't lift the boxes so they had to unload each one by hand. In about twenty minutes, they had created an open space.

Mirre, breathing heavily, said, "Do not be afraid, Rannveigh." Suddenly a hand emerged from beneath that open space and easily shifted the remaining boxes to make room. Rannveigh gasped in shock but when she saw who emerged, she nodded. The man known as Wolfsangel crawled out of his small hideout.

"So it is you? Now I get it."

"You didn't see this," he said smiling. "It's just the rambling story of a senile old lady." He put his arm around Mirre.

Mirre sighed. "Are you sure you know what you're doing?"

"I have to leave. I'm sorry, but I can't stay in Norway anymore."

Mirre looked at him and gave him a hug. "Ah, my boy, greetings to your mother and do not forget to write me another letter or postcard. And be careful."

"I will. We'll keep in touch. The very best, you too, Aunt Rannveigh. Thank you very much for everything."

Rannveigh smiled softly. "And thank you for taking such good care of my friend - may he rest in peace."

A small pang of sorrow touched Gunnar's heart. He missed the old man. Glancing at the jumble of produce on the picnic table, he said, "Here, let me help you get this back in your car." In less than five minutes, the vegetables were safely stored in the back.

Mirre gave him one more hug. "Gunnar, please," then taking him by the hands and looking him in the eyes, "You need to let go of Eirik now. You have no debt with him, certainly not now anymore. You have to take care of yourself and live your own life. God bless you."

He did not know what to say, but her words washed something clean inside. "It would be nice if Eirik were found," he said. Both old women nodded. One moment of silence, of eternity, of truth, disrupted by a railroad crossing bell. He quickly said his goodbye and waved once more and got on the train, which took him to Moss via Oslo.

Gunnar sat back in his seat and watched the world go by. The steady sound of the train made memories pop up. He thought of Hellmuth Patzschke and Obersalzberg. He recalled the parting words of Mirre and Rannveigh. He closed his eyes and drifted off while all of Norway was still on edge and the police were searching for him.

A refreshed and more reflective Gunnar arrived in Moss two hours and forty-five minutes later. A thick fog and heavy mist blanketed the city. Kjersti was waiting for him and had a taxi arranged to take them home. The two of them sat in the back in silence as the taxi wended its way into town.

Kjersti broke the silence just before they arrived. She pointed to the floating jetty. "I have found a boat for you to use. It's an interesting story, actually. I bumped into an American at the grocery store. Much to my surprise, I found out that he lives in Virginia, quite near your place. Well, one thing led to another. When he found out that his neighbour was in need of a boat for a couple of days, he was only too happy to lend his to you - for a fee, of course. Look, there she is."

"That's fantastic. Good job. Did you get any extra gas?"

"Yes, I managed to fill three jerry cans and store them in the bow. First, let's go inside the house. I have some food ready."

Gunnar stepped inside and almost instantly his saliva glands gushed. He stopped and groaned. Kjersti was alarmed. "What's the matter? Not feeling well?"

Gunnar laughed. "No. It is so good to be back here. Man, I can smell something fantastic cooking on the stove." Kjersti had completely tidied the house and on the gas stove a large pot of lapskaus, a Norwegian stew, was steaming. "Wow. This is perfect. Thank you." He gave her a hug. "I'm hungry like a bear."

"Me too. Let's hurry and eat. I don't think we have much time." It became quickly obvious they were both ravenously hungry. They each polished off two bowls full of stew. After putting the dishes in the dishwasher, they walked out of the house and enjoyed the beautiful view of the fjord. The sun was nearly behind the horizon and the moon was already visible. Yet behind them a wispy fog hovered in the background. It was still.

It was one of those rare moments when Gunnar put his guard down and was just himself. "I think I am going to miss this country. I really don't want to leave, but I have to. They know one of my identities."

Kjersti was silent for a moment. Then, grasping Gunnar's hand, "Sverre. He needs to return back to his wife and family."

Gunnar nodded.

Kjersti squeezed his hands. ".. and Eirik?" She gave him this look. She knew about Eirik. At least, she knew as much as he told her.

Gunnar realized the depth of her question, but he had not shared with her Eirik's presence deep down, his bedevilment. One day he will, but not now. "I'm hoping that Gripar, the police officer, will follow through. I've planted some seeds. I know him well enough to believe that he will push through and find him."

"You really hope he might still be alive?"

He sighed. He wasn't quite sure how to take Kjersti's statement. Did she think he was foolish to believe Eirik was still alive? Was she patronizing him or was this meant to be encouragement. He shook his head. "It's complex, I don't know. Sorry."

"It's okay. I think I understand what you are going through. It's that classic struggle between the heart and the mind. What are your plans now?"

Gunnar felt a surge of deep emotion for this woman who seemed to understand him. There weren't many people in his life who did. He was ashamed that he even considered not returning to finish this part of their plan. "We're going to sail back together to Holmestrand. I'll drop you and our cargo off there and I'll continue on south to Denmark."

There was a deep silence. Then a whisper, "What about me?" This was the part Gunnar wasn't good at. That struggle between the heart and mind thing that Kjersti referred to. "I will definitely miss you," he sighed deeply and looked at her. "But, one day, everything will be fine and we'll be together. You have to believe me."

She nodded, tears forming in her eyes.

The two of them watched as a Nornen-class coast guard boat appeared at the entrance of the harbour and slowly floated in shining its flood lights on the docks. It was a good reminder of what was at stake.

Gunnar stood up. "We have to be careful; there are police and Coast Guard out here on patrol. Doesn't matter. I am confident the crossing will go well. Come on, let's get going. It's dark enough now."

"I've already given our guest that pill, he's pretty drugged. I think we are all ready to go on that end."

Gunnar was relieved to see the Coast Guard vessel was at the far end of the harbour when they began boarding their boat. Gunnar started the engine, Kjersti released the ropes. They looked at each other, Kjersti nodded and said a prayer out loud asking God to give them a safe and uneventful journey. Gunnar smiled in amusement as Kjersti's God appeared to be working with them. Nobody seemed to pay any attention to them as they headed west into the Oslofjord, more or less hugging the coast of the Jeløya Island.

They crossed the fjord unmolested and arrived in Holmestrand. They moored out of sight at the back of the aluminium factory. Kjersti wrapped the drugged Sverre in a large blanket and put him down among some rubbish cans on the ground. The effects were starting to wear off and it wouldn't be long before he became conscious.

"It's time." Kjersti grabbed Gunnar by the shoulders and said nothing. He peered into her eyes. Outsiders might not describe this gesture as romantic, yet it felt so for both of them.

"Gunnar, Wolfsangel, I kind of like you very much as well. So, be honest with me, do you promise that we will meet again?"

He looked at her and felt a desire to keep her close to him. He nodded. Yes, that felt good. "Absolutely!" They hugged each other, holding each other tightly, neither wanting to let go. It was Sverre's cough that propelled them into action.

Gunnar hurried back to the boat. When he reached it, he turned to see Kjersti still watching him. He waved one more time and said, "See, I have returned your wooden box in the same condition as I borrowed it." Kjersti's laugh filled his heart to the brim.

Wolfsangel

He suspected that the radar of Hirtshals, Denmark, had discovered him somewhere in the night. He spotted a Danish Naval Home Guard boat that seemed to take an interest in him. Taking no chances, he took evasive manoeuvres intending to dock somewhere near Bremerhaven, Germany. As he got closer to the coast, he realised unfortunately the Wasserschutzpolizei had other ideas. They likely had been alerted by the Norwegians and the Danish. Gunnar had no choice but to come up with another plan to get him into Germany. Briefly considering his options, he decided to try the Port of Cuxhaven.

He brought the boat close to the coast, took off his clothes, and put them in a big plastic bag. He turned on the auto-navigation system and set course for due west. He pushed the throttles to half and jumped overboard. There was no way for him to double-check, of course, but if there were no obstacles in the way, that boat would run out of fuel long before it hit the English coast.

He swam to shore, towing his dry clothes in the bag behind him. He only had to swim about twenty-five meters; yet when his feet touched the ground, he was utterly exhausted. After plodding across the dike for some distance, he put on his dry clothes and made his way further to the harbour without anyone seeming to take notice of him. Fatigued and uncertain of what to do next, he spied a truck in the parking lot with 'Klokau' written on the side. The driver appeared ready to leave. Gunnar casually walked towards it and was thankful to note that the back flap was not completely closed. Acting as naturally as possible, he slipped in. Within a minute or two, the truck took off and made its way down Lower Saxony Street. Gunnar covered himself with a large piece of canvas and settled in for the ride.

Hours later, when the sun had risen and numerous miles had slipped beneath him, he woke up from a coma-like sleep to discover that he had arrived at a very familiar international airport. His luck was holding out. He chuckled to himself when he remembered that he had a locker at Schiphol Airport.

Gripar

Norway finally relaxed a bit. Wolfsangel had apparently disappeared, and Sverre had safely returned. The front pages of the Norwegian newspapers seemed less concerned about the Hurdal Three mystery, although Sloss had made it to the front page of most newspapers. In a way the papers must have decided it was time for some comic relief; a way to laugh the stress away. The picture of Aksel Sloss, bewildered and clearly distraught from the surprise fireworks at Maud statue painted a thousand words. It didn't tell the whole story of course, but the sorry sight of the big man made Gripar's and Sigrid's day.

Gripar was unable to fully relax until the case was completely solved. There were so many unknowns that puzzled him. One example was the connection between Wolfsangel and Eirik. Wolfsangel's use of the alias Gunnar Patzschke was clearly intentional, strongly suggesting that Wolfsangel was more than a vague acquaintance, a distant friend of the Tijsker family. Gripar believed that this Wolfsangel guy had to be connected to Eirik in a more intimate way, possibly even with a blood tie. But who was he? Where did this man get his motivation to highlight Eirik's life in such a way? Only someone who had personally known Eirik, and connected himself with his tragic life, could be Wolfsangel. The question was: where should they start searching for answers to these questions?

He initially supposed the answers would be found in a yellow cottage in Moss. Sigrid discovered Gunnar Patzschke had rented it for a short term. The police found evidence in the cottage to prove that three people had recently resided there. The dishwasher had been filled but not turned on. They gathered the evidence and sent it immediately to the Forensic Institute of the National Criminal Investigation Department in Oslo. There was no doubt in Gripar's mind that, in addition to the Wolfsangel, Sverre Lodbrok and Kjersti Hurum had been there. He just needed that confirmed with specific evidence.

However, there was also an interesting connection to Virginia, USA that had the potential to provide answers. The speedboat used to escape from Moss harbour was actually owned by an American who lived in Virginia. Virginia, the place where Finn Undredal's ex-wife got a postcard from. The same place where one of the two Young Lady statues was located, linking Moss with Virginia Beach.

Sloss was putting the pressure on the two of them to delve deeper and wider into Eirik's German family. He was convinced that family members had to be involved with this whole fiasco. Neither Gripar nor Sigrid found any evidence to support that theory. Gripar tried to explain that to Sloss. "Eirik himself had little or nothing to do with his extended family. His wife Marianne told me that she knew for sure that Eirik himself had never contacted his German father. He did not want to get to know him and all those others."

Gripar felt that answers to all his questions were tantalisingly close. It was like driving in a dense fog. The landmarks seem to be constantly shifting and out of place and just when you think you have figured out your location, another anomaly pops up. Gripar sighed deeply and loudly. He thought he did it in his head, but clearly did not. A startled Sigrid jumped and stared at him with an incredulous expression on her face. "Is the strain getting too much?" she asked, wide-eyed. Gripar shook his head sheepishly. "Nah, sometimes it just feels good to let it all out."

Sigrid cracked up when Walter Svendsen popped in to see what was going on.

Wolfsangel

Gunnar eventually made his way into the terminal and found a bench near a window to sit down to rest. The late-morning sun was streaming in, bathing him in a warm melancholic glow. Wasn't he supposed to get another treatment and meet with Linnea today? Or … was that yesterday? He no longer knew what day it was. Maybe he should just take his pills! He searched his pockets but there was no pill pouch. He stood up and looked around. He checked under the bench, but there was nothing. He spied his coat draped over one end of the bench. He found the pouch in one of the pockets and took a few pills, not bothering to put the pouch back.

Gunnar was keenly aware that he was sick, sick to death. Over the past couple of weeks, things were getting worse for him. There were nights when he woke up in a sweat, the darkness pressing down on his soul. He couldn't get enough air and every time he tried to take in a deep breath, he seemed to be gasping for an adequate airflow. Sometimes, when his phone alarm rang in the morning, he had trouble remembering where he was. He thought of Kjersti and how he tried desperately to hide those symptoms from her. He suspected that she knew and supposed that he was really trying to hide his symptoms from himself. He could no longer deny it. He needed to find a way to move forward into the future, as nebulous as it appeared to be. There were so many things he wanted to accomplish in his life. Things that he had put on hold; things that didn't involve Eirik or the Tyskerbarn.

'A great city, a great solitude'. Hellmuth used to say that about Gunnar. It was ironic coming from Hellmuth, who always took a 'wham-bam-thank-you-ma'am' approach to relationships. However, sitting here now, at this moment, Gunnar deeply felt its meaning. Here he was, sitting in one of the world's busiest airports, feeling utterly alone and desolate. A disease – he still refused to name it - continued to ravage his body. Sure, his doctor told him at the last visit that he was doing better than expected – the medication was starting to have an effect. Yes, the fatigue that regularly enveloped his body wasn't as debilitating as it used to be. Undeniably, he was starting to gain a bit of weight, one kilogram at a time. Despite all this, he felt hugely burdened.

It took him a moment to realise it, but Gunnar could feel his presence. He heard the whispered words that had given him his mission years ago. *Wolfsangel, you are the hook with which I catch the wolves. You are my source of life.*

"You. It's you?" He whispered anxiously.

Gunnar, swear to me that you will punish them.

Gunnar dropped his gaze to the ground. He whispered, "I have exposed them … you know that, right? All of Norway now knows the truth."

Eirik was sitting next to him now. *I'm proud of you.* Gunner could feel Eirik's arm around his shoulder. Gunnar rubbed his skull and felt enveloped by a rich sense of happiness, his melancholy seemed to be flowing away between the tiles under the steel bench. Someone above him coughed. He looked up, startled. The familiar face was replaced by that of a security guard.

"All good mate?" He asked.

"I'm going to survive."

“What do you mean?” The guard’s hand went toward his cell phone.

“I have cancer. I have cancer in my head. But, I’m going to be okay.”

The guard sized him up, suspiciously. “Why are you here, then? Are you going on a trip? Should I call someone?”

“No. I’m just resting. I just need something to eat.”

The guard continued to give Gunnar the once-over, as if he didn’t quite believe him. Gunnar felt a dormant sensation - a tingling that warned him of impending danger. He knew he had to get away from this situation. He got up and asked the guard where the nearest food court was. The guard pointed to a direction and Gunnar ambled off in search of some food.

Sitting down to eat a hamburger, he still felt like he was walking in a dream state. He saw Eirik pass by him a couple of times, saw Sverre sitting at the Starbucks, and Kjersti laughed at him from the flight info screens.

At one time, he was convinced he was sitting in his own flat in Chesapeake. He was sitting on a stool overlooking his swimming pool as he downed a can of beer. His car was standing in the parking garage and later he saw his fishing boat floating in the harbour.

He had just swallowed his last bite when he noticed a fly land on his table. He waited for Mental Theo to get rid of it. Suddenly, he spied Hellmuth, with his trademark grin, beckoning him. His best friend … or was he his brother or cousin … needed a partner. There was a situation in Africa - Central Africa that needed to be taken care of. Gunnar laughed. The two of them were going to go on an adventure again. Gunnar stood up and headed to a KLM ticket agent. He felt giddy by the prospect of going back to Africa.

The next few hours were a blur to Gunnar. Later, when he reflected to this time, he realised he must have been functioning on autopilot. He had made this trip from Schiphol to Africa many times before and his brain and hands knew intuitively what to do. He found himself with a one-way plane ticket to Johannesburg which left within a couple of hours. Somehow, he navigated through security and boarded the plane. He had no recollection of the trip to Johannesburg.

Gripar

"I think I have located a Patzschke. A Hellmuth Patzschke." Sigrid was working in Gripar's office on a laptop when she made that announcement.

Gripar got up and headed over to her. "I thought the old man had disappeared and presumed dead."

"No, this wouldn't be Eirik's biological father. However, according to this, he is a close relative. A grandson or a nephew, perhaps."

"Is there any way to track him down and have a conversation with him?"

Sigrid was studying the screen intently. "What makes this particularly interesting is that this Hellmuth has been working at Xe Service. The same company that is associated with Gunnar Patzschke's passport address. This Hellmuth has been working for the company for several years. These last two years he has been in Africa."

Gripar sighed. "I don't think Xe is going to be too forthcoming with information about its employees. Probably our best bet would be to work with Sloss. He would have the requisite connections to track this Hellmuth down. I'll see if I can get a hold of him."

Sigrid nodded. "Great. I'll continue to work with the German authorities to see if I can dig up any more information about him."

Gripar thought for a moment. "Say. Do you happen to have a picture of him?"

Sigrid searched through her database. "Not a recent one. Here is one from about ten years ago." Both Sigrid and Gripar studied the picture. It must have been from a driver's license or government record. It showed a blonde-haired guy, rough features - looked like he had a lot of acne when he was a teenager. His expression was emotionless. The eyes, however, belied the gruff exterior."

"The face doesn't look familiar," Gripar said. Sigrid agreed.

Gripar walked back to his desk and called Sloss. Gripar was astonished to find out that he was on his way to Germany. "I found Gunnar Patzschke," Sloss told him.

"What? What do you mean?" Gripar motioned with his hands and caught Sigrid's attention. She came over and Gripar put the phone call on speaker mode.

"Yeah. I got a call from the Police in Bremerhaven, Germany. They came across a boat that left Norway, hugged the Danish coastline, and arrived in German waters. They tried to flag the boat down, but it apparently made a course change and headed to the UK. A Federal Coast Guard boat said they spotted somebody jump out of the boat and head for the shore just before the boat veered East. Apparently, a few hours later, the police took Gunnar Patzschke into custody. They found him holed up in a house with ten illegal Somali men."

"A human trafficker?" Sigrid mouthed.

Gripar shrugged. That surprised him. He wasn't expecting that. "Are you sure about this?"

Sloss sounded indignant. "Yes, I am sure about this information. I have no reason to doubt the German authorities. As to whether this guy is our Wolfsangel, that's why I am heading out to Germany to talk to him. You must admit, this is a strong lead. Smuggling people is a well-paid criminal activity, which earns a lot of money. In order for this Wolfsangel to pull off what he did, he would need a lot of money and assistance."

Gripar couldn't disagree with that. Still, something didn't quite feel right. Sloss continued, "Human trafficking requires people who have a lot of connections and who are comfortable with making decisions on the fly. This Gunnar Patzschke is well-known for taking people from Africa and bringing them to Europe."

These pieces of information definitely fit the puzzle. "So, you think this is the same Gunnar Patzschke that was in Moss. What about that boat? Was it the same boat from Moss?"

"Of course it is. This just has to be confirmed by the Coast Guard."

"How come this is the first time we are hearing about this?" Sigrid asked.

Sloss became a bit defensive. "This is an international situation that has significant ties to National Security. That's our department, not yours."

As much as he hated to admit it, that reasoning kind of made sense to Gripar. Gunnar Patzschke, AKA Wolfsangel, was most likely a German citizen. He certainly wasn't a Norwegian citizen. Sigrid was able to confirm that fact. There was going to be a lot of red tape to work through in order to extradite this guy back to Norway. Better that Sloss work that out. "Ok. Are you able to keep us informed as things progress?"

Sloss uttered a non-committal grunt and was ready to disconnect when Gripar managed to ask him if he had sufficient clearance to access some background information on an Xe employee. Sloss was quite certain he did but became snarky when Gripar declined to give him a name until he got back from Germany. Which, Sloss hoped would be tomorrow.

After disconnecting, Sigrid and Gripar looked at each other. "What do you think?" Sigrid asked.

"All of this seems to fit in, more or less. But, I honestly don't see how this Gunnar could be connected to Eirik and the Tyskerbarn."

Sigrid agreed. "Human trafficking is the lowest of the low. No principles or higher morals are needed. Why would a human-trafficker even care about what happened to people fifty years ago?"

The two of them were interrupted by a knock on the door. In stepped Svendsen with a message for the two of them. "Sverre is here. I put him in the main conference room. He is waiting for you."

Gripar looked at his watch. "Crap. Lost track of time. Thanks very much. We're heading there right now."

Sverre had come in for a debriefing. Gripar was pleased Sverre agreed to do this because he was the only person they knew who had any length of interaction with the Wolfsangel. The two of them hurried to the conference room, not wanting to make Sverre wait for them.

When he entered the room, Gripar tried to hide his shock at how Sverre looked. Sverre was generally a smiling guy, full of life. He was usually quick with his humour and his bright disposition tended to put people at ease. The Sverre that was sitting down at the table was nothing like this. He looked haggard and withdrawn.

There was a tiny smile as Sverre recognised Gripar. Both Gripar and Sigrid bowed slightly and shook his hand. "How are you doing?" Gripar asked as he sat down.

Sverre shrugged. "Of course, I am very relieved to be home again with my wife and children. They picked me up from Holmestrand and now we are in our house in Voksenkollen. They have been so worried! At the moment I am still digesting everything mentally."

"I can't imagine what you went through," Sigrid said.

Sverre nodded his thanks.

Gripar got right down to business. "I'm sorry that we have to do this, but we would like to ask you some questions so that we can add information to what we already know about this Wolfsangel. You are the only one that we have that has spent that much time with him. We're hoping that with your information, we can find this guy and arrest him."

"I am happy to help, although I have no idea what this guy looked like. He always wore a face covering when we talked." There was a pitcher of water and a set of glasses on the table. Sverre poured himself a cup and then motioned to both Sigrid and Gripar if they wanted some. Both declined.

Gripar showed him a picture of the Hellmuth Patzschke. Sverre stared at it for a long time. During that time, Gripar had to suppress a smile as he watched Sverre's facial contortions. He furrowed his brow, pursed his lips, and squinted his eyes. Finally, he shook his head slowly. "I don't know. There is definitely something familiar about that face, but I can't say for sure."

For the next forty-five minutes, the three of them discussed what happened to Sverre from the time he was captured until the time he was released. The two of them probed as much as they could, cognisant of Sverre's still fragile state.

When it came to the woman that was with the Wolfsangel, Gripar suspected Sverre was holding back. Sverre could not - or did not want to - provide any details about her other than he thought the female was captured at the same time as him but was released within a few days.

When it became clear that Sverre had provided as much information as he could, Gripar asked him if he had any hard feelings towards the Wolfsangel and his cause. Sverre closed his eyes and rubbed his forehead. He then looked at Gripar straight in the eyes for several moments before he answered. "You're wondering if I have Stockholm syndrome. I can tell you very honestly that I feel no empathy for Wolfsangel as a person. Yes, we talked a fair bit about the Lebensborn in general and this Eirik Tijsker specifically. There wasn't a lot of new information - nothing I haven't already heard in the news regarding the confessions of the Hurdal Three. He never threatened me. He immediately told me at the beginning that he had no plans to hurt me. I believed him. He only needed me to draw attention to his case. So, I guess, he used me."

Gripar realised that Sverre was processing his feelings as he talked. Sverre's eyes never strayed from Gripar's. There was a pause. Gripar softly asked, "But were you able to sleep there?"

At that Sverre turned away and looked at his hands. "Very badly. Not necessarily because my bed was nothing more than a lumpy mattress. I had lots of nightmares. I heard voices, many voices. Echoes from the past, strange sounds that made me feel helpless." Sverre's voice started to crack and Gripar felt some shame in pushing Sverre this far. Sverre went on, though. "Are you familiar with Paul Simon's song The Sounds of Silence. People talking without speaking. People hearing without listening. And no one dared disturb the sound of silence."

Both Gripar and Sigrid nodded even though Sverre wasn't looking.

Looking back at Gripar, Sverre continued, "The second night, I thought I heard someone crying. I discovered that it was me."

Gripar waited for him to continue. He didn't but his eyes still focused on Gripar's. It was a bit unnerving until Gripar realised that Sverre was waiting for him to ask the question. So, he did.

"Did you understand what you were crying for?"

Without any hesitation, Sverre replied, "Injustice. I don't have any feelings for this Wolfsangel guy. Yet, he was successful in bringing me to a new perspective." Sverre paused as if he were gathering his thoughts. "You know, I want to be able to look straight into the eyes of my fellow Norwegians because one day I, along with them, will stand before God's throne, together with all Norwegians. We will be judged for how we treated these German war children."

Gripar and Sigrid gave him a moment to compose himself and then he went to the forensics department where he met with a team to see if they could get any identifying information about the Wolfsangel from him.

Sigrid and Gripar went back to his office and discussed what they heard. "So, do you really believe he told us everything he knew about the female that was with the Wolfsangel?" Gripar mused.

Sigrid shook her head. "No, I think he knows more than he is letting on. Why? I don't know."

"I agree," Gripar said. "I guess we'll have to wait until the forensics report to confirm whether Kjersti Hurum was, indeed, the third person at the cottage in Moss. Sverre thought she was released after a couple of days, but the evidence seems to suggest otherwise."

Sigrid glanced through her notes and then suddenly sat straight up in his chair. "Did Sverre say that he thought the Wolfsangel guy was very sick?"

"Yes, he mentioned that the guy was on a pretty heavy regiment of medication."

"Well, let's add that to our profile. We should be checking in with hospitals and doctors' offices around Moss to see if something comes up," Sigrid said.

Wolfsangel

Gunnar drifted in and out of consciousness. He vaguely remembered getting off a plane. He glanced around and realised he was sprawled on the floor of a terminal building. He lay back down, wallowing in a dense fog surrounded by a cacophony of voices, laughter, crying … He was driving to the mountains to bury someone; he saw Eirik walking around Fylke in white clothes, Finn and Olaf were also walking with him. Every once in a while, that woman popped in. She was laughing. She was crying. She was beckoning him. Occasionally, he even saw himself, laying on a bench. Amid the noise, he distinctly heard Linnea's voice warning him to take his medication. He had already taken his meds, hadn't he? He searched for his pill bottles but couldn't locate them. Distracted by a sudden noise that appeared right next to him, he looked up trying to focus his vision. How long has he been here? Hours, seconds, or was it days, weeks? He could sense that death was hovering nearby, like a vulture waiting for his inevitable end.

Gunnar was brought back to reality when he felt an ice pack on his forehead. The sudden cooling sensation dispersed some of the haze. Just out of focus, he saw a silhouette. He heard a familiar voice. "Easy there, old friend. You are in bad shape. You are going to be taken home, I'll take care of that."

Gunnar had words in his mind but couldn't wrap his voice around them. He wanted to express his thanks. His lips moved, but there was no sound. The voice told him not to talk but just sip from a cup of water. Instinctively, like a child, Gunnar leaned into the cup and swallowed, feeling the water trickle down his throat and into his stomach.

Eventually, he recognised the voice. He tried to form words letting Hellmuth know that he saw the email and was ready to get back into action. He eagerly looked forward to the two of them returning to the adventurous life they once shared together. The words formed in his head but refused to exit his mouth.

The next thing he remembered was feeling somebody pull him up. He felt the familiar sense of safety and he tentatively put one foot in front of the other to follow his friend.

Gripar

Gripar stared at the whiteboard in the conference room. He was having trouble connecting the puzzle pieces into a coherent picture. The ringing of his cell phone interrupted him. It was a number that he recognised. “Hi Sjurd, how are you doing?”

There was a moment of silence while Sjurd figured out how Gripar knew it was him. Then, in an excited voice, “Hey Gripar. I wanted to let you know that I found my brother. He is alive. He’s not dead. He is alive and currently in Africa. The Democratic Republic of Congo, to be exact.” There was a happy laugh at the end of the line.

Gripar was silent for a moment, processing this information. “Well, how great is that. Wow. I don’t know what to say. After all these years, you find out he is actually alive. You must be so happy. How did you come across this information?”

“I got a call from a cousin of mine, a German named Hellmuth. Apparently, Gunnar and Hellmuth have been working together for the past ten or so years for Blackwater. I guess, now it is called Xe Company. It is a private military security company. Hellmuth called me to let me know that my brother …” There was a pause and then a chuckle. “…my brother, that sounds good. I haven’t said that in a long time. Well, my brother is quite sick and he urged me to convince Gunnar to come home.”

“So, what you are saying is that Gunnar has been in DRC all this time?”

Sjurd didn’t keep the glee out of his voice. “I guess so. That’s what I gathered from Hellmuth. I did manage to speak briefly with Gunnar. He wasn’t very coherent, though. He is definitely quite sick and has agreed to come home.”

“And what now? What are you going to do?”

“I’m going there to pick him up …” Gripar heard shrieking seagulls in the background.

“What do you mean? You’re going to Africa? You going to pick him up in Africa?”

"Yes, absolutely. He is in Kisangani, sick and possibly near death. He has a medical condition but has, apparently, not taken his medication for a while. I don't even think he has any left. Helmuth figured out what he has been taking and I've talked to a doctor here. She has given me enough to get him back." There was a pause and Sjurd's voice dropped. "This is amazing. A gift from God. For years I thought he was dead, but now it turns out he is not, well, almost ... I have to pick him up. Right now! 'I'll keep you informed." With that, the call was disconnected.

Gripar shook his head. This was a completely unexpected turn of events. Sjurd's brother - Gunnar - was actually alive. That changes everything. He sighed deeply and headed to the cafeteria for a coffee.

On the way, his phone beeped. Svendsen had texted him to tune into NRK1 for an important news bulletin from the Royal Family. Returning to the conference room, he turned on the television. He was immediately taken inside of Skaugum Estates where four people were seated around a square coffee table. Sitting on a couch at one side of the table was Sverre and his wife. Seated directly across from him was Jens Stoltenberg, the Prime Minister, as well as Gripar's boss, Trina Pedersen, the Minister of Public Security.

A voice-over informed the TV audience that His Royal Highness wished to address the people of Norway on an important matter. The camera panned towards Sverre Lodbrok. Gripar thought he looked pretty good considering all that had happened to him.

Sverre's voice was clear and unwavering as he recounted to the Norwegian people what happened to him at the hands of the Wolfsangel. When he finished his factual account, he paused and took a sip of water. He glanced at his wife who smiled and nodded. Unfolding sheets of paper he retrieved from his pocket, he went on.

"Dear people, you now know the facts of the Three of Hurdal and their backgrounds. I have here an open letter to the Tyskerbarn which I have titled, 'My heart goes out to you!'"

Sverre put on his reading glasses and Gripar instinctively knew what was about to happen was going to be monumental. Up to this point, Sverre had been reading from a teleprompter. It looked like he was now going off-script - he was going to say something that he did not want anybody else to know in advance. Gripar could see the Prime Minister nervously shift his body. Gripar leaned forward in his chair.

"Today I want all Tyskerbarn to know that I feel a deep shame and guilt. I pledge to you that, moving forward from this day, I will work hard to do better. I need to change. Indeed, we all need to change. All of us Norwegians must overcome our ignorance about what you went through. I pray God to forgive me. We have neglected you. Now my heart goes out to you."

Here he paused, took another sip of water and cleared his throat. He sought his wife's eyes and nodded at her. The camera caught his hands ever so slightly shaking as he held his paper.

"Please hear me. In Strasbourg, you had asked for compensation of four hundred thousand Crowns for each of you, individually. Four hundred thousand for every lost youth. A pittance, really. In 2002, our government would only promise less than half of that. And then, to add insult to injury, the court ruled that you actually were not eligible for any compensation because of a statute of limitations. Incredible.

"Well, though the European Commission for Human Rights has rejected your case, I do not. I want you to know that I am sincere in my commitment to change. I pledge to personally make up the difference between what you have rightfully asked for and what you were given. You will get the four hundred thousand you asked for. I will pay the difference between what the government promised and what you asked for out of my personal finances. I pledge to pay all of it, even if it means I will have nothing left than the clothes on my back! With the consent of my wife, I offer you everything that we possess. Come to me, we'll work it out together!"

The camera caught the tears in his eyes and in his wife's. As it panned out, the face of Prime Minister Jens Stoltenberg, came into view. The

Prime Minister, clearly having no foreknowledge of this, was obviously shocked. His mouth was covered by his right hand, eyes popping out. Trina Pedersen was looking down at her shoes, giving her head a slight shake as she realised the enormity of the Prince's offer.

Sverre stood up and helped his wife to her feet. His eyes swept the room and then locked on the camera. Taking a deep breath, he added with conviction, "If at the end of all times we stand before God's throne, I want to be able to look straight into everyone's eyes." The two of them walked away. The announcer searched for words.

Gripar sat quietly, waiting for…yes, what? Understanding perhaps, insight? He didn't quite know what to make of all this. He was surprised, though, because he was expecting the Wolfsangel to have the last word.

He turned off the television. He made the decision to travel to the old woman in Hurdal, the widow Mirre. She definitely knows the Wolfsangel on a more personal level than she let on. If he is going to find Eirik, that's the place to start looking.

Gripar

It was around dinner time when Gripar entered Hurdal. He had eaten a pizza in Jessheim, but when he stepped into Mirre's house, a smell so delicious wafted into his nostrils, his stomach rumble audibly.

"Hello, my dear boy, what can I do for you now? Have you eaten? I still have enough left for a plate. Come sit down." Before he could respond, she shuffled off to the kitchen.

She returned with a plate of hot food. Placing it in front of him, she sat across and smiled kindly. She was very sweet, he thought, but also has her secrets.

"Thank you, Mirre, it's really great food." He finished the plate with ease and pushed back his chair. Mirre picked up his empty plate and the eating utensils and put them on the counter. "So, Mirre. I am intrigued by that porcelain candle stand." Gripar got up and took the stand from the bookcase where it was on display. "I noticed it on our first visit and did some research. I learned that these artefacts were made in the Dachau concentration camp."

Mirre's face showed no emotion as she wiped the table with a cleaning cloth. "Yes, you are correct. The Nazi's had them made by the prisoners and used them for special occasions."

Gripar nodded. "Yes. Special occasions like christening ceremonies - especially for children of senior SS officials." Mirre didn't respond. She went to the sink to put the cloth away.

"So, let me tell you what I think. I understand that a christening ceremony included both a candle stick holder and a dagger. So, is there also a dagger to go with the stand?" Mirre's face was unreadable, but she nodded. "Did you get them from Anna?" Again, a slight nod.

Gripar continued, "Well, then, I think that you must have two sets. One for Eirik and one for her sister."

Mirre took the stand from Gripar and examined it closely. "No. I don't. Anna had both sets, but somehow she lost one."

Gripar reached into the duffle bag he had picked up at the HL-Senteret on the way here. He pulled out an identical candle stand. "I think this may be the missing set." The two candle stands were identical. He turned them around, at the bottom of both was etched 'SS Allach'.

Gripar watched as the old lady took in the pair. He noticed her breathing changed slightly as she studied both carefully. Her eyes softened. "How can you be sure this belongs to Anna? That camp produced many sets of these artefacts."

Gripar paused, collecting his thoughts. "Divers found them in a lake. The Nordbytjernet Lake opposite the Romerike school in Jessheim."

At this, Mirre's eyes widened, and her mask fell. She staggered backwards forcing Gripar to quickly grab her and put her on a chair. In a whisper she asked, "The same lake where ...?"

"Yes, the same lake where Eirik's sister drowned." Pausing as he watched Mirre struggle to gain control, he looked at her. "Hellmuth Patzschke is the father of Eirik and Esther. He was a very high-ranking SS official. Hellmuth Patzschke, or Hellmuth Reinhardt as he was known during the war, went missing a few years back. Eirik married Marianne and had three children: Gunnar, Sjurd, and Anna. Furthermore, Gunnar is not dead as his family was once notified." He paused, searching Mirre's face.

She looked up tearfully at Gripar, and asked hesitantly, " ...and ... how do you know that?"

"Sjurd called me earlier. He found his brother, Gunnar, alive in Africa. He is critically ill, though."

That last statement seemed to jolt her. She opened her mouth as if to speak, but there was no sound. She then sighed deeply and seemed to shrivel. Gripar waited for her to respond. She looked at her hands. "And, what about Eirik. Where is he?" It wasn't so much a question as it was a statement.

"I'm assuming there are some things you have not told me?" She nodded her head and glanced at the dagger and standards.

The setting sun cast a brilliant red and orange canopy in the sky when Gripar drove back to Oslo an hour and a half later.

He realized the old lady was going to have a burial soon, of her husband, and maybe ...

He now knew why he, Odd Gripar, was directly involved in this matter. Wolfsangel not only sought the truth, not even only judgment, but he also sought his father.

What if there was no corpse?

There was a soft, tentative knock on the door. Gripar almost missed it. Who could it be, he wondered. Likely the neighbour two doors down. She was always popping by looking for an excuse to talk to him. Last week, she stopped by to let him know that the Kiwi Bjølsen grocery store, just down the street, had a great selection of fruit. He debated whether or not to answer when there was a second set of knocking - a little more bold this time. He strode to the door and was stunned at who he saw through the peephole.

Zofia was standing there. He wasn't expecting that. He stood there, frozen, staring at her through the peephole, unsure what to do. It looked like she was ready to walk away.

He opened the door. "Hi Odd." Zofia stood in front of him, her eyes gazing into his. Gripar could faintly smell her perfume. He shook his head. "Zofia. I wasn't expecting you. I left some messages and you didn't return my call."

"Can I come in?" she asked.

He was quite aware that he was blocking the door. He was considering whether or not he wanted to have a conversation with her right now. He was concerned about what had happened in the park, but was also puzzled by their relationship. He just wasn't sure he was ready tonight to get some tough news.

"Please," she said. "I want a chance to explain."

Gripar moved to the side and invited her in.

Zofia turned to him and took a deep breath. "That woman, you know, is my sister."

Gripar was elated at her honesty. Now, he needed to be honest as well. "Yes, I was told that her name is Kjersti Hurum. I was wondering if the two of you are related."

Zofia's head shot up and she stared at him, mouth gaping. "You knew her identity? How come you didn't say anything?"

Gripar gave her a look. She nodded. "Of course. You didn't find out until after the event. We haven't talked since then."

Gripar got up and starting pacing the deck. "How did your sister end up becoming involved with this Wolfsangel?"

Zofia couldn't stem the flow of tears down her cheek as she filled in what she knew about how her sister got involved with Wolfsangel and the kidnapping of Sverre. Yes, it was Kjersti that dropped off the letter at the HL-Senteret and it was her at the park helping to set up the Woman of Norway incident.

Gripar needed a moment to process this. He had been hoping that Zofia and Kjersti were not related. The truth of the matter, no matter how he sliced it, was Zofia's sister is an accomplice to murder and kidnapping. Leaning over the balcony railing, he said to Zofia in a flat voice, "You do know, I have an obligation and responsibility to find Kjersti in order to arrest and charge her."

Zofia nodded. "I don't know where she is. She is not at her place. I've called several times and there is no answer. I'm afraid something bad might have happened to her."

Gripar still wasn't sure what to do. He was caught between his duty as a police officer and his feelings for Zofia. His head knew what he had to do, and his heart knew what he wanted to do. While Gripar was struggling with this existential crisis, she made the first move. She got up from her chair and hugged Gripar. Gripar responded by putting his arms around her, drinking in the smell of her hair and revelling in the closeness of her body. He stroked her back. "It's going to be alright. We'll find her."

"I'm so worried about her. Tell me, how much trouble is she really in?"

Gripar couldn't minimise the truth. "A lot. Being an accessory to murder and kidnapping is pretty serious business."

Zofia loosened her arms around Gripar and stepped back. "There's no proof she was involved in the murder of those three men, is there?"

"Not direct proof. You say she was only connected with him for the kidnapping?"

"Yes, as far as I understood from what she told me, she became involved with him at the rally. Previous to that, I don't think she had never met the man."

Gripar nodded. "Well, that seems unlikely. In any case, the Wolfsangel has disappeared as well, so likely Kjersti is with him. I suspect the police are seeking arrest warrants for both of them."

"Is there something that you can do? I can't lose my sister. She is all the family I've got."

Gripar looked at her with surprise. "What do you mean? Didn't you tell me that your parents lived in Bergen?"

Zofia hung her head in shame. A pit was growing in Gripar's stomach. What was going on?

Wringing her hands, she said softly, "I wasn't being completely honest with you. I want to now, though. Please let's sit down."

Gripar slowly made his way to a chair and sat down. Waiting for her. After settling in, Zofia continued. "My father was a welder for Stavanger

Drilling Company. They were working off the shore of Scotland. He was one of hundred or so people that didn't make it when the Kielland platform collapsed. He died when I was five years old. Kjersti is a couple of years older than me. I don't really remember him much at all. We lived in Dundee at the time with my grandparents - my mom's parents. You see, my mom and dad didn't have much of a marriage. Shortly after his death, she went off the deep end. Got involved in drugs and alcohol. One day, about two years after my dad's death, she just up and disappeared. Never saw her again. Kjersti and I moved back to Norway to live with our aunt and uncle." By this time, tears were streaming down her cheeks.

Griper's eyes weren't dry either. After a pause, "I'm so sorry. Why couldn't you tell me that earlier?"

"I don't know. I guess I'm a very independent person and I… I don't know, really."

Gripar decided to forge ahead with the one burning question he was afraid to ask because he was afraid of the answer. "Can I ask you a question? You're a reporter and your job is to go out where the stories are and dig into them. Was I used as a source to fill out your story?"

Zofia looked up at Gripar and studied him. It was unnerving. He could tell she was searching for the right words. Finally, "Yes. I'm a reporter and access to information is my life blood. Yes, at first, I considered you as merely another source of information."

Gripar's face fell. He got up and leaned over the balcony rails again. Unsure of all the emotions that were coursing through his heart. Then there was a small twinge. Shaking his head, he asked, "At first? What do you mean?"

She came up behind him but didn't touch him. "Odd, I have discovered through all this that I really like you. In fact, it is becoming more than that."

He turned around. Her face radiated. She smiled tentatively and her eyes sparkled. She put out her arms and he fell into them. "I think you are becoming my M'eudai'," she whispered. They stayed like that for a while.

Wolfsangel

Dimly aware that a bear was standing in front of him, Gunnar couldn't help but admire the beast. What power! Gunnar smiled; he had no fear. The bear stood before him, bent over, he felt a big paw lifting his chin.

Again, that voice. "Brother. Gunnar, my brother. It's me. Do you hear me?"

His lips were cracked, and when he smiled, small drops of blood came out. He shook his head in tired wonder.

"Father ..."

"No, it's me, your brother, Sjurd."

"Brother? I want ..." Again he slid away, but something awoke deep inside. Strong hands picked him up. Sjurd was there. Good ...

He tasted corticosteroid tablets. He drank and drank. A cool washcloth washed his hot body, his body underwent everything as pure blessing. Dry, fresh smelling sheets, T-shirt, pillow.

Sleep, wonderful sleep ...

That evening, under the cover of darkness, Gunnar was guided by his brother onto a company plane that was to take the two of them back to Johannesburg. "Hellmuth? Where's Hellmuth?" Gunnar asked Sjurd.

"He had something he had to do. So, it's just the two of us."

Gunnar couldn't remember the last time he and his brother were together. It would have been such a long time ago and so much has happened since then. He felt estranged - his brother was acting weird but it never dawned on him that his family would have been given the same death notice as old Hellmuth.

When Sjurd told him, things got even more awkward. Gunnar was not emotionally prepared to deal with this situation. The two of them made small talk, not as brothers, but like new kids in school trying to find their place. Gunnar learned that they were heading back to Urk, his birthplace. Sjurd figured they would be able to catch a flight back to Schiphol tomorrow morning. Regularly Sjurd gave him a handful of medication. Most of the way he slept.

When they arrived at OR Tambo International, his brother took a moment to talk to his wife on the phone. Gunnar was startled as he realised that Sjurd was speaking in Urkers and he could understand what was being said. "Jannie, I realise that, honey, but everything is fine, we are safe and heading back to the Netherlands. We should be home by this evening. You don't have to worry. Everything will be fine." Clearly, she did not seem to agree, but Sjurd seemed to be able to smooth things over. "It will be okay. Goodbye, give our children a hug from me."

Sjurd went off to secure tickets back to Schiphol and came back with two coffees. Gunnar forgot how much coffee was a social event for the Dutch. Much like sitting around a campfire, coffee drinking relaxes people and opens them up. Gunnar wasn't surprised when eventually Sjurd decided to tackle the burning issue. He turned to him. "Gunnar, I am so happy and grateful to God that you weren't killed in action. You can't imagine all those years of wishing I had a second chance to talk to you and to understand who you are. So, I am going to make that effort."

Gunnar nodded. He wasn't ready to open up his heart to Sjurd. "So, what do you want to know about me?"

Sjurd stared at Gunnar. After a moment's pause. "I guess I would like to know what happened to make you so sick?"

Gunnar breathed a sigh of relief. That was a fairly straightforward question. He realized that he owed his life to Sjurd and owed him an explanation. He told his brother about the Foreign Legion, Black Water, and his accident in Sudan. It was a factual account, he tried to leave the emotions out of it. Gunnar couldn't read his brother very well. Sjurd's face remained passive. He made no gestures of sympathy. "So, what last name do you go by, then? Patzschke?"

Gunnar knew immediately this was a loaded question. It was a matter of identity and heritage and he was pretty sure his little brother didn't approve of his choices. "I wanted to leave Europe and go to the US and I finally got that chance. The first thing I did was change my last name, something I always wanted to do. I knew that Tijsker meant German in Norwegian. Our real name should have been Patzschke."

"How did you get a German passport? It's not that easy getting German citizenship. Don't you need a declaration of paternity?"

Gunnar sighed. His family had always been pretty adamant about ignoring their German roots. It was an embarrassment to them, and Gunnar really wasn't sure why they felt that way. He, on the other hand, was proud of that. His German ancestry opened many doors for him. What he was about to reveal was not going to sit well with Sjurd. "I connected with our father's father - our grandfather. He told me from personal experience that changing my last name would be the best thing for me. And he was right. He provided a declaration of paternity."

Sjurd nodded, never removing his eyes off Gunnar as he drank his coffee.

Gunnar studied the look on Sjurd's face. Was it contempt? Was it disdain? Should he even bother to explain to his brother? "Listen, I was born with three identities. A Norwegian one, Pederson, from our grandmother Anna. A German one, Patzschke, from our grandfather Hellmuth. And of course the Dutch one, Tijsker. I have no regrets. I used each one of them to my advantage. My bank account is well filled; I made a lot of money. I have a beautiful flat in Chesapeake ..." Gunnar stopped and waited.

He knew what Sjurd was going to ask. Finally, he did. "The fiasco in Norway. The Hurdal Three. Judging the living and the dead. The police are saying it was the work of a Gunnar Patzschke.' Was that your work?"

Gunnar didn't answer right away. Sjurd continued to look at him, holding his eyes, trying to pry deep into the recesses of Gunnar's conscience; Gunnar didn't flinch. Eventually, he shook his head and shrugged. "Mine? I don't know what you are talking about. Why would I be involved with that. Ask Hellmuth. He'll tell you I have been in Africa the past three years."

He could tell that Sjurd wasn't buying it. It didn't matter much. The gulf between the brothers was as wide as it ever was.

Gripar

Gripar called Sjurd a number of times but was unable to reach him. In desperation, he called Marianne. He was mildly surprised when she answered her phone. Even in her broken English, though, she made it very clear to Gripar that she wasn't going to be of any help. She didn't know if Sjurd was back from Africa and she certainly had no idea if her son Gunnar was actually alive.

Gripar felt he had no choice but to book a flight out to Holland and confront them. He desperately wanted to close this case. Ever since he found out that Sjurd's brother was not killed in action years ago, but still alive, he had absolutely no doubt in his mind that this was the person responsible for what happened in Norway. All the evidence clearly pointed to that conclusion. He and Sigrid went over everything and put together the case against him. He didn't believe for a second that Gunnar had been in Africa during all this time. What he was doing in Africa now, he didn't know, but that really didn't matter much to the case.

The only problem was that the evidence was largely circumstantial. Gripar was advised by Svendsen that he needed solid evidence that the Gunnar

Patzschke – son of Eirik Tijsker – is, in fact, the Wolfsangel. He needed proof that this Patzschke guy had killed the three men that were used for the human monument, had assaulted three men in Moss, had kidnapped Sverre Lodbrok and held him captive for several days, and had destroyed a national monument. That kind of proof might be difficult to obtain. Sjurd told him that he was planning to go to Africa and pick up his brother. Gripar's only option was to confront the entire family and fill in the missing blanks. Then he could take Gunnar back to Norway for a trial.

He decided he should let Sverre know. He called his assistant who had patched him through to Sverre. Sverre was pleased with the progress that was being made and really wanted to come with Gripar to the Netherlands. The logistical nightmare as well as the constant hounding of the press made that impossible. Sverre ended the conversation, "I appreciate you giving me an update. All the best in Holland."

Gripar boarded a KLM flight, found his seat beside the window, and settled in for the two-hour flight. His seat companion, noticing that Gripar was wearing a set of headphones, left him alone. Gripar smiled to himself. Nobody but he knew that the headphones weren't plugged into any device. It was an effective way of releasing Gripar from the social obligation of engaging in chit-chat. In a few days he would probably feel some regret for being cold, but now he nodded off.

After landing in Schiphol and going through customs, Gripar set out to find a car rental place. He knew he should have had that arranged online before leaving Oslo, but with the quick packing, the call to Sverre and everything else, he ran out of time. He caught sight of an Enterprise Car Rental sign and followed the directions to the kiosk. He asked the attendant if it was possible for him to rent a fairly large vehicle – something along the lines of a pickup truck. The attendant assured him that he had a suitable vehicle for him. Gripar ended up with a little Fiat Panda. Gripar sighed, remembering a phrase he heard several times: 'Think big, act small.' Leave it to the Dutch to drive 'small'. He made his way out of the airport complex and found a hotel to check in for the night.

Unknown to both of them, Kjersti had been on the same plane.

That morning she had paced through her workshop in Sandnes. She constantly saw her lover's face. Sometimes she laughed, sometimes she scolded and rubbed her eyes, but nothing helped.

"Oh, what's the matter with me? It can't be that I miss that soldier. Let him carry his own revenge war and leave my feelings alone."

"I do not want to miss you. Selfish bastard!" She called out in the room of her studio as she kicked the leg of her worktable.

Sandnes had been her base, but now it was the place where she had gone into hiding. In 2008 the city was the European Capital of Culture, together with Liverpool, and that thanks to her work. Her sculptures from that time were now everywhere, even in the Vigeland park in Oslo.

Kjersti was greatly bewildered by the fact the police don't appear to be looking for her. How can that be? Even now, after days, she had not been approached, she did not expect that. Either they had no idea who she was, or she was being watched.

But her life was no longer normal, anyway. She had also heard Sverre. Now she missed that Wolfsangel, that Gunnar Patzschke or 'Mister Whatever' much more than she had ever expected. He did not respond when she called his mobile. What was the matter with him?

She realized she was head over heels in love. With both her fists she hammered on her desk and shouted, "No!" But her heart laughed at her.

Then she had stormed out and purchased a ticket. Upon arrival she did not take a hotel, but immediately took the train to Zwolle and the last bus to Urk.

PART 3

THE FINAL WEEK, URK AND THE STONE FROM NORWAY

Monday

Gripar

The next morning, Gripar stuffed himself back into the Fiat and took the highway towards Amersfoort. It was true what he had heard about the Netherlands: It does not take long before you see a river or lake. After half an hour he saw the water of the IJ on the left side of the highway, the sun was playing with the water while sailing boats traversed the surface. Gripar remembered his previous trip to Urk and talking with that stranger - water as freedom in life and water as destruction in death. That's how the Urk fishermen see it. On the one hand, like a woman they are in love with and on the other hand, as a cemetery containing bodies of loved ones. It struck Gripar that maybe this is part of the reason that the village has the highest percentage of churchgoers in the Netherlands.

Zofia had once told him that the people of Urk had been the subject of some interesting research. Apparently, some scientists suspected that they were the purest Dutch. Hundreds of years before Christ was born, small groups of Celts settled on the islands around the North, East and South Sea. They subsisted on a combination of agriculture and fishing. Also, 'Urch-nay.' Orkney, the island of Urk, was much larger than just before it got diked in 1932. Urkers, she said, still see themselves as a tribe, faithful to the Bible. He chuckled to himself as he remembered a joke he heard Sjurd tell his children about how Urk was really the site of the original garden of Eden.

A strange calm took possession of him; he knew he had time. The mysterious Wolfsangel, Gunnar Patzschke, was most likely in Urk right now with his brother. He was convinced his journey which started out in Hurdal was going to end here in Urk.

The traffic was not busy. Within a short time he was in Amersfoort and had to turn to Zwolle. Driving relaxed, window partially open, he was anxiously looking forward to what was coming up. Startled, he caught a sign with his name on it. Later, he found out that his own name was anchored in a fishing village. A few kilometres north of Kristiansund, there are a few small islands, first called Gripar, later Grip, which means catching fish.

The summer warmth felt good on the open road. He opened his window all the way, enjoying the breeze on his face. Via Kampen, he entered the Noordoostpolder, on to Urk.

Wolfsangel

Although he might not admit that to anyone, Gunnar was ecstatic that Kjersti decided to join him in Urk. They had decided to stay at Sjurd's place for the night. Despite the tension in his and his brother's relationship, Gunnar was glad he was going to stay with Sjurd. He needed some time to get himself together to face his mother. Now, as he stared at solid brickwork of the ground floor and top green-painted timber cladded house, number 4/115, he wasn't sure he was ready. He had some inkling of what the Prodigal Son must have felt like when he headed home.

He stepped out of the car, oblivious to the two other occupants. He took a deep breath and started walking towards the front door.

The door burst open just before he reached it. His mother appeared. "My son, my dear son. You've come back from the dead! No, I do not yet need to know why. You are back, I'm so happy..."

Gunnar found himself embraced by Marianne. He did not say anything, yet he pulled her against him. Years ago, this woman heard her son was killed in an accident, that there was not even a dead body. It struck him how enormously selfish he had been towards his mother, his own mother! "I'm sorry, mother, so sorry." He could not give answers, not now.

"Shhh. It's okay. Come in. Oh God! How happy I am ..." At that she burst into tears. First there were silent drops crawling down her cheek. Then, deep sobs, her whole body shaking.

Gunnar looked at Sjurd. He detected both misty eyes and a twinge of a smile. Sjurd avoided returning the look. Gunnar looked at Kjersti. Tears were streaming down her cheek. They stepped inside of the house.

Sjurd decided to break the tension by doing what all good Dutch people do. "Shall I make coffee, mother?"

It was as if a spell were broken. Marianne looked up clearly flustered, first at Sjurd then at Gunnar. She facepalmed herself. "Oh, how stupid of me ... Sjurd, I am also glad that you are safe here again. Thank you. Thank you. Thank you for bringing my other son here." She gave Sjurd a hug as she wiped the stray tears from her eyes.

She finally took notice of the strange woman that had been standing there taking in the scene. She, too, was wiping stray tears. Marianne walked up to her and said in Urkers, "Welcome. Who are you?"

Kjersti looked at Gunnar, shaking her head. "What did she say? She doesn't sound happy to see me." Gunnar laughed. "That's just my mother. She wants to know who you are." Gunnar turned to his mother. "This is Kjersti, mother, Kjersti is my …, uhm …" Sjurd coughed slightly. Gunnar kept trying. "How about girlfriend? Yes, let's say girlfriend. Doesn't matter what you call it, relationship, courtship, my girl."

It was obvious to Sjurd that the two of them had a very special and unique relationship, despite the two of them trying hard not to acknowledge it. He boomed, "Brother, I think the word you are looking for is 'kalletje'." He explained the term to Kjersti in English.

She turned her head to Gunnar and looked at him happily. "Yeah, my friend. I am your 'kalletje', your girlfriend!"

Moments later, the tension broken, they sat around the kitchen table, drinking coffee. Gunnar wasn't used to drinking that much coffee, but it gave him a distraction. He was collecting his thoughts, not sure how to broach the subject of his prolonged absence. He cleared his throat. "So, mother, here we are, all home together. The family is together."

"We've got him back," Sjurd said to his mother. "Who would have imagined that?"

Marianne looked around the table with a smile only a mother could give. "It may sound crazy, Sjurd, but I knew deep down in my heart that he was still alive."

At that moment, it was like a switch had been turned on and the guilt hit him. What a blow to their mother if something would have also happened to Sjurd. What a blow to his wife and children. All his life, he was pretty much unconnected. He had never actually stopped to consider what his death might have meant to his family. It's not over, though. That disease was still ravaging his body. He stared at the coffee grounds at the bottom of his cup. "There is something you need to know, mother. I am sick. Really sick." Gunnar looked up at her. She nodded hesitantly. Gunnar went on to explain what had happened. Gunnar could see in her eyes how devastated she was at this news. Just when she had regained her son, he was telling her that he was dying.

"Don't worry. I am going to beat this," Gunnar said with conviction. Last night, he, Sjurd, and Kjersti discussed strategies for doing that. It involved seeing a world-renowned specialist in Amsterdam and implementing a strict regimen of medication, diet, and exercise. They all felt better in the end, having articulated a plan. For Gunnar, it was like the old days, developing a battle plan to attack the enemy. He knew it was partly psychological. It gave a sense that the players had a measure of control. It gave everyone an ease of mind. Now, as he recounted their earlier discussion, he could tell everyone around the table bought into that belief. They talked as if this disease was a minor inconvenience and would be taken care of. However, deep in his heart, Gunnar wasn't entirely convinced.

After his third cup of coffee, Sjurd stood up, put his hand on his brother's shoulder. "Well, brother, I have to go home. We will see each other soon." He gave his mother a kiss on the cheek and stepped out the door. That left the three of them sitting around the table. The conversation had died out. It was an emotionally exhausting morning. Marianne got up to clear the table.

Gunnar could tell that his mother was puzzled by Kjersti. Gunnar had never been much of a ladies' man. It wasn't that women weren't interested in him. There were a few of them that had their hearts broken. When they would start to get serious, they discovered the well of anger and frustration deep in Gunnar's soul and escaped. Some unscathed, but most of them not. The best thing he did was join the Foreign Legion.

His mother was probably wondering what kind of a relationship the two of them had and how long Kjersti was going to last. In a rare display of affection, he grabbed Kjersti's hand, and said to his mother, "Kjersti. She's going to stay with me here on Urk! She'll keep an eye on me." Behind those big glasses, those sharp and intelligent eyes shone. She really did have a delightful and honest smile. His mother was probably wondering how they got to know each other. He would tell that later, not now.

He realised how tired he suddenly was, physically and emotionally. He found himself unable to keep his eyes open. Desperately wanting to lie down for a bit, he stood up, a bit unsteady on his feet. Quickly, Kjersti moved in to help him, supporting Gunnar as they climbed the stairs. They made their way to his old, childhood bedroom, where Marianne had prepared a bed for him. He lay down, Kjersti ruffled his hair, and he fell immediately asleep.

Later that night he woke up, sweating profusely. He had a great need for fresh air. He opened the window, stuck his head out and took a deep breath. He felt a presence in his room. He turned around and there was Eirik standing at the door.

"Father …"

Eirik looked around, confused. He stared at Gunnar as if wondering where they were.

"I am home, father, I am home …"

For a brief moment it looked like Eirik was smiling at him, then he was gone.

That night Gunnar whimpered in his sleep.

Tuesday

Wolfsangel

'A man's gotta do what a man's gotta do.' It was one of the few mantras he learned as a boy growing up on Urk that Gunnar still lived by. That disease wasn't slowing down like he hoped and expected. Okay, maybe he didn't follow the instructions given to him by Linnea as closely as he should have. Now that he had taken care of events in Norway, it was time to turn his attention to another important matter. It was not too late; he had to do what he had to do.

After breakfast, he and Kjersti travelled to the AMC in Amsterdam, where they met with Dr. de Vries. Kjersti had made arrangements for him to receive Gunnar as a patient. She also made sure that his office had received all necessary medical information from Oslo.

In true Dutch fashion, the bespectacled bald man did not beat around the bush. "I studied your test results. I'll be honest. I believe that you have a brain tumour which was undetected earlier. You have been infected with HIV and, in a small number of cases, this can lead to a lymphoma. Based on the symptoms you have described, I think we need to consider that."

Gunnar asked what the next steps should be.

"Well, we need to do some more testing to be sure. We should schedule, at minimum, a CT scan and a lumbar puncture. These will confirm whether or not a brain tumour exists. The lumbar puncture will allow us to analyse the spinal fluid to determine the existence of tumour cells and if there are, we can start to narrow down the type of cells. Based on that information, we can develop a treatment plan."

"If he does have lymphoma cancer in his brain, what are the symptoms? And, will they get worse," queried Kjersti.

The doctor studied Gunnar for a moment. "Well, you will notice behavioural and cognitive changes as well as movement impairment."

Gunnar nodded. "Yes, I've noticed that for sure."

"What about blurry vision, incontinence, or decreased libido," the doctor asked.

Kjersti's eyebrows perked up. She was clearly interested in how Gunnar was going to answer this. Gunnar coughed slightly. "I haven't pissed my pants, if that's what you're asking. No blurry vision either." He didn't feel like answering the third one. The last time he was aroused sexually was when he was talking with the bikini-clad girl on the 'stand-up board'. He figured it would be safer to leave that alone. Wasn't he also sexually attracted to Kjersti? He hoped that Kjersti didn't pick up his thoughts.

Kjersti saved the moment. "You mentioned cognitive changes. What would that look like?"

The doctor shrugged. "Irrational behaviours. Difficulty making decisions. Confusion. Hallucinations. Memory loss."

Kjersti nodded. Gunnar knew he had definitely experienced these symptoms to a lesser degree these last few days. He asked for the chances of a successful treatment. At this question, Dr. de Vries paused to consider what to say. "It's okay, doctor, just give it to us straight. You've been forward with us and we appreciate it," Gunnar responded.

The doctor avoided looking at them. "Worst case scenario. If it is confirmed that you indeed have Primary Central Nervous System Lymphoma, the average survival is less than four years. Long term survival is achieved in about fifteen percent of all cases. All of this depends on you engaging in a fairly rigorous protocol. If you do nothing, the survival is less than one year, one hundred percent of the time."

At this Kjersti gasped, covered her mouth, and then looked at Gunnar. Gunnar returned the look. He was expecting news like this. He had heard most of this already from Linnea. It was a bit different now, though. He had come to really fall for Kjersti and, as much as he refused to go there, his thoughts had been drifting towards his future. Could he dare hope to even have a future with her? He noticed a tear starting to form in the corner of his right eye. Damn. He didn't want to wipe it and he certainly didn't want it to escape and run down his cheek. He did the only thing he could, he pretended to relieve an itchy eyelid.

Kjersti must have caught that. She put her arms around him and hugged him tight. The fight suddenly became real for him. Hearing the doctor confirm pretty much what Linnea told him and having Kjersti wrap her arms around him, convinced him that his ‘ignore it and it will eventually go away’ philosophy wasn’t going to work. Besides, he had to admit to himself that he was scared when he heard from Sjurd how he tried to book a flight to the Congo. He had virtually no memory of how he ended up in Africa.

Kjersti released Gunnar, cleared her throat and asked, “Doctor, are there examples of survival of this disease? Does he have any chance?”

The doctor looked intently at her, probably seeing what he often does in this situation, a mixture of despair, fear and craving. “Yes Madam. I have read that there are survivors, and I will do my utmost to keep him alive.”

“Please doctor, give us hope …”

“There are rare, almost incredible cases of healing. You can be assured that I will do my very best. There is on-going research and we have an excellent facility here. Your job is to take good care of your man. Take good care of him, yes?”

“I will stand with my man.”

They left the hospital and drove back to Urk. Kjersti took the wheel this time. The first half hour they did not speak to each other. Then he turned his head to Kjersti and saw the grief on her face. “Sorry, Kjersti, I’m sorry. I am sick, very ill, maybe you better go back to Sandnes. I’m really sorry.”

Kjersti glared at him for a moment. Gunnar thought it was necessary to outline the situation and went on, misunderstanding her look of fury. “I know. I really can’t go back to Norway. I am in a lot of trouble with those Norwegians. They know who I am.”

“So what? What exactly are you saying to me?”

Gunnar sighed from the depths of his heart. “You have a life of your own. If you stay with me, it will not be easy for you. Didn’t you hear the doctor? I’m dying.” Relationship issues were challenging for him. He could stalk the most fearsome members of the Boko Haram and bring them down with a KA-BAR knife without the slightest hesitation or trace of fear. Yet, when it comes to navigating relationships, he was a probie. He could sense her anger but had no idea where it came from. He looked outside without seeing anything.

Suddenly, without warning, Kjersti unexpectedly jerked the wheel; the car screeched into a parking lot at a great speed. There she hit the brakes and Gunnar felt his seatbelt strain against his shoulders. The car jerked to a complete stop. He felt Kjersti's big hands firmly grasp his head and turn it to her.

He looked into tear-struck fierce eyes as she raised her voice. "Now you keep your mouth shut, Gunnar. Do not speak death. You be strong and focus on getting better. Do you hear me? Do not get slack now!" By the time she got to the end of her tirade, she was shouting at him.

He blinked at her in alarm. "Yes, but, I'm thinking of you …"

"Do not worry about me. I am here because I have chosen this. I have chosen you."

"Why?" Gunnar was genuinely puzzled.

Her voice softened. "I'm crazy about you." She was trying to blink back her tears but was losing the battle. "I'm not sure why. I must be nuts. But, it is true." As if to underscore, she threw the car into gear, gunned the engine and pulled back into traffic again. It took great effort, but Gunnar did not gasp and close his eyes as she nearly rubbed out the car behind her.

The floodgates had opened. Gunnar's heart soared because Kjersti articulated what he came to realise he was so desperately desiring. With their eyes fixed on the cars in front of them came the words, the sentences. They talked heart to heart for the first time. Both were as uncomfortable as can be talking about love. It was as if they were exploring an uninhabited exotic island, together, for the first time.

They returned to Urk around two o'clock in the afternoon. He had to go to bed immediately. Like last time Kjersti helped him up the stairs but this time, tucked him in. For the first time in as long as Gunnar could remember, he fell into a peaceful sleep.

Gripar

Gripar wasn't sure how he was going to confront Gunnar. Just showing up on the doorstep of Marianne's house didn't seem like a good idea. He decided to watch the house and see if he could catch Gunnar alone.

He felt like one of those American cops doing surveillance work surreptitiously in his car. The place was pretty quiet. He decided to kill some time by touching base with Sigrid. She was working on the Eirik angle. They were pretty sure now they knew where he was roughly located.

"So, is this is looking like a possibility," he asked Sigrid.

Sigrid was obviously drinking something hot because he could hear her expel some air then curse under her breath about something still being hot. "I think so. It is about four kilometres to the north. There is a stream that goes to the Lake Hersjoen. That lake goes back to Hurdalsjoen and other places. The municipality is actually amenable to this project."

Gripar still couldn't believe they were exploring the possibility of draining a lake in order to find a body. "Okay, that's good. But is it physically possible?"

"Yes, it is," Sigrid replied, taking another sip of her hot drink which she punctuated with another expletive. "This lake can be pumped out. I have talked extensively with a specialist from Grundfos. She said that they have the equipment we would need to make it work. There are a few challenges they still need to work out, but they seem quite confident there was nothing they couldn't handle."

"What kind of challenges?"

"Mostly having to do with where to pump the water. The best solution would involve running hoses over road systems."

Gripar was trying to think of all angles. "Would we have to divert traffic? Are we going to upset commuters?"

"Well, traffic will have to slow down, for sure. We would have to do what we can to minimize the amount of time it will take to pump it to a level where they could determine if our suspicions are correct. It's not a terribly big lake and shouldn't take too long."

Gripar was impressed at how thorough Sigrid was. "So, the municipality is on board with this? What about the ecosystem? The fish? There must be fish and other water creatures in the lake. What will happen to them?"

Sigrid was ready with an answer to this one as well. "Well, the municipality has been in discussions with the Department of Nature Management. It turns out that both have been concerned about the rising level of toxicity in the lake. This toxicity has significantly impacted the ecosystem in the lake. The fish population, along with other water creatures, have been decimated. As you know, there has been a significant increase over the years in the dumping of toxic chemical waste in the lake - waste from the production of MDMA drugs. Over the past few years, there has been a constant pungent odour emanating from the lake. The residents nearby have been complaining. So, when we approached them with our request, they felt this was a golden opportunity to clean the lake and take care of a growing problem."

Gripar chortled. "How often does it happen that the police and the environmental authorities agree to work together?"

Sigrid agreed. "They definitely are leaning towards approving our project. We don't have to pump the lake totally dry as we first thought. We can drain it to a level where our forensic team can work efficiently and effectively to locate Eirik's remains - if they are indeed there."

Gripar was confident that their suspicions were on track. Sigrid expressed some doubt. "I don't necessarily trust Mirre, though."

"What do you mean?"

Sigrid paused for a moment. "Now you find out that she might have given Eirik the dagger and candle standard when he came to visit in 1977. How come she never mentioned that to us. She never even mentioned that she knew Eirik. I feel like we are playing a game of chess. I'm just not sure if she is the chess master or the Wolfsangel is."

Gripar wasn't too worried. "I'm not sure it really matters because I think they are almost out of moves. I need to somehow connect with Gunnar. I'm sitting outside of his house waiting for him to come out so that I can talk to him alone."

The two hung up. Gripar rubbed his eyes and temple contemplating the herculean task of emptying a lake.

Tuesday afternoon

Wolfsangel

A bombinating noise aggravated his ears. Gunnar opened his eyes and, for a brief moment, he was disorientated. He looked around the room wondering where the heck he was and where that noise was coming from. After realising he was back in his old bedroom, he set out to locate the source of the highly annoying noise. He discovered it was from an alarm clock. He fumbled for the button. When he couldn't find it, he yanked the cord from the outlet. He lay back down in bed. Strange to be back on Urk. Gone for nearly twenty years living the life of a mercenary, then Eirik's revenge in Norway, and now back in my birthplace. Strange, alienating, yet connected.

He pushed himself out of bed and sat on the edge. He apprised himself in a mirror across the room. He hardly recognised the person he was staring at. His once robust, ripped, physique was fading away. He felt miserable, his testicles ached, and a bleeding wart parked itself on his chest. He was used to taking quick naps and waking up fully rested. Not now. Lately, he woke up weak and lethargic. He couldn't focus his mind on his task. He sighed deeply. He really wanted to crawl back under the covers.

He lifted himself off the bed and struggled with putting on his clothes. It dawned on him that it was awfully quiet in the house. Kjersti was probably out with one of the family members. Remembering this morning, he felt sure she'll manage just fine. He stepped out of the house and headed towards the sunny harbours. He felt a bit unsteady on his feet and, just to be safe, he stayed a few meters away from the water side.

Outside he was being followed by a Norwegian policeman, who had waited an hour just around the corner for this opportunity. Gripar knew he had no jurisdiction here, but he finally had the chance to meet face to face with the Wolfsangel.

Gunnar eventually found the place he was looking for - it was more instinctual because he really couldn't remember the route he had taken. He stepped inside the Wabu Café and immediately felt he had entered a time warp. Not much had changed since the old days. It looked like the same wallpapered walls held the same old posters. He found a table by the window. The hell with his health. Instead of a coffee, he ordered a whiskey neat.

Wolfsangel / Gripar

It didn't take long before the door opened and Gripar strode in. He walked straight to his table. It flitted across Gunnar's mind to question how Gripar knew where he was. The policeman took a seat directly across from him. Gunnar winced slightly as Gripar's green eyes took him in. "Odd Gripar,

I presume? The policeman from Norway? You're a long way from home. We meet again."

Gripar looked quizzically at Gunnar.

Gunnar smiled sardonically. "Did we not meet once on the road to Lillehammer many years ago?" Gunnar watched as Gripar searched his memory. "I would have thought you'd remember. You were searching for answers at the side of the road." Gunnar was pleased as he watched recognition dawn on Gripar's face. "Did you ever find what you were looking for?"

Gripar paused as the memory of that event filled his mind. Yes, he remembered now. At that time, he was in a very dark place and this guy, not much older than him, stopped and helped him out. He studied the face in front of him. He couldn't be sure that this was the same guy, so many years had passed. There was, however, something familiar about him.

Gripar decided not to answer right away. Beckoning the waiter, he also ordered a whiskey, neat. He wasn't technically on duty anyway and right now he felt he needed that. Prior to arriving here, he was convinced that the Wolfsangel wasn't a sociopath even though he couldn't wrap his head around what motivated him. Now, as he took in Gunnar, he was less convinced. "You know, I am not quite sure. I'm still on that journey. As, I'm sure, Wolfsangel would understand."

Gripar took the whiskey from the waiter. He took a deep swallow. "Let me tell you a story, perhaps you might consider it a myth. Somebody has shaken Norway to its foundations. For me it all started on a foggy morning in Hurdal." Gradually he unfolded everything he had discovered. He told Gunnar about the witness reports, the backgrounds of the Hurdal Three. Everything he heard about Lebensborn and injustice. He weaved together the stories of Mirre and Olaf, Robert, and the girlfriend of Finn Undredal.

Gunnar listened carefully without interruptions. He noticed that Gripar purposefully evaded directly answering the question. Nevertheless, he was impressed at how Gripar got pretty much all of the details correctly. Eirik's story was in good hands. All the planning and execution worked better than he had hoped.

Gripar continued to carefully watch Gunnar's face through all this. To his dismay, he still couldn't read it very well. This guy was pretty smooth. He remained as puzzled as ever with Gunnar's emotional investment in all this.

When he was finished, Gripar gave Gunnar a frank appraisal. "That this all happened is a good thing in itself. I mean, it gave an opportunity for the Norwegian people to evaluate their history and reflect on their responsibility. Many people took that opportunity. Really, I understand what drove Wolfsangel. He was looking for truth, justice..." Gripar trailed off, hoping that Gunnar would pick it up from here.

No such luck. Gunnar was well aware of what Gripar was trying to do. Hadn't he done that many times to his own captives. Gunnar felt a tickle in his throat and coughed, trying to clear his throat. "So, Lodbrok had a harrowing experience. How's he doing?"

"Sverre is alive, he is physically healthy, but ..."

"Did I hear that correctly? He wrote a letter, an open letter?"

"Ah, you heard about it? Sjurd told you, or ...?" Gunnar did not respond, so Gripar went on. "Does not matter. Something has touched Sverre's Norwegian conscience, his heart. Maybe it's love?"

"Ha, love!" Gunnar spat out. "For what? For whom? He is an aristocrat. Privileged. What does he care?"

Gripar remained silent, his green eyes drilling into Gunnar's. "You obviously care. Why?"

Gunnar could feel his anger agitating at the pit of his stomach. Maybe that's what Gripar was hoping for. "Yes. I also happen to think that what happened in Norway is important. But, not in the way you might think.

Do you imagine this Wolfsangel is a son of Norway with a deep love and compassion for its well-being? Do you think he has this deep desire to see reconciliation?" Gunnar snorted with derision. "From what I have been told, Norway is reaping what it has sown. This Wolfsangel guy is dealing in the currencies of revenge and death. I doubt Sverre understands that."

Gripar looked out the window into the harbour. He could see the fishing boats tethered to the dock. He thought about Sjurd and how he seemed so completely different from his brother. Revenge and death were the currency of the mercenary. "I disagree. Sverre is now sowing forgiveness. What do you hope he will reap? Justice?"

Gunnar shook his head. "I actually don't really care. If you ask me, it's all backwards. You can't reap justice by sowing forgiveness. You have to sow justice in order to reap forgiveness."

The two lapsed into silence, each nursing their drink.

Finally, Gunnar broke it. "So, you haven't answered my question yet. When we first met, you were searching for something. Did you ever find it?"

Gripar continued to gaze out the window. He didn't quite know how to answer it. He was aware of the note that the Wolfsangel sent him. It was in his pocket. He slid his hand into it to make sure it was there.

Gunnar decided to wait for an answer. He knew that Gripar had heard him. He noticed Gripar's hand stealthily making its way into his pocket as if searching for something.

"No. I can't say that I have," Gripar finally answered, still looking out the window.

"If I recall our conversation so many years ago, you were looking for justice. Not revenge. But if you wanted justice, why weren't you willing to pursue it?"

Gripar shrugged. He had asked himself that question many times. What is the line between justice and revenge? "How do you know I haven't pursued it?"

"You're evading my question. That tells me you likely haven't and you are wondering why."

Gripar snorted. "Ok. Fair enough. Isn't it the job of the state to do that on behalf of its citizens?"

"What if the state doesn't? Then what?"

"Ah," said Gripar nodding. "That's what this is all about. The state isn't doing its job, so the Wolfsangel needs to do it for them."

"I don't know anything about this Wolfsangel, but from what I have heard, I kind of like him. If the state isn't doing its job in seeking justice, shouldn't the individual assume the obligation to seek it?"

Gripar shrugged his shoulders. "I'm not sure what you're driving at. Obligation to who? As far as I am concerned, justice is about ensuring people take ownership of what they did. It's about restoration and balance. It is not an individual perspective; it is a social perspective. That's why the state needs to pursue justice."

Gunnar leaned back. Nothing so far surprised him. In all those years since they first met, Gripar's views are essentially unchanged. It was this perspective so many years ago that convinced him of that. "But, I ask again, what happens when the state fails to seek justice? Then what?"

Yes, then what, thought Gripar. He had to admit to himself that there was no justice in the death of his family. Nobody took ownership. There was no restoration and balance. Gripar shrugged again. He was becoming more and more uncomfortable with this line of questioning.

"So, don't you ever want to know what happened to your parents?" Gunnar pressed.

"I know what happened. More or less. They got run off the road by a drunk driver."

Gunnar leaned back and gave a slight smile. He raised his eyebrows.

Gripar caught the look. "Oh. Okay. I know what you're thinking. Justice is about me seeking revenge against the driver. I don't agree. Justice is finding out who did it and bringing him - or her - to court where a proper punishment can be handed out. It's not about me. It's about society expecting that people who transgress the laws of land are held accountable." Gripar's hackles were starting to rise.

Gunnar figured it was time to change directions. "I'm wondering. Did you ever check out the file in the police records that concerned the death of your parents? You should, you know. You might find there is more to the story than meets the eye."

Gripar did not respond. Gunnar continued, 'You convinced yourself that everything had been done to find out the truth, and that's where you left it. An entire family, save one person, wiped off the face of the earth as the result of another person's actions. Your life irrevocably changed in the blink of an eye. Where is the justice?"

Gripar could feel anger bubbling up inside.

Gunnar was pleased. He reached into his backpack and took out a single sheet of paper and handed it to Gripar. Gripar hesitated and then grabbed it and started reading. His heart was racing and he could feel droplets of sweat form on his forehead. He glanced through the words on the page and looked up. "Olaf Andersen? Where did you get this?"

Gunnar shrugged noncommittedly. It was part of the confession of Olaf. In this particular section, Olaf describes how he left Hurdal to go north. He had been drinking before he left and then he got to Lillehammer and decided to grab another drink. Olaf wasn't exactly sure how it happened, but he remembered being blinded by the headlights of an oncoming car. Olaf, too drunk to realise that he had drifted into the other land, watched the other car swerve into the other lane and smash into a concrete guard. He went to check on the occupants. One of them was still breathing – the little boy in the back seat. Olaf didn't bother calling an ambulance. He had no regrets, that Olaf. It was all part of the circle of life.

Gripar was stunned. He didn't know what to think. When he read the police report, he found out that two of the three occupants died instantly. The third one just passed away when the emergency crew arrived. Now he found out it was his little brother who might still be alive if Olaf Andersen had called for an ambulance right away.

He got up from the table and walked back and forth. He looked outside and recalled his first visit to Urk some months ago and how he was astounded at the stability of this community whose whole existence depended on the fruits which an unyielding and temperamental ocean was willing to give up. His father often reminded him of what C.S. Lewis said: Adversity often prepares people for an extraordinary destiny.

Gripar wasn't sure how long he had been looking outside lost in thoughts, he heard somebody coughing. It was Gunner. Wemmick's drawbridge. He pushed his emotions to the side. He would deal with them later. He turned to face Gunnar. "All right, that came up hard. Yet I thank you. Now it's my turn. Your father, Eirik. I think I may have found him."

The reaction on Gunnar's face couldn't have been more palpable than if he had just been told his symptoms had been misdiagnosed. His eyes narrowed and his jaw dropped slightly. Gunnar grabbed Gripar's arm. "What do you mean?"

Gripar shrugged off the hand. He studied Gunnar's face as he explained. "An SS dagger and candlestand were found at the bottom of a lake near Jessheim. I think the lake is located very close to the Romerike School." He could see Gunnar's eyes twitch. "Mirre confirmed to me that this set actually belonged to the Tijskers. It was a set of artifacts used in a Nazi christening ceremony. An interesting tidbit to this story is that after the war ended, she was given two sets by the family for safekeeping. She returned one set to Eirik when he visited her at the end of 1977."

Gunnar was genuinely puzzled. He didn't know Eirik had visited her in 1977. Why didn't she tell me that? She knows I was looking for him. "So, do you think he threw them in the lake? Or …?"

"Our forensic department has reasons to believe there are human remains located at the bottom of the lake. Our specially trained dogs picked up a scent but neither sonar nor our divers have been able to conclusively determine the location. There is a great deal of soft sediment at the bottom. At this very moment the lake is being drained; the pumps have been on for hours."

Gunnar's jaw dropped and his eyebrows raised as the implications of what Gripar just told him dawned on him. "So, you think…" His voice trailed off but his lips kept moving. The throbbing in his head began to intensify. He grabbed his head and retired again into his world of pain.

Gripar noticed the change in Gunnar. It was enough for one day. He started walking to the exit, but turned around. Gunnar had drifted away, hands still on his head. He felt no sympathy for the man. "Gunnar Patzschke, you should know that one way or another, I will ensure you are brought back to Norway to face charges for the crimes you have committed." It wasn't an idle threat. Sigrid was busy working with Sloss and the Dutch authorities on the paperwork for a European Arrest Warrant. Once that was complete, Gripar would need to work with his department on getting resources here to escort Gunnar back.

Gunnar ignored him. Gripar waited for a response. When there was no reaction, he resumed his leave.

Gunnar just sat there for a long time. He had counted on Gripar solving the mystery of his father's disappearance. However, he had to admit to himself now for the first time, he had still expected that they would find Eirik alive. Certainly not at the bottom of a lake. He could feel a rage building up. He closed his eyes. Voices screamed through his head. He looked up but his eyes did not see the water. Inside his head he shouted it out. "Eirik, are you really dead? No!" The rage was threatening to engulf him. "Eirik, you must be alive! I know, I feel it! You are alive!"

Gunnar felt a new energy surging through the rage. It was a sense of revenge. There was a clammy chill creeping up his spine. He reached for his glass and the one from Gripar, still partially filled, emptied them in his mouth, swallowed, grimaced and ordered another one.

Wolfsangel

How he managed to get home, he wasn't sure. He stumbled through the door where Marianne was able to hold him and guide him to the couch in the sitting room. Kjersti made him some herbal tea and it was one of the few times he actually appreciated the hideous liquid. He lay back on the couch and dozed off in a deep slumber.

He was eventually awakened by the sound of Kjersti's laughter. He sat up and looked at his watch. He had been sacked out for about forty-five minutes. Glancing in the kitchen, he saw Marianne, Kjersti, and his brother Sjurd conversing around the kitchen. As he caught snippets of the conversation, he realised they were all talking in Norwegian. They were talking about Kjersti's art and sculptures. It was a world completely alien to Marianne. She was an Urker. Her life was defined by the moods of the sea. The art world was esoteric to her and Gunnar could tell that his mother was fascinated by it. Gunnar hadn't really considered what it would have been like for his mother to be married to Eirik - a man who struggled so deeply with his identity. He thought about Sjurd - the good son. The one who continued on in the family tradition.

He started to get up from the couch but immediately lay down again. A wave of dizziness crashed over him and he closed his eyes, waiting for it to subside. He must have drifted off again, because the next thing he saw when he opened his eyes was Kjersti bending over him, a huge smirk on her face.

He sat up again and tried to orient himself. Kjersti's smirk faded and replaced by a look of concern. She put her palm on his forehead and gently rubbed it for a minute or two. When the two of them made their way to the kitchen, he was greeted by looks of concern from both his mother and his brother. Gunnar raised his arms. "I'm okay. I'm doing good." He wasn't going to mention the fact that he consumed too much alcohol earlier.

He sat down and stared at a scented candle burning in the middle of the table. The flames flickered as a tiny column of grey smoke headed towards the ceiling. He looked at all three of them individually. Nobody returned the look, they all seemed preoccupied with examining their hands or starting at the dark liquid in their coffee cups. He sighed softly. This was as good a time as any for him to finally tell his story. Finally, "If you want … I … Let me tell my story." They all immediately fixed their eyes on him.

At first hesitantly, then becoming more comfortable, he told them everything from the beginning to the end. He started at Eirik and ended at Eirik. He was able to tell his story uninterrupted.

When he was finished, he simply shrugged. "I don't think I had a choice. It was something I had to do." Nobody spoke, each person seemed lost in their own thoughts.

The silence unnerved Gunnar. "Father. It's about father. I need to know what happened to him. Did he really kill himself as he wrote in his note, or…?" He shook his head. "I searched everywhere, for years, but I didn't succeed. I hope that Inspector Gripar succeeds. They are pumping. The whole lake is being pumped out."

Marianne's head popped up, shocked. "Are they … You mean … Eirik's body … in the lake?"

Gunnar nodded. Sjurd was still trying to understand. "But how? Why you? Where did you find out about those Hurdal Three?"

"Remember, Sjurd, when you, mother and I would go to the hospital hoping to visit him. We usually had to wait outside while they checked to see if he would accept visitors. There was that one time, I think it was around 1978, that it seemed to take forever. I started exploring and I found a side door on the outside of the basement that was open. I snuck in and somehow found father's room. He was in a feverish state, but he immediately recognized me. He was glad to see me. I know that he considered me his confidant. I'm not sure why, but he always shared stories about his past. I … I guess, he didn't do that with you or the others. I enjoyed being with him, listening to his stories.

"I thought he was going to tell me more stories. This time was different. He seemed hurried and distracted. He had something on his mind. He told me he was glad to see me, but he didn't have much time. Father asked me if I knew what a sacrifice was. I nodded. I told him that I knew the stories in the Bible about the Israelites sacrificing their animals. Father became excited. Yes, yes, son. That's right. A priest slaughters a sacrifice on a stone and the blood makes it all right again. I remember being confused, though. He went on about blood on a stone, the final judgment, justice, revenge and much more. He talked about Jephthah from the Old Testament. I became a bit scared because he seemed to be in a trance. Of course, my eight-year-old brain couldn't truly understand what he was getting at.

"Later on, Mirre helped me to understand that he had a higher purpose in sharing those stories. They were more than stories. I was being initiated into a mission he expected me to fulfil."

There was a deep silence as the group processed what they just heard. The weight of that mission hung heavily in the air. Gunnar leaned back in his chair. Those memories still haunted him. He didn't realise it then, but as an eight-year-old, he was being set up for a task much larger than himself. Recounting the story to his family for the first time, the enormity of that dawned on him. He grew silent. Kjersti reached over and touched his arm. He put his hand over hers and smiled at her.

Marianne, silent up to this point, spoke up. She had tears streaming down her face. "I think I remember that day. We searched for you frantically until a nurse came and told us you were in his room. When we met you there, you definitely were not your normal self. In fact, I don't think we ever saw the real Gunnar since. Now I know why."

Sjurd grasped his head in his palms. "I wish I had known. I never really knew him. I was just four or five … He shut himself off to me."

Gunnar reached over and touched Sjurd on the shoulder. "That was probably for the best. Look at where you are now. You have a beautiful family. Look at me. I can't get away from his legacy."

"I had no idea," Marianne murmured. "Your father told me about what happened to him and his mother. I never knew, though, that he was seeking justice for the actions of those three men. I never knew that Mirre was involved with all this."

Before Gunnar could respond, Sjurd spoke up abruptly. "However you might interpret father's stories and the purpose behind them, I really don't believe father had revenge and manslaughter on his mind."

Gunnar's irritation at his brother rose. "He was looking for reconciliation through satisfaction. Do you remember?"

Sjurd shook his head. "No. That refers to Jesus. He is the one that judges the living and the dead."

Gunnar cleared his throat, took a sip of water. How can he make them understand? "You're wrong. It is possible for us humans to judge the actions of others, even if they are dead. The three men have been convicted by the action of the Norwegian people. Those three deserved to be judged and found guilty! The truth is that nobody in Norway feels they are guilty for what happened to our father and grandmother, but they are."

Silence fell again. This time Kjersti broke it. "If you see injustice being done, but you close your eyes and look away, are you not also guilty?"

Marianne nodded at Kjersti. "Yes, that's how it is if you close your ears and eyes to injustice. Not only in Norway, but in many places around the world."

Sjurd was clearly struggling to understand. "Yes, father experienced it that way, right? Injustice, impotence. He … his story had to be told. But, why you? … Now the police want you. Was there no other way, brother?"

Gunnar chuckled humorously. "You don't know those three as Father knew them. As I know them. I am a soldier, a mercenary. I know those kinds of men, they will never confess voluntarily. There was no other way." Then he closed his eyes and from the depths of his soul, sighed. "I am … Sometimes I see our sister Anna Esther through an ice layer. I, her oldest brother, had not been watching her." He swallowed and added softly, "It was my fault."

"No, Gunnar, you can't say that. You are not guilty of her death," said his mother. "You shouldn't think that. Do you have …?"

Gunnar, eyes still closed, felt his mother grab his arm with her work hands. He opened his eyes to look at her. "Father threw his pain on me like Elijah's cloak … as well as the sacrifice, maybe even the stone." His eyes turned and looked at his mother, brother and Kjersti hard for a moment. He took a very deep breath and hissed. "I sacrificed the bastards. Their blood is the redemption he seeks."

It was now completely silent. Marianne stroked his hands and nodded her head. She understood him better than he would ever know. She too had hated the monsters who had driven her husband to insanity.

Gunnar recovered. He took a sip of his cold coffee. He knew that his brother did not approve of his actions. They were from very different worlds. His God did all the judging while the people stood back impotently. He, Gunnar, was a hardened mercenary. He was a man of action. He did not hesitate to take the lives of the guilty. They deserved it.

This entire day sucked the energy out of him. He thought he would fall quickly asleep, but that wasn't to be. Even two hours later, he could still hear the sounds of the pumps at Jessheim. He could see the water was receding. Peering through the darkness, he hoped to spot the shape of a body lying on the lake bed.

Wednesday

Wolfsangel

Gunnar had a restless night. By the time the sun was peeking over the horizon, it was five in the morning. He had little sleep; his legs felt leaden and his arms could hardly push himself into a sitting position.

His thoughts kept returning to the lake. Eirik is not there, lying in the mud. Impossible! Gunnar had seen enough people trapped, unable to free themselves, dying a slow, agonising death. He could not believe it.

Yet, what if Gripar was right? What if his father was lying there, trapped? What if the first person to see him there was a stranger who decided to walk away? He had to be there.

Without thinking, he stood up. There was an emotion surging through his heart that was alien to him. It wasn't anger or fear. It wasn't love either. He had always known, right from the start, that Eirik was going to be part of this journey. First the first time, however, he had a nascent realisation that this journey was greater than the sum of its parts. His emotional connection to Eirik, to his father, was more profound than he understood.

His primordial mind directed him to head to the lake where his father supposedly lay. He needed a way to get there. Slipping on his clothes, he staggered outside. Nobody seemed to notice him. He headed towards Van Slooten for a car rental but when he got there his plans were halted by a locked door. Why was the door locked? He rattled the door and started banging on it. Nobody answered his knocking. He wandered up and down the sidewalk several times before he realised that it was still too early in the morning for the place to be open. He sat down on a bench and waited like a zombie until someone arrived at half past seven. To this day, he can't figure out how he managed to adequately fill out the paperwork, but he must have. Before long, he was cruising along the N50 in a Ford Mustang.

He ignored the alarm bells ringing in his head. He ignored Linnea's piercing gaze. He was focussed on the sound of diesel pumps. He was like a heat seeking missile once it had found its target. Nothing else mattered. He was going to drive north to the Nordbytjernet Lake! He would show them…

Delirium, confusion of mind, fits of melancholy, shame, and deep anger darted and swirled around his head. He tried blocking it out with some music, but it didn't seem to help much. He drove on.

Crossing the German border at Meppen, his vehicle seemed to instinctively target Bremen and Hamburg. It had been nearly three hours of straight driving. His mind was still locked on his target, nothing else mattered. Before Hamburg he turned to the north, towards Denmark. At Flensburg, the E45, he did not turn to Copenhagen, but to the north, to Aalborg.

After Aalborg, his mind continued to block all other distractions. He was operating, not on reasoning, but on pure instinct. He was possessed with one single thought: he had to get to Norway as soon as possible. He saw Eirik struggling in the mud, arms lifting in a plea for help. He needed Gunnar. He needed his son to rescue him!

The Mustang purred along, not at all fazed by the nine hours of straight driving. He had already stopped once for a tank of petrol. He glanced at the gauge, dimly aware it was time to fill up again. Gunnar arrived at Hirtshals at six o'clock in the evening, totally exhausted. He parked the car and then stepped out. He staggered about the parking lot wallowing in the cool, fresh air. The cool air carried him back to reality. Not all the way, just enough for him to realise his body was asking for food. He found a kiosk that sold him a hamburger and cola.

The sound of the pumps had briefly receded when he arrived but now were in full force. He became disoriented, not knowing what to do. He looked at the sky. The clouds were gathering together and had turned a menacing deep blue-grey. The wind had picked up and whitecaps were hurtling towards the shore. He was separated from Eirik by the Skagerrak. It was almost as if the sea was warning him not to cross. He had to, though. He had to get to Eirik. His body protested, screaming out to him in pain and exhaustion.

A face flashed through his head, reminding him of his cousin Hellmuth! Of course, Hellmuth. Yes, his friend in dangerous times. But was he not dead? Was he still alive? There was danger, bullets … No. Suddenly he had to know. He spotted an old-fashioned telephone booth. He had to call. Currency? Yes. Strangely, the number appeared before his eyes and he dialled. His cousin would understand…!

Someone picked up. Yes! It is him! "Hellmuth, cousin, how are you …? You're still alive?" Gunnar howled with laughter. "We're going to meet again, that fucked up Norway. That rotten brain cancer will not win. I'm a dead man. Thank for you did in Africa. Will you come to me again?" Gunnar laughed again. Suddenly, he broke down sobbing.

It was quiet on the other side. Eventually, he could hear Hellmuth say, "Gunnar, everything is fine with me. I am safe. I took a bullet to the shoulder and am on leave. I'm okay. How about you? You don't sound normal, my dear friend."

Gunnar made a guttural noise. "It's over, but …" He started mumbling incoherently. It was like random words of a drunken teenager coming out of his mouth. "I will kick that cancer into the mud. I must win. I am the best. Oh God, Kjersti, mother…"

Hellmuth understood. Gunnar knew he would. He heard Hellmuth say soothingly, "You're right, show them who's in charge. Where are you, by the way?"

Gunnar looked around. Where was he? He didn't know. Oh, yes. "Hirtshals, selbstverständlich, at the boat." Gunnar started laughing again. "That's where it always starts. How did it work in the Congo? Are they also emptying lakes over there?"

His laughter suddenly died in his throat. He smelled diesel fumes from the pumps. He heard water being sucked through pipes. Those sounds came back to haunt him. "Hey cousin, I can't understand you anymore. The pumps make too much noise. Hang in there..."

Gunnar collapsed, sobbing. It was too much. The weight of the cloak. He let go of the receiver. He could hear Hellmuth calling to him. His stomach starting heaving and he puked out the hamburger he had just eaten.

He was surrounded by a haze and dense fog. He couldn't locate his car. After a few minutes of stumbling about, he discovered his rental car. He put the seat down and curled up.

Gripar

Gripar just got off the phone with Sjurd. Sjurd told him that Gunnar took off without saying a word to anyone early this morning. His cellphone was still on his night table, his medication was sitting in its usual spot, and no clothes were missing. He simply vanished. Later that evening, he received a phone call from Hellmuth, Gunnar's cousin and Xe comrade. Apparently, Gunnar called him in Hirtshals, Denmark, at the ferry terminal. He is on his way to Norway. Sjurd recounted the strange conversation Hellmuth had with Gunnar.

Sjurd pleaded with Gripar to do what it takes to pick Gunnar up when he arrived. He was convinced that Gunnar was mentally sick, delusional, and even suicidal. "Please, Gripar, he is my only brother. He doesn't know what he is doing. He needs to be protected from himself before he does something even worse. I trust you."

Gripar immediately called Sigrid and filled her in. Her grasp of technology was above and beyond his. She called him back in half an hour to let him know that Gunnar's credit card had been used in Van Slooten to rent a vehicle. The agency said he was driving a dark blue Ford Mustang with registration plate number 6-DBJ-53. From what they could tell from the GPS unit, that car is currently sitting in Hirtshals, Denmark. Sigrid also contacted the ferry terminal to see if they had CCTV feeds that might confirm the whereabouts of Gunnar. They weren't very forthcoming but did promise to look into it.

"Do we call Sloss?" Sigrid asked.

That was a good question. When Sloss returned from Germany having discovered that Hellmuth Patzschke, the human-trafficker, was not the Wolfsangel, he was in a foul mood. On the other hand, given Hellmuth Patzschke, the son of Eirik Tijsker, is actually a German citizen and arresting him in Norway will require the services of the PST, Gripar felt they had no choice.

Gripar made the call. Within the hour, Sloss had contacted the police branches in Kristiansand, Bergen, Larvic and Oslo. He also requested that all the ferry ports in Norway and Sweden be on high alert for Gunnar. Sloss' message was clear: This man has killed before and will kill again. He is a trained mercenary and highly dangerous. He is also suffering from a mental condition which makes him even more dangerous.

The trap was set. The moment Gunnar stepped on Norwegian soil, he would be arrested. After calling Sjurd as a courtesy to let him know that he was doing everything he could to safely capture his brother, Gripar and Sigrid waited for the call confirming Gunnar had arrived in Norway.

Unbeknownst to Gunnar at the time, it was his girlfriend that sprang into action. He shouldn't have been surprised at that. Kjersti was as bold then as she was at the Holmestrand rally.

The phone rang at Marianne's place. Kjersti watched Marianne jump to the phone and answer. Then, while on the phone, she staggered as her legs seemed unable to support her. Kjersti was alarmed and stepped in to steady her. The two of them were already a nervous wreck because of Gunnar's sudden disappearance. When the phone rang, they were both hoping for good news.

This didn't look like good news to Kjersti. "Who was that? Something about Gunnar? Is he okay? Is he alive?"

Marianne had grief and heartbreak written all over her face. "That was Sjurd. Gunnar has gone berserk. He is still in Hirtshals, Denmark. If he crosses over into Norway, the police are waiting for him. He will get arrested right away. My son will be going directly into prison." Marianne began sobbing as Kjersti wrapped her arm to console her. "Gunnar is completely confused. Hellmuth told Sjurd that Gunnar has gone nuts talking about some pumps. What can we do? Kjersti, please help me."

Kjersti held her close for a moment. Then with a determined look on her face, she backed off to face Marianne. "We are going there to pick him up. You have got a car? Let's go!"

Marianne's face registered shock then surprise. A smile slowly crept in. Within half an hour, another car from Urk raced past Meppen on to Denmark. Inside sat two people, scared of driving in the dark, but even more scared of the darkness in Gunnar's mind.

Wolfsangel

Gunnar drifted in and out of consciousness. He had no idea how long he had been here. When he arrived, the parking lot had been full of cars waiting to board the ferries. Now, the lot was nearly empty as other cars were coming in hoping to catch the next boat. He was feeling feverish and sweaty; his brain had been replaying memories. Weakened and totally confused, he slipped into a delirium. Anger and revenge prevailed in his head. He was tied down in the jungle of Africa; face down, naked, with his legs spread out. Sitting there, he felt the violation again. He smelt the nauseating stench of drugs, booze, and garlic on their breaths. He drifted back into a comatose sleep; the darkness mercifully closing in on him.

The morning light woke Gunnar. He became aware of a persistent pain in his groin. It took him a moment to realise he had to take piss so badly his bladder hurt. It took him another moment to realise he was lying down in his car. He found the door handle and pushed open the door. He stared at the pavement, confused. Shaking his head, he rolled out onto the pavement. With considerable effort and concentration, he managed to push himself up.

Leaning against his car, he opened his fly and let it go. The pain started to dissipate. He heard a noise. Looking up, he noticed the rows of cars all waiting to board. He caught a movement in one of the car windows. It was the face of elderly woman, completely horrified at what she was seeing. He jerked his head around as he heard a voice yelling at him. He didn't catch what the man was saying. Clearly the man was angry. Gunnar shouted an obscenity and then cursed as he noticed that the front of his pants was damp. He had splattered all over himself.

His lungs caught some fresh air! He stumbled about, moving up the rows of cars that were parked, waiting their turn to board. He breathed in deeply, absorbing the oxygen and the scent of the ocean. When he got to the end of the row, he looked around, confused. "Hellmuth, where are you? Sjurd ... Where are you? Where is my car?" He started making his way back down the row.

He found his car. The blue Mustang. The driver's door was still wide open. He sat down, closed his eyes, his mind still tossing and turning in a maelstrom of memories. A few minutes later, rows of cars disappeared onto the ships, again without him. And a little later the ships left. Emptiness and silence returned.

Not far from him a car careened into the parking lot and came to a sudden halt. There was a panicked look on both occupants. Marianne and Kjersti jumped out and ran to the ferries praying they weren't too late. It certainly looked like Gunnar had crossed the Skagerrak. The parking lot appeared to be quite empty. Even the gulls were screeching at the large empty terrain.

Kjersti didn't want to think the worst. She looked at Marianne and pointed to the right. Marianne understood and ran off in that direction. Kjersti went to the left.

Within a few minutes, Kjersti spotted what she was looking for. Parked off to the side was a car with a Dutch license plate. She hollered at Marianne and broke into a hundred metre sprint towards the car.

Gunnar heard a high-pitched scream of delight. He opened his eyes and caught the sight of a well-built woman yank open the door and stick her head inside.

"There you are! My stubborn, sick little man. I've found you. And none too soon." She pulled the keys from the ignition contact and ran to the other side of the car. Before Gunnar knew what was happening, she grabbed Gunnar under his arms. Although he weighed almost 90 kilos, she swung him over the centre console like he was a sack of potatoes. He landed in the passenger seat with a thud.

Gunnar squinted through the fog and focused his eyes on the woman. "Kjersti? Is that you? Are we on the boat?"

"No. You're not going to sail. You're not going to drive either," Kjersti said sternly.

"But… I need to be on that boat. I need to get to Norway. Eirik. They might have found Eirik." Gunnar was trying to articulate his words.

"What are you thinking? You're not going to sail. You must do nothing, my beloved, nothing anymore." She leaned over to kiss him on the top of his head. Then, tousling his hair like he was a little kid, "No boat to Norway for you. You're going back to Urk with us."

"No, no. I'm not going…" He began to fill with panic. He tried to lift himself out of the car, but Kjersti gently pushed him back. He lifted his leaden hands, almost too tired to finish his sentence, "… home".

Gunnar really didn't have the strength to resist Kjersti right now. He leaned back in his seat and sat passively as Kjersti wrapped the seat belt around him. She smiled at him, wrinkling her nose. "Man, you stink like piss."

He was too tired to be embarrassed.

By this time Marianne had arrived. Her relief at seeing her son was palpable. Like a good mother, she took a water bottle out of her purse. "Here is some water. You're dehydrated." She pushed a plastic water bottle into his mouth. Gripar was thirsty. He drank and drank until his mother took the bottle out of his mouth. "Stop, not too much water at once. You'll get sick."

Kjersti had three bottles of medication in her hand. She shook two pills from each bottle into the palm of her hand and passed them on to Gunnar. "Here, before you finish all the water, take these." Then wagging her finger at him, "Make sure you swallow all of them."

Marianne jumped into the driver's side of the car. "Kjersti, you drive my car. I'll take this one. We'll stop every two hours. Switch once in a while, if you like. Not much speed, as long as we get home. I am so happy with you, girl!"

Kjersti laughed. "Let's get out of here."

They started their cars and drove quickly from the empty terrain.

They did not know this at the time. On the other side of the water, because of Sjurd, the Norwegian police were ready to arrest the Hurdal killer, sick or not, the moment he stepped off the ferry. The CCTV video feed had confirmed that Gunnar was there.

However, Marianne, Kjersti and their sleeping fellow traveller eventually found their way back to the Netherlands. It took forever. Neither Kjersti nor Marianne were experienced drivers. They kept hanging behind trucks, glued to their bumpers, afraid to pass. Had Gunnar not slept the entire way home, he would have demanded to take the wheel.

They eventually turned off the A1 at Bremen. It was early morning when they arrived at Urk. Supporting him between them, they carried a sleepwalking Gunnar to his bed. They undressed him, washed him and made him comfortable in his bed. Again, they forced him to swallow his medicine. When they left his room, they closed the door behind them.

Both were dead tired but not quite ready to sleep. Kjersti had a glass of wine with Marianne and then crashed on the couch, snoring loudly. Only then did Marianne think of Sjurd, she called him to let him know that his brother is back home, here on Urk. He seemed relieved with this good news.

Friday

Gripar

Gripar was disappointed that Gunnar didn't make it back to Norway. He wanted Gunnar to face charges. However, the truth was they didn't have a lot of direct evidence that Gunnar was responsible for the death of those three men. Sverre hadn't made a firm decision yet on how he wanted to proceed with the deprivation of liberty charges. As well, Gunnar Patzschke was actually a German citizen. The Germans would likely put up a fuss. They would prefer to deal with him in their court system rather than in Norway's.

"How are things going at Nordbytjernet Lake," Gripar asked Sigrid on the phone

"They are working bloody hard to get the job done. Four huge pumps are pumping out the lake water. They have been busy for several hours and the water level has dropped significantly. It caused a bit of an attraction for the locals. Many people have come to watch. I guess it is quite something, they had never seen the water level of their well-known lake that low! The bottom is already quite visible in most places."

"That must be quite a bizarre sight." Gripar was trying to imagine what that looked like.

"Yes. This'll likely never happen again."

Gunnar

Gunnar's condition was more or less stable again. A good sleep had done him much good and the medication seemed to have fully kicked in. Marianne and Kjersti were surrounding Gunnar's bed discussing the situation with him. Suddenly, there was a loud bellow from downstairs. Kjersti, startled, looked up at Marianne with wide eyes. Marianne laughed at her reaction. "Oh, don't worry. That's just the baker. I ordered some lekkers and he is dropping them off."

"For a moment, I thought a hippopotamus was in heat," Kjersti said, under her breath and in English. Gunnar burst out laughing while it was Marianne's turn to look at them with wide eyes.

Gunnar told them to go downstairs so he could shower and change into some street clothes.

By the time he finally got downstairs, he was greeted by a table full of goodies, the smell of rich, Dutch coffee, and a hug from his sister-in-law. His mother had organised a welcome home party for him and, despite feeling a bit anxious about so many people in the house, he enjoyed talking with his extended family members.

One of his nephews asked him, "Hey, Uncle, how is America?"

"America is great, but don't you have school? It's Friday," Gunnar asked with a glint in his eye. The children took him seriously and took great pains to assure him they were not skipping school. Yes, it was so cozy, so good to be here.

"Have I ever told you about my work in Africa as a private security guard?" A gaggle of nephews and nieces crowded around him. He talked and talked, not about guns, not about the screaming of women and children being slaughtered, not about the three of Hurdal. No, he told them about beautiful forests, strange animals and happy African children. And when they asked him about it, he even invited them to come to his flat in Chesapeake.

At around two o'clock, Gunnar was starting to feel like he had enough of all these people. Sjurd must have sensed that because he walked through the crowd and towered over Gunnar. "Hey there, little brother, what say the two of us spend some time working on that motor boat?" There was a heavy emphasis on the word 'little'.

Gunnar shook his head and looked at the kids. "You do realise, don't you, that your dad may be bigger than me. However, I was the one gifted with both brains and good looks." The children didn't quite know what to make of that. They didn't know their uncle well enough to figure out that he was joking. Gunnar turned his attention to Sjurd. "Our boat? Do you still have it?"

"Yes, of course. It has not been used for a while and needs some work, a bit of sanding, painting, but above all it needs to be cleaned. She's probably slimy green from tons of leaves."

Gunnar's mind was brought to happier times when the two of them, as teenagers, pooled their money together, and like all good Urkers, bought an open motor boat. It was rundown and not really seaworthy. But the two of them spent a lot of hours refurbishing it. It was really the only time in their lives when the two of them spent any length of time together. "Is it still in the werkhaven, near the lock?" he asked.

"That's right. So, do you want to go, or would rather sit here and drink more coffee?"

Gunnar grinned. "Let's go."

Of course, the children begged to come along, but Sjurd firmly put a stop to that. This was going to be brother time.

Excited and armed with a thermos of coffee and some leftover 'lekkers', Gunnar walked with Sjurd to the werkhaven. The boat was pretty much as Gunnar remembered. The hull was originally painted bright blue, but over the years the colour had faded to a dull brownish-blue. Most of the riggings were still there, coated with a thick rust. Gunnar looked at the deck and was dismayed to find it buried under a pile of debris. They had their work cut out, that's for sure. The two of them stripped to their waist and got at it.

After an hour or so, the boat was clean enough. The men washed their hands in the harbour water and wiped them on an old towel. Gunnar started the engine. Both of them grinned like schoolboys when the motor eventually caught. His eyes watering from the dense exhaust smoke, Gunnar gave the thumbs-up. "It is good enough to go for a trip. Let's take her out."

Gunnar took the helm. It was coming back to him. He headed for the locks.

"So tell me, did you ever meet our German grandfather and talk to him?" Sjurd asked when they settled in.

"Hell yes!" said Gunnar. "That man was as crotchety as a stubborn mule."

"He was a real Nazi – Gestapo, SS, and all that stuff – if I'm not mistaken?"

"Yep, fanatical until the end. If you know how those guys grew up with the Nazi dogmas, you can understand it better. Really, though, there are good things to say about that man too. He loved Eirik and Anna."

Sjurd studied Gunnar's arm. "Hmmm. That tattoo. What's that all about?"

"That's a Leben-rune, a very old symbol, from before Jesus Christ. It came from the Scandinavian world of the Vikings."

"And the other? That hook, what do you call it again?"

"That is a wolfsangel, to catch wolves." He turned to the right and saw the light towers which marked the entrance of the harbour go by. "Look there! The lighthouse."

They sailed out of the harbour and turned to the Urker lighthouse. Gunnar, who was behind the wheel, gave full throttle and the sloop picked up speed. After ten minutes they passed the lighthouse, then turning towards Enkhuizen, they headed away from Urk at full speed. It was a fantastic trip, a chance for the two brothers to spend time on the open water - something they hadn't done in years. Sjurd was able to explain to Gunnar how things were going in the fishing industry. It was completely different from life as a mercenary. The two brothers really had drifted apart in so many ways and Gunnar was grudgingly grateful for this opportunity to reconnect.

That evening they all went to Sjurd's place and devoured a huge quantity of fried fish and – over Kjersti's protestations – beer. In between all that eating, there were plenty of stories and a lot of laughter. They celebrated life as a family for the first time in a long time.

At half past ten in the evening the doorbell rang. "Who would that be? A stranger I guess, an Urker would just walk in," Sjurd's wife, Jannie, said as she walked to the door. The rest of the family held their breath so as to not miss any of the exchange in the kitchen.

Gunnar heard Jannie ask who it was and what did they want. There was a slight catch in his breath when he heard the reply and recognised the voice.

"I am Sverre Lodbrok and I come from Norway. May I talk to Gunnar for a moment, please." Kjersti and Gunnar looked at each other. Kjersti had a look of concern on her face and grabbed Gunnar's hand.

"Who are these two men behind you?" They heard Jannie ask.

"They are my security detail. I am just here to talk, nothing more. I promise you."

"I'm not sure that is a good idea," Kjersti said softly with a worried look on her face.

Gunnar stood up and so did Kjersti. "Come", he said to her, "let's see what he wants."

The two of them walked to the kitchen and stood in front of Sverre. They looked at each other in silence. Jannie walked back to the living room.

Sverre broke the silence first. "I have come here to your home in peace. I need your help."

Gunnar didn't know what to make of it. He looked into Sverre's eyes and saw no deception. What possible help could Sverre want from him?

"Then what are those two guys behind you doing?" Kjersti couldn't help herself. Gunnar could tell she was upset and suspicious.

Sverre smiled reassuringly. "Well," shrugging his shoulders, "there is this little matter of my being provided alternate accommodations against my will. Now, my father won't let me go anywhere without some protection. I can assure you, though, that they won't do anything to you."

Kjersti, shamefaced, looked at Gunnar. Gunnar asked, "What can I do for you?"

Marianne's voice came from the living room. In Urkers, she chastised Gunnar, "Gunnar, invite the man inside. There is plenty of food and drink." Gunnar decided to remain at the door, so his company did as well. Sverre had a winsome smile on his face. It was pretty clear to him what Gunnar's mother had said. Yet Gunnar didn't step away from the door.

Sverre nodded, accepting Gunnar's decision. "Thank you. As I said, I come in peace. I do not want anything from you, just your attention and, if you are willing, your assistance." Sverre explained to them in Norwegian what had happened since returning home. He explained his open letter to the people of Norway and the response that he has so far received.

Gunnar kept waiting for the punch-line. He was expecting that Sverre was going to offer him a deal of sorts to bring him back to Norway for a trial. Sverre didn't. He opened his palms to Gunnar. "My heart goes out to you too, Wolfsangel. What happened to your family is unforgivable. But I want you to know that I have forgiven you for kidnapping me. I didn't enjoy those few days with you sitting in a cage. I learned something, though, about myself and my convictions." Grabbing Gunnar by the shoulder, he spoke earnestly, "Come to Norway and help me."

Sverre was silent as he watched Gunnar process that. For some strange reason, the usually suspicious Gunnar Patzschke believed that Sverre was sincere. "Dear man, I believe you, but your country is sick."

"Help me to heal it."

Gunnar shook his head. "You cannot change the past."

Sverre looked at him in surprise. "How can you, of all people, say that. The testimonies of those three men have acquitted your father and exposed the wounds of my country. You should come with me. I need your help to finish what you started."

Gunnar, still shaking his head, looked at him with disbelief. "What can I do? I come to Norway and am immediately arrested. I'll spend the rest of my life rotting away in a prison. Not even you can prevent that. Are you trying to curse me, man?" Gunnar rubbed his face with the palm of his hands. "Besides, I won't be your poster boy."

Sverre was silent for a moment. "No, Wolfsangel," he said softly. "We want your forgiveness, not your curse."

It was so surreal. Those words echoed in his mind. Suddenly, Gunnar felt dizzy and had to lean against the wall behind him. He closed his eyes. Kjersti checked him out, glanced at Sverre. "I am actually glad you came by, but I don't know if he can do what you are asking."

Sverre nodded in understanding and shook hands with Kjersti. There was a shy smile on her face as he tacitly acknowledged his nurse and protector. He walked to the door, his relieved bodyguards ready to follow him out. He stopped, reached into his pocket, and pulled out an envelope. Passing it to Kjersti, "Oh yes, before I forget. Here's a letter. Inspector Odd Gripar has something he wanted to tell you. I suggest that when you decide to read it, you should be sitting down."

When Gunnar and Kjersti stepped back into the living room, all the merriment had disappeared. Marianne, Sjurd, and Jannie were all looking at their hands, unsure what to do.

"Are you okay, son?" Marianne asked finally.

It took a moment, but Gunnar stirred and nodded. He took some deep breaths. "Let's read that letter."

Kjersti read it aloud. It was pretty obvious that it was written by a police officer. It was very factual and emotionless. Kjersti shook her head. "The police found a body at the bottom of a lake. It was buried under a layer of mud and plant growth. So what?" Kjersti asked, looking around the room for more explanation.

It was Marianne who spoke up. "It seems like the body was located exactly on the spot where that hole in the ice was, years ago." She looked at Gunnar. "Where divers found the dagger and well-known candle standard some years ago."

Sjurd, taking the letter from Kjersti, nodded. "He writes that a body was found under a leaky plastic inflatable boat, with weights attached. He is pretty sure they have recovered the body of Eirik Tijsker, but they will have confirmation from their forensic lab tomorrow."

Gunnar stared out into space. In the distance he heard Kjersti asking again what this all meant. She was clearly confused.

In the middle of the night, Gunnar woke up, bathed in sweat and short of breath. He sat up and took a deep breath.

No! Eirik was alive. He was sure of that.

Saturday

Gunnar

It was Saturday. The day before Pentecost, the feast of the Spirit. Tomorrow was a day of rest in honour of the Creator; today was a day from and for Urkers.

Kjersti and Gunnar walked quietly through the crowds along the harbours and the main street. He had woken up this morning restless and unsettled. He had a slight headache and some brain fog. These were his constant reminders that he was in the midst of a battle, fighting for his life.

The two of them enjoyed the day. They found a place to snack on fried and smoked fish and drink fresh coffee. Gunnar was brought back to his earlier life in Urk. Fishermen smoked fish, local artists sold their art and a boat full of young Urk women emitted some nostalgic sounds. It was a beautiful day; the sun was kind enough to show its face and provide a soothing heat.

An elderly man in traditional Urker clothing stopped in front of their table. "Gunnar, son of my old friend Eirik. Welcome back home. Say, at twelve o'clock, I'll be singing with the men's choir. We'll be singing Hallelujah in the Bethel church. Why don't you come too!"

Gunnar grinned. "I'll take it under advisement." He had no intention of setting foot inside a church.

The man laughed. Gunnar could tell from the expression on Kjersti's face that she didn't have a clue what the two of them were talking about. They were speaking in the Urker dialect - apparently the original language spoken in the Garden of Eden. "I know," the man said, "You're not ready yet. Listen to me son, you are not the only one. We are all on our way to Damascus. Come with us and do as we do. Your father would have liked it too, I know that."

After the man left, Kjersti asked Gunnar what he had said. He translated the conversation and added, "Urkers and singing go together like fish and beer."

She laughed. "I want to be there. Come, do it for me." Gunnar shook his head at first but changed his mind a bit later. Why? He did not know, probably Kjersti's influence? But strangely enough he felt good about it.

The two of them arrived at the Bethel church about ten minutes before noon. Kjersti was concerned because the church was full. They stood at the entrance and scanned the pews hoping to catch an open spot. A man stood up and waved them over. "Here. Son of Eirik the Norwegian and Marianne Weerstand, come, sit down here!" A spot was created by a well-built man and woman who shifted to the right in their pew, until two on the other side were squeezed out. They were sore but laughed and were immediately given a place somewhere else.

Many men, all dressed in Urker traditional dress, stood up and looked around quietly. The organ began and although the Urk people were used to it, the heavy tones caused shivers in everyone's spines. Then the men's choir sang. Glancing at Kjersti beside him, he could tell that she had never experienced such a thing. Her face was transfixed, her eyes were glowing. It was hard, yes raw, and straight from the heart. One hundred men's voices!

He put his arm around her and found himself transported to a different time. He focused on a blond man singing in the back row. He saw his own father. The man sang as only Urkers can sing, full of faith and certainty, and with a loud voice: "Beautiful home for weary pilgrims, coming from the sandy desert, where they rest from their works, at the springing well."

The next hour he completely lost himself, all worries, tensions, and fears. The compelling urge to perform, to avenge, to fight no longer existed. Beside him sat his woman; his arm resting over her neck, his hand gently caressing her shoulders.

When it was over, they decided to stroll through the streets and along the harbour. Kjersti did not stray from Gunnar's side; she was constantly giving him side glances. Gunnar pretended not to notice, but inside, he was beaming. He leaned in towards her and gave her a kiss on her soft lips. That took her by surprise and she squeezed his hand. "Next week to the hospital in Amsterdam, and then probably to the United States for further treatment. I'm going with you, whether you want it or not, but I wish we could stay together here, Gunnar. I'm enjoying myself here."

Gunnar's eyebrows shot up. "You want to live here on Urk? Well, that is daring."

"Ha, I fit here, I am a natural born Urker." She laughed as they walked up to the door of Marianne's house.

After chatting with the rest of the family over coffee and lekkers, Gunnar suggested that they go out for another sail. The weather was beautiful and yesterday's trip out with Sjurd rejuvenated his soul. He didn't realise how much he missed being on the water. He supposed that was due to his mother's genes.

Jannie begged off because she had some work to do. So Sjurd, Kjersti and Gunnar, armed with a bag of fresh smoked salmon, a bottle of white wine and a few cans of beer, went to their boat. Gunner felt good. The wind gently tousled his hair and the sun warmed his arms as he gripped the wheel. He guided the boat through the harbour, past the green-and-red harbour lights, and onto the IJsselmeer. There, he pushed the throttle to full and the boat leapt forward.

Gripar

Gripar, Zofia, and Sverre watched the boat leave the harbour. Gripar was hoping to catch Gunnar and talk about what they found out at the lake. Zofia had decided to join Gripar in Urk, partly to spend some time with him and partly to do some research on her story of Eirik Tijsker. Gripar had spent the evening talking with Zofia and Sverre. Sverre specifically requested that Gripar drop all charges against Gunnar and Kjersti, but Gripar wasn't sure that would be possible. Sloss, especially, would balk at that.

The three of them sat on the terrace outside of De Kaap restaurant. Sverre's two associates had found a spot nearby where they could keep an eye on their boss. Zofia told them that she had nearly completed her research on Eirik and how this was one of the most difficult stories to capture in words that she had ever done. Sverre filled them in on his conversation with Gunnar and at the same time outlined the assistance he was requesting from Gripar.

"I think they are heading back," Zofia said. Gripar took out his binoculars and confirmed. "Yes, they are definitely heading for the stone. Let's meet up with them there." The five of them quickly walked through the crowded streets of Urk, towards the lighthouse.

Gunnar

The boat was about a hundred meters from the coast. By this time, Sjurd had replaced Gunnar at the helm and the three of them soaked up the sun. Gunnar was one again brought back to his early years. When the weather cooperates - no wind, clouds, and rain - there is no nicer place on the whole world than the Urker beach with a view of the waving flag in front of the lighthouse.

Gunnar cleared his throat. “Man, it feels good to be here with you, brother. I know we have still have our differences, but this is, indeed, a great feeling to be together as a family.”

“Same to you, brother. It’s been a blessing for my kids to get to know their long-lost uncle. And mother … Well, I haven’t seen her beam so much as these past couple of days.”

Kjersti smiled at the two of them. “You guys do have a great family.”

“Even, Sjurd?” Gunnar smiled and took a sip of his beer, slightly uncomfortable with all this emotional stuff. He was feeling this deep need to connect and he wasn’t sure where that was coming from. He sighed. “Sverre. He wants me in Norway. To help, he says.”

Sjurd nodded. “Your heart’s not in it? You’d rather be galivanting in the African jungle doing somebody else’s dirty work?”

Gunnar grunted. That’s a bit harsh. He and Kjersti spent a lot of time talking these past few days about their future. He didn’t know what to do. He just knew that he needed to make a change.

Sjurd noticed the slight change in Gunnar. “I didn’t mean to be a jerk. I just think that maybe it’s time to look at life differently.” He turned off the outboard and grabbed a beer for himself. The sloop gently touched the large rock that was located just off the shore. Sjurd turned to Kjersti, “So, this is where Gunnar came from.”

Kjersti looked around, puzzled. “What do you mean?”

Gunnar guffawed as Sjurd told her the story that all Urker children are told. “This rock is known as the midwife of Urk. It is called the Ommelebommelestien. We know that Norwegian children come from the cabbage patch and American children are brought in by a stork. But, did you know that Urker children come from this stone?”

Kjersti looked as confused as ever. Gunner put his arm around her. "What my little brother is trying to say is, according to legend, the future father has to row to this stone with the midwife and arrange to pick up the baby."

Kjersti laughed. "Oh. That's a neat legend. But, I don't quite get it. Your father isn't an Urker. He is Norwegian. How did that work?"

Sjurd and Gunnar looked at each other and laughed. "It's complicated," Gunnar said. "Our mother is Urker, this rock and our father are Norwegian, our Grandfather is German."

"You poor thing," Kjersti said as she pressed Gunnar's head to her shoulders. "No wonder things are a bit messed up for you."

"Well, whether Gunnar realizes it or not, he is a true Urker," Sjurd said. "Our father rowed to this stone and made the required payment for him. It's true, though, father didn't have to pay full price. He got a discount. So now, Gunnar is bonded for life to this stone." Sjurd gave Gunnar a friendly punch on the arm.

At that moment, Sjurd's phone rang. He took it from his pocket, looked at the screen, then quickly to Gunnar and turned around. "Yes, what's up?"

Gunnar saw the look on his brother's face. He felt tension rising.

"Are you sure?" He heard Sjurd say, and suddenly felt sick. Gunnar put down his bottle of beer and got a sudden urge to vomit.

"Okay. Thanks. See you soon." Sjurd ended the conversation. He looked at Gunnar. "It was Inspector Gripar. He got the test results back. It was confirmed that the body in the lake was our father's – Eirik Tijsker."

At that news, Gunnar kneeled on the bench, put his hands on the gunwale, and leaned over. He started to hyperventilate. He felt a set of strong arms grabbing his shoulders. "What's the matter? Are you not feeling well?" Kjersti asked anxiously, but Gunnar frowned and held up his hand as if feeling irritated by the sound of her voice. He cleared his throat and then asked, "Was he sure? He was absolutely sure?"

"Yes. Absolutely. It's definitely father's. He … He's dead …" Sjurd's voice trailed off.

Gunnar could see them but felt disoriented. He tried to speak, but no words came out of his mouth. His unblinking eyes then fixed on the lighthouse. Kjersti tried to get his attention and rubbed his back. With great difficulty he uttered words from his distorted mouth, "No. He's not dead. He is still alive. He needs me. That policeman knows where he is."

"No, honey, your father is dead. They finally found him."

Gunnar caught a movement out of the corner of his eye. He saw Sjurd stand up and make his way over to him. Quickly, turning to the movement, Gunnar shoved him back. The boat rocked from the force, and Sjurd, unbalanced, slipped and fell backwards nearly hitting his head on the opposite gunwale.

Without a thought to his brother, Gunnar jumped overboard and waded to the shore. The sloop continued to rock wildly making it difficult for both Sjurd and Kjersti to steady themselves. "Come back!" Kjersti screamed, but Gunnar continued walking to the shore.

Gunnar / Gripar

By this time, a crowd of people noticed what was going on and stopped what they were doing to watch how this would play out. Gripar watched Sjurd get up off his hands and knees and rest on the bench in the boat. After a couple of deep breaths, he threw the anchor into the water. He jumped out of the boat, determined to catch up with Gunnar.

Gunnar had arrived at the shore and Gripar strode up to meet him. He gasped as he watched helplessly as Gunnar slipped on the wet rocks on the shore and slammed head-first into them.

Before Gripar could reach him, Gunnar had managed to stand up, a bit unsteady on his feet. His vision was blurry and he glanced around him trying to focus. He took a couple of steps forward but immediately found himself unbalanced. His left knee collapsed and he reached down to take hold of one of the rocks to regain his balance. Where was he? Gunnar looked wildly around hoping to find him. He could feel anger swirling up inside him. He focussed on Gripar. “Where is he? What did you do with him? Leave him alone! Leave my father alone,” he shouted.

“Your father isn’t here. But we did find him,” Gripar replied. He started walking toward Gunnar, hoping to calm him down.

Gunnar found his balance and moved toward Gripar. The two were less than ten meters apart. “He finally found me, and now, you’ve taken him? You stay away from him!”

Gripar kept calm and made no sudden movements. He kept walking slowly towards Gunnar. “He is not here, Gunnar. I didn’t take him away.” Gripar tried to keep his voice soft and non-threatening.

Surprisingly quick, Gunnar took a hold of Gripar’s arm and swung him onto the rocks. Without a backward glance, he moved towards Sverre. Sverre froze. One of the bodyguards jumped forward to place himself between Sverre and Gunnar. Gunnar laughed. He had been in this situation many times before. Instinctively, he responded. He drove his knee into the man’s crotch and as the man bent over double, Gunnar gave him a head butt. The one bodyguard was down. Gunnar turned around and saw the second one coming at him. Gunnar turned back to Gripar and jumped towards him.

Gripar had his back turned to Gunnar. He had landed painfully on the rocks. He was up on one knee, assessing the damage.

From behind, Gunnar grabbed Gripar's arm and twisted it behind his back. Gunnar then lifted the arm higher and higher as Gripar screamed in pain. Just before the bone cracked, Gunner released him and kicked him into the water.

Gripar fell headlong. He pushed out his arms to break the fall. Gripar fought to control the pain. He sat there on his hands and knees, water nearly up to his chest, as he took some deep breaths.

Gunnar looked back at the shore. For a brief moment he saw his father looking at him with a bewildered look on his face. Gunnar ran into the water and put his hand on top of Gripar's head and pushed it under the water. When he looked up to see where Eirik was, he disappeared. There was a crowd of people gathering near Sverre, yelling at him. The two body guards started walking towards him.

It all happened so quickly. One moment, he was flung into the water and the next moment, his head was shoved under. Gripar's one arm was too sore to do anything, so with his good arm, he reached for Gunnar's leg to trip him. Gunnar was able to evade the roving arm. Becoming desperate, Gripar tried to rise out of the water. The harder he pushed up, the harder Gunnar pushed down. With his lungs screaming for air, Gripar made one last attempt to break free. Without warning, Gunnar let go. The restraint was gone and Gripar's head shot above the water. He took in gulps of air.

Gunnar watched as the two burly men strode towards him. He grabbed a large rock and raised it above his head. Then, he spotted Gripar's head popping up above the water. A primordial rage took hold of him and he was ready to smash it down on Gripar's head.

"Gunnar. Stop!" The voice ripped through Gunnar's synapses, freezing his muscles. He felt two hands violently shove him backwards. Shocked and caught off-balance, Gunnar stumbled back. Sjurd was towering over him and just before he fell into the water, Sjurd grabbed his arm and pulled him up.

"What the hell are you doing?" Sjurd yelled at him. "Get back to the boat."

Gunnar was dazed. The rage that suddenly overtook him, just as suddenly dissipated. This gave enough time for Sjurd to give his brother a hard push on his chest. Gunnar let go and fell back into the water. Sjurd then pulled Gripar up above the surface of the water with a mighty bear grip and brought him up to the high side.

He turned to Gunnar. "Gunnar, go back to the boat!" he ordered.

Gunnar faced Gripar. "Father? Father? Where are you? What did you do to him?"

Gripar didn't answer. He was still in shock over the violence of nearly drowning.

Sjurd gently grasped Gunnar's arm. "Go back, brother, go to the sloop."

"But father …?" He begged his brother. "Father?"

"Father is dead. He is really dead. They know for sure." Pulling him closer, Sjurd leaned into Gunnar's face. "Listen brother: Eirik, our father, is dead!"

He heard Sjurd speak, but the words did not immediately touch him. He looked around again, searching. He saw Sverre but no Eirik. He struggled in his mind to make sense of this. Eirik? No more? He no longer had a father? No Eirik? He no longer lived, his voice, his image, they would never be there again? In vain, Gunnar sought Eirik in his head. He could feel his presence nearby, but couldn't see him. Where was he?

Gunnar blocked his ears and closed his eyes. The world became dark and silent. He could feel the ground tremble and a sound began to build somewhere out in the distance. The trembling became more intense and the sound began to crescendo. Fear. A great fear took hold of him. There was more fear than he ever felt in the jungle.

He needed to leave. He had to leave. Heaving his chest forward, head up, clawing hands in the air, he opened his eyes and cried out his suffering, fear and pain. All his impotence raged against the world.

He took a deep breath, shook his head again, looked around, detached from reality. Back to the boat, which had flattened itself against the old primal rock. His head glowed, his body shook. He saw Kjersti and her outstretched arms, but it didn't register. He was focussed on the stone. Its grey surface drew him like a black hole in the universe. He saw, with amazement, that the colour of the stone had dissolved and transformed from grey to black and then to blood red. He laughed out loud when he comprehended. The stone was his destination. Eirik's stone was his stone.

He pushed himself forward through the water and reached the stone. Firmly grasping it, he climbed on and tried to get into a standing position. He was unsteady and uncertain. When he glanced down, he saw the raging waters circle the stone, threatening to wash him off.

He addressed the stone, whispering, "You are Eirik's stone. His sacrificial stone." Gunnar could feel the ancient stone had been patient. It was enveloped in its own mystery, layered in legends and riddles of ice ages, enormous floods and gigantic meteors. In its past, temperatures sank from subtropical to ice cold. The stone did not know time and temporality.

In shadows of this stone, Gunnar felt the emotions envelop him – emotions created by the oath sworn by a man in a cell thirty-two years ago desiring blood for satisfaction and victory. Gunnar understood without words. The stone … himself … the sacrifice. Suddenly, a burden fell off him. He found Eirik and became one.

He opened his eyes, threw back his head, and laughed uproariously. Slowly, his vision sharpened as the fog lifted. He saw the white lighthouse standing as a sentinel over the waters. A movement from the crowd caught his attention.

Sverre had stepped forward, reaching both hands to the man who called himself Wolfsangel. Gunnar-Eirik focused his gaze on Sverre. He lifted his arm up and pointed directly at Sverre. "You, from Norway. I am the son of your shame, but I curse you, man from the north!"

Sverre walked to the edge of the water and stepped in. Gunnar-Eirik watched as the man lifted his arms to heaven. The man's mouth opened and Gunnar-Eirik heard the words and felt them in his soul. "Vennligst! Tilgi synder mitt folk, tilgi deres synder, tilgi dem det onde de gjorde!"

Gunnar-Eirik reeled back, those words hammered deep inside him: 'Please! Forgive the sins of my people, forgive their crimes, forgive them the evil they did!'

An anguished cry penetrated the air. It came from a woman that had just run up to Sverre. She begged, "Gunnar, my son! Stop speaking, stop fighting, please stop it all! Step from that rock and come to me. Come home. I have already lost a husband and a daughter, why should I lose you too? I love you, my son, I love you!"

Gunnar-Eirik turned to her. "Marianne, do you know what they did to me there? They…" pointing to Sverre, "…are now talking about love, peace and tolerance, but in their own backyard they pissed on me, raped us. Norway was hell!"

Marianne nodded.

Gunnar-Eirik reached for his side. He found the sheath that held a Zwilling fillet knife. Whipping it out, he waved the knife at Sverre. "I am a Tyskerbarn! You will not treat us like we're offal."

The wind started to pick up as the clouds, for the past hour or so, had been drifting in from the Ijsselmeer. The winds carried with it the soft voice of a girl.

Gripar

Gripar sat on his haunches on the shore. He was still shaken up after his near drowning at the hands of Gunnar. He had never seen anything like this. It was so totally unexpected. Zofia stood behind him with her arms wrapped over his shoulders. Beside him stood Sverre. He couldn't read his expression. Sverre was motionless, his eyes fixed on Gunnar. There was an expression of pain lurking on his face. It occurred to Gripar that perhaps Sverre was the only one who knew why that man was standing there on that stone. That man carried the pain of the Lebensborn children of his country, Norway.

Gripar stood up as Zofia moved to stand beside him. She grabbed his hand and clasped her in his. The words of Gunnar struck Sverre to the core. The anguish of Sverre's response and his plea for forgiveness brought a shiver down his spine. He noticed, in the unnatural silence that followed those words, the sound of singing. Just behind the lighthouse there was a male choir singing in the old Bethel church scattered around the town. The words were carried by the wind and floated around the crowd. It was a surreal moment as the crowd heard 'Rock of Ages, cleft for me, let me hide myself in Thee; Let the water and the blood … … make me pure …'

Gripar glanced at Sverre. It was the moment that he was released. Sverre shoulders sagged and his head fell forward. He dropped down to his knees and closed his eyes. Sjurd came over and put his hand on his shoulders.

The silence was broken by the sound of Marianne's anguished cry. Sverre stood up as Sjurd moved to his mother's side. Gripar's mind was brought back to the day when he found out his parents and his little brother had been killed. Tears started to well up in his eyes as he fought to resist the deluge of emotions that was teetering on the brink.

He watched as Sjurd started wading through the water to reach the stone. It was Kjersti who gestured at him from the boat to not intervene. She pointed to herself. Sjurd understood and nodded. Kjersti moved to the front of the sloop. She called out to Gunnar, "Gunnar, my love, come to me." She put out her arms as if she was a mother letting her child know that it is safe to jump. Gripar glanced around. Marianne was sobbing, the crowd seemed to be praying, and the seagulls circled indecisively under the growing grey cloud cover. He was suddenly startled by the sudden collective gasp of the crowd. Gripar turned back to the stone.

A wave, whipped up by a sudden gust of wind, swept over the stone. Gunnar lost his balance and slipped, his feet slid back, his body fell forward. He instinctively tried to break his fall with both hands, his right hand still held the filleting knife.

Kjersti screamed and with superhuman strength jumped out of the boat. Sjurd howled and ran into the water towards the stone. Kjersti reached Gunnar just as he fell. Time seemed to slow down. Gripar watched as the knife was poised to enter Gunnar's chest. Everyone froze. Kjersti let out another primordial scream as she stretched out her hand and dove in intending to bat the knife into the water.

Gripar thought he saw red rivulets stream over the rock just as another wave washed over it, cleansing it. Both Kjersti and Gunnar were swept off the rock and into the water. Just then, Sjurd had reached the stone and managed to grab the legs of both Kjersti and Gunnar.

Sjurd dragged them to the shore. Kjersti was sobbing uncontrollably while Gunnar lay motionless on the beach. For a moment, a briefly surprising moment, completely unexpected, light from the lighthouse flashed straight to the stone. Some spectators later swore that they had seen a fiery flash of lightning coming from the stone towards heaven. The rock washed completely clean.

The crowd made a wide circle around the three of them. Sverre, Zofia, and Gripar rushed to help out. Marianne sat down with Kjersti at Gunnar's side. The two of them were shaken up and softly sobbing.

All that remained in the water was an empty sloop thumping against an old stone that long ago was transported by ice from Norway.

1978, Jessheim, Norway

Eirik

He had filled the cheap inflatable boat with air from his lungs and put it on the water. He looked up at the empty building of the Romerike School, there was no one yet. Of course not, it was very early.

Yet he heard a girl singing, from the laughing water, where the early morning sun was playing with the surface. Another life sparkled to him, through death. The thoughts of his mother, sister and daughter touched him deeply to the marrow of his bones. 'I am coming …, I am coming …'

He felt a strange calm, a kind of curiosity, coming over him. He sat down in the boat and as it wobbled, he laughed. Who would have thought that he, a man who made his living from great steel cutters, would end up in a wobbly inflatable toy boat?

No, he was not afraid anymore.

Gently humming along with the girl's singing, he tied a rope through the paddle holes, then through the holes of the weights he had bought in a sports store. First, he tied his feet, then he fixed the rest of his body as much as possible. His hands were still loose; he grabbed the dagger and candlestick that Mirre had kept for him. Then he took the little paddles and pushed off.

The boat floated to the place where Esther had drowned. Another voice started singing along with the first. It totally overwhelmed him. That was his daughter, Anna Esther.

'Ah, my daughter, my dear, dear sweet one. Are you here too?'

He prayed to heaven to forgive him. 'God! Be with Marianne, Gunnar and Sjurd. I am grateful, so much I have received from you. Do not be angry and receive me.'

The boat stopped. Eirik took the SS dagger and struck the boat. It was over. With a smile on his face he sank to where there was no mourning and no tears.

The sinking boat turned over just before it reached bottom, covering him.

For a moment his body protested, but his mind was strong.

2010, Virginia Beach, USA

Gunnar

He stood on the boardwalk, overlooking the beach. It was late morning, and sun seekers were still drifting in, filling the beach and marking out their territory. He could hear the laughter of children playing. Seagulls were circling around, swooping down every time it looked like somebody was throwing some food on the ground. He watched as a brown mottled gull found an abandoned hotdog but before he could feast, two large white gulls charged in. The mottled gull put up a small fight but was no match for the larger white ones. It could only stand back and watch from the sidelines.

Gunnar turned around and scanned the Norwegian Lady Statue. It seemed like a lifetime ago when he and Kjersti used the Norwegian Statute Lady in Moss to accomplish their goals. He had moved on.

It was only three weeks ago this chapter of his life came to a close at the funeral of Eirik in the village of Urk. Even though this wasn't the first time the village held a funeral for people lost through water, Urkers treated this one as solemnly as they always had. The entire village came out to pay respects to Marianne and the family. Mirre and her dear friend had wanted to come out, but the trip would have been too much for them. They sent their regrets.

Gunnar recalled how that day had started drizzly and cloudy, but when Eirik's casket was lowered into the ground, the sun suddenly broke through and its resplendent rays bathed everyone in warmth and hope.

There was a special delegation from the Norwegian government and some from the Tyskerbarn, the German war children. Sverre wanted to come, but it was felt he would make the funeral too political. He was working with the government to ensure that the Tyskerbarn got their full compensation, just as he had promised. The Prime Minister was publicly speculating about the government committing to covering the full cost. He didn't want Sverre to pay anything.

The Tyskerbarn deeply appreciated the affirmation of their suffering. They, like the rest of the country, wanted to move on and finally allow the past to settle to the bottom of the nation's collective pool of memories.

Gunnar smiled as he remembered seeing Hellmuth and the gang. They were all dressed in expensive suits and wearing Ray-Ban sunglasses; those tough, burly guys. It felt good to be among them again.

After the funeral, Gunnar and Kjersti made plans to fly back to the US so that he can begin a series of treatments. Hellmuth was skeptical that Gunnar would manage to stick to the medical protocols and drug regime.

"I'll tell you what, old friend," Gunnar had grinned. "I bet that in five years I will have beaten this disease. Let's set a date and meet up in Bangui at the same cafe we stopped in so many years ago." Then wrapping his arm around Kjersti, "The same place where I told you about this wonderful woman."

Hellmuth had stuck out his hand. "You're on. This time, I'll buy the beer."

Gunnar's laugh startled a group of birds perched on the statue. He turned back to the beach and searched for his 'kalletje'. It took a bit, but he found her. She was attempting to learn how to SUP in the light surf. He watched as she struggled to keep balance, but a surprise wave caught her off guard and she fell. When she got up, he could hear her distinct laughter. He became disquieted. He knew the journey ahead was going to be arduous and inconstant, but he was ready to take it on.

Five thousand kilometres across the Atlantic Ocean, under the ever-present sentinel of the lighthouse, the eternal stone remained constant and firm as the turbulent waves crashed over it.

AFTERWORD

After my book was first published, it immediately became apparent that the historical background of the story fascinated many people. They asked me, 'Did this really happen? In Norway?' Yes, there are many historical facts in the book 'Blood out of stone', perhaps much more than the readers first suspect; therefore this afterword.

The Lebensborn Project, source of life

The project was set up by Heinrich Himmler on December 12, 1935, with the aim of giving "racially pure" women the opportunity to secretly give birth to a child. Born children were then handed over to the SS organization that took care of the education and adoption of the child. The first Lebensborn House was opened in 1936 in Steinhöring, a small village not far from Munich. Ultimately, there were ten Lebensborn homes located in Germany, nine in Norway, two in Austria and one in Belgium, the Netherlands, France, Luxembourg and Denmark.

The persistently low birth rate and the fear that the Germanic race would be hit hard if German soldiers were killed led Himmler in 1939 to direct orders to all SS men and the police to father as many children as possible. War cost human lives, these had to be replenished.

This thought led to the large-scale kidnapping of children who were 'racially good', especially from the eastern occupied countries. Many children were stolen from families and transferred to the Lebensborn Centers to become Germanic. In Poland alone, 100,000 children may have been stolen. The Nazis went far: In 1942, an SS unit destroyed the entire male population of a small village called Lidice in retaliation for the murder of SS Governor Reinhard Heydrich in Prague. During this operation, SS men made a selection: 99 children were considered good enough to be Germanized and sent to Germany. It is estimated that more than 250,000 children were kidnapped and sent to Germany. Only 25,000 were recovered after the war and returned to their families.

The number of children born in Lebensbornhuizen is somewhere around 20,000 to 25,000, of which about 12,000 are in Norway. Germany really wanted to take them in as their own children after the war, but Norway didn't release them. Some children already lived in Germany after the war, but were forcibly sent back to Norway to be tortured there. Many German fathers wanted to acknowledge their children, but were prevented from contacting them. If successful, the mothers and children received alimony through volunteers, but a significant amount of restitution paid by the Germans to Norway for the Lebensborn disappeared without ever reaching the children.

After the liberation, many Norwegian Lebensborn children were imprisoned with their mothers in psychiatric hospitals, labeled as "mentally defective and prone to perverse behavior." They were hated, despite the fact that they were innocent. Some fled from Norway. The dark-haired ABBA singer, Anni-Frid Lyngstad, fled from Norway to Sweden after the war with her mother and grandmother. But the many left behind had a hard time. Many Norwegian Lebensborn children were abused and neglected until the 1960s. Apparently nobody cared. They were hated, the tyskerbarn, the German war children. In 2007 they hoped in vain for justice and recognition through the European court in Strasbourg. The worst must have been that the mothers were officially described by a doctor, Else Vogt Thingsstad, as retarded and their children as hereditary weak. This was published in the Arbeiderbladet in December 1945. Another doctor backed this up with, "These kids are just as likely to grow up to be normal citizens as basement rats could become pets."

Witnesses described how there was no escape for many Lebensborn children. "If the mother was a German whore, then the child was the same and you could do with it whatever you wanted," said Tor Brandacher, spokesperson for the War Child organization about the Lebensborn. He says everyone hated them, everyone beat them, and everyone abused them and urinated on them. Every perversion known to man was exercised on them, according to Brandacher. A boy was raped by nine men, who then urinated on him. Another woman told him that when she was four and living in foster care, she was hanged in a barn when the farmer needed oral sex. At a children's home in Trysil, young people were force-fed until they vomited and had to eat the vomit. A war child himself, Brandacher began researching the subject in 1987 when adoption laws changed so that people could find out the identities of their biological parents. He says elsewhere people were let in through the back doors at night to abuse the children. They paid the staff half a ham and a bottle of alcohol. A group of men burned a girl's forehead with a swastika. It is clear from various sources that these children were not protected from sadistic nurses and 'host' parents. They were leashed like dogs, locked up with false dogs and between pigs, tortured with boiling water, hot fire pokers and lit cigarette butts. Children and their mothers were abused – fully supported by the Norwegian government – by the Norwegian and American secret services CIA for medical experiments, open brain surgeries where brains were removed from living persons, LSD experiments, et cetera. Fortunately these terrible things did not happen to all Lebensborn, Thorleiff Blatt, the chairman of the Lebensborn Federation of Norway assured me, but it is clear that many Lebensborn children have suffered greatly.

Eugenics

Germany is given the blame, but the idea of improving a human population has been the goal of many since the nineteenth century. Francis Galton, cousin of Charles Darwin, already focused on developing the idea of selective breeding of humans to improve the breed over generations. Galton distinguished positive eugenics, which encourages the most capable to reproduce, and negative eugenics, which discourages or prevents the less able from reproducing.

The Kaiser Wilhelm Institute of Psychiatry was supported for millions by the Rockefeller Foundation from America. One of the leading psychiatrists at the German Psychiatric Institute was Ernst Rüdin, who later became the director and eventual architect of Hitler's systematic medical suppression. From 1940 onwards, thousands of Germans who were taken from old people's homes, psychiatric institutions and other reception facilities were systematically gassed. Leon Whitney, executive secretary of the American Eugenics Society, praised Nazism at the time. Verschuer, head of the German Eugenics, not only survived the war, he was even reinstated. His assistant Joseph Mengele, the angel of death of Auschwitz, probably also remained active from Argentina and Brazil. He died in 1979, but there is evidence that he continued to experiment until his death. A connection with McGill University under the Paperclip arrangement is therefore a possibility. Many clever Nazis were brought to the United States and deployed in the scientific world. One of the influences of eugenics is forced sterilization programs. This happened well into the 1970s in the United States among African Americans and in Canada among Native Americans. In Canada, more than 2,800 sterilizations were performed in the province of Alberta between 1929 and 1972. It was also common in Norway and Sweden, there as well, the original population, the Sami, were viewed as inferior. Unfortunately, it is far from over: the Republic of China is still working on it on a large scale.

Attack Oslo

On 25 September 1942, Oslo was attacked by Havilland Mosquitos during the day, targeting the Gestapo headquarters in Oslo and carried out at the request of the Norwegian government in exile. The aim was to destroy the data that the Gestapo had about the Norwegian resistance. The attack was carried out by four Mosquitos (Type B Mk IV) of No.105 Squadron, commanded by squadron leader George Parry. Each aircraft was armed with four 500-pound bombs with fuses with a delay of 11 seconds. Four bombs hit Gestapo headquarters. Unfortunately, three of those four bombs bounced out of the building before exploding and the only bomb that remained in the building did not explode.

Hellmuth Reinhard

Hellmuth Reinhard (born 24 July 1911) was head of the Gestapo in Norway (1942–1945), and was partly responsible for the deportation of at least 532 Norwegian Jews. He was sentenced in 1967 to 5 years in prison for complicity in murder. Born Hermann Gustav Hellmuth Patzschke on July 24, 1911, he became a member of the Hitler Youth and studied in Vienna, Leipzig and Berlin. In 1934 he became a member of the SD, the intelligence service of the SS and the NSDAP. He became leader of the SD-Hauptamt, Partei und Staat in 1938. On April 25, 1939, he changed his surname to Reinhard. During the war he was stationed in Prague and later, in August 1941, he became leader of the Zentralstelle für judische Auswanderung in the Netherlands. During 1941/42 he was in Einsatzgruppe C for about three months, after which he went to Norway to become head of the Gestapo, Abteilung IV, from January 28, 1942, under the leadership of the leader of the Security Police in Norway, Heinrich Fehils. He remained in this position until February 1, 1945. After the war, he changed his name back to his original name, avoiding further investigation from authorities regarding his activities at the time. It was not until 1964 that his true identity became known to the West German police and he was prosecuted in 1967. He was released in 1970 and presumably died in 2001. (source: Wikipedia et al.) I have taken the liberty of including him in this made-up story, because I do not misuse his name. In this story he remains a SS man in his heart, like so many old SS men, who remained convinced Nazis until their death. His relationship with Anna and his death in this book are made up. I got the facts about him from various sources and incorporated them into the story.

Locations

The towns of Hurdal, Holmestrand, Oslo, Sandnes and Moss all exist, of course, including the streets, the Romerikeschool, Nordbytjernetmeer, the farms, the campsites and the restaurants. I was even allowed to visit the Lebensborn baby room in Hurdal, it was still in its original condition! I have tried to hang the story on and between real facts. To give an example of details those actually exist: the stairs outside the Fylke psychiatric hospital where Gunnar slipped into the story, the grounds of the Hurdalbunker. In Moss there really are (at the time of my research) that yellow house, the harbor, the statue and story about it and other places. Mr. Thorleif Blatt, chairman of the Norwegian Lebensborn Federation, has checked the story for historical truth. He confirmed that near Holmestrand, in Grefsrud to be precise, an SS training camp had been built; the dining hall is still there, he said. The base for the German soldiers was Mrs. Hedvig Rosing's school building for deaf children in Holmestrand. He convinced me to use the name Sverre Lothbrok instead of Haakon Magnus. In the Netherlands such a thing is allowed, but he had his doubts about Norway in that regard. I haven't been to most of the African places mentioned, except Wonderboom Airport near Pretoria. But I know Vanderhoof Airport in B.C. Canada well, having lived in Smithers B.C. for five years and been to the Vanderhoof Air Show several times. Yes, and Urk of course: I was born there and I feel privileged I was allowed to live there for the first nine years of my life.

Personal and thank you

Writing this book has kept me busy for ten years. It started on my bicycle. I cycle to Zwolle every day, where I work as an English teacher at a secondary school. I often get lost in fantasy and meditation and one day I saw a man standing on the Urk stone in my mind. He yelled at people standing on the side. Of course I didn't know why and challenged myself to come up with an explanation. So to my great surprise I stumbled upon the story of the Norwegian Lebensborn children. That summer my wife and I were on vacation in Norway where I investigated the case. We visited the

Norwegian Center for Holocaust and Religious Minority Studies, which is located in the former Villa Grande, in Oslo. 'Gimle' as it was then known was the residence of the Norwegian Nazi leader, Vidkun Quisling, during World War II. There I spoke to Norwegian historians Terje Emberland and Sigurd Sørlie and the writing began.

First in English, but then it turned out that I really couldn't just write a book out of my sleeve, and I switched to Dutch. Klaas Wierenga and Janna IJmker, both experienced writers, helped me enormously; without them it would not have been possible. I visited Norway again when the book was almost finished to revisit all the places where the story takes place. Oslo, Trondheim, Hurdal, Drammen, Sandnes, Jessheim, and so on. Writing is plowing the rocks, making up the story is fun, but what comes next ... what a job! You have to be stubborn and believe in the value of your story. This story had to be told and as a writer I had to experience it myself and feel the emotions. Eight to ten hours a week I went into quarantine to build and renovate a house in my spirit world, just as I had done in the physical world. Through the latter I gained great respect for plumbers, masons, kitchen builders. Try to earn your money this way! Respect! The respect for writers has grown enormously by doing it myself.

Urk! I am proud to be an Urk, I still like coming here. The Ommele Bommele stone, the Norwegian primeval stone that lies diagonally in front of the lighthouse, has great significance for me, just like my birthplace: district 4 no. 115. I could not have done without the support of my wife, Alie, without her faith in me. I already mentioned a number of important people above, and I would like to add a few more names: the capable textual 'checkers' and writers Linda Bruins Slot and Anita Franschman, Thorleiff Blatt, chairman of the Lebensborn Federation Norway, cousin Klaas, and Arno van den Kieboom of Publisher Keytree. My friend from Canada: Rob Vanspronsen did much more than translating, he gave the whole story a great make over.

Finally, I would like to thank my main characters, sorry that it sometimes took me so long to find and understand you. If any of you, dear readers, would like to write a review or article about this book, welcome! I tried to write a thriller as best I could, at times I succeeded.

Bram Verhoeff

Hasselt (The Netherlands)

bloodoutofstonebook@gmail.com

Acknowledgement – Rob vanSpronsen

When Bram approached me in 2020 asking me to help him take his original version of this book and develop an refreshed, up to date English version, I was thrilled. I have known Bram for over thirty five years. We were colleagues at Christian school in Carman, Manitoba, Canada. There, Bram was well-known for his master story-telling. Students absolutely loved hearing them. I knew then that any story coming from Bram was going to be great and worth telling. I was not wrong.

It was an absolute pleasure to work with him on this project. He gave me a lot of freedom in making over his original story, which was written in slightly old-fashioned English, since he left Canada in 1993. I also used my freedom to shape some new aspects to the story, so this English version is fairly different than the Dutch 'Bloed uit steen', published by Keytree in 2020. While doing this, I learned so much about Norway, the Tyskerbarn, and WWII history. He was magnanimous in his patience with me. I am very grateful for this opportunity.

I wish to also express a huge debt of gratitude to my beloved wife, Agnes, for being along side of me on this project.

Lightning Source UK Ltd.
Milton Keynes UK
UKHW011841090223
416719UK00001B/100